IMPLICATING
THE SYSTEM

IMPLICATING THE SYSTEM

JUDICIAL DISCOURSES IN THE SENTENCING OF INDIGENOUS WOMEN

ELSPETH KAISER-DERRICK

UNIVERSITY OF MANITOBA PRESS

Implicating the System: Judicial Discourses in the Sentencing
of Indigenous Women
© Elspeth Kaiser-Derrick 2019

23   22   21   20   19   1   2   3   4   5

University of Manitoba Press
Winnipeg, Manitoba, Canada
Treaty 1 Territory
uofmpress.ca

Cataloguing data available from Library and Archives Canada
ISBN 978-0-88755-828-3 (PAPER)
ISBN 978-0-88755-555-8 (PDF)
ISBN 978-0-88755-553-4 (EPUB)

Cover and interior design by Jess Koroscil
Cover image: Linocut by Elspeth Kaiser-Derrick

Printed in Canada

This book has been published with the help of a grant from the
Federation for the Humanities and Social Sciences, through the Awards
to Scholarly Publications Program, using funds provided by the
Social Sciences and Humanities Research Council of Canada.

The University of Manitoba Press acknowledges the financial support for
its publication program provided by the Government of Canada through
the Canada Book Fund, the Canada Council for the Arts, the Manitoba
Department of Sport, Culture, and Heritage, the Manitoba Arts Council,
and the Manitoba Book Publishing Tax Credit.

Funded by the Government of Canada | Canadä

CONTENTS

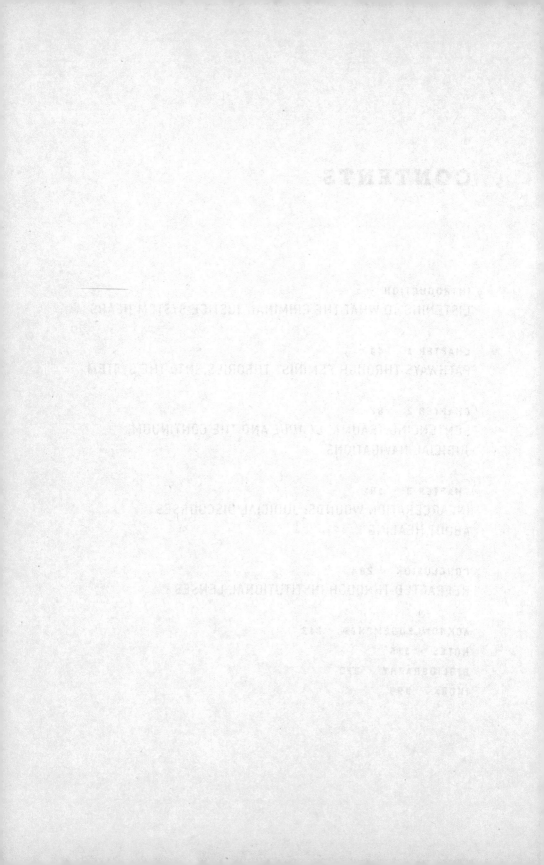

LISTENING TO WHAT THE CRIMINAL JUSTICE SYSTEM HEARS

While obtaining my law degree at the University of Alberta, I worked extensively with the clinical program Student Legal Services of Edmonton. In one of my capacities there, for the Legal Education and Reform Project, I regularly attended outreaches at Kindred House. Kindred House is a drop-in centre for street sex workers (women, including cis- and transgender women, over eighteen years old). It is grounded in the philosophy of harm reduction, which in this context means "meet[ing] the clients where they're at."[1] Kindred House offers a safe place for its clients to take respite from the stress and exposure of the streets, supplies various health and other resources, and provides a sense of community to alleviate some of the isolation instilled by poverty and marginalization. I would sit with a fellow law student during these outreaches, sometimes offering legal information and pamphlets, periodically opening files for women who lacked other access to legal representation, intermittently talking to women who just wanted someone to talk to, and constantly aware that this space belonged to those who have been pushed to the periphery of public spaces and services.

It was apparent that these women lived very hard lives, with very little support and resources, and many had been criminalized. I was appalled that the overwhelming majority of clients were Indigenous.[2] Program coordinator Shawna Hohendorff reported to a parliamentary subcommittee on sex work that of her clients at Kindred House, roughly 80 percent are Indigenous.[3] This overrepresentation was also evident in separate support outreaches for street sex workers that I volunteered for with the PAR Foundation and Crossroads,[4] conducted in large outfitted vans in Edmonton. It was evident that this overrepresentation is inter-generational; for example, during one outreach, an Indigenous mother and daughter approached the van together to access resources.

Referring to the overrepresentation of Indigenous peoples in the criminal justice system, the Royal Commission on Aboriginal Peoples (RCAP) concluded in 1996 that "over-representation is linked directly to the particular and distinctive historical and political processes that have made Aboriginal people poor beyond poverty,"[5] in a deeply entrenched "process of colonization."[6] Hohendorff commented to the parliamentary subcommittee that her clients felt unheard and alienated from institu-tions with power, as if "their particular life stories" did not matter.[7] She explained, "I don't know all of the answers, and I think it's a complex set of problems," but what "we need to do is to listen . . . so that they are part of our community, not separate."[8] Similarly, in its review of the crimi-nal justice system released in 2018, Department of Justice of Canada reports from consultations with various stakeholders (including lawyers, judges, organizations supporting criminalized persons, and Indigenous leaders and communities) that women in the system (particularly wom-en appearing in capacities as victims and also Indigenous women gener-ally) "often feel their experiences are not believed and have therefore lost confidence in the justice system."[9] Participants in the Department of Justice Canada review also point to insufficient information about "specific gendered experiences" of women in the system, and that "data collection through a gendered lens" is needed, adding that Indigenous women must have access to "approaches that consider the historical and oppressive contexts"[10] that are engaged. In this book, I strive to dem-onstrate the importance of Hohendorff's insight, and these findings by the Department of Justice Canada, by exploring the limited histories of criminalized Indigenous women as these narratives appear in their sentencing judgments, such as those presented through pre-sentence reports (PSRs) and *Gladue* reports, and how judges respond. Often, these narratives reveal layered experiences of victimization, including sustained victimizations (frequently occurring throughout these women's lives) and diverse forms of victimization (often involving violence, such as physical and sexual victimization, but also other types of victimization, including emotional abuse, neglect, and substance abuse, and systemic, state-based victimization). This prevalence of victimization (and state oppression) makes the interrelationship between the victimization and criminalization of Indigenous women central to my book. Indeed, participants in the criminal justice review told the Department of Justice Canada that the government should legislatively require various actors within the system, including judges, "to take into account the underlying factors contributing to offending and victimization."[11] My focus on sentencing judgments does not go far enough to respond to Hohendorff's suggestion; it remains necessary for legal and policy-based work to engage and incorporate the actual voices and directives of Indigenous women themselves. Nonetheless, the presentation of criminalized Indigenous women's histories to the courts is one of the few ways that their lives might be "listened to" in the criminal justice system, and it impacts how the system responds.

Sherene H. Razack suggests "storytelling in law" for its narrative-based "potential as a tool for social change," with its orientation toward "putting the context back into law."[12] The "stories" examined in this book are those written by, and for the purposes of, the criminal justice system, about the Indigenous women ensnared by that system. Razack observes that Indigenous women prisoners query whether their "stories of oppression are even 'translatable' for the court's benefit."[13] I am interested in what information the sentencing judge hears, and how this influences sanctions. The context in which sentencing judges learn about the criminalized Indigenous women appearing before them includes the legislative requirement that they consider the unique circumstances of Indigenous peoples and reduce reliance on incarceration—s. 718.2(e)[14] of the Criminal Code—and the direction by the Supreme Court of Canada (SCC) in *R. v. Gladue* and *R. v. Ipeelee* establishing a judicial framework for sentencing Indigenous peoples. Gillian Balfour writes, "The disconnect between restorative justice sentencing practices—a seemingly progressive legislative initiative—and the unrelenting coercive punishment of Aboriginal women lies, to a great extent, in the exclusion of women's narratives of violence and social isolation in the practice of sentencing law."[15] For Balfour, to meaningfully import the experiences of Indigenous women into sentencing law, courts must situate these women's criminality "in the context of gendered conditions in Aboriginal communities"[16] by considering (within the factors comprising the *Gladue* analysis) how past experiences of violence may have contributed to their criminalization and coming before the courts. Balfour concludes that the ways defence counsel present their cases and how sentencing judges use *Gladue* factors both fail to "recognize the gendered conditions of endangerment in Aboriginal women's communities as a systemic factor"[17] (where such conditions refer to "violence against women and feminization of poverty").[18]

My review of the cases I have identified is guided by related questions about how the presentation and interpretation of Indigenous women's histories impact sentencing determinations. It is imperative to examine how judges present and use criminalized Indigenous women's histories to assist with sentencing determinations because the overrepresentation of Indigenous women in the system is steadily increasing, and across all types of correctional custody/supervision ("remand, sentenced, and other").[19]

Overrepresentation: The Numbers, Growing from Colonial Roots

Indigenous peoples are grossly overrepresented in correctional admissions, and this disparity is even wider among Indigenous women than men. I offer various statistics here to provide some scope for this overrepresentation, while recognizing Carmela Murdocca's caution that there is danger of further "erasures" of colonial violence where "appeals to justice" are rooted in sterile statistical snapshots, given that Indigenous peoples have long "been utilized as Canada's 'raw data' for national incentives (such as policy and law)," such that "this kind of quantification continues the colonial project."[20]

The overrepresentation of Indigenous women in the Canadian criminal justice system is stark, given that a report from Statistics Canada analyzing information from the 2011 National Household Survey shows that only 4 percent of the total population of Canadian women and girls are Indigenous.[21] In its 2016–17 annual report, the Office of the Correctional Investigator cautions that women are "the fastest growing population in Canadian corrections," and especially so are Indigenous women whose numbers in federal prison increased by 60 percent in the decade preceding 2017.[22] The Correctional Investigator reports in 2016–17 that Indigenous women comprise 37.6 percent of women in federal custody.[23] In a Juristat report analyzing 2015–16 data, Julie Reitano identifies that 38 percent of women admitted to sentenced custody at the provincial and territorial levels are Indigenous (whereas Indigenous men account for 26 percent of male admissions).[24] In terms of other types of dispositions, Statistics Canada reports from 2011–12 data that 25 percent of persons admitted to remand and 21 percent of those admitted to probation and conditional sentences are Indigenous.[25] The overrepresentation of Indigenous women within these figures is again even more pronounced than for Indigenous men, as Indigenous women comprise 37 percent of all women admitted to remand (Indigenous men account for 23 percent of male admissions).[26] These figures vary substantially by province and territory; Indigenous overrepresentation is most extreme in the prairie provinces and the northern territories. These statistics may also underrepresent the Indigenous population in the criminal justice system, in part because the percentages exclude persons whose Indigenous identity was unidentified.[27] Nonetheless, the fact of overrepresentation of Indigenous peoples (both women and men) in prison is "consistent across all provinces and territories."[28]

Research demonstrates that Indigenous peoples are also overrepresented as victims of criminal offending,[29] and that Indigenous women experience particularly high rates of violent victimization.[30] The United Nations Committee on the Elimination of Discrimination against Women (UN Committee) locates violence against Indigenous women within an international human rights framework, declaring that the Canadian government has failed in its obligations and thereby "violated the rights of [Indigenous] women victims of violence."[31] Jillian Boyce finds from 2014 data that Indigenous women are three times more likely to report spousal violence than non-Indigenous women, and are at elevated risk of victimization through this type of violence.[32] Shannon Brennan reports that in 2009 Indigenous women "were almost three times more likely than non-Aboriginal women to report having been a victim of a violent crime" (irrespective of the type of relationship, or whether it involved stranger violence).[33] Brennan writes that Indigenous women also report having experienced proportionally more emotional or financial abuse within their spousal relationships than non-Indigenous women.[34] These figures are likely lower than the true numbers, in part because the 2009 data exclude the territories,[35] and perhaps also due to some Indigenous women's fears about (and/or decisions to refrain from) reporting to police. Moreover, Patricia Monture-Angus suggests that statistics about violence against Indigenous women are necessarily deficient because "focusing on a moment in time or incidents of violence, abuse or racism, counting them—disguises the utter totality of the experience of violence in Aboriginal women's lives."[36] This bolsters the need to understand victimization vis-à-vis Indigenous women in a broad, comprehensive way instead of limiting the parameters of what constitutes "victimization."

In a report based on 2014 information, Samuel Perreault concludes that "Aboriginal identity itself remained a key risk factor for victimization among women, even when controlling for the presence of other risk factors."[37] Perreault indicates that factors "strongly associated with the risk of violent victimization" (including "childhood maltreatment," homelessness, mental/physical disabilities, and substance use) contribute to explaining the elevated rates of violent victimization among Indigenous men, "but could not completely explain higher rates experienced by" Indigenous women.[38] This suggests that specific vulnerabilities to victimization are systemically attached to Indigenous women.

The overrepresentation of Indigenous peoples in the criminal justice (and particularly correctional) system must be understood as directly connected to processes of colonization put in motion by colonialism. Joyce Green defines colonialism as "both an historic and a continuing wrong. A term that encompasses economic and political practices, it refers to the appropriation of the sovereignty and resources of a nation or nations, to the economic and political benefit of the colonizer. The practices by which colonialism is normalized and legitimated include racism, which is encoded in law, policy, education and the political and popular culture of the colonizer."[39] Maori scholar Linda Tuhiwai Smith describes colonialism as a manifestation of imperialism[40] and outlines that the interrelated "imperialism and colonialism brought complete disorder to colonized peoples, disconnecting them from their histories, their landscapes, their languages, their social relations and their own ways of thinking, feeling and interacting with the world."[41] She highlights how colonialism produced the "process of systemic fragmentation"[42] that is felt by Indigenous peoples through the "fragmentation of lands and cultures," as well as through having their "identities regulated by laws and our languages and customs removed from our lives."[43] She explains that this systemic fragmentation remains "something we are recovering from."[44] Imperialism and colonialism are together systems of domination and control, which Tuhiwai Smith articulates as "the specific formations through which the West came to 'see,' to 'name' and to 'know' indigenous communities."[45]

Similarly, other writers understand colonialism as an instrument of structural (institutional) oppression as well as cultural oppression, which often manifest in the same practices.[46] For example, the residential school system in Canada functioned as both structural and cultural colonialism, affecting Indigenous peoples, as Tuhiwai Smith writes, "physically, emotionally, linguistically and culturally."[47] The Royal Commission on Aboriginal Peoples describes the residential school system as consisting of "a three-part vision of education in the service of assimilation. It included, first, a justification for removing children from their communities and disrupting Aboriginal families; second, a precise pedagogy for re-socializing children in the schools; and third, schemes for integrating graduates into the non-Aboriginal world."[48] Tuhiwai Smith states that these institutions "were designed to destroy every last remnant of alternative ways of knowing and living, to obliterate collective identities and memories and to impose a new order," and had the effect to "silence (for ever [sic] in some cases) or to suppress the ways of knowing, and the languages for knowing, of many different indigenous peoples."[49] This coercive seeing, naming, and knowing continues to have devastating effects on Indigenous communities in Canada, including the virtual extinction of many Indigenous languages.[50]

In Canada, according to John O'Neil, colonialism refers to the "long history of assault from Euro-Canadian political, economic, religious, and educational institutions on the social and cultural integrity of Aboriginal communities."[51] The Royal Commission on Aboriginal Peoples reports that several governmental policies directly produced the reverberating effects of colonialism. These policies include the Indian Act, which established systematic discrimination between the legal rights of most Canadians and those of certain identified Indigenous peoples ("status Indians"); the residential schools system, which fragmented families, attempted to strip Indigenous children of their cultures, and fostered widespread abuse and neglect of those children; and the relocation of Indigenous communities, which further alienated and disempowered peoples whose collective sense of home, culture, and spirituality is intimately tied to the land.[52] These events have deeply entrenched intergenerational effects, both on-[53] and off-reserve.[54] Green suggests that colonialism has had a gendered impact on Indigenous women, who "have suffered from colonialism similarly to Aboriginal men, but also in gender-specific ways, including the loss of culture, traditional territories, identity and status, children and culturally respected gender roles."[55] Jodi-Anne Brzozowski, Andrea Taylor-Butts, and Sara Johnson write that the persisting, pervasive effects of governmental policies and laws pertaining to colonization and the assimilation of Indigenous peoples have produced "the marginalization of Aboriginal peoples, which is reflected in high unemployment rates, low levels of education, low income and inadequate living conditions."[56] The overrepresentation of Indigenous peoples in Canadian prisons must also be added to this list. As Joane Martel and Renée Brassard explain, "overincarceration is one of the consequences of the enduring fragmentation and loss of identity" experienced by Indigenous communities through colonization.[57]

Overall, there is overwhelming evidence that colonization has decimated Indigenous communities, set in motion the conditions that render Indigenous persons vulnerable to criminalization and incarceration, and produced the overrepresentation of Indigenous peoples in the system.

Book Pathways and Research Questions

In Chapter 1, I discuss the feminist theory of the "victimization-criminalization continuum," which suggests that women's criminality should be understood as connected to their experiences of victimization, and that women's responses to victimization can lead to criminalization.[58] Smita Vir Tyagi states that "violence and victimization play a significant role in women's trajectories of offending."[59] Indigenous women continue to be overrepresented in the criminal justice system as both victims and criminalized persons.[60] The relationship between systemic victimization and overrepresentation suggests the suitability of the victimization-criminalization continuum as a lens to consider judgments sentencing Indigenous women. For Indigenous women, the continuum should be framed in terms of how (personal, collective, and state-based) experiences of victimization are marginalizing and constrain the life options available to them, which may leave them vulnerable to criminalization. These issues must be situated within the processes of colonization that ricochet through Indigenous women's lives. Colonization and the victimization-criminalization continuum lay the groundwork for my focus on how sentencing judges understand and use information about Indigenous women's histories of victimization within the *Gladue* analysis.

In Chapters 2 and 3, I analyze decisions in which Indigenous women are sentenced and, where possible, focus on those processing offences for which conditional sentences are or were previously an available sanction. This sanction offers the most meaningful direct alternative to imprisonment to assist in ameliorating the overincarceration of Indigenous peoples (at least, the most meaningful of those alternatives within our current criminal justice system). My overarching interest in these chapters is whether and how Indigenous women's experiences of victimization and criminalization contribute to punitive sanctions that are judicially characterized as treatment-oriented sentences. The histories of victimization presented at the sentencing hearings of criminalized Indigenous women are often quite extensive. This underscores the importance of considering how sentencing judges process these histories, and how they ultimately impact sentencing determinations. Judicial understandings of victimization and criminalization are often visible in their reasoning, and may or may not combine with judicial consideration of *Gladue* factors. (My usage of "histories" is not intended to suggest reified past experiences, as of course such experiences of victimization have ongoing personal significance to the women's lives, resurface in the sentencing process, and may recur in the same or other forms, including in victimization by the state during the criminal justice process itself, and in related systems of control. Further, I do not mean "histories" to be correlated with concepts of objective truth, as they are interpreted and written by state actors for state purposes.)

In Chapter 3, I discuss how judicial understandings of victimization, criminalization, and *Gladue* factors influence sentencing outcomes. I focus particularly on a tendency to translate discourses about victimization, criminalization, and *Gladue* factors into a judicial approach that characterizes both conditional sentence orders and prison sentences as healing-oriented. There is ample evidence that imprisonment exacerbates pre-existing difficulties (mental health and otherwise) and engenders new problems. While I focus on discourses about rehabilitation, given its place in sentencing, I intend the expanded context signalled by Laurence J. Kirmayer, Gregory M. Brass, and Caroline L. Tait, who suggest that, "framing the problem purely in terms of mental health issues . . . may deflect attention from the large-scale, and, to some extent, continuing assault on the identity and continuity of whole peoples. To these organized efforts to destroy Aboriginal cultures are added the corrosive effects of poverty and economic marginalization."[61]

In the Conclusion, I highlight the importance of the role of the sentencing judge in the broader project to ameliorate the overrepresentation of Indigenous peoples in prison. *Ipeelee* encourages judicial creativity to respond to overrepresentation. Because sentencing judges act after systemic issues have already failed Indigenous women, there is clearly also the simultaneous need for real change at the community level.

I am interested in how judges negotiate the task of sentencing Indigenous women, particularly given ubiquitous histories of victimization and the s. 718.2(e) directive and *Gladue* requirement to consider the unique backgrounds of Indigenous persons on sentencing. Where possible, I focus on cases in which conditional sentences were either an available sentencing outcome or discussed as unavailable, because they offer the most meaningful (in terms of approximate functional equivalency) alternative to a sentence that would otherwise be a term of institutional incarceration. The overrepresentation of Indigenous women in prison is accelerating concurrent with incursions into the conditional sentencing regime. As the need for alternatives to incarceration for Indigenous women has intensified, amendments to the Criminal Code have eroded the availability of those alternatives. Tuhiwai Smith writes, "Research is not an innocent or distant academic exercise but an activity that has something at stake and that occurs in a set of political and social conditions."[62]

To study the discourses in judicial reasoning, I consulted the largest body of cases I could reasonably amass—175 decisions in total (sentencing 177 Indigenous women, given two sets of co-accuseds). Many provincial/territorial-level sentencing judgments are not published,[63] which limits the scope of research that may be conducted on sentencing practices.[64] Because of my focus on judicial treatment of criminalized Indigenous women's histories of victimization and *Gladue* factors, I isolated sentencing decisions for Indigenous women spanning between the date *Gladue* was decided (23 April 1999) and the final date of my searches (31 December 2015). I focus exclusively on sentencing decisions issued by courts of first instance (I reference any appeals when relevant). I do not differentiate between decisions issued by provincial/territorial courts and those by superior courts or by jurisdiction, although another study specific to Saskatchewan has found a disparity in how *Gladue* is applied there in Provincial Court versus that in the Court of Queen's Bench.[65]

These decisions include many in which conditional sentences feature prominently, although I also consider cases in which the only sanction discussed is incarceration in a federal institution. For example, in some judgments dealing with manslaughter, the judges did consider conditional sentences, whereas in other manslaughter cases with facts closer to murder, the judges exclusively considered longer terms of federal imprisonment; I include both types of cases. My further reasoning to include cases that contemplate only federal sentences is because Indigenous women often experience pressures to plead guilty, which becomes even more problematic on sentencing where they were overcharged. Also, what the Criminal Code declares as offences deserving of federal time are constructs, the product of political decisions, and could be otherwise conceived (at least theoretically, and certainly through any potential amendments), making any strict demarcation between cases dealing with provincial and federal sentences less necessary or logical. Additionally, the utility of conditional sentences (as an alternative to imprisonment) to respond to *Gladue* has been undercut with each amended restriction, first in 2007,[66] and again in 2012.[67] As such, it is useful to also examine cases where conditional sentences are dismissed, to further explore judicial discourses about the victimization and criminalization of Indigenous women. It remains helpful to foreground the conditional sentence order because of its restorative justice orientation in order to examine how judges connect histories of victimization and *Gladue* factors with this arguably more healing-oriented sanction.

Indigenous Women Along the Victimization-Criminalization Continuum

Indigenous women experiencing victimization are at heightened vulnerability to criminalization in part because their intergenerational marginalization already narrows their options. In her 1996 report for the Commission of Inquiry into Certain Events at the Prison for Women, Justice Louise Arbour identifies systemic limitations experienced by criminalized Indigenous women, who generally "enter the prison system at a younger age, have lower levels of education and employment, deal with greater problems of substance abuse which in turn plays a greater role in their offending, and experience higher incidences of physical and sexual abuse."[68] It is useful to think about the sentencing of Indigenous women with reference to the victimization-criminalization continuum because of the disproportionately extensive histories of victimization many criminalized Indigenous women experience. Additionally, because these histories must effectively be presented to courts sentencing Indigenous persons in the form of *Gladue* factors, it becomes important to understand the interplay between how judges discuss and use Indigenous women's histories of victimization and their *Gladue* factors (in terms of whether/how the goals of *Gladue* are furthered). The UN Committee on the Elimination of Discrimination against Women finds that

Canada's "justice and law enforcement system is not sufficiently responsive to the particular needs of aboriginal women, whether as victims of violence or as offenders."[69]

Acknowledging the interwoven issues comprising the victimization-criminalization continuum, particularly for Indigenous women, I use the term "victimization" expansively throughout this book. As I use it, "victimization" often describes experiences of violence, as well as other personal, accumulated, collective, intergenerational, and systemic, state-based traumas. The term further encompasses other difficulties that may accompany Indigenous women's responses to individual and governmental/institutional abuse and neglect (whether through numbing or attempting to regain control), such as (but not limited to) through substance use. I have chosen to adopt this expansive approach to the term "victimization" (effectively, victimization as commonly understood, victimization through systems of control, and victimization-adjacent responses) because I believe these catalysts are so interlaced they are impossible to disentangle, and it would therefore be artificial to consider them in isolation. Further, adopting a more restrictive characterization of victimization would not reflect the judicial reasoning that takes the broader view. Connected to colonization, the impact of addictions is of particular relevance to criminalized Indigenous women;[70] for example, Maria Yellow Horse Brave Heart suggests that addiction should be understood with reference to mass trauma.[71] Similarly, Nancy Poole emphasizes that "violence against women is . . . clearly implicated in the development of addiction and mental health issues."[72]

It is particularly necessary to employ an expansive definition of victimization for criminalized Indigenous women. Monture-Angus situates Indigenous women's experiences of violence within colonization, explaining that, as a Mohawk woman, "my experience of violence transcends my gender and also includes my experience of the state."[73] She writes, "The general definition of violence against women [that perpetrated by men] is too narrow to capture all of the experiences of violence that Aboriginal women face."[74] Monture-Angus criticizes prevailing definitions of violence against women "relied on by dominant institutions, structures and groups" (including feminist bodies) as being themselves "colonial" because such definitions omit the larger picture of colonization.[75] She explains that these dominant definitions preclude Indigenous women's own representations of the violence they experience. Monture-Angus suggests that such dominant, limited conceptions of violence against Indigenous women constitute and represent a further manifestation of violence in the form of "ideological violence."[76] The expansive definition of victimization that I adopt accommodates differential (but interlocking) impacts of colonization (including from the systemic violence of colonization, related interpersonal violence, and Indigenous women's responses). Further broadening the concept of "victimization" that I have articulated so far, Monture-Angus also includes "the failure to adequately resource Aboriginal community healing"[77] within her understanding of violence sustained by Indigenous peoples. This failure is implicit and at times explicit in my discussion of judicial discourses regarding victimization through colonization and available community sanctions.

Notwithstanding my expansive articulation of the victimization-criminalization continuum, I retain some lingering discomfort with the term "victimization." Some of that hesitancy relates to my inclusion of addictions, in that defining addiction as victimization may impede attention to the agency of Indigenous women. Similarly, Renée Linklater establishes a need to respect Indigenous resiliency in decolonizing trauma work, and cites Rupert Ross, who observes that "despite sustained assaults on the physical, mental, emotional and spiritual health of so many aboriginal people, the majority are *not* in jail, nor are their lives swamped by addictions, violence and despair."[78]

My unease in using the victimization-criminalization continuum arises primarily because this concept was not originally developed for the specificity of Indigenous women. Maria Yellow Horse Brave Heart and Lemyra M. DeBruyn frame various intergenerational impacts of colonization on U.S. Indigenous communities (such as violence and addictions) in terms of "historical trauma" and "historical unresolved grief,"[79] concepts originally derived from post-traumatic stress disorder and applied to mass trauma. This formulation has been challenged. For example, Joseph P. Gone argues that it essentializes Indigenous experiences of and responses to trauma, and that its orientation shifts focus away from systemic, structural inequalities,[80] and Aaron R. Denham suggests that this approach remains pathologizing.[81] I mention the concept of "historical trauma" here because, while acknowledging the substance of Gone's and Denham's critiques, I appreciate its articulation as collective in its impacts on Indigenous families and communities, cumulative in its compounded harm and weight, and intergenerational[82] in how it permeates and affects successive generations.

As applied to Indigenous women in the criminal justice system, the victimization-criminalization continuum should attend to the particular nature of the trauma of colonization as collective, cumulative, and intergenerational. Moreover, in applying the victimization-criminalization continuum in this context, I seek to delineate the specificity of the critical elements of systemic state-based assimilationist, marginalizing, control-oriented, and decimating processes, practices, policies, legislation, and institutions that comprise colonization. Ultimately, I am hopeful but uncertain as to whether defining the term "victimization" expansively is sufficient to encompass these dimensions. There is a need for further work to consider whether it would be more appropriate to refer to the "traumatization-criminalization continuum" (which might better connote the breadth and complexity of traumatizing experiences through families, communities, and generations, although, like "historical trauma" above, might also be critiqued as pathologizing), or, alternatively, to the "institutionalization-criminalization continuum" (which might better foreground the role of colonizing state forces in impelling and perpetuating the continuum). However, because the phrase "victimization-criminalization continuum" is widely used in work pertaining to Indigenous women in the criminal justice system, I have retained it—with slight reservations—for this work.

The Purpose and Principles of Sentencing

Prior to 1996, the Criminal Code of Canada specified sentencing maxima and options, but the principles of sentencing were largely judge-made. Parliament radically changed the sentencing regime with amendments to the Criminal Code that came into force in 1996.[83] As noted by Justices Peter Cory and Frank Iacobucci in *Gladue*, these amendments constitute "the first codification and significant reform of sentencing principles in the history of Canadian criminal law."[84] Aspects of these amendments signal parliamentary intention to reduce reliance on imprisonment for all criminalized persons. Section 718.2(d) provides that "an offender should not be deprived of liberty, if less restrictive sanctions may be appropriate in the circumstances."[85] The iteration of section 718.2(e) engaged in the cases I analyzed directed that sentencing judges must consider "all available sanctions other than imprisonment that are reasonable in the circumstances," "for all offenders," and "with particular attention to the circumstances" of those who are Indigenous.[86] Through the passage of the Victims Bill of Rights Act[87] in 2015, section 718.2(e) has since been amended such that now consideration of such sanctions should also be "consistent with the harm done to victims or to the community."[88] The conditional sentence order was introduced by section 742.1, which gives meaning to the requirement that judges look to alternatives for imprisonment by allowing judges to order sentences that would otherwise be prison terms to be served in the community (where appropriate).

The purpose and principles of sentencing are set out in s. 718 of the Criminal Code. The main purpose of sentencing is "to protect society and to contribute, along with crime prevention initiatives, to respect for the law and the maintenance of a just, peaceful and safe society by imposing just sanctions."[89] Section 718 lists that these sanctions must incorporate one or multiple of these itemized objectives: (a) denunciation; (b) deterrence, general and specific; (c) separation from society; (d) rehabilitation; (e) reparations for harm to the victim(s) or larger community; and (f) responsibility for the harm done.[90] Denunciation, as described by Chief Justice Antonio Lamer in *R. v. Proulx*, signifies societal "condemnation of the offender's conduct,"[91] and often accompanies deterrence (the need to discourage future such conduct) in judicial reasoning. Although imprisonment is commonly associated with the promotion of deterrence (both in the public consciousness and the courts), the Supreme Court of Canada has held that "empirical evidence suggests that the deterrent effect of incarceration is uncertain," further suggesting that conditional sentences can operate to deter with punitive conditions and public awareness.[92]

Rehabilitation is considered more restorative justice-oriented for its basis in and prioritization of healing and personal/behavioural change and emphasis on reintegration into society.[93] This is often in tension with denunciation and deterrence because, as Justices Cory and Iacobucci observe in *Gladue*, "restorative sentencing goals do not usually correlate with the use of prison as a sanction."[94] Any friction among the purposes of sentencing may be written into the sentencing process, reflecting that "sentencing, like the criminal trial process itself, has often been understood as a conflict between the interests of the state (as expressed through the aims of separation, deterrence, and denunciation) and the interests of the individual offender (as expressed through the aim of rehabilitation)."[95] However, the interests of the state and those of the individual should not be understood as wholly polarized. The purposes of denunciation, deterrence, and rehabilitation should be interpreted as interconnected processes, because most prisoners will eventually return to the community. This understanding is consistent with the restorative justice paradigm.[96] Anthony Doob and Cheryl Webster state, "Canada has never given primacy to any one specific sentencing purpose," affording judges the discretion and responsibility to determine which should be foregrounded, depending on each case[97] (although determinations by sentencing judges about how to weight the various objectives may also be guided by the tone of judgments by the appellate court of that jurisdiction, which may operate to suppress judicial intention to emphasize restorative justice principles on sentencing).[98] This is consistent with the inherently individualized process of sentencing.[99] While some sentencing decisions involve factors that point toward a sentencing response guided by denunciation and deterrence over a more rehabilitative approach, other judgments emphasize the rehabilitation of the woman before the courts as the overriding concern. Paradoxically and problematically, the latter sometimes still produces a punitive sanction, albeit under the guise of "healing." I use the terms "healing" and "rehabilitation" interchangeably, as seems consistent with the reading and usage of both terms in *Gladue*.[100]

In the review of the criminal justice system by Department of Justice Canada, participants suggest that to reduce overincarceration and to promote alternative measures beyond the system, the government could reorient sentencing with rehabilitation as the primary "goal"[101] of the process. This could involve a lesser overall concentration "on guilt or innocence," and a greater focus "on helping to rehabilitate and reintegrate people with mental illness and addiction,"[102] and particularly so in the context of the overincarceration of Indigenous persons. In the current system, section 718.1 requires sentences to be proportionate to both the seriousness of the offence and the degree of responsibility of the offender.[103] Proportionality is the fundamental principle of sentencing and is always engaged in sentencing (however judges resolve the remaining purpose and principles of sentencing).[104] In *R. v. Nasogaluak,* the Supreme Court of Canada held, in a decision delivered by Justice Louis LeBel, that proportionality predates its codification in the 1996 sentencing reforms, rooted in a "long history as a guiding principle in sentencing."[105] In an Alberta Court of Appeal decision thoroughly detailing the sentencing regime in Canada, Chief Justice Catherine A. Fraser, Justice Jean E.L. Côté, and Justice Jack Watson write for the majority that Parliament positioned proportionality as the required overarching principle to propel the determination of sentence because it provides a "common standard" "to guide the exercise of sentencing discretion."[106] This prevents the "arbitrary application of state power," constituting the "blunt tool of punishment" as "valid" and "morally acceptable."[107]

The "secondary principles"[108] in s. 718.2 combine to bolster the proportionality principle and form part of the proportionality analysis.[109] Section 718.2(b) is the parity principle, which implicates the degree of moral blameworthiness of the offender and is necessary to the proportionality analysis. It directs that sentences should be similar for similar offenders and similar offence circumstances.[110] Sections 718.2(d) and (e) should be read together and jointly constitute the restraint principle.[111] As above, section 718.2(d) states that less restrictive sanctions should be ordered where appropriate, and s. 718.2(e) specifies that imprisonment should be ordered as a last resort where reasonable and given harm caused, and particularly for Indigenous persons before sentencing courts.[112] Both these restraint and restorative justice–oriented principles are inherent in and consistent with the proportionality principle.[113] The justices for the majority in *R. v. Arcand* hold that "the object of the sentencing exercise is to draw on all sentencing principles in determining a just and appropriate sentence which reflects the gravity of the offence and the degree of moral blameworthiness of the offender."[114] These principles operate within and guide s. 718.3, subsections (1) and (2), which ensure judicial discretion on sentencing within any restrictions on available sanctions for the specific offence.[115]

The purpose and principles of sentencing operate in conjunction with one another in an "integrated framework."[116] The objectives of sentencing listed within the purpose of sentencing must conform to the proportionality principle.[117] Sentencing judges determine how to weigh the various objectives in relation to the gravity of the offence and the offender's degree of responsibility (proportionality).[118] Effectively, the objectives and secondary principles of sentencing inform sentencing determinations, but in service of the proportionality principle.[119]

Of the various sentencing principles, s. 718.2(e) is critical to the discussion in this book. I also periodically refer to how aggravating and mitigating factors are presented in the judgments. Judges must adjust sentences by accounting for aggravating or mitigating circumstances (further sentencing principles) arising from the offence or specific to the offender per s. 718.2(a) of the Criminal Code.[120] Although various aggravating factors are (non-exhaustively) listed in the Criminal Code, there are no legislatively itemized mitigating factors.[121] Instead, mitigating factors (and additional aggravating factors) develop through judge-made law. Justice Iacobucci states in *R. v. Wells* that *Gladue* factors "are mitigating in nature,"[122] and this formulation is affirmed in *Ipeelee*.[123] *Gladue* explains that "aggravating circumstances will obviously increase the need for denunciation and deterrence,"[124] which then has potential implications for judicial decisions about the severity of custodial sanctions ordered in terms of duration and the form of sanction. David Milward and Debra Parkes observe that aggravating and/or mitigating factors propel much decision making in sentencing, and that the case law suggests "aggravating factors are seen to cast the offence—and the individual—in such a negative light as to render *Gladue* inapplicable."[125]

Clayton C. Ruby, Gerald J. Chan, and Nader R. Hasan explain that the weight judges attribute to aggravating and mitigating factors they find in a specific case ultimately "shapes and determines the sentence imposed,"[126] rendering the relative weighting of those factors

cruciallysignificant.Whilevariousfactorsarestipulatedas "aggravating" in
s. 718.2(a), the section is expansive and still affords judicial discretion, as
the weight of any aggravating factors must be contexualized and considered alongside available mitigating factors, against other circumstances
of the person before the court, and all within the fundamental principle
of proportionality. That is, even where a legislatively enumerated aggravating factor may be identified in the facts of the offence, a judge may
determine that when balanced against other complex sentencing considerations, that aggravating factor should not produce a demonstrable,
quantifiable effect on the type and/or duration of the sanction imposed.

None of the statutorily specified aggravating factors are gender-
specific, although they may have gendered effects, such as those arising through the operation of s. 718.2(a)(ii). The statutory wording of
this provision indicates that in sentencing a judge "shall also *take into
consideration*" that "a sentence should be increased or reduced to account for any *relevant* aggravating or mitigating circumstances relating to the offence *or the offender*," including that evidence of partner
abuse in the commission of the offence shall be deemed aggravating.[127]
As Ruby, Chan, and Hasan observe, the principles in s. 718.2 are broad
and "provide no mechanism for resolving the inevitable conflicts that
arise" among competing principles within specific cases.[128] It thus remains available to judges to determine that partner abuse committed
by a criminalized woman in the context of a relationship in which she
has herself been abused carries only minimal or negligible weight as an
aggravating factor, effectively displaced by the potentially mitigating effect of the abuse she has experienced and given overall reduced moral
blameworthiness. However, as observed by Justice Alexander Sosna in
R. v. McIntyre, "the courts have repeatedly held that domestic violence
perpetrated on a partner is an aggravating factor."[129] This judicial norm
may create harsher penalties for Indigenous women criminalized for offences involving violence against their abusive partners, if this contributes to the perceived need for greater denunciation and deterrence at
the expense of mitigation through *Gladue* factors. It must also be remembered that much of Indigenous women's violence occurs in this domestic context,[130] so they may be disproportionately subjected to this aggravating factor. In thirteen judgments within my research in which the

offence involves violence against the Indigenous woman's partner, judges find this circumstance to be aggravating per s. 718.2(a)(ii), despite extensive histories of intimate violence that the women experienced both within that relationship and elsewhere.[131] I suggest judges should be cautious and strongly disinclined to give meaningful weight to s. 718.2(a)(ii) when sentencing a woman whose offending arises within the context of partner abuse wherein she has been victimized.

The specific issue of whether partner violence should be given compelling weight as aggravating in cases where women become criminalized for their own violence after surviving extensive violence within that relationship (or within similar other relationships) should be explored in greater depth than the scope of this book allows. In Chapter 2, I highlight a sentencing decision[132] in which the judge comments that this aggravating factor may be less persuasive in such cases. For now, it is worth noting that the violence committed by Indigenous women often arises against a distinct background of victimization,[133] demanding a contextual understanding of both ends of this spectrum of abuse to enable sensitive sentencing legislation and judicial reasoning.

R. v. Gladue: Fleshing out Section 718.2(e)

In its 1999 decision *Gladue*, the scc gives direction to judges sentencing Indigenous persons in the post-1996 regime by discussing the context of and parliamentary intention behind s. 718.2(e) and explaining how judges should engage in the analysis required by this provision. Delivered by Justices Cory and Iacobucci in a unanimous judgment, *Gladue* explains that s. 718.2(e) was intended in part to ameliorate the overrepresentation of Indigenous peoples in the criminal justice system, and particularly its prisons. Justices Cory and Iacobucci decried this overrepresentation as a national "crisis."[134] Broadly, they held that the parliamentary intentions motivating s. 718.2(e) were primarily to reduce overreliance on incarceration as a sanction, expand usage of restorative justice principles to guide sentencing, and promote consideration of how to better design sentences that will be more appropriate for and meaningful to Indigenous persons.[135]

Justices Cory and Iacobucci held that while the 1996 sentencing amendments signify a general amplification of restorative justice principles, restorative justice is particularly critical in the sentencing of Indigenous persons because "most traditional aboriginal conceptions of sentencing place a primary emphasis upon the ideals of restorative justice. This tradition is extremely important to the analysis under s. 718.2(e)."[136] Rooted in "a model of healing rather than of punishing,"[137] as Tuhiwai Smith suggests, restorative justice presents a different paradigm for sentencing.[138] This paradigm implicates different goals because it is relationships-oriented, expanding the view of justice processes to include interconnections among the criminalized person, the victim(s), and the broader community, and striving to balance and respond to each party's needs through the sanction ordered.[139] (In the context of decolonizing trauma work, Renée Linklater states, "relationships are a significant aspect of Indigenous healing.")[140] Often, sanctions consistent with restorative justice are community-based.[141] Justices Cory and Iacobucci explain that community-based sanctions are important for criminalized Indigenous persons because they "coincide with the aboriginal concept of sentencing and the needs of aboriginal people and communities."[142] Such issues are complex; Indigenous women's groups made submissions in opposition to the alternatives to incarceration proposed within Bill C-41, which included s. 718.2(e) and the conditional sentence order, and, in Carmela Murdoca's words, "warn[ed] that so-called 'culturally appropriate' (or community-based) legal mechanisms did not have any 'cultural relevance' to certain communities," and that non-carceral sentences issued for men would extend "serious and violent implications for the women"[143] in contexts of intimate violence, who may feel unsafe or revictimized.[144]

Gladue directs "sentencing judges to undertake the process of sentencing aboriginal offenders differently, in order to endeavour to achieve a truly fit and proper sentence in the particular case."[145] Justices Cory and Iacobucci explain that this different mode of sentencing arises from a necessary change in the "method of analysis,"[146] because s. 718.2(e) "suggests that there is something different about aboriginal offenders which may specifically make imprisonment a less appropriate or less useful sanction."[147] *Gladue* finds that Indigenous peoples may be "more adversely affected by incarceration and less likely to be 'rehabilitated' thereby, because the internment milieu is often culturally inappropriate and regrettably discrimination towards them is so often rampant in penal institutions."[148] As a result, judges must be apprised of the options available in or outside the community that could function as alternatives to imprisonment.[149]

This observation about the inappropriateness of incarceration for Indigenous peoples is borne out by research finding that they are assessed as having higher needs in prison,[150] which translates to their being assessed as presenting higher risk (to the institution, and/or of reoffence), often grounding a harsher experience of imprisonment due to institutional decisions such as isolation through segregation or being classified at a higher level of security[151] (which imports stricter controls and supervision).[152] In *Gladue*, Justices Cory and Iacobucci hold that the judicial search for alternatives to imprisonment for Indigenous peoples should be expansive, such that "even if community support is not available, every effort should be made in appropriate circumstances to find a sensitive and helpful alternative. For all purposes, the term 'community' must be defined broadly so as to include any network of support and interaction that might be available in an urban centre. At the same time, the residence of the aboriginal offender in an urban centre that lacks any network of support does not relieve the sentencing judge of the obligation to try to find an alternative to imprisonment."[153]

Gladue directs that the s. 718.2(e) analysis involves both consideration of systemic and background factors related to each Indigenous person coming before the courts, and how his or her Indigenous heritage or connection should influence the form of sanction.[154] Specifically, judges must determine whether the sanction would be meaningful (in terms of denunciation and deterrence) to the criminalized person's community, often implicating restorative sentencing principles.[155] Recognizing that Indigenous communities and their customs, traditions, and beliefs are not monolithic but vary across nations, *Gladue* finds that sentencing concepts are often inappropriate for criminalized Indigenous persons.[156]

Justices Cory and Iacobucci direct that it is particularly important for judges to structure community-based sentences for less serious or non-violent offences.[157] They indicate that for more serious or violent offences, sentences will be more similar in type and duration for

Indigenous and non-Indigenous persons, as is more likely to be consistent with both Indigenous and non-Indigenous conceptions of sentencing.[158] Although "there is no single test that a judge can apply,"[159] much as all sentencing must be individualized, the sentencing of Indigenous peoples engages a number of questions specific to each case:

> For this offence, committed by this offender, harming
> this victim, in this community, what is the appropriate
> sanction under the *Criminal Code*? What understanding
> of criminal sanctions is held by the community? What is
> the nature of the relationship between the offender and
> his or her community? What combination of systemic or
> background factors contributed to this particular offender
> coming before the courts for this particular offence? How
> has the offender who is being sentenced been affected by, for
> example, substance abuse in the community, or poverty, or
> overt racism, or family or community breakdown? Would
> imprisonment effectively serve to deter or denounce crime
> in a sense that would be significant to the offender and
> community, or are crime prevention and other goals better
> achieved through healing? What sentencing options present
> themselves in these circumstances?[160]

To answer these questions, judges must take judicial notice of the relevant systemic or background factors involved, but also may require evidence about the criminalized Indigenous person's circumstances, at minimum through the pre-sentence report.[161] Ultimately, Justices Cory and Iacobucci characterize the duty of a judge sentencing an Indigenous person as being engaged in a process of substantive equality: "The fundamental purpose of s. 718.2(e) is to treat aboriginal offenders fairly by taking into account their difference."[162]

R. v. Ipeelee: Underscoring and Bolstering *Gladue*

The SCC has since delivered a judgment strongly affirming *Gladue* and adding some clarity. Decided 23 March 2012, *Ipeelee* addresses two appeals concerning Indigenous men designated long-term offenders involving breaches of their long-term supervision orders. Writing for the majority (Justice Marshall Rothstein dissented in part), Justice LeBel notes that "the overrepresentation and alienation of Aboriginal peoples in the criminal justice system has only worsened"[163] since the 1996 amendments, and references that "courts have, at times, been hesitant to take judicial notice of the systemic and background factors affecting Aboriginal people in Canadian society."[164] Justice LeBel reiterates *Gladue*'s directive to judges, underscoring that to provide the necessary context to engage in sentencing, "courts must take judicial notice of such matters as the history of colonialism, displacement, and residential schools and how that history continues to translate into lower educational attainment, lower incomes, higher unemployment, higher rates of substance abuse and suicide, and of course higher levels of incarceration for Aboriginal peoples."[165]

More rigorous deployment of judicial notice may also assist with one of the two problems *Ipeelee* identifies with the jurisprudence post-*Gladue* that have "thwart[ed] what was originally envisioned by *Gladue*":[166] "some cases erroneously suggest that an offender must establish a causal link between background factors and the commission of the current offence before being entitled to have those matters considered by the sentencing judge."[167] This incorrect interpretation of *Gladue* functions as an "evidentiary burden,"[168] which goes much farther than the *Gladue* directive to "give attention to the unique background and systemic factors which may have played a part in bringing the particular offender before the courts."[169] This practice is inappropriate because a causal link will be prohibitively difficult for Indigenous persons to disentangle and establish, given the complexities and interrelationships within the continuing effects of colonization.[170] Justice LeBel adds that it does not even make sense to demand a causal connection, because *Gladue* factors "do not operate as an excuse or justification for the criminal conduct" but instead contextualize the judge's reasoning.[171]

The second problem *Ipeelee* discerns in the post-*Gladue* jurisprudence is the "irregular and uncertain application of the *Gladue* principles to sentencing decisions for serious or violent offences."[172] Justice LeBel explains that *Gladue*'s reference—that sentences will be more similar for Indigenous and non-Indigenous persons the more serious or violent the offence—has led to "unwarranted emphasis" on this proposition, prompting "numerous courts" to "erroneously [interpret] this generalization as an indication that the *Gladue* principles do not apply to serious offences."[173] This is problematic because what constitutes a "serious" offence is not defined in the Criminal Code,[174] and it undermines the overriding *Gladue* direction that judges must consider the background and circumstances of each Indigenous person on sentencing.[175] Judges have a *duty* to apply s. 718.2(e),[176] and to fail to apply *Gladue* when sentencing an Indigenous person "runs afoul of this statutory obligation," producing "a sentence that was not fit and was not consistent with the fundamental principle of proportionality."[177] Therefore, it is not sufficient for sentencing judges to detail the personal history of an Indigenous person before them but to then fail "to consider whether and how that history ought to impact on her sentencing decision."[178]

Both errors *Ipeelee* finds in the post-*Gladue* jurisprudence feature in the cases in my research. *Ipeelee* provides helpful comments about how *Gladue* factors conform to the overarching sentencing regime (instead of presenting a deviation): "Canadian criminal law is based on the premise that criminal liability only follows from voluntary conduct. Many Aboriginal offenders find themselves in situations of social and economic deprivation with a lack of opportunities and limited options for positive development. While this rarely—if ever—attains a level where one could properly say that their actions were not voluntary and therefore not deserving of criminal sanction, *the reality is that their constrained circumstances may diminish their moral culpability.*"[179] Because these systemic issues may cause Indigenous peoples to have diminished moral culpability[180] (which strikes at the heart of the foremost principle of sentencing—proportionality—in terms of the degree of responsibility of the offender), *Gladue* factors are framed as mitigating.[181] Moreover, following *Gladue,* Justice LeBel explains that "the existence of such circumstances may also indicate that a sanction that takes account of the underlying causes of the criminal conduct may be more appropriate than one only aimed at punishment per se."[182] Restorative justice sanctions may be necessary, as "the *Gladue* principles direct sentencing judges to abandon the presumption that all offenders and all communities share the same values when it comes to sentencing and to recognize that, given these fundamentally different world views, different or alternative sanctions may more effectively achieve the objectives of sentencing in a particular community."[183] *Ipeelee* clarifies that the most important consideration—as with all sentencing—should be the individualization of sentencing decisions. As such, s. 718.2(e) does not require judges to produce an artificial reduction of incarceration rates.[184] Quite the contrary; *Gladue* merely requires an "individualized assessment of all of the relevant factors and circumstances, including the status and life experiences, of the person standing before them," which for criminalized Indigenous persons requires consideration of their unique circumstances.[185] This, "to endeavour to achieve a truly fit and proper sentence," is "the fundamental duty of a sentencing judge."[186] Additionally, this must be done "in a manner that is meaningful to Aboriginal peoples" because "neglecting this duty would not be faithful to the core requirement of the sentencing process."[187]

Although this book focuses on the text of sentencing judgments, it should also be noted that appellate courts exert a hovering influence that may either constrain attempts by sentencing judges to give full effect to *Gladue* analyses or permit sentencing judges to engage in shallower *Gladue* analyses, complicating the already challenging task of sentencing. For example, James Scott finds that the Saskatchewan Court of Appeal has undermined the likelihood and effectiveness of proper *Gladue* analyses at the sentencing level by demonstrating "very little to no support" for ameliorating Indigenous overrepresentation through restorative justice principles, including s. 718.2(e),[188] and by allowing "the lower courts to rely on the 'lip service' of *Gladue* principles" without requiring judges to explain their reasoning or to list the sentencing principles considered.[189] (Other research suggests that many other appellate courts "have recently shifted towards requiring express reasons from sentencing judges" regarding their *Gladue* analyses.)[190] As such, it should be kept in mind that sentencing judges render their decisions within this institutional hierarchy, with the prospect of being overturned, and/or the potential knowledge of appellate permissiveness of less robust *Gladue* analyses, depending on the jurisdiction. Even more broadly, it should also be remembered that all sentencing judges operate within the function and limits of the overburdened criminal justice system. Formerly of the

Provincial Court of Nova Scotia and since appointed to the Nova Scotia Court of Appeal, Justice Anne S. Derrick describes the work of frontline judges: "The work is hard, regularly relentless, the problems that propel people before us often seem intractable, the narratives are frequently heartrending, and . . . they read as indictments of the inequalities in our society. The available resources are stretched thin, [and] the tools we have at our disposal are blunt. It has been my experience that the judges serving these courts and facing their perennial challenges keep trying their best to do justice, to find the right balance, to craft solutions, with compassion, common sense, and courage."[191]

In *Gladue*, Justices Cory and Iacobucci describe that the systemic or background factors contributing to overrepresentation "flows from a number of sources, including poverty, substance abuse, lack of education, and the lack of employment opportunities for aboriginal people. It arises also from bias against aboriginal people and from an unfortunate institutional approach that is more inclined to refuse bail and to impose more and longer prison terms for aboriginal offenders."[192] They also cite loneliness, dislocation, and community fragmentation as factors contributing to the overrepresentation of Indigenous peoples in the system.[193]

Although Justices Cory and Iacobucci do not name "colonialism" or "colonization" or any variations thereof,[194] the sources of Indigenous overrepresentation in the system *are* products of colonization, the reverberating effects (and/or continued strategies) of colonialism. In *Ipeelee*, Justice LeBel explicitly names colonialism as part of "the distinct history of Aboriginal peoples in Canada"; Justice LeBel writes, "The overwhelming message emanating from the various reports and commissions on Aboriginal peoples' involvement in the criminal justice system is that current levels of criminality are intimately tied to the legacy of colonialism."[195]

Alternatives to Imprisonment: Conditional Sentence Orders

As part of the 1996 amendments to the Criminal Code, the conditional sentence order (CSO) was implemented to provide an alternative to provincial incarceration because it remains a sentence of imprisonment, but served in the community and with an amplified restorative justice orientation. The conditional sentence of imprisonment offers a particularly important alternative for the sentencing of Indigenous peoples.[196] *Gladue* describes the advent of conditional sentences as "alter[ing] the sentencing landscape" for its ability to give real meaning to ss. 718.2(d) and (e).[197] The leading judgment on conditional sentences is *R. v. Proulx* (issued before the 2007 and 2012 CSO amendments), in which Justice Lamer holds that conditional sentences were intended "for less serious and non-dangerous offenders."[198] The 1996 iteration of the conditional sentencing regime required judges to evaluate four factors when deciding whether a conditional sentence order was appropriate: conditional sentences were available only for individuals who would otherwise be sentenced to terms of less than two years' imprisonment; offences that had minimum terms of imprisonment were ineligible; the presence of the individuals could not present a danger to the community; and the sentence must be consistent with principles of sentencing.[199]

Conditional sentences are associated with a restorative justice approach because they are orders of imprisonment served in the community, although punitive elements are incorporated through supervision and attached conditions that restrict liberty, with the further punitive potential that a judge will commute the sentence to a prison sanction for persons who breach conditions without reasonable excuse.[200] *Proulx* underscores the punitive quality of conditional sentences, but notes the simultaneous ability for the sanction to respond to rehabilitative, denunciatory, and deterrent goals. This combination of rehabilitative and punitive features of conditional sentences distinguishes them from probationary orders,[201] because probation "has traditionally been viewed as a rehabilitative sentencing tool."[202] Additionally, a judge can order an offender to participate in treatment as a condition of a conditional sentence order, whereas this can be accomplished only with the offender's consent for a probation order.[203] (Probation, by itself or attached to another type of sanction, including conditional sentences, is the most frequently ordered disposition.)[204] For the Indigenous women in my research receiving conditional sentence orders, treatment conditions are often attached.

As the conditional sentence is available to certain criminalized persons who otherwise face jail, *Proulx* holds that conditions that constrain liberty (such as house arrest or strict curfews) "should be the norm, not the exception."[205] Such conditions, alongside the stigma of living in the community under strict controls,[206] ensure that "a conditional sentence may be as onerous as, or perhaps even more onerous than, a jail term, particularly in circumstances where the offender is forced to take responsibility for his or her actions and make reparations to both the victim and the community."[207] Nonetheless, Justice Lamer still maintains that prison is generally more onerous, which encourages the imposition of lengthier conditional sentences to approximate a shorter duration of jail.[208] These and other impacts of the conditional sentencing regime have been criticized for effectively widening state control and presenting a risk of "the increased use of imprisonment," primarily due to what Kent Roach describes as the "extraordinary breach provisions that give the state administrative powers generally not seen in the criminal law."[209] (In the British context, Pat Carlen refers to proposals for non-custodial sanctions as "state transcarceralism," part of "a policy designed to bring the pains of imprisonment into the 'community'" in a manner "so punitive that sentencers would have more confidence in awarding them.")[210]

The conditional sentence order remains critically needed within the sentencing options available to judges. It is an especially needed sentencing alternative for Indigenous persons because, as Elizabeth Adjin-Tettey writes, against the backdrop of colonization and its continuing manifestations and effects, "the ineffectiveness of incarceration creates a cycle of victimization, which is partly manifested in the overincarceration of Aboriginal people."[211] The Truth and Reconciliation Commission (TRC) reports that it "believes that the recent introduction of mandatory minimum sentences and restrictions on conditional sentences will increase Aboriginal overrepresentation in prison. Such developments are preventing judges from implementing community sanctions even when they are consistent with the safety of the community and even when they have a much greater potential than imprisonment to respond to the intergenerational legacy of residential schools that often results in offences by Aboriginal persons."[212] Additionally, according to Juristat, research shows that "the representation of Aboriginal adults is growing only in admissions to provincial and territorial sentenced custody"[213] (the level at which conditional sentences are relevant). *Ipeelee* also recognizes that the overrepresentation of Indigenous peoples in prisons, which prompted s. 718.2(e), "was generally worse in provincial institutions."[214]

The availability of conditional sentences is also particularly important for Indigenous women specifically. Justice Arbour has noted that the overrepresentation of Indigenous women is even more stark in provincial prisons than federal penitentiaries[215] (although they are also highly overrepresented in federal institutions).[216] This suggests that restrictions on this alternative to provincial/territorial incarceration are likely to exacerbate the overrepresentation of Indigenous women where it is already most pronounced. It is necessary to have alternatives to imprisonment at this level because proportionally more women (both Indigenous and non-Indigenous) are admitted to provincial/territorial prisons than to federal penitentiaries. In 2015–16, according to Juristat, women comprised 16 percent of all admissions to provincial and territorial corrections, and "accounted for a higher proportion of community admissions (20%) than custody admissions (13%)" (the latter figure seems to include admissions to remand), whereas women represented 7 percent of overall admissions to federal custody (which also appears to include remand).[217] It is helpful to understand the greater proportions of women in provincial/territorial custody and alternatives to custody through Justice Arbour's comments: "As an overview, I think it is fair to say that women commit fewer crimes than men, and that the disproportion is immense and has remained more or less historically constant. Women commit fewer violent crimes than men, and even when they are convicted of the same crime as a man, the factual underpinning of the offence is often considerably different, and tends to point to a much lower risk of re-offending. Women pose a lower security risk than men. They have primary childcare responsibility in numbers vastly disproportionate to male offenders."[218] In this context, restrictions on the availability of conditional sentences may have gendered effects. Comments by Cynthia Chewter, Ellen Adelberg, and Claudia Currie, issued a few years after the introduction of this sanction, remain equally salient today: "Conditional sentencing legislation offers a powerful new tool for those who advocate for women in conflict with the law. The legislation also helps to alleviate some of the most serious burdens that women face in the correctional system: inability to serve their sentences close to their communities, loss of their children, and potential access to a greater variety of programs and counseling."[219] Limitations on the availability of conditional sentences risk reinforcing these burdens on criminalized women, burdens carrying weight that can fracture their families (and it must be remembered how processes of colonization have fractured and continue to fracture specifically Indigenous families and communities). Altogether, the ongoing attenuation of judicial discretion to order conditional sentences is a cause for concern generally, and specifically for criminalized Indigenous women.

The 2007 and 2012 Conditional Sentencing Amendments

The conditional sentence has been contentious throughout its lifespan, in the political domain and within the public consciousness.[220] Objections to or discomfort about the conditional sentencing regime primarily relate to the use or perceived use of conditional sentences for violent offences. Statistics Canada reports that in 2008–09 the vast majority of conditional sentences were ordered for non-violent offences (including 28 percent related to property offences and 21 percent to drug offences), whereas 26 percent of conditional sentences pertained to violent offences.[221] In this climate, Parliament passed Bill C-9: An Act to amend the Criminal Code (Conditional Sentence of Imprisonment),[222] which received Royal Assent on 31 May 2007, with its amendments coming into force six months later.[223] Still more restrictions have supplanted the 2007 amendments as part of Bill C-10,[224] which received Royal Assent on 13 March 2012 and entered into force as the further amended s. 742.1 on 20 November 2012.[225] The content of this newly enacted version of s. 742.1 is much more restrictive than prior iterations. All such restrictions on judicial discretion in the conditional sentencing regime undercut the utility of the sanction to respond to the overincarceration of Indigenous peoples.

Currently, the conditional sentencing regime is governed by s. 742, comprising s. 742.1 to s. 742.7.[226] Section 742.1 retains the original parameters: conditional sentences are still available only for imprisonment terms of less than two years and are subject to compliance with conditions; offences with codified minimum punishments are ineligible; community safety should not be endangered; and the sentence must be consistent with the purpose and principles of sentencing. The 2007 amendments made additional restrictions, but the added restriction of greatest potential relevance to criminalized Indigenous women was the stipulation that the commission of serious personal injury offences, as defined in s. 752,[227] rendered conditional sentences unavailable. In the main, section 752 defines "serious personal injury offence" as an indictable offence (excluding treason and first- and second-degree murder) "for which the offender may be sentenced to imprisonment for ten years or more" and involving "the use or attempted use of violence"; conduct likely to endanger or endangering another person's life/safety; or conduct likely to inflict or inflicting "severe psychological damage" on another.[228]

Because the violence for which Indigenous women are criminalized is often serious, the 2007 amendment that removed conditional sentences as an option for cases involving serious personal injury offences may have had a disproportionate impact. This aspect of the 2007 amendments was of particular relevance because, as noted by Justice Arbour, Indigenous women are often imprisoned for more violent offences and experience more periods of incarceration than non-Indigenous women.[229] Their experiences of imprisonment are also more punitive. As Karlene Faith and Anne Near indicate, Indigenous women are overall "more likely than white women to be classified as maximum security, to be locked in segregation and to be denied parole."[230] The Office of the Correctional Investigator reports in 2017 that Indigenous women federal prisoners constitute 50 percent of women in maximum security.[231] In the previous year, the Correctional Investigator reports that Indigenous women federal prisoners comprised 50 percent of women held in segregation,[232] and, in the report from 2015, that Indigenous women are "more likely to be classified as [having] low reintegration potential" than non-Indigenous women.[233] Allison Campbell suggests that the overclassification of Indigenous women is "because of the violence they experience outside the prison walls, and because of their resistance strategies inside them."[234] For these and other reasons, the experience of incarceration may be understood as more punitive for Indigenous women than for other prisoners, and the stakes of not receiving community sanctions greater. Some have argued that the impacts of the 1996 sentencing reforms have been gendered,[235] contending that, as Robyn Maynard writes, "more Indigenous men [than women] have benefitted from sentencing provisions for conditional sentences."[236] Nonetheless, because a conditional sentence order most readily replaces what could otherwise be a carceral sentence, conditional sentences provide a valuable tool to address the overrepresentation of Indigenous women in prisons.

The 2007 erosion of the conditional sentencing regime is deepened by the 2012 amendments, which engage similar problems. After it entered into force, Bill C-10 detaches s. 742.1 from the above connection to serious personal injury offences in s. 752, but now further restricts s. 742.1 by adding subsections that remove the sanction for the following offences (where they are prosecuted by indictment): those with maximum terms of imprisonment of fourteen years or life; those with a maximum term of imprisonment of ten years where the offence resulted in bodily harm, involved the trafficking/production of drugs, or involved a weapon; and those identified within the list[237] of offences provided (which, among other offences, include theft over $5,000 and breaking and entering). I identified which of the cases in my research would no longer be eligible for conditional sentence orders after the 2012 amendments following the passage of Bill C-10. The results are sobering: for the most part, the amendments effectively all but eliminate conditional sentence orders as a possible sanction. In the Department of Justice Canada's review of the criminal justice system, participants suggest that the government legislatively expand judicial discretion to "deal with the restrictions on conditional sentences that mandatory minimum penalties create," and contend that "conditional sentences should be used more often but are usually unavailable for more serious offences."[238] At this juncture, where conditional sentences have become increasingly less available, it is of continued importance for courts to heed the direction from *Ipeelee* to not overly fix on the idea (misapprehended from Justices Cory and Iacobucci's comment in *Gladue*) that more serious or more violent offences will more often produce sentences similar between Indigenous and non-Indigenous persons.[239]

Restrictions on Judicial Discretion: Preliminary Problems

The various permutations of the respective legislative texts of bills C-9 and C-10 culminating in the 2007 and 2012 amendments to the conditional sentencing regime exceed the scope of this book, although concerns voiced within the pushback against restrictions on judicial discretion did manifest to some degree in the cases I studied. In September 2006, the National Criminal Justice Section (NCJS) of the Canadian Bar Association recommended that Bill C-9 (the first set of amendments) should not be enacted.[240] The NCJS cautioned that Bill C-9 encroached on judicial discretion, impeding the ability of judges to "achieve a just result," and set the stage for "a disproportionate impact on populations already over-represented in the justice system, notably the economically disadvantaged, Aboriginal people, members of visible minorities and the mentally ill."[241] The NCJS expressed concern that the incursions into judicial discretion would impact the proportionality of sentences where judges are compelled to sentence more[242] or less[243] punitively to conform to the proposed legislation. The version of Bill C-9 that passed had been amended, differing from the iteration criticized by the NCJS.[244] However, the NCJS concern about proportionality has manifested in some of the cases in my study in which probation replaces the now-unavailable conditional sentence order.[245] Other decisions indicate that, when precluded from delivering the conditional sentence order they would have otherwise imposed, judges also resort to imposing terms of incarceration.[246]

In my case law research, the effects of the conditional sentencing amendments are inconsistently represented, as each case varies in terms of when the offence was committed and how long the criminalized woman had been in remand or on judicial interim release, for example, before the hearing. Because the timing of the offence relative to the 2007 and 2012 amendments varies, it may still be slightly premature to find trends in the case law for the effects of the amendments. This issue implicates the principle of legality, which, as noted in *Arcand,* "has not been expressly codified in Canada," but is protected by the judiciary.[247] Sentencing must comply with the legality principle,[248] which "requires that the law must be (1) accessible, that is understandable; (2) foreseeable in its consequences; and (3) non-arbitrary in its application."[249] In my research, the original conditional sentencing regime (enacted in 1996 and preceding the first set of amendments) operates as late as 2012,[250] and even 2014.[251] Further, while the earliest case that deals with the version of s. 742.1 enacted through Bill C-9 in the 2007 amendments is a 2008 decision,[252] my searches also produced cases engaging this conditional sentencing regime as recently as 2015.[253] I believe the first decision from my research that relies upon the version of conditional sentences that entered into force in 2012 through Bill C-10 is a case decided in 2014.[254] As such, because the offence dates are variable and only several years have transpired since the 2007 and 2012 amendments, it is difficult to reliably track the impacts on Indigenous women through the sentencing decisions. Nonetheless, many decisions specifically comment on the unavailability of conditional sentences for the women facing sanctions due to the 2007 and 2012 amendments. Moreover, such restrictions on judicial discretion hamper fulfillment of the *Gladue* analysis required by s. 718.2(e), while the legislative reasons mobilizing s. 718.2(e) (over-representation and broadening of the use of restorative justice) remain unchanged. Conditional sentence orders offer a critical alternative to imprisonment for Indigenous women.

Law's Complicity with Oppression and Capacity to Promote Progressive Social Change

Suggesting broadly that law is implicated in social and political practices of institutional violence, Robert Cover argues that legal interpretation (particularly such work by judges) should be understood as an act of violence in itself, and also facilitating further violence.[255] Cover contends that legal interpretation (such as in sentencing) and its implementation (such as through the administration of prison sentences) each consist of distinct acts of violence,[256] but are interconnected in the sense that judicial pronouncements induce and empower action by other institutional bodies[257] in a manner that produces the violence of domination.[258] As Fran Sugar and Lana Fox observe, the prison system replicates "the violence that it is supposedly designed to manage" for Indigenous women sentenced to carceral terms who are often already "victims of long-term and systematic violence."[259] Jonathan Simon argues that Cover's work insufficiently theorizes punishment, and that without examining the shifting conditions of the work of judges,[260] given "changing mechanisms and purposes of punishment"[261] through increased punitiveness at the political level in the United States, Cover assumes an implicitness in the violence of law, which elides "consideration of whether law's violence could be mediated."[262] Simon's analysis renders the political context of sentencing significant, given the need for greater (and incursions into existing) legislative and community-based provision for alternatives to incarceration in Canada.

Cover's depiction of law as an oppressive force with inherent power to cause harm remains salient for its recognition that institutional practices of sentencing and incarceration are necessarily interrelated, not insular, and that the effects of sentencing (especially where producing a prison sentence) must be understood in the context of the lives and security of individuals coming before the law. Yet, this capacity within law should not be regarded as an inevitability. Much as Marianne Constable suggests, Cover's formulation of the violence of law obstructs "law's aspiration to justice."[263] Angela Davis observes about the criminal justice system in the United States that "sentencing practices . . . are immediately responsible for the huge number of people that are behind bars."[264] While further illustrating that law enables oppression and exclusion, such recognition of the direct relationship between sentencing practices and overincarceration creates space for what Davis describes as "the dual strategy of taking up the law and recognizing its limitations."[265] Similarly, I suggest that to view law and its judicial interpretation solely as enabling oppression overlooks law's (often unrealized) potential to defend individual (and, ultimately, collective) dignity and hold state institutions accountable. The power of law to cause harm is useful in supporting ethically minded legislative and judicial interpretive practices, but the potential of legal interpretation and reform to contribute to social change must also be recognized.

The capacity of law to engender substantive change remains challenged due to internal frameworks and dynamics. Given continued Indigenous overincarceration in Manitoba despite s. 718.2(e) and *Gladue*, Milward and Parkes suggest that "the individualizing tendencies within law," together with "the tension between competing approaches to justice (retributive versus restorative) and the general primacy of retributive approaches," hinder the capacity of law to alleviate overincarceration and other systemic issues.[266] In Chapters 2 and 3, I discuss elements of individualizing judicial narratives/reasoning and judgments in which restorative justice objectives recede that tend to support this analysis. Equally, I also examine cases in which judges engage in contextualized reasoning that seeks to respond to the spirit of *Gladue*, including where judges engage in forms of resistance (such as when departing from risk-based analyses in sentencing instruments, and when directly decrying legislative limits on their discretion). Such cases offer some measured promise for the ability of *Gladue* to ameliorate Indigenous overincarceration where properly, consistently, and sensitively applied, and given adequate resources (particularly in terms of accessibility of *Gladue* reports and community-based services).

Interpreting and expanding upon the conception and dimensions of law they discern within Michel Foucault's work, Ben Golder and Peter Fitzpatrick offer a way to understand law that allows for the possibility of resistance and progressive change. They examine Foucault's work to find a characterization of law that functions through two interconnected modes: through its "definite content" and simultaneously through its "responsive dimension," which "extends itself illimitably in its attempt to encompass and respond to that what lies outside its definite content."[267] I understand this to mean that law operates both through its written form (such as in statutes) and also reciprocally and reflexively, where, for example, judges interpret legislation by reference to the ever-shifting content and reach of law expressed through the jurisprudence, seeking to apply and extend it to the unending variability of facts and contexts coming before the courts, and where legislators amend the law due to related jurisprudential findings and various socio-political forces. Golder and Fitzpatrick propose that through this dynamic within and comprising Foucault's articulation of law, law becomes "receptive of resistances that constantly challenge its position."[268] Given that the text of s. 718.2(e) does not, on a plain reading, incorporate gendered understandings of its objectives (and neither does its interpretation in *Gladue*), I suggest that where sentencing judges do engage in reasoning that productively resonates with the victimization-criminalization continuum and situate this within overarching *Gladue* analyses, this functions as a moment of resistance that contains some degree of hope to mitigate the trajectories of Indigenous women in the system, and to ultimately propel changes in the law and its ongoing interpretation.

In this manner, there is potential inherent in law for incremental social change, in its fluidity and receptivity to be expanded to circumstances that exceed (and resist) its defined parameters (though still dependent on political will and judicial decision-making). Given this responsiveness of law, Golder and Fitzpatrick contend, law has the capacity to provide "the constituent source of our sociality, of our being-together," to "form and iteratively re-form the social bond,"[269] through an ethical lens. In this reflexive model, given that this "social bond" has also been formed through processes of colonization, including by operation of law, inversely, legislative and judicial efforts to orient the law toward decolonizing objectives become possible and necessary to contribute to our collective unmaking and remaking in an ongoing movement (through dedicated institutional and community-based striving and action) toward reconciliation and equality. Essentially, the interpretation and adaptation of law to changing social contexts is not unidirectional. Much as law has functioned to underwrite, entrench, and perpetuate practices of colonization, law also has the capacity to engender social change, promoting social justice, through both the common law and legal reform, even as it also adapts in response to change. Murdocca observes that "scholars and legal practitioners caution . . . that simply concluding that the aspirations of section 718.2(e) have been ineffective obscures a more nuanced consideration of sentencing reform, institutional legal practices, and systemic forms of racism."[270] This book strives to participate in that space, to illustrate that the interpretation of law has tangible effects on criminalized Indigenous women's lives (for whom law and legal institutions may constitute oppressive forces within "illegitimate political structures"),[271] but also to insist upon the progressive potential of legal and institutional reform, primarily in support for judicial discretion in service of the fulsome implementation of *Gladue*.

CHAPTER 1

PATHWAYS THROUGH FEMINIST THEORIES, INTO THE SYSTEM

The Public Inquiry into the Administration of Justice and Aboriginal People of Manitoba (also called the Aboriginal Justice Inquiry), created to examine certain and systemic criminal justice failures toward Indigenous peoples in that province, produced a report by its co-commissioners in 1991 in which Justices Alvin C. Hamilton and C. Murray Sinclair indicate that the overrepresentation of Indigenous women in prison "can be traced, in part, to the victimization"[1] they experience. Justices Hamilton and Sinclair suggest that of the Indigenous women incarcerated in a provincial prison within their purview, "the most significant factor that caused them to be there" seemed to be related to experiences of abuse, particularly childhood sexual abuse and intimate partner abuse, and that "many felt trapped in an impossible economic and social situation from which there was little chance of escape."[2] The co-commissioners further state that "none of the women we spoke to wanted to be involved in criminal activity, but they often believed it was necessary to do so," and frequently in relation to caring for their children.[3]

There is ample research suggesting, in the words of Joycelyn Pollock and Sareta Davis, a "link between victimization and violent offending."[4]

As Sugar and Fox comment about Indigenous women, "there is no accidental relationship between our convictions for violent offences, and our histories as victims," as "for us, violence has begotten violence."[5] Although I focus on judicial understandings of the relationship between experiences of victimization and criminalization for the Indigenous women they sentence,[6] it must be recognized that, as Tyagi notes, "women are involved in the justice system more as victims than offenders."[7] Additionally, as Lisa Muftic, Jeffrey Bouffard, and Leana Bouffard describe in an American study of intimate partner violence, the forms of violence women actively engage in often differ in significant ways from those of men in terms of "the seriousness, context, and outcomes of violence."[8] There is much support for Pollock and Davis's proposition "that violence by women is very likely to take place in the domestic sphere."[9] Muftic, Bouffard, and Bouffard find that, "overall, research points to the potential conclusion that not only are women less likely to engage in severe physical violence but also the types of violence women resort to within an abusive intimate relationship are typically more self-defensive in nature."[10] Myrna S. Raeder writes, "While the continuum from victim to offender is most clearly evident in cases of women who kill their abusers, a much wider range of female crime has ties to domestic violence."[11] In the cases I analyzed in my study, women's criminalization seems frequently connected to past experiences of victimization (including state-based victimization through processes of colonization), and often involves intimate partner violence or experiences related to this abuse. Moreover, violations of the law committed by women are often non-violent. Elizabeth Comack observes that women are "most likely to be charged with property-related crimes,"[12] and that "the vast majority of offences committed by women are 'poverty crimes' that reflect the systemic inequality, discrimination, and marginalization emanating from their class/race/gender locations."[13] Justices Hamilton and Sinclair suggest that Indigenous women "are often going to jail for unpaid fines" without access to childcare support to enable their completion of various alternatives through "fine option programs."[14] The ways in which Indigenous women become criminalized must also be connected to processes of colonization.

Feminist discourses are significant to criminology because, as Raeder says, "it has not been fashionable to treat female offenders as victims, even if their crimes have a direct relationship to their violent victimization."[15] This is particularly true among groups such as "traditional victims' advocates" who continue to "see a sharp break between victims and offenders."[16] In the American context, Raeder calls for the victims' movement to include criminalized women within the purview of the victims' community, programs, and advocacy,[17] and urges the creation of "a fairer sentencing regime for offenders whose criminality is linked to the domestic violence they have suffered."[18] Canadian political and judicial institutions and actors should similarly develop more nuanced understandings of victimization and criminalization so that policy, law, and sentencing practices can better respond to the specificity (and diversity) among criminalized Indigenous women's lives.

I draw from many feminist writers to provide the theoretical background that will undergird my discussion of the cases in subsequent chapters. Various feminist criminological theories describe how women's victimization may contribute to their criminalization. Although I argue that these theories are substantially equivalent, I use the language of the victimization-criminalization continuum. There are criticisms of this theory, but these criticisms should subside when the theory is framed expansively. As Tuhiwai Smith writes, "The framing of an issue is about making decisions about its parameters, about what is in the foreground, what is in the background, and what shadings or complexities exist within the frame."[19] Criminalization and overincarceration of Indigenous peoples operate as reverberations of colonization (or, rather, are more appropriately regarded as ongoing—active, and more indirect—processes of colonization).

Blurred Pathways: Directions for the Victimization-Criminalization Continuum

Developed in the 1990s and onward,[20] several feminist criminological theories about criminalized women share the basic premise that women's experiences of violence and other forms of victimization should be understood as connected to how women enter the criminal justice system as accuseds.[21] In her review of feminist criminology, Joanne Belknap finds that "perhaps the single most important contribution of feminist criminology is in the development of the 'pathways' perspective or approach," which she defines as advancing the proposition "that traumas and victimizations are risk factors for offending," noting the widespread research documenting "the extensive trauma and abuse histories"[22] of women who have been sentenced. Meda Chesney-Lind also emphasizes the significance of this insight, identifying that feminist research has pointed to sexual and physical victimization, gender, and race as generating particular (and, I would add, interconnected) pathways leading to criminality and criminalization.[23] These modes of pathway generation are accelerated in communities struggling with substance abuse and overincarceration.

Also responding to accumulated research indicating the prevalence of prior experiences of victimization for criminalized women,[24] related streams of thought convey similar ideas to the pathways theory. For example, Amanda Burgess-Proctor writes that "feminist research identifies the concept of 'blurred boundaries' between women's victimization and offending experiences."[25] According to Dana Britton, the "'blurred boundaries' thesis argues that women's offending is intimately linked to their previous victimization."[26] This theory tries to "[disrupt] the dichotomy"[27] between "victim" and "offender," noting the instability between these ideas and identities because, as Elizabeth Comack states, "the boundaries between the two categories are more often than not blurred ones."[28] Similarly, Wendy Chan and Dorothy Chunn point to work that refers to "the multiple statuses" inherent in those who may be "simultaneously threatening and threatened," posing risks and at risk, and how thoses multiple, shifting statuses "are connected or disconnected at a given moment," which can be understood through contextualization of criminal acts and making visible experiences of victimization.[29]

While these theories convey the same concepts I use, I primarily draw from (and use the language of) the related feminist concept of the "victimization-criminalization continuum" to consider whether and to what extent such ideas are understood in judicial discourses about Indigenous women, and what this means for the sentencing of Indigenous women. Balfour discusses the initial relationship between early "standpoint theory and method in feminist criminology"[30] and analyses that connected women's law-breaking on a continuum between victimization and criminalization. Balfour finds that this early formulation suggested that "women's lawbreaking behaviours (drinking and drugging, prostitution, and violence) were understood to be strategies to cope with the impact of abuse," and "women's victimization (sexual exploitation, domestic violence, rape) was viewed as a cause or pathway into violence, addiction, prostitution, or fraud."[31] This formulation has been criticized. However, notwithstanding problems various feminists have identified with this theory, it remains useful to understand how many women in the system may have come into heightened vulnerability to criminalization through their experiences of victimization. Balfour contends that the victimization-criminalization continuum "has not been adequately theorized or debated,"[32] which leaves the possibility to expand it beyond problems associated with and identified within it. I use the victimization-criminalization continuum to signify that Indigenous women's experiences of (personal, state-based, and related) victimization constrain their available options, which—particularly for already marginalized women—magnifies their vulnerability to criminalization.

For my purposes, I do not observe any substantial difference among the blurred boundaries, pathways, and victimization-criminalization continuum theories. All allow for nuances within the blurriness, branching paths, and shifting continuum of identities, experiences, and structural locations. Additionally, in substance, all three modes of understanding emerge from evidence connecting women's experiences of victimization to their criminalization and support this formulation. Moreover, because I have chosen to adopt an expansive definition of "victimization" to include a range of traumatic and marginalizing experiences (often connected to violence, but not limited to that experience), any nuanced distinctions among these theories dissipate. I primarily refer to the victimization-criminalization continuum simply because it most explicitly connects these experiences, although I periodically reference the pathways theory interchangeably. Ultimately, these feminist theories all seek to explain the same issues, all sharing the fundamental premise that the culmination of life experiences, including victimization, contributes to women's criminalization (and I seek to simultaneously emphasize systemic and structural forces channelling and limiting women's available options). Much as the issues within and dynamics surrounding women's lives are impossible to disentangle, these feminist theories are necessarily enmeshed with each other, and not isolable.

The Victimization-Criminalization Continuum: Constraining Options and Support

The victimization-criminalization continuum has been criticized on the basis that it suggests a determinative relationship between women's victimization and criminality (that women's law-breaking can be directly explained through their experiences of victimization, and dealt with likewise).[33] Balfour writes that this "recent feminist scholarship has challenged the over-determined role of abuse in women's lives, cautioning that such a strategy renders women responsible for how they cope with abuse, justifying the imprisonment of women based on their assumed need for treatment."[34] This work also contends that the victimization-criminalization continuum "follows the psychologizing and individualizing logic of the criminal justice system."[35] In support of these challenges to the basic formulation of the victimization-criminalization continuum, in my analysis of the cases to follow, I examine where such individualization of systemic problems contributes to judicial discourses about prison as a necessary place for healing. These criticisms of the continuum share similar foundations and impulses as the concept of "responsibilization," which features in much feminist writing about women in the correctional system. Kelly Hannah-Moffat outlines that responsibilization is the process through which "individuals (as opposed to the 'state') are increasingly expected to be responsible and accountable for their own risk management and self-governance."[36] This focus deflects attention and responsibility for supporting women's needs in the community away from government provision of funding and services.[37]

Related criticisms argue that the victimization-criminalization continuum does not leave sufficient space for recognition of women's expressions of agency, as agency disrupts the problematic determinative idea that victimization leads to criminality. Tyagi writes, "That women offenders experience such high degrees of abuse and trauma, which often form pathways into offending, should not be assumed to translate into

45

women's lack of agency. One should not infer that women offenders are simply the sum total of their victimization, addictions and traumatic life experiences."[38] Comack explains that incorporating agency is useful to subvert essentialist ideas about victimization and criminality, because historically the categorization of women as victims has had the effect of devaluing feminist insights and focus.[39] Comack suggests that "dualistic thinking"[40] elicits and propels criminal justice-oriented responses (such as decisions about the degree of punitive response warranted by offending behaviour) instead of more careful thought and attention to "the wider contexts in which people encounter their troubles" and the necessity of making changes at that level as opposed to merely the reactive end.[41] I understand "agency" to mean, in Emma LaRocque's words, "our capacity to make choices."[42] Philosophically, LaRocque expands that this translates into "moral agency," which is rooted in "what makes us human."[43] Because agency is fundamental to our sense of humanity, autonomy, and self-determination, the denial of our abilities to make choices strips that away. As such, because, as LaRocque states, "colonization or any other form of coercion is a form of dehumanization"[44] that undercuts Indigenous peoples' right and ability to exercise self-determination (at both individual and collective levels), the issue of agency takes on greater significance for Indigenous women.

To avoid the agency-denying conception of the victimization-criminalization continuum and allow for fuller appreciation for how women enact violence and other forms of legal violations, feminist conceptions of female offending must incorporate fuller understandings of how experiences of violence and other victimizations impact women and how these experiences constrain women's available options and support. This assumes particular significance for Indigenous and other marginalized women whose range of choices is already circumscribed by the structural limits of their lives (such as the narrowed options and resources available to low-income women in small, remote communities). Dana M. Britton notes the delicacy required to achieve this conceptual balance: "Mirroring overall trends in feminist theory, the best of this work is moving toward a nuanced and contingent conception of women's agency, one that sees women neither exclusively as victims nor as unfettered actors."[45]

The idea that agency is expressed within the constrained options available to victimized women is reflected in various studies of criminalized women. For example, Dana DeHart finds that "most women in our sample possessed a component of choice in committing their crimes,"[46] and that recognizing the "cumulative impact of victimization" is necessary to understanding "why women chose illegitimate over legitimate pathways."[47] As such, thinking about victimization in terms of marginalization and the morass of limited options and support/resources that women must navigate allows for the element of agency that the victimization-criminalization continuum has been criticized for precluding. The issue of agency is nonetheless still fraught in this context, because although no one makes life choices unencumbered by externalities, for many victimized women, their remaining options are extremely few and augment their precariousness and vulnerability to coming into conflict with the law. Tyagi writes, "Violence and victimization play a significant role in women's trajectories of offending. Studies have repeatedly shown that women's pathways into crime most often involve running away from physical and sexual abuse or abusive relationships. The trajectory into criminal behaviour is motivated by survival and as a response to victimization."[48] For many of these women trying to escape violence or other forms of victimization, there is not much to run to in terms of government resources, social services, and other needed community supports.

In their research, Kathleen J. Ferraro and Angela M. Moe illustrate the degree of constraints and dearth of community support for some women. Ferraro and Moe find that some women view prison as a reprieve from the threats in their lives on the outside (including feeling safe from abusive partners while incarcerated,[49] receiving the shelter and minimal care that women who live on the street otherwise lack,[50] and experiencing relief at being removed from their community triggers for substance abuse).[51] Where imprisonment functions as something of a respite, women become vulnerable to criminalization, having nothing left to lose. Ferraro and Moe highlight that this perception of imprisonment speaks more to the "complex problems"[52] marginalized women face in the community with minimal supports that cannot be fixed through sentencing initiatives.

I do not want to overemphasize this depiction of prison as a refuge, in part because much evidence suggests that imprisonment generally exacerbates pre-existing life and mental health difficulties and foments new such issues.[53] Additionally, I am quite uncomfortable with this depiction of prison as a refuge because where the views of the Indigenous women sentenced become visible in the judgments, I did not see evidence of this perspective on prison, and instead found many indications that the women experienced prison as a source of anxiety, oppressiveness, and even illegitimacy. Defence counsel routinely seek alternatives to imprisonment where appropriate and available, and past periods of imprisonment in the women's lives as reported in pre-sentence reports and *Gladue* reports and otherwise presented to the courts generally read as threatening and damaging experiences for both the women and their families. Further, Ferraro and Moe study the narratives of thirty women in a southwestern county prison in the United States, and the dissonance between social issues (such as health care and other aspects of the social security net) in this context versus the Canadian context means their findings cannot be directly transposed onto the lives of criminalized Canadian women. Nonetheless, their findings speak to the scope of just how narrowed some women's options can be, and within which these women are vulnerable to criminalization.

Most federally sentenced women are mothers. In its 2013–14 report, the Correctional Investigator outlines that 75 percent of women in prison have children under the age of eighteen, with almost two-thirds of these women acting as "single caregivers" at the time of their arrest, and more than half having experienced some involvement with Children's Aid, "often due to substance abuse, mental health concerns or issues of abuse/neglect."[54] It is more difficult to obtain information about the profiles of women serving sentences in provincial prisons,[55] although there is research showing that the majority of women serving time in the provincial correctional system are also mothers, and usually single parents.[56] My own research includes Indigenous women ordered to both provincial and federal sanctions. In determining the proportion of women who are identified in the judgements as having children, I found that approximately 80 percent are mothers. Motherhood and its associated responsibilities and financial demands (including how it can constrain life options and choices) becomes difficult for incarcerated women whose abilities to maintain relationships with their children are compromised by their separation, and may also be challenging for women to balance alongside compliance with supervisory orders once they are released into the community.[57]

In their interview-based research, Ferraro and Moe find that issues relating to the custody of criminalized women's children are interrelated with other issues, predominantly substance use. For some women in Ferraro and Moe's study, their substance use occasioned the removal of their children.[58] Those women who lost their children to state care (due to a variety of reasons) often simultaneously lost motivation to seek treatment or otherwise regain control over their addictions, and became further embroiled in these struggles.[59] Women's senses of control over and agency within their own lives are undermined when the state removes their children into its custody. The context of state apprehension of women's children also has a deeper significance for Indigenous mothers, given the role of this government practice within ongoing processes of colonization. Substance use may represent an attempt to reassert some form of control. Alternatively, distressed women forcibly separated from their children may turn to substance use having, as Ferraro and Moe state, "nothing [remaining] to lose,"[60] or may simply use because that feels better (and is more readily achievable than other ways of coping) than their challenging realities. At these junctures, women become more susceptible to criminalization, so issues related to motherhood can impact women's pathways to prison or other criminal sanctions (and certainly impacts their experiences of such modes of punishment).

Taking these varying experiences into account, it becomes apparent that women have different, and sometimes very constricted, options, depending on where they are located socio-economically and in other ways. Accordingly, victimization can be seen as narrowing women's options such that criminality looms larger as an option—perhaps more accessible (even necessary), less distasteful, or less catastrophic where violence and other traumas have been felt in women's lives. Alternatively, often, victimization isolates women from social supports and narrows their options such that few options exist at all for these women, who then become more susceptible to becoming criminalized. (Of course, victimization by the state through past and continued processes of colonization exacerbates this cycle, already constricting options available to Indigenous women and systemically isolating them from social supports and opportunities, and within fractured communities.) This depiction is different from suggesting a determinative relationship between victimization and criminalization; instead, it points to the strains in marginalized women's lives, and how they exercise limited agency in navigating those strains.

In this context, the victimization-criminalization theory remains helpful in understanding women's criminalization and socio-legal responses to it. Karlene Faith explains that "victimization cannot be named as 'the' cause of crime," in part because although many criminalized women have experiences of victimization, the proportion of victimized women who later offend is small relative to the number of victimized women who do not.[61] She contends, "The continuum, then, does not follow deterministically from victimization to criminalization."[62] Instead, Faith suggests, "the continuum from victimization is arbitrarily drawn according to power relations as constructed through racially divided and class-based social structures, in tandem with the authority of law and other dominant discourses such as medicine, social sciences and welfare, which all serve selective law enforcement practices."[63] In this light, a woman's criminalization is more properly seen as connected to her experience(s) of victimization as refracted through her (shifting) intersectional structural positioning within various systems, institutions, and power dynamics.

"Intersectionality" is a feminist theory holding that feminism is not advanced by a focus exclusively on gender as an analytical category for "understanding and combating inequality," according to Joanne Conaghan.[64] Instead, intersectionality posits that gender is just one category of identity that operates in conjunction with other such categories to create a distinct experience,[65] an experience of "'interlocking' oppressions," as Conaghan puts it.[66] Intersectionality offers a more complex way to advance feminist goals because it permits nuance and can better explain and be applied to the different experiences and situations within the multiplicity of women. For example, intersectionality seeks to provide the framework to understand how gender, race, and class are interrelated experiences within interrelated systems of oppression that fuse together and bolster each other. Justices Hamilton and Sinclair report for the Aboriginal Justice Inquiry of Manitoba that Indigenous women incarcerated in a provincial institution there described feeling "discriminated against both as women and as Aboriginal persons."[67] These interconnections are complicated and personal; for example, as Lorelei Means comments about feminist priorities from the United States context, "We are *American Indian* women, in that order. We are oppressed, first and foremost as American Indians, as peoples colonized by the United States of American, *not as women*."[68] Although the relationships among the various intersections within Indigenous women's lives are encumbered by complexity, as processes of colonization are not severable from other oppressions, Rauna Kuokkanen explains, "the subjugation of Indigenous communities depended on the subjugation of women."[69] The UN Committee articulates that "intersecting forms of discrimination and their combined negative impact" on Indigenous women "reproduce[s] a multi-level oppression that culminates in violence" against Indigenous women.[70]

Faith's inclusion of intersectional ideas in the victimization-criminalization continuum is useful for its incorporation of systemic factors, including poverty and colonization, which contribute to women's vulnerability to victimization. I envisage the continuum as non-linear, with many incursions and redirections from external forces (broad, structural forces like colonization and interrelated poverty, as well as events within Indigenous women's lives often stemming from those structural forces, such as the removal of their own children by the state). Visually, perhaps the continuum would look something like a web instead of a vector, but more of a branching, inverted, cage-like web that traps (constrains) Indigenous women rather than the security of the web of the social net that catches those of us who are structurally positioned to not slip through. The linocut print I created for the cover of this book represents this concept of complex, snarled pathways into and through the system, ultimately ensnaring Indigenous women.

Faith rejects notions that the "victim" identity indicates passiveness or powerlessness, but instead offers that the myriad ways women navigate and survive abuse are demonstrations of their agency and choice.[71]

Criminality should be understood as manifesting within these modes of orientation and survival, indicating, in Faith's words, "women's resilience and capacity for positive action as well as negative reaction against social injustices."[72] The agency that can be inferred from women's criminal behaviour may take different forms, and criminalized women's choices are and will continue to be constrained by systemic forces. That is, the victimization-criminalization continuum should reflect the often limited options available to women who become criminalized. These constricted options can be related to Danielle Dirks's suggestion that "women's experiences in the criminal justice system have been thematically linked by abandonment."[73] Such neglect and abandonment can be conceptualized both at the personal level (such as from women's families or communities) and as marginalization at the state or structural level (such as through the deplorable condition of many under-resourced and underfunded Indigenous communities, the lack of access to resources more broadly, and colonialism itself, the very assertion of the state as an entity unilaterally deeming itself entitled to exert power and control over Indigenous nations and peoples).

Notwithstanding criticisms of the victimization-criminalization continuum, it remains a helpful lens through which to understand women in conflict with the law. Moreover, the inverse offers an important dimension; Kim Pate suggests that our current "framework . . . is that women are not in conflict with the law," but "laws are increasingly in conflict with women."[74] It is instructive to take a wider view (from a singular focus on women's criminalization) to incorporate discussions about how manifestations of the continuum operate in (or fail to enter) judicial reasoning on sentencing. I use the victimization-criminalization continuum in the latter respect in this book to explore discourses of victimization, criminalization, and where they intersect and impact Indigenous women at sentencing. I return to Justice LeBel's words from *Ipeelee* again here to emphasize the importance of judicial thinking about the relationship between victimization and criminalization in the sentencing of Indigenous women: "Canadian criminal law is based on the premise that criminal liability only follows from voluntary conduct. Many Aboriginal offenders find themselves in situations of social and economic deprivation with a lack of opportunities and limited options for positive development. While this rarely—if ever—attains a level where one could properly say that their actions were not voluntary and therefore not deserving of criminal sanction, the reality is that their constrained circumstances may diminish their moral culpability."[75] This scc identification that colonization produces constrained circumstances and can reduce moral culpability signifies an entry point for judicial analysis of how victimization limits Indigenous women's options/ choices and renders them more vulnerable to criminalization, and how the two factors (*Gladue*-related and those connecting to the victimization-criminalization continuum) should be understood as interrelated.

Shifting Pathways: Structural Dislocation and Layered Victimizations

Dana D. DeHart calls attention to expanding research that positions victimization as a pivotal force that may propel women along a "'pathway' to crime," singularly or alongside "other factors such as poverty, family fragmentation, school failure, and physical and mental health problems."[76] DeHart identifies a direct correlation between victimization and criminality for some women in her study.[77] Her research consists primarily of interviews with sixty women (approximately half African-American, half white) at an American maximum-security state prison, and also includes various prison demographic and criminal record documentation, and some related media reports.[78] The women's lives include "a range of victimization and criminal experiences"[79] and their convictions vary in type and severity from shoplifting to murder. The open-ended interview approach used in her study engaged responses pertaining to "family and relationship history, physical and psychological victimization, lifetime delinquency and crime, and interactions with social service and justice systems."[80]

DeHart draws from earlier work to underscore that victimization and its effects "serve to 'structurally dislocate' women from 'legitimate' social institutions" such as "push[ing] girls and women out of families and peer groups, homes, schools or workplaces, and institutions of worship,"[81] as well as creating family disruption experienced by mothers whose children are removed into state care.[82] Through this process, victimization further marginalizes women by limiting or removing access to aspects of our social structure and resources, which restricts their available options for support.[83] Without these avenues, it becomes even more difficult for women to leave abusive relationships, particularly for women who lack independent financial stability or housing.[84] Victimization impacts women's physical and mental health,[85] and women's support networks may have already been contracted within controlling, abusive relationships.[86]

While DeHart's research emerges from the United States, it applies to the effects of victimization for women in Canada. The Native Women's Association of Canada (NWAC) reports that with few options available to Indigenous women in or leaving abusive relationships, they become "forced into situations or coping strategies that increase their vulnerability to violence," including remaining in abusive situations or entering new ones, sex work, homelessness, and substance abuse.[87] Research documents a specific nexus between intimate violence and substance abuse, particularly for marginalized women.[88] Statistics Canada reports that substance abuse may be used as a coping mechanism to deal with experiences of victimization, and can increase an individual's vulnerability to reacting with inappropriate violence or being herself further victimized.[89] Statistics Canada also describes the frequent connection between substance abuse and criminalization (such as committing offences to support an addiction or where substance abuse becomes entwined within a broader experience of criminality).[90] Chronic poor housing situations in Indigenous communities (falling beneath the criteria of "safe, secure, affordable or appropriate") also constrain the options available to women struggling with these issues.[91] According to NWAC, criminalized persons generally demonstrate a prevalence of "dual, multiple, or overlapping sources of vulnerability,"[92] and processes of colonization deepen and tighten these entwined vulnerabilities for Indigenous women.

DeHart's work is also helpful to understand the victimization experiences of criminalized Indigenous women because her study highlights that the "*cumulative* impact of victimization over the life span"[93] of incarcerated women differentiates their histories and experience from those of non-incarcerated women.[94] This finding is highly relevant for

Indigenous women whose extensive histories of victimization are disproportionately high.[95] Experiencing high volumes of victimizations also contributes to how women become dislocated from social supports. DeHart states, "Most of the women suffered multiple traumas and were victimized in multiple ways (e.g., child abuse and neglect, adult relationship violence, sexual violence). The varied impacts of polyvictimization (i.e., experiencing simultaneous episodes of different types of victimization) had potential to create ripple effects in multiple arenas in the women's lives, causing overall disruption and pushing the women out of the mainstream. Often, the intersection of losses seemed to create uniquely difficult situations."[96] Describing "polyvictimization" as "unrelenting trauma,"[97] DeHart reports the conclusion from related quantitative studies that the "sheer number of victimizations" is more indicative of the difficulties women may experience than "any particular type."[98] In similar language, but specific to Indigenous peoples, Maria Yellow Horse Brave Heart relies on the concept of "historical trauma," which she also refers to as "massive cumulative trauma," to describe "cumulative emotional and psychological wounding, over the lifespan and across generations, emanating from massive group trauma experiences."[99] DeHart suggests the accumulation of victimizations produces "a tangle of barriers that the women faced in finding legitimate pathways in life,"[100] accelerating their structural dislocation.

As in my imagery above (and on the cover) of a cage-like web, experiences of victimization often do not unfold in a linear manner, where victimizations directly and indirectly lead to criminal activity; instead, in DeHart's words, these experiences may overlap and fluctuate in an "entanglement of victimization and crime,"[101] knotting ever more tightly the more women become enmeshed in the system. In their study comparing physical and sexual revictimization (adult victimization following experiences of child abuse) of incarcerated women against those of inner-city non-incarcerated women, Chantal Poister Tusher and Sarah L. Cook find that incarcerated women were more likely to experience revictimization.[102] While they acknowledge that it is "currently unclear how patterns of violence and incarceration intersect throughout women's lives,"[103] the finding that there *is* an intersection between victimization and incarceration is significant and deserves attention.

DeHart suggests that understandings about how the cumulative impacts of multiple victimizations may influence options available to women have import at a variety of stages of processing through the justice system, such as "implications for rehabilitation and accountability, including recommendations during pretrial services, sentencing, correctional programming, and conditions of release."[104]

Violence Against Indigenous Women

In their 2017 report about women in the criminal justice system, Tina Hotton Mahony, Joanna Jacob, and Heather Hobson reference much research finding that Indigenous women "are more likely to be affected by all types of violent victimization" than non-Indigenous women,[105] including "the most serious forms of sexual and physical violence," experience substantially higher rates of partner violence, and "fea[r] for their lives at a greater frequency."[106] These findings do not include data from the Northwest Territories, Yukon, or Nunavut, but other research from Juristat indicates Indigenous women living in the territories experience "higher proportions" of partner violence than Indigenous women in the provinces.[107]

DeHart's articulation of "polyvictimization"[108] and "unrelenting trauma"[109]—continuous and various experiences of victimization—is also experienced by many criminalized Indigenous women, and should be situated within the broader context of processes of colonization, as does Brave Heart's usage of "historical trauma" and "massive cumulative trauma."[110] These levels of violence speak to how Indigenous women experience colonization in a gendered way. In her capacity as the vice-president of the National Action Committee on the Status of Women and a member of the Aboriginal Women's Action Network (BC), Fay Blaney commented in 2000 about the "systemic and institutionalized discrimination" faced by Indigenous women that "we do have patriarchy and we have colonization within our Aboriginal communities, not only historically, but that's the case today."[111] Joyce Green writes that "some Aboriginal cultures and communities are patriarchal, either in cultural origin or because of incorporation of colonizer patriarchy."[112] Green understands colonialism in an intersectional way, noting it is "closely tied to racism and sexism."[113] She writes that these "isms" have been "directed at Indigenous people," but "have also been internalized by some Indigenous political cultures in ways that are oppressive to Indigenous women."[114] Douglas A. Brownridge explains that "the elevated risk for violence against Aboriginal women is not due to any single risk factor but, rather, a constellation of variables that may be linked to the larger experience of colonization."[115] Andrea Smith, a Cherokee scholar, also suggests violence against women in Indigenous societies is necessarily connected to colonization.[116]

Most of Indigenous women's experiences of violence are not reported to the police.[117] This mirrors the general data that most violence against women goes unreported; also, incidents that are reported are not always recorded in police files, often not producing a conviction, and, as Kim Pate indicates, "rarely result in incapacitation"[118] of the perpetrators. The UN Committee too notes "low prosecution rates for crimes against" Indigenous women,[119] and relates this "environment conducive to impunity"[120] for violence against Indigenous women to broader access to justice barriers for Indigenous women needing support. As Indigenous women's experiences of victimization are generally underreported to police, the pre-sentence reports or *Gladue* reports of criminalized Indigenous women may often signify the first time these experiences enter the consciousness of the criminal justice system. This is significant to how Indigenous women's histories of victimization are understood and shaped in judicial reasoning in sentencing decisions, because these histories are often substantial, having accumulated before the women come into conflict with the law. That is, Indigenous women's experiences of violent and other victimizations may become apparent to state institutions only when the women themselves are sentenced, some time after the continuum has been impelled into motion (and at a juncture when their law-breaking is viewed to overdetermine their victimization due to the nature of the criminal justice system).

Any discussion of the victimization of Indigenous women must address missing and murdered women in Canada, as they are disproportionately Indigenous women. Canada ratified the Optional Protocol to the Convention on the Elimination of All Forms of Discrimination against Women in 2003, permitting the United Nations Committee on the Elimination of Discrimination against Women to conduct an inquiry examining submitted information pertaining to "grave or systematic violations"[121] of this Convention by an implicated state. The Feminist Alliance for International Action and NWAC initiated this process in 2011. Following its own consequent inquiry, the UN Committee issued its report with findings and recommendations in March 2015, declaring that the Canadian federal government has demonstrated a "protracted failure . . . to take effective measures to protect"[122] Indigenous women. Noting "continued reluctance of the federal government" to establish an independent national public inquiry into missing and murdered Indigenous women and girls despite "repeated calls to do so"[123] by various governmental, non-governmental, Indigenous, and other bodies, the UN Committee includes among its recommendations that the Canadian government establish this inquiry. On 8 December 2015, the Canadian government announced it would conduct a federal public inquiry into missing and murdered Indigenous women.[124]

The National Inquiry into Missing and Murdered Indigenous Women and Girls (MMIWG Inquiry) officially commenced on 1 September 2016, amid criticism, and as women continued to be killed.[125] The MMIWG Inquiry articulates it seeks ongoing feedback and input from Indigenous communities "into the design and implementation" of the conduct of its process "throughout,"[126] and identifies various preliminary challenges in performing its mandate, which offers a hopeful self-reflexivity. Through research and publicly and privately convened hearings across Canada, the MMIWG Inquiry is engaged in what it refers to as a "Truth-Gathering Process"[127] involving three phases: hearings with families, affected community members, and Indigenous women survivors of violence; hearings with Indigenous, grassroots, and governmental institutional bodies regarding institutional and systemic violence against Indigenous women; and hearings with experts, including Indigenous Elders. Guided by the belief that "we need to understand how social structures and laws have so devalued the lives of Indigenous women and girls,"[128] the objective of the MMIWG Inquiry is to gather findings and produce recommendations in relation to "the systemic causes of all forms of violence against Indigenous women and girls."[129]

Preceding the implementation of this national inquiry, to address lacunae in available information about missing and murdered Indigenous women and to give voice to the stories of silenced women, the Sisters in Spirit initiative within NWAC produced a report in 2010. The Royal Canadian Mounted Police (RCMP) based the time frame for its own subsequent findings on this report, and drew on the work of Sisters in Spirit when cross-referencing police records with that data and further research compiled by Maryanne Pearce. In 2014, from its review of its own investigations related to Indigenous women reported to the RCMP as murdered or missing between 1980 and 2012, the RCMP suggested that there are 1,181 Indigenous women in total (of which 1,017 Indigenous women were determined to be homicide victims, 164 women remained missing at the time of the report, and the cases of 225 additional women were then still unresolved).[130]

The RCMP report identifies that, of both women homicide victims and of women missing, Indigenous women are overrepresented, and acknowledges these figures may still be lower than the actual extent of these forms of violence against Indigenous women.[131] Indeed, in its 2015 follow-up report, the RCMP adds a further eight missing Indigenous women who were not included in its previous report due to problems related to data collection (and an additional eleven Indigenous women had gone missing in the time between the reports).[132] Based on concerns and information from involved families, NWAC has since determined that these figures do not encompass the real numbers of missing and murdered Indigenous women.[133] Indeed, the actual numbers may be exponentially higher: activists with Walk 4 Justice have since sought to gather names of the women, and, according to CBC's John Paul Tasker, "stopped counting when they got to 4,232" in 2011.[134] NWAC suggests some families do not report their missing loved ones to police due to long-entrenched mistrust of institutions of law enforcement, and other families maintain that certain deaths were wrongly classified as effected by natural causes.[135] (In 2015, witnesses appearing before the parliamentary Special Committee on Violence Against Indigenous Women about missing and murdered Indigenous women reported that "they had been victims of misconduct and improper treatment at the hands of police officers.")[136] In 2017, the MMIWG Inquiry released its interim report, and states that "with all the information we have, we still don't know how many Indigenous women and girls are missing or have been murdered,"[137] suggesting only that "the general consensus is that the numbers are staggering."[138]

The 2014 RCMP report finds that the overwhelming majority (89 percent) of all women victims of homicide (both Indigenous and non-Indigenous) within its review were killed by men, and men known to the women through varying types of relationships.[139] In its follow-up report, the RCMP emphasizes that women "are most frequently killed by men within their own homes and communities."[140] Lacking complete information about the victims and any sex work involvement, Sisters in Spirit indicates some prevalence of sex work among missing and murdered Indigenous women.[141] The RCMP includes sex work within circumstances contributing to women's vulnerability to becoming missing or being killed, but is careful to indicate that while the percentage of Indigenous women victims involved in sex work is "slightly higher" than those who are non-Indigenous, it is not a "significant difference."[142] Sisters in Spirit cautions that sex work is not causally related to these women becoming missing or murdered, but instead that "many women arrive at that point in the context of limited options and after experiencing multiple forms of trauma or victimization."[143] Particularly among those who have experience in the survival of street sex trade, as Larry Campbell, Neil Boyd, and Lori Culbert describe, many have "suffered some tragic life event that led them to the streets."[144] These depictions reflect my interpretation of the victimization-criminalization continuum: many of these women have been pushed out of or away (in DeHart's words, "structurally dislocate[d]"[145]) from safe social spaces.

Sisters in Spirit locates the problem of missing and murdered Indigenous women in the aftermath and continued effects/processes of colonization, which necessitates attention to traumas faced by Indigenous men, too, as well as women.[146] Although Sisters in Spirit could obtain family information for only about a third of the women within its study, it finds that most of those women were mothers, which, it observes, produces intergenerational effects in the loss experienced by their children.[147] Overall, the TRC reports that more research is needed, but the available information suggests a devastating link between the large numbers of missing and murdered Aboriginal women and the many harmful background factors in their lives. These include: overrepresentation of Aboriginal children in child-welfare care; domestic and sexual violence; racism, poverty, and poor educational and health opportunities in Aboriginal communities; discriminatory practices against women related to band membership and Indian status; and inadequate supports for Aboriginal people in cities. This complex interplay of factors—many of which are part of the legacy of residential schools—needs to be examined, as does the lack of success of police forces in solving these crimes against Aboriginal women.[148]

Gendered Intersections

As victimization functions to displace women from the social institutions that support and connect us to each other, it further marginalizes women who are already marginalized within a confluence of intersectional, systemic disadvantages. Some scholars identify limits of intersectionality to the feminist project because, as Conaghan suggests, it "tells us little about the wider context in which such experiences are produced, mediated and expressed"[149] and specifically is not sufficiently instructive about how inequalities form or regarding the "relations of subordination" in which they are produced.[150] Sherene Razack moves in this direction when advocating an approach "to ascertain how, at specific sites, patriarchy, white supremacy, and capitalism interlock to structure women differently and unequally."[151] Andrea Smith and Luana Ross contend that "the colonial process itself is structured by sexual violence,"[152] which informs how Balfour articulates the victimization-criminalization continuum. Balfour locates violence by and against Indigenous women on a continuum "situated in historical, cultural, economic, and political practices that deny Aboriginal women their dignity and respect, autonomy, and self-determination, thereby contributing to their endangerment."[153]

Using this expanded, structurally based framework (as opposed to an identity-based lens), intersectionality remains of assistance in thinking about the sentencing of Indigenous women. Its utility is evident in Balfour's argument that colonization has created uniquely vulnerable conditions for Indigenous women to be victimized, contributing to the uneven application and effects of the 1996 sentencing amendments for Indigenous men versus Indigenous women, and permitting the "incarceration spiral"[154] of Indigenous women to persist.

Identifying the dissonance between sentencing practices that have restorative underpinnings and the goal to address the overincarceration of Indigenous peoples—through s. 718.2(e) and, at least in its originally enacted form, s. 742.1—and Indigenous women's escalating imprisonment rates, Balfour explores "the exclusion of women's narratives of violence and social isolation in the practice of sentencing law."[155] In the 1980s and '90s, the federal government prompted Canadian police departments to use mandatory charging policies for domestic violence calls to address violence against women, except the incidental effect became that marginalized women (often racialized and poor) were increasingly charged within these policies, too.[156] Often, Indigenous women (particularly in remote areas) did not receive proper police responses when they sought assistance for the violence to which they were subjected in their relationships, which sometimes resulted in their being later charged for their own violence in self-defence.[157] Balfour also notes that Indigenous women living on reserves are charged in much higher proportions than Indigenous women living off-reserve.[158] Balfour situates Indigenous women's vulnerability to victimization within processes of colonization, describing that the "legacy of colonialist policies such as the reserve system and residential schools, as well as the destruction of traditional economies and cultural institutions, have created such conditions."[159]

Balfour characterizes the mandatory charging policies as retributive strategies that fail to respond to feminist concerns and fail to protect Indigenous women.[160] Restorative sentencing practices included in the 1996 sentencing amendments have also failed to alleviate the overincarceration of Indigenous women. Noting that Indigenous women's rates of incarceration are increasing at a greater rate than those of Indigenous men (as remains true today), Balfour suggests that these amendments have produced gendered effects.[161] As a result, Balfour writes, there is a "fault line"[162] between retributive and restorative justice policies, and Indigenous women have "fallen between the cracks,"[163] because neither punishment philosophy has managed to reduce the overrepresentation of Indigenous women in the system. Balfour describes these issues as "the confluence of victimization, criminalization, and incarceration of Aboriginal women."[164]

Significantly, Balfour argues that the systemic and background factors required for consideration by *Gladue* should include gendered understandings of violence experienced by Indigenous women, but are not sufficiently recognized as such in sentencing decisions.[165] For example, in the transcripts from *Gladue,* she finds that evidence of domestic abuse to which Jamie Gladue was subjected was not taken into account on sentencing, whereas Gladue's own violence (for which she was charged) was aggravating because the victim was her partner.[166] (Balfour also notes that her sentence appeal was dismissed due to that same aggravating factor and offence seriousness.)[167] Moreover, the Crown dismissed Gladue's own experiences of violence within her relationship, and the trial judge supported this erasure.[168] I discuss above the frequency with which the spousal violence committed by Indigenous women sentenced in the decisions I consulted is judicially deemed to be aggravating under the Criminal Code, but is not situated within the context of their own (often extensive) experiences of abuse. To respond to these problems, Balfour suggests, defence counsel must change their "lawyering strategies" such that they actively engage with Indigenous women's histories of victimization and incorporate these histories as *gendered* systemic and background factors that must be considered within the s. 718.2(e) analysis.[169] For these strategies to be effective, there must also be meaningful alternatives to incarceration available.

Revisiting the Colonization That Never Left

Douglas A. Brownridge explains that "colonization theory essentially argues that the problems faced by many Aboriginal peoples have their roots in Aboriginal peoples' historical experiences."[170] Those "historical experiences" were institutionally imposed and perpetrated in and by

Canada. After several years of compiling stories and information offered by over 6,000 Indigenous witnesses (most with direct residential school experience), the TRC finds in its series of reports issued in 2015 that "for over a century, the central goals of Canada's Aboriginal policy were to eliminate Aboriginal governments; ignore Aboriginal rights; terminate the Treaties; and, through a process of assimilation, cause Aboriginal peoples to cease to exist as distinct legal, social, cultural, religious, and racial entities in Canada. The establishment and operation of residential schools were a central element of this policy, which can best be described as 'cultural genocide.'"[171]

As Indigenous peoples continue to suffer the effects (and ongoing manifestations) of colonization, understandings of these processes must inform criminal justice laws and policies affecting them. Jodi-Anne Brzozowski, Andrea Taylor-Butts, and Sara Johnson reference research suggesting "that the long-term effect of colonization has been the marginalization of Aboriginal peoples, which is reflected in high unemployment rates, low levels of education, low income and inadequate living conditions."[172] Brownridge references research connecting substance abuse to "the social and cultural distress of Aboriginal peoples' past and continuing colonization."[173] All these marginalizing effects have been correlated with both victimization and criminalization.

Processes and effects of colonization are felt both for Indigenous peoples living in urban/rural environments as well as those living on-reserve, as recognized in the *Gladue* proclamation that alternatives to incarceration must be explored for Indigenous peoples living in urban, rural, and reserve settings,[174] because s. 718.2(e) applies to all Indigenous peoples irrespective of where they live.[175] Statistics Canada reports that in 2016, of Indigenous persons "with registered or treaty Indian status, 44.2% lived on reserve," the remainder living off-reserve, and half in the western provinces.[176] Research suggests Indigenous peoples often leave reserves because their communities lack necessary support to care for their baseline needs, especially health and social services.[177] For many Indigenous peoples, this urbanization carries with it feelings of isolation and alienation from their cultures, while often failing to convey access to the resources and services needed.[178] However, some authors, such as Heather Howard and Craig Proulx, also point out that Indigenous peoples living in cities "actively make the urban place their space"[179] (such as through participating in friendship centres),[180] and that it is essentializing and misrepresentative to confine Indigenous experiences to more traditional, stereotypical settings.[181] Instead, Indigenous communities and individual and collective identities shift, change, and may be amorphous.[182]

As observed by the TRC, "despite being subjected to aggressive assimilation policies for nearly 200 years, Aboriginal people have maintained their identity and their communities," and maintain assertions of their "rights to self-governance."[183] Nonetheless, although there are many positive ways through which Indigenous peoples exercise resilience, reassert control, and reclaim their identities and governance structures, the over-representation of Indigenous peoples in prisons is a stark reminder that their communities continue to suffer the effects of colonization.

In terms of the Canadian government compelling control over Indigenous land, the TRC notes that the government negotiated some treaties, but these inegalitarian processes were "often marked by fraud and coercion," and that the government "was, and remains, slow to implement their provisions and intent."[184] In other locations, "the land was simply occupied or seized" by the government from Indigenous peoples.[185] The TRC further identifies that in other instances, the government forcibly moved Indigenous peoples from "agriculturally valuable or resource-rich land onto remote and economically marginal reserves."[186] The government coercively restricted Indigenous peoples to these reserves in the 1880s through a "pass system" and "without legal authority or foundation."[187] Further, the TRC also reports that the Canadian government unilaterally substituted structures of Indigenous governance with "relatively powerless band councils" over which Canada retained control; through this, it "disempowered Aboriginal women, who had held significant influence and powerful roles in many First Nations."[188]

The Canadian government's forced relocation of Indigenous communities is one of many events that has relegated Indigenous peoples to the margins. Processes of colonization were executed without consultation, and practices, including these forced relocations of Indigenous communities, worsened a "decline in living standards, social and health problems, and a breakdown of political leadership."[189] The Royal Commission on Aboriginal Peoples reports that the relocations "must be seen as part of a broader process of dispossession and displacement, a process with lingering effects on the cultural, spiritual, social, economic and political aspects of people's lives."[190] This "may have contributed to the general malaise gripping so many Aboriginal communities and to the incidence of violence, directed outward and inward."[191]

Occupying a pivotal position in the Canadian federal government's Indigenous policy,[192] and in one of this colonialist policy's most damaging forms, the government and Christian churches jointly instituted the residential school system in the 1800s. The TRC identifies that the primary religious denominations were Roman Catholic, Anglican, United, Methodist, and Presbyterian, and that these churches were "involved in the administration of the residential school system" in direct "partnership" with the government until 1969.[193] Residential school closures began in the 1940s,[194] with most closed by the 1980s,[195] but the final such institution was not closed until 1996.[196] During this period, many thousands of Indigenous children were effectively "legally kidnapped," and forced into residential schools—often far away from home, for many years,[197] and separated from their siblings.[198] In its reports, the TRC indicates the federal government has estimated that, at minimum, 150,000 Indigenous children were involved in the residential school system,[199] describing that these children "lived in a world dominated by fear, loneliness, and lack of affection."[200] The TRC characterizes the residential school system as, "at best, institutionalized child neglect,"[201] establishing that it was constructed "not to educate them, but primarily to break their link to their culture and identity."[202] The residential school experience persists as a painfully entrenched part of Indigenous nations and communities.

Replete with horrific neglect, abuse of every sort, and preventable deaths[203] (and deaths "in tragically high numbers," the TRC reports),[204] these institutions attempted to eradicate Indigenous culture,[205] and Indigenous communities were left without resources to attempt to cope with the various involved and resultant traumas.[206] This process of forced assimilation profoundly disrupted Indigenous community coherence; educational systems; cultural integrity; and family, legal, and political structures.[207] Andrea Smith suggests that Indigenous peoples "individualize the trauma they have suffered" through the experience and aftermath of abuses in residential schools in a manner that intensifies their individual and collective feelings of shame, and isolates them from pursuing support.[208] (This trauma and shame-propelled isolation can also be integrated with DeHart's analysis that compounding experiences of victimization marginalize women and impede their access to supportive social and institutional structures.) Smith draws a direct line between state violence against Indigenous communities and "oppressive behaviours that we have internalized,"[209] noting that she observes Indigenous peoples themselves tend to connect residential school abuses to "the onset of violence in their communities."[210] As cited above, the TRC finds that the residential school system was paramount within an Indigenous policy that constitutes cultural genocide. In their book written nearly ten years prior to the TRC's reports, Roland Chrisjohn, Sherri Young, and Michael Maraun also argue that the "Residential Schools were genocide."[211] They assert that the forced transfers of Indigenous children, suppression of Indigenous culture, forced assimilation practices, and the infliction of serious mental harm on Indigenous peoples as members of a group constitute genocide because "cultural genocide is genocide."[212] Chrisjohn, Young, and Maraun contend "the federal government of Canada bears primary responsibility for adopting and implementing an explicitly genocidal policy,"[213] although they also locate responsibility with the churches.[214]

The TRC has since determined that the residential school system was indeed "an integral part of a *conscious policy of cultural genocide*."[215] In the words of the TRC, "Residential schooling was only a part of the colonization of Aboriginal people. The policy of colonization suppressed Aboriginal culture and languages, disrupted Aboriginal government, destroyed Aboriginal economies, and confined Aboriginal people to marginal and often unproductive land. When that policy resulted in hunger, disease, and poverty, the federal government failed to meet its obligations to Aboriginal people. That policy was dedicated to eliminating Aboriginal peoples as distinct political and cultural entities and must be described for what it was: a policy of cultural genocide."[216] Pointedly, the TRC explicitly declares, "The Canadian government pursued this policy of cultural genocide because it wished to divest itself of its legal and financial obligations to Aboriginal people and gain control over their land and resources."[217] The systematic and widespread rupturing of community and family relationships, destruction of Indigenous governance and economies, and suppression of Indigenous languages and cultures continue to have corrosive effects for Indigenous peoples. These and related lingering/continued effects of colonization are often called "intergenerational effects" or "intergenerational trauma."[218] In addition to the scars and unhealed wounds remaining for Indigenous peoples and communities, the TRC also underscores, Canada's "policies of cultural genocide and assimilation have left deep scars" on all of Canadian society, and have profoundly "damaged the relationship between Aboriginal and non-Aboriginal peoples."[219] Here, we all bear active and ongoing responsibility, and in many capacities (as individuals, and through social, legal, and political institutions).

The Indian Act was enacted in 1876 as a legal instrument through which Indigenous peoples could be controlled in everything from their lands and resources,[220] to restricting their mobility,[221] to limiting their very membership in Indigenous nations (the latter by creating status laws that excluded Indigenous peoples who do not meet "legislated identity criteria").[222] The TRC also finds that, through this legislation, "the Aboriginal right to self-government was also undermined."[223] Historically, this statute had many additionally oppressive features, including its attempts to suppress Indigenous culture by such provisions as that prohibiting potlatches and other ceremonies[224] (the TRC identifies the banning of "Aboriginal cultural and spiritual practices" as further evidence of an extensive "assault on Aboriginal identity").[225] The Indian Act remains in existence today, retaining much of its oppressiveness and power over Indigenous peoples "from cradle to grave,"[226] and requiring Indigenous communities/nations, according to Marianne Ignass, to "still face up to the essentialized legal norms of Indian-ness perpetuated" by this legislation.[227]

Membership status is significant for Indigenous peoples on a number of levels, including the impacts on their individual and collective senses of identity and the legal repercussions (as the Indian Act connects status to Aboriginal rights and title).[228] Without suggesting that all Indigenous societies were devoid of gender oppression before colonialism,[229] the Indian Act is also said, as Joyce Green states, to have "abolished the traditional matriarchal society for a patriarchal one,"[230] disrupting traditional

Indigenous social orders and reducing the standing of Indigenous women.[231] The status laws have been particularly deleterious for Indigenous women whose Indigenous status became contingent on their marital state.[232] Further, while 1985 amendments to the Indian Act through Bill C-31 permitted the reinstatement of membership status to Indigenous women whose status was previously rescinded, if an Indigenous woman who had married a non-Indigenous man reclaimed this status and they had a child who later also married a non-Indigenous person, her child lost Indigenous status.[233] Additionally, the government did not provide the resources necessary to reserve communities to be able to support the increased numbers of Indigenous peoples who returned after the reinstatement of their status following these amendments, adding strain to already compromised communities.[234] Compelled by a 2015 Quebec superior court decision[235] finding related gender-based discriminatory sections of the Indian Act unconstitutional, Parliament passed Bill S-3,[236] which received royal assent on 12 December 2017, and amended those elements such that the transfer of status is gender-neutral.[237]

Amendments to the Indian Act in 1951 also permitted provincial and territorial child welfare authorities to remove Indigenous children from their homes and reassign them to generally non-Indigenous families, causing dislocation, cultural loss, and sometimes abuse.[238] Thousands of Indigenous families were subjected to this upheaval, particularly between 1960 and 1980.[239] Even against this history, NWAC reported in 2010 that there are more Indigenous children in state custody than ever before.[240] In another form of Indigenous overrepresentation (and pointing to the interrelated, indissoluble nature of colonization, in that it cannot be restricted to particular institutions or practices), Indigenous children remain vastly disproportionately represented within the number of overall Canadian children in care.[241] The MMIWG Inquiry also indicates that Indigenous children in provincial and territorial state welfare systems "receive poorer services than non-Indigenous children in care."[242] Indeed, in a 2016 decision, the Canadian Human Rights Tribunal finds discrimination by the government against Indigenous children in the provision of state welfare services on reserves and in the Yukon on grounds of "race and/or national or ethnic origin."[243]

Sisters in Spirit identifies that child welfare policies must be revisited because Indigenous children are generally removed into care for different reasons from those for non-Indigenous children—predominantly for neglect (more frequently than for abuse), and stemming from substance misuse, housing shortages and inadequacies, and poverty generally[244] (perhaps also from oversurveillance of Indigenous families and communities). As the TRC writes, "Aboriginal children are still taken away from their parents because their parents are poor."[245] It is necessary to recognize that such phenomena (substance abuse, poor housing, and poverty writ large, among other social conditions) combine in different ways for Indigenous communities from those for other, non-Indigenous communities struggling with the same problems. This is where ongoing processes and effects of colonization have distinct, intersectional impacts. For example, there is research demonstrating that controlling for these issues (i.e., when these social conditions are found in other families and communities), Indigenous families and communities remain more likely than non-Indigenous families and communities to be subjected to intervention by child welfare authorities.[246]

Blackstock et al. emphasize that "the institutionalization of Aboriginal children is a profound concern for Aboriginal peoples."[247] I would add that this is also a profound concern for the criminal justice system (and, ethically, it should be a societal concern), as the intergenerational trauma and fragmentation in Indigenous communities contribute to the criminalization of Indigenous peoples. Additionally, there is research connecting being removed into state care in childhood with coming into conflict with the law.[248] This research also suggests a relationship between being involved in state child custody and later becoming involved in sex work.[249] Further, it should be reiterated and spelled out that in both these two institutional structures (the state child custody system and the criminal justice system, particularly its prisons), Indigenous peoples continue to be alarmingly overrepresented (and ever increasingly so in both systems, as the TRC indicates),[250] and both structures implicate ongoing state control over Indigenous peoples and are directed against some of the most marginalized people in our society.

Criminalization: Complicit in Colonization

Patricia A. Monture argues that "criminalization of Indigenous populations, which results in the present rates of overrepresentation, is in fact a
strategy of colonialism and it is therefore seen globally."[251] She contends
that Indigenous peoples "are the commodities on which Canada's justice
system relies," and if all were "released from custody tomorrow, prisons
would be empty and forced to close."[252] The term "strategy" should be
unpacked, because it implies deliberateness, defined generally as "a plan,
method, or series of maneuvers or stratagems for obtaining a specific
goal or result."[253]

Historically, there have certainly been government-designed and
-implemented strategies that have been consciously and actively directed
toward various abhorrent goals, including that of assimilation and the
cultural destruction of Indigenous peoples, ostensible ownership of the
land comprising the territories of Indigenous nations, and control over
Indigenous peoples. The TRC explicitly characterizes "these measures"
as constituting "part of a *coherent policy* to eliminate Aboriginal people
as distinct peoples."[254] Like the TRC above, NWAC, too, describes such
strategies as "by all definitions, cultural genocide."[255] These strategies
continue to have reverberating effects in the lives of Indigenous peoples.
Such reverberations are certainly evident in the mass poverty within
many Indigenous communities and the overrepresentation of Indigenous peoples in the justice system, among other definitive indicators.
On the surface, it seems these continuing problems function more as
tidal ripple effects than express strategies in the way that previous iterations of colonization have been articulated (such as the residential
school system). Equally, however, the various forms of related colonization strategies today may be simply less visible (and perhaps involve less
consciousness about and/or acknowledgment by the implicated institutions) than were such blatant historical statements as where Deputy
Minister of Indian Affairs Duncan Campbell Scott expressed to a parliamentary committee in 1920 that through assimilationist policy, "our
object is to continue until there is not a single Indian in Canada that has
not been absorbed into the body politic."[256]

Certainly, the criminalization of Indigenous peoples is a manifestation of how processes of colonization are extended. In this context, processes of colonization seem to be maintained variously: initially, because colonization-induced traumas and the widespread, pervasive poverty effected through colonization create conditions that render Indigenous peoples vulnerable to criminalization; subsequently, because the effect of criminalization (particularly incarceration) is to exacerbate problems associated with colonization (such as continued cultural alienation and the ongoing disruption of Indigenous families and fragmentation of their communities); and generally, because criminalization (especially incarceration) represents and functions as an ongoing mode of control over Indigenous peoples. NWAC emphasizes the relationship between the cultural/familial devastation characteristic of residential schools and that inherent in the overincarceration of Indigenous peoples: "Canadian correctional institutions continue the legacy of separating Aboriginal children from parents, while holding them in environments where racism and discrimination thrive."[257]

The issue of whether criminalizing practices are representative of strategies of colonization may seem difficult to affirm in the face of such initiatives as the government's legislating s. 718.2(e) to ameliorate the overincarceration of Indigenous peoples. At the same time, this governmental response represents a decision and was not the only possible initiative (within the criminal justice system and beyond) that might have been implemented in addition or in its place. As Carmela Murdocca argues, regarding a broader view of state responsibility, "Promoting community justice models to address overincarceration rates obscures the onus incumbent upon the state to address the relationship between historical injustice and contemporary incarceration."[258] For its part, the effectiveness of s. 718.2(e) remains contingent upon resources that may not be readily (or at all) available, such as fulsome *Gladue* reports and culturally appropriate, properly funded community services. Parliament also undercut this sentencing reform with the 2007 and 2012 conditional sentencing amendments (and by legislating various mandatory minimum sentences, which also function to remove the availability of CSOs). While those regressions may be motivated by an ostensible concern for victims (i.e., not specifically directed against Indigenous peoples), they likely—even almost inevitably—have the effect of contributing to the further overincarceration of Indigenous peoples.

As *Gladue, Ipeelee,* and s. 718.2(e) recognize, the overrepresentation of Indigenous persons in the criminal justice system must be addressed through institutional consideration of the ways in which they have been generationally impacted by colonization—that is, criminalized Indigenous persons must be treated differently from criminalized non-Indigenous persons. This imperative motivating the law is not rigorously recognized in various political discourses running through further legislation. In particularly the Bill C-9 parliamentary debates that ultimately produced the 2007 amendments first restricting conditional sentences, various political discourses fail to recognize this need to specifically and differentially attend to criminalized Indigenous persons. For example, former member of the Conservative Party of Canada Vic Toews (who in 2014 was appointed as a judge to sit on the Manitoba Court of Queen's Bench) stated in the Bill C-9 parliamentary debates that "some have expressed concern that this bill would potentially increase the overrepresentation of aboriginal offenders. However, when considering this, we should also note that aboriginal Canadians are also overrepresented as victims of crime. Bill C-9 is aimed at providing protection to those victims and their communities."[259] Similarly, in response to related concerns about the overrepresentation of Indigenous women in the system, another former Conservative member, Pierre Lemieux, declared in the same debates, "Mr. Speaker, while I thank the hon. member for her comments and thoughts, particularly on how this bill applies to our first nations people, my concern is that this particular bill is *for all Canadians.* While I do understand her concerns and I thank her for having voiced them here in the House, this particular bill is to get tough on crime *for all Canadians.*"[260] These and similar such comments flatten concerns about overrepresentation into the suggestion that a bill characterized as of benefit to "victims" will be equally beneficial to Indigenous victims, and that a bill purporting to be for "all Canadians" will also support the needs of Indigenous persons (and it must, of course, be noted that those Indigenous victims may themselves be or become criminalized). Such comments are completely misaligned with the intentions behind s. 718.2(e) and its further articulation through *Gladue* and *Ipeelee*. In this sense, wherein (then proposed, now enacted) sentencing legislation neglects to specifically consider criminalized Indigenous persons, concerns about overrepresentation are relegated to the margins. Through this form of marginalization, such legislation may not be designed to directly target Indigenous peoples in the manner of previous iterations of governmental systems of control over Indigenous peoples. However, by collapsing concerns about Indigenous overrepresentation into the idea that all "victims" and "all Canadians" will be served by that legislation, the criminal justice/correctional system of control remains intact. That is, whereas previous government systems of control over Indigenous peoples may be more clearly recognizable as being oriented by strategies of colonization, criminal justice legislation that fails to attend to the specificity of how colonization continues to impact criminalized Indigenous persons can also be understood as strategic in a subtler, more diffuse manner. This diffuseness can be almost imperceptible. I mention above that s. 718.2(e) has been recently amended through the Victims Bill of Rights Act, which now includes that "the harm done to victims or to the community"[261] must form part of judicial consideration for alternative sanctions and particularly for Indigenous persons. The then Minister of Justice and Attorney General of Canada for the Conservative Party, Peter MacKay, declared that part of the goal of this amendment is "to reinforce the sentencing principle of restraint"[262] in s. 718.2(e), which seems implausible. During the parliamentary debates, multiple concerns were raised about how this amendment is both redundant (given that the harm done to victims and the community was already contemplated within the existing objectives of sentencing by s. 718[f]),[263] and that it could dilute the capacity of s. 718.2(e) to respond to the overincarceration of Indigenous peoples by potentially shifting the balancing of sentencing objectives and principles. Notwithstanding such pushback, and even without a strong narrative to counter those concerns, the amendment passed, which could be conceptualized as something like strategic drift.

It is helpful to consider that Sisters in Spirit decries the child welfare system's apprehension strategy inherent in removing children from Indigenous families for its inattention to the long-term consequences of this practice. Sisters in Spirit describes this as a "focus"[264] of state custodial services and do not use the term "strategy." However, as these removals represent action predicated on an institutional focus, they should be regarded as a form of strategy. In this light, it is useful to consider incarceration as another form of strategy, at least because it represents an institutional focus wherein the mode of dealing with social problems (with colonialist foundations) in Indigenous communities is to remove people from the community and confine them. This is not, as Antony Duff and David Garland state, merely a matter of "ask[ing] what it is about crime that makes punishment an appropriate response to it,"[265] but, rather, "What about the crime of Indigenous peoples makes incarceration viewed as an appropriate response." Indeed, *Gladue* responds to this question, following s. 718.2(e), that "there is something different about aboriginal offenders which may specifically make imprisonment a less appropriate or less useful sanction."[266]

Despite legislative and judicial pushback signalling that the overrepresentation of Indigenous peoples in prisons is a "crisis"[267] that must be addressed from a number of avenues, not least at sentencing, Indigenous peoples continue to be disproportionately represented in Canadian prisons. Monture argues that colonialism and imprisonment share "power, control, and isolation" as "key components" that "are now embedded."[268] Continued overincarceration in the face of attempts at the opposite may speak to processes of institutionalization that persist independently of discrete law and policy changes because they become inveterate, both hardened and retaining momentum within these structures. This kind of institutionalization is built into the continued overincarceration of Indigenous peoples, evidenced by its resistance to attempts to address the problem. It is conceptually helpful to consider Kimberlé Crenshaw's depiction of intersectionality here. Crenshaw suggests that forms of subordination such as classism, racism, and patriarchy are enacted in repetitive ways that leave tracks through which the "traffic" of power and decision making travel, creating patterns and conditions where these dynamics are replicated and become systemic.[269] This framework is useful to understand how legal and policy processes and decisions become institutionalized, solidified, and resistant to change.

Angela Davis identifies the prison as "an institution deeply connected to the maintenance of racism," which, in the United States, "reproduces forms of racism based on the traces of slavery that can still be discovered within the contemporary criminal justice system."[270] Similarly, Michelle Alexander powerfully argues that "something akin to a racial caste system" still operates as a form of race-based institutionalized control within the United States,[271] concretized by mass incarceration. Alexander explains that "African Americans repeatedly have been controlled through institutions such as slavery and Jim Crow, which appear to die, but then are reborn in new form,"[272] and are based in different types of control (exploitation, subordination, and marginalization/warehousing).[273] Quoting Loïc Wacquant, she states that each iteration of these successive racial caste systems "is less total, less capable of encompassing and controlling the entire race."[274] This also makes the racial control underpinning successive systems less visible and, as Alexander alarmingly suggests, "more durable than its predecessors."[275] Davis, too, writes that "racism hides from view within institutional structures,"[276] questioning whether its embeddedness in "the institution of the prison" renders it even "possible to eliminate one without eliminating the other."[277]

Citing the words of Luana Ross, Davis notes further that the function of prisons is to "keep Native Americans in a colonial situation."[278] Balfour indicates that other "feminists and critical race scholars have [also] denounced the prison system as the neo-colonial reserve."[279] In Canada, there have been various institutional practices that have predominated in different historical periods and that (functionally) seem to supplant each other (or to bleed into the next) as the primary modes of retaining control over Indigenous peoples. For example, Lindy-Lou Flynn writes that as the pattern of removing Indigenous children into residential schools began to dissipate in the 1950s, the child welfare system "quickly rose up to take its place."[280] As explained by the TRC, "the residential school experience was followed by the 'sixties Scoop'—the wide-scale national apprehension of Aboriginal children by child-welfare agencies."[281] For the Aboriginal Justice Inquiry of Manitoba, Justices Hamilton and Sinclair explain that the "Sixties Scoop" persisted into the 1980s, and comment that "the child welfare system was doing essentially the same thing with Aboriginal children that the residential schools had done."[282] The UN Committee, too, registers its concern "at the continuing discrimination, originally evident during the time of the residential school system and now perpetuated in child welfare practices."[283] The TRC concludes that "Canada's child-welfare system has simply continued the assimilation that the residential school system started."[284] Indeed, the TRC articulates a sense of overlapping and interconnected systems of control, suggesting that through their imposition of "strict discipline, religious indoctrination, and a regimented life," residential schools functioned more as "a prison than a family," and were simultaneously effectively "more a child-welfare system than an educational one."[285] Moreover, the TRC cautions that "similar acts of violence" to those perpetrated in the residential school system are at further risk of "recurring in new institutional forms" if Indigenous peoples are not properly recognized by the state "as holders of Treaty, constitutional, and human rights . . . entitled to justice and accountability from Canada to ensure that their rights are not violated."[286] Additionally, given the interconnectedness of shifting forms of colonial violence, the MMIWG Inquiry reports that "there is also a direct link between child welfare apprehensions and missing and murdered Indigenous women and girls,"[287] and finds "strong links between the child welfare system and violence against Indigenous women and girls"[288] generally.

Whether because of a form of "strategy" or merely that colonial gutters in the institutional landscape resist being redirected and successive policies flow through these same channels, there have been governmental forms of control over Indigenous peoples that preponderate in any given time. The disproportionate criminalization and incarceration of Indigenous peoples is one of the primary institutionalized ways through which Indigenous peoples are controlled in today's Canada, and this effect of continued forms of control remains significant whether it is designed as a direct or indirect strategy. As one of the Indigenous women prisoners interviewed by Sugar and Fox comments, "Most of us were raised in residential places like prisons and the judges convict us for that. I believe we are victims of being victimized," adding that "all we have ever done is run away from institutions."[289] Further, the Aboriginal Healing Foundation reports that residential school survivors in Ontario indicate experiencing revictimization (the reproduction and re-experiencing of past abuses) in "any institutional environment or setting" evoking the "hallways, closed doors, and sterile" context of residential schools, "where rules are inflexible, appear arbitrary" and well-being is treated as secondary to bureaucratic interests, where restraint practices are deployed to prevent self-harm, when the perceived "problems" of Indigenous peoples are deemed solvable only through reference to non-Indigenous knowledge, when "human rights, basic necessities or opportunities" afforded to the wider public are "denied or inaccessible" to Indigenous peoples, and in "any situation of prejudice."[290] All of these revictimizing institutional conditions are engaged in prison.

Kiran Mirchandani and Wendy Chan suggest that the very formulation of categories and definitions of "crime" and "criminality" "maintain gender, race, and class divisions," and connect such labelling practices to repressive and control-oriented strategies that are "inherently political."[291] In terms of whether criminalization is an institutional strategy, for example, referring to the "motives" of the developers of the residential school system, Chrisjohn, Young, and Maraun argue that even if they could be known, they "don't explain anything. . . . There is no need to posit and argue about the personal attitudes, values, morals, or 'whatevers' of these men, when the political, economic, social, and legal inducements for them to act in a particular manner are so crystal clear."[292] Moreover, Alexander discerns there is "widespread and mistaken belief that racial animus is necessary for the creation and maintenance of racialized systems of social control."[293] In this view, it is immaterial whether a "racial animus" can be definitively attributed to our criminal justice system, in that it still persists as a racialized system of control perpetuating the overrepresentation of Indigenous peoples within it. Indeed, Andrea Smith describes the criminal justice system as a form of "state violence," which "cannot provide true safety for women, particularly women of colour, when it is directly implicated in the violence women face."[294] The criminalization of Indigenous peoples is much muddier and more complex now, because the government and judiciary have both framed it as an appalling national problem. Murdocca contends that even "reparative legislation and reconciliation are new techniques in the management of racial and cultural difference," particularly in how they contribute to the creation of the identity of liberal white settler nations "through the regulation and governance of the colonized body."[295]

Essentially, the institutionalization of ways of controlling Indigenous peoples functions as colonization, whatever its intents. For example, the Indian Act sanctioned the removal of Indigenous children into state care, and this should be regarded as an institutional strategy of colonization. Because there were three times as many Indigenous children in state care in 2004 as at the peak of the residential school system[296] (*after* the period in which such child removal was a more express policy), it is clear that this strategy of colonization that ostensibly reached its height between the 1960s and through to at least the late 1980s (as above, the "Sixties Scoop")[297] has continued (and accelerated) in much the same form through today.[298] Indeed, in a 2017 report by the Representative for Children and Youth in British Columbia, Bernard Richard finds that of children and youth in state care in that province, over 62 percent are Indigenous, and that this form of overrepresentation extends to child welfare systems across Canada.[299] In this respect, while it may be useful and productive to call criminalization a "strategy" of colonization, it matters more that Indigenous peoples continue to suffer similar (and intergenerational) effects from today's policies and laws. Whether Indigenous peoples experience an extension of colonization strategies or are marginalized by different strategies that convey similar effects (by exacerbating long-standing problems or creating new problems), in the end it all begins to blur together.

I suggest locating the concept of "strategy" within the meaning of state complicity with ongoing processes of colonization. A framework based in "complicity" permits more diffuse understandings of "strategy," and can thereby accommodate ostensibly decolonizing initiatives by the government such as s. 718.2(e) that render the idea of "strategy" slightly unstable. Redirecting the analytical and political focus from the strategic actions of the state toward notions of state complicity may offer greater potential to demand state accountability and responsibility for how its policies, laws, and institutions continue to decimate Indigenous peoples and communities. That is, the concept of complicity can encompass the idea that criminalization is a strategy (through actions, omissions, and misdirections) propelling colonization, but also may produce greater opportunity for seeking state reflexivity, in terms of how it must examine and mitigate the colonizing harms propagated by its own control-based institutions (including but not limited to the criminal justice system), and operate from a place of consistent accountability and responsibility, moving forward.

In addition to considering whether criminalization is a strategy of colonization, in terms of practicality, it may be helpful to think about how colonization, as a series of institutionalized processes, resists developments in law that seek but fail to produce decolonizing ends. Deborah Bird Rose's concept of "deep colonizing"[300] practices is instructive here. Rose explores how institutions that are motivated by decolonizing objectives or organizing principles (such as truth and reconciliation commissions) can actually bolster the very processes of colonization they strive to dismantle.[301] In the context of Indigenous land claims in Australia, Rose examines one such claim to find that the experiences of Indigenous women were not properly considered in the institutional process of collecting evidence about their society, and the contributions the women did make were required in a form that was in contradistinction to the gender norms within their community.[302] This had the result of denying them full participation in otherwise decolonizing institutions, and thereby compounding the very processes of colonization that were challenged.

Applying Rose's analysis to the overincarceration of Indigenous peoples in Canada, s. 718.2(e) and *Gladue* are together a manifestation of the institutional decolonizing strategy to ameliorate the overrepresentation of Indigenous peoples in prisons, and over twenty years after the implementation of the 1996 sentencing amendments, Indigenous peoples continue to be vastly overrepresented in the system. Following Rose's example, perhaps one of the intrinsic problems with these decolonizing strategies is the minimal (if any) opening for meaningful "engagement"[303] with Indigenous communities (where existing, and insufficient, forms of "engagement" seem primarily restricted to, for example, limited usage of sentencing circles and any band representation in *Gladue* reports, neither of which constitute participatory roles in determining the process or the forum itself). Another intrinsic problem might be the operation of these strategies within the very adversarial legal system in which Indigenous peoples are overrepresented. More effective might be broader initiatives to consult Indigenous communities regarding sentencing practices, equally or preferentially incorporating

Indigenous justice traditions appropriate to specific communities, and, moreover, greater support for and movement toward Indigenous self-government. Indeed, Murdocca identifies that in "testifying before the Standing Committee on Justice and Legal Affairs" in regards to the then proposed sentencing amendments that produced s. 718.2(e), Indigenous women's groups registered their belief "that 'restoring Aboriginal models' of justice was not only a historical impossibility and a fallacy but also, more critically, legal and government shorthand for the continued [colonial] management of indigenous peoples."[304] Overall, at minimum, colonization has certainly cut deep tracks that current socio-legal practices are routed through, and deep enough that even attempts to divert them—such as s. 718.2(e)—have not yet proved successful.

Importantly, vis-à-vis criminalization as a strategy of colonization, Monture suggests that criminality by Indigenous peoples cannot be reduced to individualistic understandings, but must instead be situated within the colonialist past.[305] In this sense, colonization is reinforced by criminalization. Other Indigenous activists, such as Tuhiwai Smith, elaborate that "such things as mental illness, alcoholism and suicide, for example, are not about psychological and individualized failure but about colonization or lack of collective self-determination."[306] Similarly, the TRC underscores that "violence and criminal offending are not inherent in Aboriginal people," but instead "result from very specific experiences that Aboriginal people have endured, including the intergenerational legacy of residential schools."[307] Monture explains that widening the lens past the individual "is not intended to make victims of Aboriginal people or of all prisoners but rather its purpose is to provide a necessary and historic, contextual and structural analysis of the problem at the centre of the question being examined."[308] This analysis is fundamental to the *Gladue* framework. For Indigenous women, as NWAC indicates, colonization has produced conditions in which they are "affected by higher levels of poverty, lower educational attainment, higher unemployment, poorer physical and mental health and lack of housing,"[309] all of which are further strained for Indigenous single mothers.[310] The victimization of Indigenous women must be contextualized against the backdrop and landscape of colonization,[311] which is critical in the face of what Monture describes as the lack of a "sustained

[Canadian] analysis" of the relationship "between colonialism and the oppression of women."[312]

From Gladue Factors to Risk Factors to Treatment

In reviewing eighteen judgments sentencing Indigenous women from 2005 to 2006,[313] Toni Williams seeks to understand how Indigenous women continue to be overincarcerated despite the mutual goals of s. 718.2(e) and the conditional sentencing regime to reduce reliance on imprisonment. Williams argues that because s. 718.2(e) effectively requires judges to identify and weigh such factors as "emotional trauma, familial failings and community dysfunction" through application of the *Gladue* test, this provision imports a contextualized, intersectional analysis into the sentencing process.[314]

Williams concludes that, despite feminists' best intentions for the use of intersectionality, the "intersectionalized constructions" of Indigenous women in the cases "may not reliably shield them from imprisonment in part because of how courts have integrated intersectionality claims into decision-making processes that are organized around controlling risk."[315] That is, calculations of the degree of risk presented by the criminalized person (risk of reoffence, risk to public safety, and, in the prison context, risk to institutional security) have assumed increasing prominence in penal policies and in the sentencing process,[316] and the factors used to assess those levels of risk are largely the same as those engaged by the *Gladue* analysis.[317] (In my research, I find some sentencing judges do look behind such assessments of risk, presenting some hope toward *Gladue* analyses reflecting Monture's direction that offences committed by Indigenous peoples must be firmly contextualized within colonization and not individualized.)

The concept of risk assessment manifests in different forms in the sentencing domain from its manifestation in prison, although ultimately both are concerned with ensuring public safety.[318] On sentencing, judicial decisions are informed by risk assessment instruments including projections of the risk of reoffence in pre-sentence reports[319] and psychiatric reports, which assist particularly with determining whether, and for what duration, a sentenced person must be separated from society. In her research analyzing decisions sentencing Indigenous men and women for violent offences, Balfour identifies that "risk functioned as a composite of the following: aggravating factors such as lack of compliance with police or remand treatment program requirements; a not guilty plea and/or a lack of remorse; and a criminal record for violence"[320] (and, in the cases I examined, a very high percentage of those Indigenous women pleaded guilty, amidst various pressures to do so). "Risk" operates in prison variously, but the most obvious form of risk management occurs when correctional authorities assess prisoners through a series of standardized questions to determine what level of security is needed to contain any threat they are deemed to pose. This takes place at both federal[321] and provincial[322] institutions.

It should also be noted that against the increased prevalence of risk instruments and analysis in the justice system, particularly in the prison setting, the idea of risk itself may be incongruous with Indigenous knowledge and world views. Patricia Monture-Angus writes that risk management "is contrary to how I was raised as an Aboriginal person to think about relationships."[323] Monture-Angus writes that these "individualized instruments" are inherently flawed because they fail to incorporate "the impact of colonial oppression on the lives of" Indigenous peoples.[324] She argues that risk instruments (such as the scales used to help determine a prisoner's security classification level) do not really measure the risk presented by that person, but instead "merely [affirm] that Aboriginal persons have been negatively impacted by colonialism."[325]

Williams suggests that because primary factors evaluated in institutional decision making are alternately *Gladue* factors in the sentencing process and risk factors in prison machinery, there is dissonance producing a conflict between the goal of *Gladue* factors to reduce overincarceration and that of penal risk factors to inform the necessary level of punitiveness.[326] Moreover, this conflict becomes effectively internalized in sentencing discourses. Judges must navigate between the level of risk and personal needs assessed for the convicted individual (as determined primarily based on the pre-sentence report and the judge's own evaluation) and the *Gladue* directive to look to alternatives for imprisonment for criminalized Indigenous persons.[327] For example, a convicted woman may be assessed to present a high risk because of her criminal history and substance abuse, which may militate toward a punitive sanction designed to separate her from society. However, this may be in tension with *Gladue* factors that would formulate these (otherwise perceived as risk-related) factors in the context of colonization and might point to the inappropriateness of a prison sanction. Williams asserts that s. 718.2(e) functions as a conduit for intersectional concerns to become retranslated as risk factors, which in turn undercut the ability of s. 718.2(e) to ameliorate the overrepresentation of Indigenous peoples in prison because elevated risk projections suggest harsher sanctions.

In her study, Williams finds that judges making community orders (largely conditional sentence orders) resolve the tension by either formulating sentences that are guided by rehabilitation and reintegration (healing-oriented, including imposing minimal confinement and discretionary conditions) or by focusing on the risk assessed for the person before the court and amplifying the punitive features of the conditional sentence (such as ordering lengthier sentences with more restrictive terms).[328] For some cases in her study in which judges order incarceration, Williams finds that judges paradoxically cast their decisions in a restorative light, focusing on rehabilitation, but then deliver a punitive sanction, while "construct[ing] the prison at least to some extent as a therapeutic environment, a place of safety, healing and growth for a defendant whose life in the community marks her as both victimizer and victimized."[329] Williams expresses concern that the *Gladue* analysis facilitates a stereotypical representation of criminalized Indigenous women in which they are "over-determined by ancestry, identity, and circumstances."[330] She writes that sentencing courts translate the intersectional inquiry required by s. 718.2(e) into "claims about Aboriginal women with a simple narrative that constructs Aboriginal families as incubators of risk, Aboriginal communities as containers of risk and the prison as a potential source of healing intervention in the defendant's life."[331]

These judicial discourses about the victimization and criminalization of Indigenous women are instructive because overemphasis on one of these aspects of women's pathways can impact sentencing outcomes. Comack writes that the dichotomy some discourses construct between victims and offenders is "premised on an individualistic focus," producing a dynamic framing that "victims require therapy and counseling;

offenders deserve punishment."[332] It must again be remembered here that Monture suggests Indigenous criminalization cannot be understood in reductive, individualized terms. Judges are most directly in a position to determine whether a sentence should be more rehabilitative or punitive.

The dynamic in which judges focus on rehabilitation in sentencing reasoning, but then order a punitive sanction, speaks to how institutional structures become embedded and solidify in ways that are resistant to feminist-inspired initiatives. The fixed nature of such structures, impervious to feminist strategies (or, alternatively, retranslating them such that they act opposite to the goal of women's equality), is also seen above in Balfour's discussion of how mandatory charging policies served only to criminalize already marginalized women. Similarly, Colleen Anne Dell, Catherine J. Fillmore, and Jennifer M. Kilty demonstrate how the Correctional Service of Canada has implemented the philosophy of women-centred corrections recommended by the Task Force on Federally Sentenced Women (TFFSW)[333] in ways that are antithetical to that gender-sensitive vision (such as by constructing women's self-harm as an institutional threat and responding with punitiveness).[334] These examples demonstrate where rigid institutional structures cannot accommodate feminist impulses, which becomes even more troubling as the already limited options available to Indigenous women on sentencing have continued to be curtailed by government conditional sentencing amendments.

This idea of feminist concepts being translated when introduced into an institutional and procedural framework that is not itself motivated by feminist concerns is critical to my thinking about how the judges in my study cast and respond to Indigenous women's histories of victimization. Parallel to Williams's analysis, my research suggests that pre-sentence reports and associated *Gladue* factors and *Gladue* reports operate as entry points for judicial cognizance of how these women's experiences of victimization relate to their criminalization, and how judges resolve these experiences has direct implications on the kind of sanction ordered. The respective histories of Indigenous women (including violence experienced and committed) are presented to and received by sentencing courts in various forms (such as counsel submissions, pre-sentence reports, *Gladue* reports, and judicial notice) that often include recommendations regarding the level of risk that a given woman is likely to pose to the community if she is given a conditional sentence. The very structure of pre-sentence reports in particular renders it difficult to read these women's backgrounds (including any experiences of victimization) as anything *but* connected to their offending.

The Pathway to the Cases in This Study

Judges sometimes use something of a victimization-criminalization continuum lens to process and evaluate the Indigenous women before them; at other times, judges do not adopt this lens and instead simply de-emphasize or bracket past experiences of victimization. When judges do employ a kind of victimization-criminalization lens, they sometimes do so to infer risk (or accord with that projected in pre-sentence reports) and sentence more harshly. Critically, in most cases the women's histories are presented and read as if their criminalization is related to their experiences of victimization, but judges are informed by and respond to these depictions in different ways. Balfour describes that sentencing law excludes "women's narratives of violence and social isolation," producing the "disconnect" she describes between "restorative justice sentencing practices" and "the unrelenting coercive punishment of Aboriginal women."[335] Examining how institutional representations of women's histories (of victimization, offending, and other) are deployed in the cases gives insights into how they impact sentencing outcomes.

Given that these Indigenous women are received by and "known" to the courts in their criminalized capacity, and given my examination of judicial narratives pertaining to their (institutionally authored) histories of victimization and criminalization, in a further effort to not individualize or reduce them to these experiences, I want to extend these words of the TRC about survivors of residential schools to all the women in the cases that follow: "Survivors are more than just victims of violence. They are also holders of treaty, constitutional, and human rights. They are women . . . who have resilience, courage, and vision."[336]

CHAPTER 2

SENTENCING TRAUMA: *GLADUE* AND THE CONTINUUM, JUDICIAL NAVIGATIONS

The histories of victimization of the Indigenous women sentenced in the cases I have identified become part of judicial reasoning through such instruments as pre-sentencing reports and/or *Gladue* reports. As such, these histories of victimization should be understood as only partial, as they are filtered and recorded through institutional instruments, bodies, and structures oriented around the purpose of sentencing, and are interpreted through various actors in the criminal justice system and ultimately by sentencing judges. A lawyer who represented one of the women in the following judgments on a prison matter disclosed to me that the violence to which that woman had been subjected in her life was much more extensive and harrowing than described in the decision sentencing her. This serves as a reminder that the text of judgments does not and cannot represent or encapsulate the victimization histories of the Indigenous women being sentenced. The fragments of women's stories that follow are, of course, institutional renderings circumscribed for institutional ends, not biographies.

As histories of victimization generally overlap with elements of *Gladue* factors, often concepts related to the victimization-criminalization continuum lens and *Gladue* factors will be intertwined. However, while both the continuum and the *Gladue* analysis often share *information* about Indigenous women's lives in the form they are presented to the courts, the analytical *focus* of each differs: the victimization-criminalization continuum most directly focuses on gendered vulnerabilities and responses to victimization, whereas the *Gladue* analysis most directly focuses on reverberations of colonization (and how that should impact sentencing). Additionally, the *Gladue* analysis is necessarily, through legislation and SCC direction, part of the process for sentencing Indigenous women, whereas the victimization-criminalization continuum is a lens that may or may not be introduced or read into this sentencing matrix. Each of the cases I examine features the sentencing of an Indigenous woman. I identified and reviewed 175 cases in total through my various case law searches in online databases, involving the sentencing of 177 Indigenous women (as there are two sets of co-accuseds). I do not discuss all of them, but instead draw out the decisions that offer the clearest discourses related to victimization, criminalization, and the *Gladue* analysis. Some of the decisions I discuss below are laudable for their nuanced navigations within these issues, whereas other decisions are hampered by shallower understandings.

For the most part, I strive to deal with the judgments in a self-contained way, by delving into detail for each case and exhausting that discussion before moving to the next case. I discuss the decisions within various identified themes, but the structure of my discussion still presents particular judgments largely separately. I have chosen this format primarily to retain the individual integrity of each Indigenous woman's life (at least in the partial and institutionally filtered form her life manifests in the sentencing process) and sentencing narrative. Program Coordinator Shawna Hohendorff at Kindred House (the daytime shelter for street sex workers in Edmonton) has emphasized that her clients felt that institutions with power consider "their particular life stories" peripheral and insignificant.[1] Because part of my goal is to foreground the victimization histories of criminalized Indigenous women such that they are pulled in from that periphery and recognized for their intrinsic significance, it seems appropriate to organize my discussion around these aspects and refractions of each woman's story, as told to the courts through institutional instruments, instead of partitioning the narratives and disconnecting them from the women at the centre. Hohendorff stated we must "listen . . . so that they are part of our community, not separate."[2] By focusing on each judgment in its distinctness, I aim to "listen" to what the criminal justice system hears, in terms of what information judges receive about the women's histories of victimization and criminalization (within colonization), and how judicial understandings connected to these issues influence sentencing reasoning.

The Indigenous women I discuss in this chapter have experiences of victimization that often relate to abuse within families of origin and intimate relationships (which must also be connected to colonization), and these experiences and relationships have profoundly isolating effects that can augment vulnerabilities, including vulnerabilities to criminalization. We all have a deeply human need for healthy, loving relationships with others and to feel a sense of belonging, and being harmed within and isolated from those spaces of safety and support is often devastating to our mental health, general functioning, and abilities to navigate (and options available within) other challenges we encounter. Elements of these stories of devastation and isolation manifest in various judicial narratives discussed below. More broadly, some of the judicial narratives reveal systemic isolation, which calls back to the structural alienation and aloneness felt by the Indigenous women street sex workers at Kindred House, who, as Hohendorff related, felt abandoned and unheard.[3] Moreover, this systemic isolation signifies the individual, family, and community fragmentation and alienation propelled by colonization.

Judicial Navigations Along the Victimization-Criminalization Continuum

Some decisions in the cases I identified maintain a rigid dichotomy between "victim" and "offender," while others suggest that "victim" and "offender" are not mutually exclusive categories. In an explicit example of the latter, Justice Peter T. Bishop writes that Janet Masakayash "has been both the victim and perpetrator of violence," indicating this "is reflective of Mishkeegogamang," as her community suffers from "endemic" violence, a "dysfunctional" level of substance abuse, and "very few internal resources."[4] Various judges directly correlate histories of victimization with later offending. When sentencing Georgina McNabb for the manslaughter of her sister (prior to which she had no criminal record) in *R. v. McNabb*, Judge Lawrence Allen comments that "she comes from a family and a community that has been bedevilled by alcohol addiction, the same problem that in Ms. McNabb's life has lead [*sic*] to the tragic situation before the court."[5] The judge adds, "Clearly, Ms. McNabb's history handicapped her and is directly linked to the criminal act which brings her before the court," noting that "these factors are relevant from a *Gladue/Ipeelee* perspective."[6] In another case, declaring mindfulness of the intergenerational effects of residential schools on Janine Firth's family, including the related "direct impact"[7] on Firth herself, Judge Karen Ruddy suggests that "not surprisingly, her history of victimization, for want of a better word, has also led to a lengthy history of self-medication," and that her substance abuse "is evident in most of the offences that are before me and in her record as well."[8]

Some judges also articulate women's pathways to criminalization by recognizing the constrained choices in Indigenous women's lives where they contend with victimization. In sentencing Chantelle First Charger from the Blood Reserve, Judge J.N. LeGrandeur acknowledges, "I have no doubt that her presence before this Court at this time has been fundamentally impacted by the social and economic deprivation that has come as a result of her Aboriginal circumstances and the factors described in *Gladue* and *Ipeelee*, none of which she is responsible for. These circumstances left her with a lack of opportunities and limited options for positive development."[9] In *R. v. Chartier*, in sentencing a "reclusive" woman from the impoverished, "small isolated community of Chemawawin Cree Nation"[10] for Internet-based offences, including extortion and personation, Judge Ryan Rolston suggests Shelly Chartier's Internet activities functioned as "a coping mechanism," and that "the context of the offender's background evidently does bring perspective to her present circumstances."[11] In connecting her constrained circumstances to her level of culpability, the judge comments she "clearly acted voluntarily, however it is equally clear that her background factors contributed to her offending behavior to an extent that her moral blameworthiness is diminished."[12] In *R. v. Morgan*, Judge Michael Cozens points to Dawn Morgan's guilty pleas and her counsel's submissions that she did not have a defence of duress and therefore "had other choices but to commit these offences."[13] The judge later adds that this Nacho Nyak Dun First Nation woman "has had a difficult life, some of it as a result of the choices she has made, but these choices have been made from the position she stood in," and explains that "this is not an excuse for her actions, simply a context."[14] Judge Anne Krahn finds in *R. v. McKenzie-Sinclair* that the young Opaskwayak Cree Nation and War Lake First Nation woman, Heather McKenzie-Sinclair, who acted as a lookout while her boyfriend committed an impulsive break and enter, felt under "pressure . . . to go along with him . . . , particularly since he had been physically violent with her in the past," which "would have been very hard for her to resist."[15]

Broadening the lens to the cyclical nature of victimization and criminalization, in *R. v. R.K.*, Judge Marva J. Smith relates the victimization in M.P. and her co-accuseds' past to their offending and comments broadly on how victimization is often then reproduced as violence. Noting M.P.'s Indigenous heritage, Judge Smith describes her personal history: M.P.'s life involved abuse and neglect in her biological family, after which she cycled through group homes via Child and Family Services in her youth. She has two children with a substance-addicted man, "who subjected Ms. M.P. to a great deal of physical abuse" that she never reported "out of fear of further reprisal."[16] One of her children was removed into state care and another died.[17] Stating, "Obviously, she has suffered from disadvantage and is a product of her difficult background,"[18] Judge Smith later notes, "None of the three offenders before me had the loving, nurturing start in life that every child in our community deserves. Far from it. All were criminally victimized as children and adolescents."[19] Judge Smith clearly connects this victimization to later criminality: "Could more have been done to protect them in their formative years or to help them overcome their dysfunctional backgrounds? It is not for me to say. I only make the observation that the community should be concerned with the fact that too often children are victimized. Violence, cruelty and mistreatment in childhood and adolescence so often beget violence and cruelty to others when these children grow up."[20] This judicial representation of the victimization-criminalization continuum foregrounds the significance of victimization in early life and depicts a causal relationship between early victimization and later offending (the experience of violence/cruelty "beget[ting]" the commission of violence/cruelty), in that M.P. is described as "a product of her difficult background."[21] Judge Smith also recognizes the limits of both the role of the sentencing judge and judicial comments about the cycle of victimization and criminalization in the observation that "it is not for me to say"[22] whether the cycle could have been averted.

Some judges in my study characterize the personal histories of the Indigenous women being sentenced in a manner that reflects Dana De-Hart's finding that the intersection of cumulative, "unrelenting"[23] traumas constitutes the type of victimizations that often pervade the lives of criminalized women, and Maria Yellow Horse Brave Heart's depiction of "massive cumulative trauma across generations"[24] for Indigenous trauma. Such judicial acknowledgements of polyvictimization include Judge Cunliffe Barnett's comment in *R. v. Lilley* that Diane Lilley's pre-sentence report "tells the story of a woman who has had a life characterized by continuous trauma, the sort of life that most people would just shake their head at in disbelief," because she "has suffered a lot of abuse."[25] In *R. v. Batisse,* Justice Robbie D. Gordon writes that Brenda Batisse, living on the Matachewan First Nations Reserve and later on the Timiskaming First Nations Reserve, "has seen and experienced more grief than any one person should."[26] Sometimes this language and the inherent understanding of the cumulative effects of repeated experiences of violence emerge directly from sentencing instruments, and judges adopt the same framework. For example, in *R. v. Chouinard,* the pre-sentence report expressed that "the count is not in years of abuse, but in a lifetime of it."[27] Justice Lynn D. Ratushny incorporated this understanding from the pre-sentence report into her reasoning by adopting the phrase "lifetime of abuse"[28] and using that framework to situate her decision within rehabilitative concerns instead of imposing a sentence of incarceration.

Justice Ratushny recognizes the polyvictimization in Chouinard's life, using a lens akin to the victimization-criminalization continuum to find that Chouinard was enmeshed in a "life's cycle of substance abuse and victimization,"[29] and positions her criminalization within this cycle. Other judges discuss the unrelenting traumatization in many Indigenous women's lives by locating it within the general context of the reverberations of colonization. For example, in *R. v. Pépabano,* Judge Normand Bonin comments, "No doubt the accused has unfortunately lived in a dysfunctional milieu, in relation with [*sic*] the numerous traumas experienced by many First Nations communities."[30] Other judges fail to contextualize Indigenous women's victimization and criminalization within colonization.

In this section, I more closely examine cases featuring various judicial discourses related to the victimization-criminalization continuum. In *R. v. George,* the judge articulates an almost direct line from the experience of victimization in the life of the woman being sentenced to her becoming criminalized. In *R. v. Shenfield,* the judge offers a sensitive appreciation for the vulnerabilities of this woman with respect to her victimization and the offence for which she is being sentenced. In *R. v. Woods,* the judge's decision includes a clear judicial statement about the victimization-criminalization continuum, although this becomes more complicated where the judge situates issues related to that woman's victimization within both mitigating and aggravating factors. *R. v. Dennill* offers some problematic reasoning by decontextualizing the experiences of victimization of the woman being sentenced (and by decontextualizing her broader experience as an Indigenous woman). The judge's attribution of that woman's problems to her choices and not systemic factors should have been informed by the victimization-criminalization continuum, in terms of how victimization narrows women's alternatives. The largely very nuanced decision *R. v. Chouinard* articulates various issues related to victimization. *R. v. Kahypeasewat* engages several important issues. The judicial discourse is generally attentive to this woman's experiences of victimization. The judge decides that she has "battered woman syndrome," and also importantly finds that her offence is derivative of such experiences, although problematically also finding her offence aggravating because the victim was her (abusive) spouse. Looming over the whole decision is the troubling possibility that her offence was actually self-defence, which connects to broader concerns about pressures for women to plead guilty. *Kahypeasewat* is noteworthy for its pronouncement that Indigenous peoples individually and collectively internalize the violence of colonization. This critical point is seldom explicitly made in the cases in my study; in fact, I did not find any other judgments specifically highlighting this concept in those clear terms.

Summur George

The judge in *R. v. George* draws on the "heartbreaking"[31] and "very helpful"[32] *Gladue* report provided, and explicitly connects the experiences of victimization experienced by Summur George to the offence for which she is sentenced, including situating that connection within the victimization histories (embedded in colonization) that extend through her immediate and extended family. George is a "status Indian and member of Chippewas of Kettle & Stony Point"[33] who had no criminal record until this robbery charge for which she pleaded guilty. Justice Jonathon C. George outlines that George's father was in residential school, her mother grew up in foster homes after being removed from her own family, and her half-sister committed suicide at thirteen years old (which, the judge notes, "sadly is a common occurrence in First Nation communities").[34] George and her family have confronted alcoholism and mental health problems.

After dropping out of school (where she had experienced bullying and racism), George's own two young children were apprehended into state care, which, Justice George observes, "seems to represent the beginning of Ms. George's serious problems which has ultimately led to this offending behavior."[35] One of her children died from a health condition. Justice George comments with compassion, having "tried to imagine what that would be like," that "it's hard to believe anyone, regardless of their circumstances, would be well equipped to deal with this."[36] The judge indicates George experienced "essentially a mental breakdown" as a result, quoting her explanation from her *Gladue* report that she was "feeling extremely depressed and out of control and drank alcohol to suppress my feelings."[37] George's depiction of her own experience mirrors Kathleen J. Ferraro and Angela M. Moe's findings about the interrelationship between the removal of women's children by the state and these mothers' use of substances to cope with the loss of their children and of control over their lives.

Justice George describes the robbery, during which George—visibly intoxicated and pregnant with her third child—pointed a toy handgun at a store employee. She later "provided an inculpatory statement" to police, identifying "her motivation as simply being 'mad at life.'"[38] Justice George writes that the offence was "in all likelihood a cry for help,"[39] and states, "I have yet to be involved in a case where it is so clearly obvious what has led to the offending behavior."[40] I have suggested that the victimization-criminalization continuum might be visually represented as a web, given the many complexities along women's pathways to and within the criminal justice system. However, in this judgment, Justice George articulates an almost linear relationship between George's experiences of victimization (her own, those of her family, and all rooted in colonization) and her ultimately becoming criminalized for the first time for this offence. Given that a conditional sentence order is unavailable due to amendments to the regime, the judge orders a thirty-day prison sentence, followed by two years of probation.

Jillian Shenfield

In *R. v. Shenfield*, there is a nuanced judicial portrait connecting Jillian Shenfield's offence to her vulnerabilities, contributing to her receiving a suspended sentence for the duration of an eighteen-month probation order for trafficking. In response to their request to purchase cocaine, Shenfield had informed two undercover police officers that she could contact someone. She physically transferred the cocaine to the officers when that person arrived and insisted he would only "go through her."[41] Judge L.G. Anderson found this constituted trafficking, but notes that her "primary motivation was to assist the persons posing as users, herself being a user."[42] In this case, for the purposes of discussing the victimization-criminalization continuum and judicial understanding of those dynamics, victimization primarily refers to addiction (and the ways it amplified her vulnerabilities).

Although her experiences from her childhood and youth are not disclosed in the decision, it identifies that Shenfield is "of aboriginal origin with ties to the Saddle Lake First Nation," and she now has children who are "no longer in her care."[43] She is described as having "trouble coping with many aspects of life," and an addiction to cocaine.[44] On sentencing, Judge Anderson reflects on Shenfield's pathway into sex work and criminality, commenting that "her addiction led her to the street and all of the dangers, exploitation and vulnerabilities that surround life on the street."[45] The judge expands this view: "This is not a case where Ms. Shenfield exploited the vulnerabilities of others to enrich herself. On the contrary, she was targeted precisely because of her own obvious vulnerabilities and her predictably easy exploitation. She was a known drug user, selling herself on the street to support her drug habit. She was not on the street to promulgate the sale of drugs. Ms. Shenfield epitomizes the victim of the very exploitation that our drug laws, including the harsh sentencing guidelines for commercial predators, strive to prevent."[46] Judge Anderson here recognizes that Shenfield was a vulnerable person who depended on others (to support her addictions), implicating the power imbalance inherent in her interactions with the undercover police officers and the dealer. This depiction further fleshes out the analysis of the victimization-criminalization continuum by integrating how others perceived and capitalized on her vulnerabilities with the judge's understanding of her status as a vulnerable drug user, culminating in a fuller picture of how Shenfield's victimization contributed to her offence.

Judge Anderson also recognizes Shenfield's vulnerability and victimization when deciding that, although it was unclear from evidence at trial whether Shenfield kept a piece of cocaine for herself, nothing "turns on that in relation to sentence," and that "if she did capitalize on this event to get a small amount of drugs without having to turn a trick, I am not going to punish her for that."[47] This recognition of Shenfield's vulnerable, intersectional experience, and the limited options available to her, demonstrates judicial sensitivity that meaningfully impacts sentencing and shows judicial recognition of the importance of not extending the meaning and scope of her punishment to her victimization/vulnerability. This decision represents an unusual judicial portrayal of the victimization-criminalization continuum for its holistic view of that Indigenous woman's vulnerabilities. It illustrates how that expansive interpretation of what it means to be a criminalized person, including the contributory role of victimization, can impact sentencing.

Candace Woods

The overlap between *Gladue* factors and the victimization-criminalization continuum is intimated in *R. v. Woods*, where the judge effectively substitutes a version of the victimization-criminalization continuum for *Gladue* factors to guide the sentencing analysis. Judge S.P. Whelan sentences Candace Woods to a conditional sentence of two years less a day for robbery, among other lesser offences. Woods had displayed a knife and demanded money from a restaurant till. She was a sex worker and carried the knife "for protection,"[48] and her "counsel advised that she was high on morphine and had not slept in several days."[49] Judge Whelan describes that she "is a member of the Muskoday First Nation,"[50] whose parents are Elders and had separated when she was young, precipitating a cycle in which she would have conflict with her mother over her substance use until her mother "insisted on her leaving the home" in her early adolescence.[51] She "became involved in the street and drug culture" and sex work.[52] When she was four years old, Woods was sexually abused by a family friend. Her addictions began in her youth, which also fluctuated through periods of treatment and sobriety. One of her relapses was triggered by the grief and guilt Woods felt over the murder of her sister, after having introduced her sister to the street and drug culture.[53] Her addictions persisted through her relationship with her common-law partner, who was also mired in substance abuse. However, after completing the Women's Substance Abuse Program in pretrial custody and following her release on an undertaking, Woods maintained sobriety. She was the primary caregiver for her baby.

Judge Whelan explains that Woods "committed the substantive offences to support her drug habit."[54] Contextualizing this pattern when discussing mitigating factors, Judge Whelan cites that she "was repeatedly victimized at an early age," and notes that "experience in this Court has shown that the pattern of behavior, evidenced in her record and the offences for sentencing today, is typical of many young persons who have been sexually abused. Her offences are related to a lifestyle of substance abuse and prostitution."[55] This analysis represents a clear judicial pronouncement on the operation of the victimization-criminalization continuum in Woods's life, and notably situates it within mitigating factors.

However, equally and seemingly paradoxically, Judge Whelan also positions Woods's substance abuse (itself a form of victimization, within my definition, and, as the judge states, connected to Woods's experiences of victimization by sexual abuse) within aggravating factors, as her "addictions problems" have "been a significant factor in her offending and unstable lifestyle."[56] This complicates the narrative about victimization and criminalization, because it seems that the judge connects Woods's substance abuse to her victimization as a child and finds this mitigating, while simultaneously finding her substance abuse aggravating when decontextualized and connected to "her offending and unstable lifestyle."

Nonetheless, it is noteworthy that Judge Whelan engages in an analysis that largely resonates with the victimization-criminalization continuum and then likens it to the *Gladue* analysis. The judge states, "I believe that the Pre-Sentence Report, submissions, and my discussion of aggravating and mitigating factors, above, reflects something of the type of analysis anticipated in *R. v. Gladue.*"[57] Judge Whelan does not mention taking judicial notice of *Gladue* factors. However, her description of "the type of analysis anticipated in *R. v. Gladue*" is otherwise broadly consistent with the *Ipeelee* reiteration of the *Gladue* direction about this analysis: in addition to a judge's taking "judicial notice of the broad systemic and background factors affecting Aboriginal people generally," "additional case-specific information will have to come from counsel and from the pre-sentence report."[58] Because there is no explicit discussion of the *Gladue* analysis outside of this reference, the victimization-criminalization continuum discourse that emerges from the reasoning (via the discussion of the pre-sentence report and the mitigating factors, including Woods's history of victimization) effectively substitutes for the *Gladue* analysis, or is at minimum emphasized over a more explicit *Gladue* analysis. Generally, *Woods* offers an example of how permutations of the victimization-criminalization continuum may function in place of a more definitive, circumscribed discussion of *Gladue* factors. This underscores the utility of thinking about how the victimization-criminalization continuum and *Gladue* factors interact and overlap in judgments.

The *Gladue* analysis is not presented as explicitly as would be helpful, although Judge Whelan does position rehabilitation and alternatives to incarceration as "weighty considerations."[59] Within the brief direct reference to the *Gladue* analysis, Judge Whelan notes having "been mindful of the seriousness of this robbery, especially given the threat of violence."[60] This is the type of statement that risks the problem *Ipeelee* distills from the post-*Gladue* jurisprudence that judges have incorrectly interpreted: that serious offences preclude the *Gladue* analysis.[61] However, noting that Woods "has experienced disadvantage but she has also experienced the benefits of a strong cultural heritage through her parents who are Elders,"[62] alongside her rehabilitative progress and compliance with restrictive bail conditions, ultimately, Judge Whelan decides to craft a sentence consistent with Woods's further rehabilitation, in the community.

Kara Dennill

In *R. v. Dennill*, *Gladue* factors are de-emphasized and the victimization-criminalization continuum that emerges from the judgment does allow for recognition of agency, but in a way that effectively supplants systemic factors. Kara Dennill is sentenced to nineteen months' imprisonment cumulatively for two separate trafficking offences after she twice sold cocaine to undercover police officers. Lauding the PSR as "very thorough and, in my view, a balanced pre-sentence report,"[63] Justice V.A. Schuler discloses its contents: Dennill is "an Inuit woman"[64] who "grew up in a supportive and encouraging adoptive family."[65] However, "interventions by Social Services" began after her "difficult behaviour" when Dennill "began to drink and use drugs" as a youth.[66] Ultimately, she became involved in the youth criminal justice system.[67] She was a "victim of abuse by individuals outside her family."[68] Dennill has a young child who is cared for by her parents due to "her unsettled lifestyle,"[69] which the judge later clarifies: "By that I mean drinking, taking drugs, and staying out late at night and because she does not follow through on things."[70]

Justice Schuler notes, "It appears that many resources have been tried but she has not always followed through with them and has from time to time run away from home and from facilities she was placed in."[71] Justice Schuler later comments, "Although Ms. Dennill has clearly had some traumatic experiences in her life, as described in the pre-sentence report, she has also had a supportive family and, it seems, a good family life. The difficulties she has had appear to have resulted, at least in part, *from choices she has made* about the people she associates with *and the lifestyle she leads rather than any systemic factors* that have affected her as an aboriginal woman."[72] Dennill's experiences that precipitate her "unsettled lifestyle"[73] and "difficulties"[74] would be understood through a victimization-criminalization lens as relating less to pure "choices she has made,"[75] as the judge declares, and more to how her experiences of victimization have limited her range of choices, and how she has navigated her life within those narrowed options. The *Gladue* analysis should augment this understanding by providing the context of the role of colonization in constricting her life options.

It would be illuminating to know the circumstances of Dennill's Inuit birth family. There are myriad reasons she may have been put up for adoption, but it is possible that systemic factors arising from colonization were involved. It is difficult to understand how Justice Schuler decides that her experience as an Indigenous woman is effaced or largely irrelevant because she was raised in "a supportive family" within "a good family life."[76] Furthermore, there is insufficient information provided (perhaps in the pre-sentence report, but certainly in the judgment) about how Dennill may have been culturally affected by growing up in an adoptive, perhaps non-Indigenous (unspecified) family. Her tendency to "run away from home and from facilities she was placed in"[77] is presented merely within the general discussion of her youth, and may relate to the judge's comment that she "does not follow through on things,"[78] although, in fairness, the judge does not expressly connect this perception of her failure to follow through with her history of running away. It is conceivable that Dennill felt alienated from her birth family and culture, unsettled within her adoptive family, and disconnected from the institutions that were interceding in her life.

While this is all mere speculation, it remains difficult to understand how Justice Schuler links her "difficulties" with "choices" and "lifestyle," "rather than any systemic factors that have affected her as an aboriginal woman."[79] In this respect, the judgment seems to overly focus on Dennill's (decontextualized) agency at the expense of further consideration of systemic factors, which is not consistent with the lens of the victimization-criminalization continuum or the *Gladue* analysis. It seems that the judgment evinces a portrait of a woman who has struggled, despite being raised in an ostensibly "good" family, and therefore a woman whose struggles are of her own making, and *Gladue* factors are deemed to fall away at this juncture. Within this framework, effectively, personal choices are held as antithetical to systemic factors, whereas the framework would be better aligned with understandings of victimization and criminalization within the *Gladue* analysis if Dennill's choices were understood to be circumscribed by systemic factors.

Josée Chouinard

R. v. Chouinard offers a particularly sensitive judgment where it deals with the experiences of victimization in Josée Chouinard's life and how that background informs her sentence. I highlight some judicial comments that do not comport with the later direction from *Ipeelee*, although it appears that Justice Ratushny's contextualization of Chouinard's victimization plays a significant role in fashioning an appropriate sentence otherwise. Chouinard is sentenced after pleading guilty to being an accessory after the fact to manslaughter, and receives a three-year sentence of imprisonment, the balance of which (after pretrial custody) is to be served conditionally in the community, followed by a two-year probation order. Justice Ratushny comments that the pre-sentence report details a life that "almost takes one's breath away with sadness."[80] The judge elaborates that Chouinard was repeatedly sexually assaulted in her childhood, but had "some good years in foster care."[81] Then, Chouinard "drifted into new abusive relationships and substance abuse,"[82] including her relationship with the victim. He was the father of her two children, and "would beat her when he drank."[83] Her two daughters were removed from her care when she was charged.

Justice Ratushny decides to orient Chouinard's sentence around rehabilitation concerns instead of imposing incarceration. A significant part of this orientation derives from Justice Ratushny's consideration of Chouinard's "lifetime of abuse," and that in her childhood Chouinard "accepted serious abuse as part of her normal life and simply went on living."[84] Justice Ratushny uses this context to inform her understanding of Chouinard's conduct after having been present for the brutal beating adjacent to her own offence, which involved assisting with the disposal of the body "while in a drunken haze"[85] (in that Chouinard continued to drink and laughed about it with the other parties involved). Against the backdrop of Chouinard's extensive history of victimization, the judge finds that "it is not surprising she found herself reacting as she did to the abuse of the victim that night."[86] This recognition prompts Justice Ratushny's "focus on an individualized, restorative approach to sentencing to try to deter Ms. Chouinard from drifting again into criminal behaviour and to try to assist in her rehabilitation, away from her life's cycle of substance abuse and victimization."[87]

The judge's formulation of the victimization in Chouinard's life (her "lifetime of abuse," her "life's cycle of substance abuse and victimization," and that her reaction to the offence "is not surprising")[88] reflects the general concept behind the victimization-criminalization continuum. Additionally, it encourages understanding of how victimization constrains women's options—and choices within those options—particularly when read with Justice Ratushny's further comments that "alcoholism was part of her mother's life, part of her father's life and became part of Ms. Chouinard's life and along with the alcoholism, came an inability by either mother and daughter to prevent or leave a life filled with physical abuse."[89] These insights are consistent with Marilyn Brown's conception of agency within constraints: "The pathways perspective[90] also needs to consider the degree of autonomy which women can exercise within relationships that are often marked by dependence, abuse, and victimization."[91]

Despite this articulation of the accumulation of polyvictimization and how these experiences created barriers for Chouinard, the interrelationship between a victimization-criminalization lens within the *Gladue* analysis here is slightly weakened by one of the problems identified in the post-*Gladue* jurisprudence by *Ipeelee*. Justice Ratushny does recognize per *Gladue* that "the principle of restraint is particularly applicable to Ms. Chouinard as an aboriginal offender"[92] and sentences accordingly, ordering a just sentence consistent with *Gladue*. However, Justice Ratushny also mentions that "it is difficult to specify which elements of Ms. Chouinard's background might be attributable to her heritage. Only her mother was aboriginal."[93] The facts do present issues that may well be attributable to colonization. However, neither the difficulty ascertaining which aspects of Chouinard's background relate to her heritage nor the fact that "only" her mother was Indigenous should have any bearing on the *Gladue* analysis (and, on 14 April 2016, the Supreme Court of Canada held that persons who are Métis and non-status are "Indians" under s. 91(24) of the Constitution Act, 1867).[94] Judges should not artificially restrict the multiplicity of Indigenous identities and experiences, and (given the clarification from *Ipeelee*) they must neither expect nor require the establishment of a causal connection between *Gladue* factors and the offence in question.

Valerie Kahypeasewat

In *R. v. Kahypeasewat*, the judge attributes Valerie Kahypeasewat's offence to her past experiences of victimization in a way that seems to endorse the victimization-criminalization continuum as a lens, both in the judicial discourse about these issues and also in how this discourse meaningfully impacts the ultimate sentence. Judge Bria Huculak offers a nuanced understanding of the experiences underlying the manslaughter for which the judge orders Kahypeasewat to serve a conditional sentence of two years less a day followed by two years of probation. Kahypeasewat pleaded guilty to manslaughter after killing a man with whom she had been in an abusive relationship after he repeatedly and aggressively "attempted to engage in intimate physical contact despite her demands to be left alone," and she finally swung at him with a knife.[95] I describe the circumstances of the offence in some detail because although there is judicial sensitivity to her victimization, the facts troublingly suggest that Kahypeasewat acted in self-defence. Within a self-defence frame (and even outside it, within the actual confines of the judgment), it is clear how Kahypeasewat's experiences of victimization have constrained her options, both broadly in her life and in the specifics of the offence circumstances.

At the sentencing circle convened for Kahypeasewat, the Crown read in the circumstances of the offence.[96] Judge Huculak describes Kahypeasewat's "on-off relationship"[97] with the deceased, spanning several years. On the night of the offence, Kahypeasewat and the deceased, Frank Nadary, had been drinking with others at Kahypeasewat's brother's apartment. Nadary was harassing Kahypeasewat, and had refused to leave after being asked to do so multiple times (by Kahypeasewat, and it seems by others, too), including when she wanted to sleep. Nadary persisted in trying to initiate unwanted sexual contact with Kahypeasewat, who left the room, opened the front door, and again asked him to leave, physically trying to push him out. Kahypeasewat explains her frustration in her statement to the police: "How many times I told him to leave, 'get out, leave me alone,' he just wouldn't listen."[98] She threatened to call the police if he refused to leave.[99] Judge Huculak writes that Nadary then "attempt[ed] to smother the accused by wrapping his arms around her," and grabbed her neck, "pulling her hair."[100] After Nadary refused to leave, Kahypeasewat discloses, "I was like—it was like I couldn't breathe, like, you know."[101] In a later statement to police, Kahypeasewat expands about her feelings of anger and fear, explaining it felt "like you're having a panic attack or something. Like for me it was like that smothering feeling, anger plus it's kind of hard to breathe for me, you know, when I'm trying to get him away and I can't, it's pretty frustrating."[102]

The judge continues that Kahypeasewat "was able to escape his grasp and began to throw various objects in his direction to deter him."[103] In her police statement, Kahypeasewat explains that she had been throwing cups, but

> I kept missing him, I was trying to get him to get out and
> he wouldn't leave. He kept moving around so I wouldn't hit
> him with the cups. That's when I grabbed the knife. I was
> looking, first thing I seen like, I would take it and throw it
> at him, but those were the cups. And then all of a sudden I
> had this knife and I was missing him with that, and I didn't
> know I connected because it was fast. I was trying to scare
> him out of there but I didn't realize I'd connected and it
> became a major big thing.[104]

The judge explains that Kahypeasewat "swung at Mr. Nadary three times, with the second strike inflicting a mortal wound on the victim."[105] Judge Huculak notes, "Despite the fact that Valerie was swinging the knife at Mr. Nadary, he continued to attempt to grab her. Valerie had intended to scare Mr. Nadary and the motion that the knife was swung was toward his arms."[106] Kahypeasewat told the police, "But I didn't mean to connect, I just tried to scare him, tried to get him out of the house, the apartment. But he wouldn't leave."[107]

It is critical to understand these events in the context of Kahypeasewat's having been in four relationships that "involved physical violence," including her relationship with Nadary—he "had been convicted of unlawful confinement and assault" against her[108] ("assault causing bodily harm," which resulted in a "condition of no contact").[109] Additionally, the judgment indicates that Nadary "had been released from jail about a month before the alleged offense and he had come looking for her," and that Kahypeasewat "knew that although he was not supposed to have any contact with her, it would not deter him."[110] (That is Kahypeasewat correctly anticipated this legal order against him would fail to protect her.) The entire basis of their relationship was founded on Nadary's abuse: Kahypeasewat reported to the doctor authoring a report for the court that "the victim had 'decided' on their relationship and added, 'He would find me and drag me out or scare me to the point of going out with him.'"[111] Kahypeasewat disclosed, "'I felt I had to act accordingly . . . so I didn't get hit or screamed at.'"[112]

The doctor reports that the deceased "tried to control" Kahypeasewat and emotionally abused her, and that "she was in fear of the victim throughout most of their relationship and said he frequently threatened to kill her."[113] Kahypeasewat also reported to the doctor that during the incident, after throwing cups at Nadary had no deterrent effect on his advances, and she grabbed the knife, "'that's when I started swinging at the same time I had my eyes shut tight because I figured he would throw punches.'"[114] She opened her eyes only after realizing she had "hit something."[115] The facts speak to an Indigenous woman not merely with constrained choices, but with no meaningful choice in how to react to and contend with the ongoing abuse, harassment, and fear induced by the deceased. This is the troubling context of her criminalization that led to her guilty plea to manslaughter. Joycelyn M. Pollock and Sareta M. Davis write about violence committed by women that "there are a number of narratives that sound much more like self-defence than aggression

initiated by the female offender."[116] The circumstances of Kahypeasewat's offence certainly conform to this analysis.

Judge Huculak details Kahypeasewat's personal history, which includes experiences of racism; extensive sexual, physical, and emotional
abuse beginning in her violent home life as a child and continuing
through several violent intimate relationships; and the murders of her
mother and one of her daughters. She developed substance abuse issues,
culminating in the removal of her children by Social Services. Judge
Huculak finds that Kahypeasewat "suffer[ed] a form of battered woman
syndrome,"[117] and includes this as mitigating alongside her history of
complex abuse, resultant post-traumatic stress disorder, and her *Gladue*
factors. However, Judge Huculak also notes having "taken into account"
aggravating factors, including that "the victim was a spouse."[118] This is a
reference to s. 718.2(a)(ii) of the Criminal Code, which the judge cites
within the sentencing principles considered. While such consideration
is legislatively required, uncritical application of this principle is problematic in this context, wherein Kahypeasewat has extensive experiences
of violence in relationships, including in her coerced relationship with
the deceased. Indeed, Judge Huculak even explicitly cites that "she was
victimized by Frank Nadary"[119] among the mitigating factors engaged.
It seems incongruous for the judge to consider battered woman syndrome and victimization by Kahypeasewat's abusive partner as mitigating factors while simultaneously finding it aggravating that this offence
involved violence against that same abusive partner. In fairness, Judge
Huculak simply notes having "taken into account"[120] various aggravating factors including this one, and does not directly comment on the
weight accorded to that consideration. Nonetheless, to avoid making
this finding per s. 718.2(a)(ii), perhaps, among other alternatives, the
judge could have decided that this was not a relationship contemplated
by this provision (which seems readily available on the facts because, as
noted above, Kahypeasewat comments that the deceased "had 'decided'
on their relationship," and "'would find me and drag me out or scare me
to the point of going out with him,'"[121] indicating that it was abuse and
duress that constituted the relationship as "spousal"). Depending on the
facts, I suggest that s. 718.2(a)(ii) is generally neither informative nor
appropriate in contexts such as Kahypeasewat's offence or in any context

where an abused partner is being sentenced for an offence against her abusive partner.

Notwithstanding this incongruence, considering Kahypeasewat's life overall, Judge Huculak clearly recognizes how her experiences of victimization and other struggles have left her vulnerable to criminalization. The judge indicates that "these socio-economic factors figure significantly into sentencing considerations, since Valerie Kahypeasewat's tragic upbringing, the murder of her child, racism, victimization, abuse, addictions, family dislocation, poverty, fragmentation, lack of education and employment, family dysfunction, and her shattered life all contributed in a major way to her criminal record."[122] Elaborating on how the violence permeating Kahypeasewat's life also informs her sentencing, Judge Huculak declares, "I find that [her] stabbing of Frank Nadary was a *derivative crime* borne of the unresolved effects of past conditions of abuse, indignities and profound grief."[123] The idea that this stabbing is a derivative crime stemming from the trauma suffusing Kahypeasewat's life relates quite a profound judicial statement. Additionally, it conforms well to the conception of victimization and criminalization operating along a continuum. The judge concludes with further such contextualization, noting the limits of sentencing because "the socio-economic and environmental back-drop to domestic violence must also be addressed which is beyond the scope of this court."[124] This comment reflects a recurrent theme that judges identify in the cases I reviewed: the criminal justice process is inadequate to respond to issues rooted in fundamental, entrenched societal inequalities and oppressions that act as destabilizing forces.

Judge Huculak elaborates: "Domestic violence in the aboriginal community is a serious issue. The factors contributing to this are complex. What sentence the accused receives will not change this. The *Gladue* factors play a prominent role in creating the conditions where violence is turned inward toward family, friends and self. The tragedy is that without significant resources and a change in the socio-economic conditions, little will change."[125] These comments are significant, representing judicial understanding of the role of colonization in the internalization of violence. Tuhiwai Smith explains the process of the internalization of colonization as a form of violence that is corrosive to Indigenous peoples' individual and collective senses of self and well-being, expressed as both internally and externally directed violence:

> Often there is no collective remembering as communities were systematically ripped apart, children were removed for adoption, extended families separated across different reserves and national boundaries. The aftermath of such pain was borne by individuals or smaller family units, sometimes unconsciously or consciously obliterated through alcohol, violence and self-destruction. Communities often turned inward and let their suffering give way to a desire to be dead. Violence and family abuse became entrenched in communities which had no hope. White society did not see and did not care. This form of remembering is painful because it involves remembering not just what colonization was about but what being dehumanized meant for our own cultural practices.[126]

The internalization of colonization is a complex process, and it is important that Judge Huculak makes reference to this process by stating as above that "*Gladue* factors play a prominent role in creating the conditions where violence is turned inward toward family, friends and self." The judge's comments about the intractable nature of these issues, absent fundamental societal shifts, is also critical for its recognition of how—like other forms of victimization—colonization constrains Indigenous women's choices and the options available in and to their communities at a systemic level. This framework, heeding the internalization of colonization and its expression through inward and outward violence (and connected to Monture's contention that Indigenous offending must be contextualized within colonialism and not viewed through an individualistic lens), should undergird the sentencing of all Indigenous persons.

Taken as a whole, *Kahypeasewat* represents a complicated judgment, and particularly as pertains to the victimization-criminalization continuum. On one hand, it presents a nuanced understanding of how Kahypeasewat's own experiences of victimization (situated within colonization) have contributed to her "derivative crime,"[127] and yields an appropriately sensitive community sentence. However, equally, it involves the sentencing of an Indigenous woman whose offence reads as self-defence on the facts, which is amplified by her experiences of abuse in relationships generally and specifically in her relationship with the deceased.

Kahypeasewat was charged with manslaughter. It is unclear what pressures she may have experienced in her decision to plead guilty. Studies have found that women are generally more likely than men to plead guilty.[128] Additionally, the Canadian Association of Elizabeth Fry Societies (CAEFS) and NWAC have emphasized that their advocacy work reveals "women are susceptible to entering guilty pleas at a very high rate."[129] Elizabeth Sheehy indicates Indigenous women experience heightened pressures to plead guilty.[130] She identifies possible reasons for this, including having to contend with portrayals in court material that they were the aggressor (which could result from such issues as addictions affecting memory or linguistic usage inadvertently insinuating mutual aggression), pressures arising from lengthy or serious criminal records, and access to justice issues.[131] For the Aboriginal Justice Inquiry of Manitoba, Justices Hamilton and Sinclair report that "a number" of Indigenous women incarcerated at a provincial prison described that "they did not understand the court procedures," sometimes related to not understanding the language used, and "some knew nothing other than that they were told to plead guilty, so they did."[132] Some research, as reported by Murdocca, indicates Indigenous women "charged with the homicide of abusive partners often plead guilty in higher number and forego the use of possible defences, such as self-defence," fearing lengthier sentences if such arguments fail at trial.[133] CAEFS and NWAC raise concerns "that women face additional pressures in plea-bargaining . . . especially when the context is a battering relationship,"[134] as were Kahypeasewat's circumstances. CAEFS and NWAC explain that some of these pressures derive from women's striving to "protect their children and sometimes to protect the batterer," noting that overcharging also leads women to pleading to more serious charges.[135] Kahypeasewat had several children, two of whom were present at the apartment on the night of the offence (a factor the judge found to be aggravating,[136] which is problematic in the context of the abusive relationship, given that Kahypeasewat did not voluntarily choose to expose her children to the deceased at all, and made strenuous, repeated efforts to induce him to leave the apartment on the night of the offence). CAEFS and NWAC point to the lack of available statistics about the pressures within which women plead guilty, which means "systemic arguments cannot be made in courts that would assist women who have faced or are facing these circumstances."[137]

The degree to which Indigenous women may be overcharged is often not readily visible. This invisibility obscures related pressures for women to plead guilty to more serious charges than they might otherwise confront, and situations in which women may feel compelled to plead guilty to lesser included offences instead of proceeding to trial. I canvassed the sentencing decisions in my own research and tabulated the number of Indigenous women who pleaded guilty, seeking a sense of the prevalence of guilty pleas. There are 175 judgments in my study, involving the sentencing of 177 Indigenous women (two judgments sentence Indigenous women co-accuseds); of these, 136 women pleaded guilty (five additional cases each involve both guilty pleas and convictions after trial to different charges, but I elected not to include them in that total because the most serious charges were disposed of through trial). In seven judgments within my study (for the sentencing of eight women, given one case involving two Indigenous women co-accuseds), the judges note that the women were initially charged with second-degree murder, and instead pleaded guilty to manslaughter.[138] In two of these cases, the women entered these guilty pleas after initiating the trial process: Jessica Hanley pleaded guilty at the beginning of her fourth week of trial,[139] and Janet Masakayash entered her plea on the first day of her preliminary inquiry.[140] The invisibility of the problems of overcharging and related (or separate) pressures to plead guilty also obscures circumstances in which women enter guilty pleas but may have otherwise been acquitted or convicted of lesser offences following trial. For example, when Justice René Foisy sentences Mary Martin (alongside her two Indigenous male co-accuseds) for simple possession of cannabis, the judge comments that Martin's "involvement appears to have been more on the periphery,"[141] and adds about all three Indigenous persons that their "guilty pleas were entered before trial in circumstances where it is not at all certain that the Crown would have been successful."[142]

Kahypeasewat is not the only judgment over which the issue of self-defence silently and unsettlingly lingers. Another such example involves the sentencing of Roxanne Simms, who has Inuit heritage through her mother, for aggravated assault on her former partner. Judge Donald S. Luther determines this is "not a case of self-defence," finding that she "had a realistic opportunity to escape."[143] However, this determination seems to rest unsteadily and uncomfortably on the provided, albeit limited, facts. Simms was convicted at trial, in what appears to be an unreported judgment. The sentencing decision indicates that the offence took place while Simms was "attempting to retrieve her belongings from the apartment" that she and her former partner "had once shared" (implying she wanted and was actively trying to leave), which, the judge comments (without clarifying the relevance), was an apartment "no longer, technically speaking, hers."[144] Moreover, Judge Luther writes that Simms's former partner "weighs about 25 kilograms more than the offender and is significantly taller than she," adding that "he assaulted her viciously by pounding her in the face, pinning her to the floor, elbows surrounding her throat, and kicking her. She almost lost consciousness."[145] This is the context in which Simms stabbed him once in the arm, "rather than leave when she could,"[146] as the judge suggests. Judge Luther also comments, in reference to the determination that self-defence is not engaged, that "neither was she defending family or friends, or even her personal property,"[147] which is a perplexing qualification, given that the provided facts suggest she *herself* was under extreme and immediate threat. Perhaps Simms's self-protection was not viewed as sufficient, or that the violence against her was otherwise "naturalized."[148] Razack writes about the persistent and dehumanizing narrative of "the squaw" as it operates in sexual assault trials, wherein, on the Indigenous woman victim's body, "violence may occur with impunity."[149] Additionally, Judge Luther quotes an email her former partner sent to both Simms's lawyer and the probation officer, in which her former partner explains, "'I feel that I have introduced her to a dark world of alcohol and drug addiction'" (during the offence, both of them remained affected by alcohol and/or other substances consumed previously), and that "'it is regrettable to also inform you that I knowingly pushed her to act out in violence by initiating it myself.'"[150] Judge Luther's response regarding this letter is simply that "what is most regrettable, in my view, about her life thus far is the relationship she had with" her then-partner.[151] Without further information about how the judge did not find self-defence at trial, it is at minimum unclear as to why this set of facts did not produce such a finding, and, overall, troubling. *Kahypeasewat* and *Simms* both involve Indigenous women engaged in what read as desperate, self-defensive acts of violence. Justices Hamilton and Sinclair report for the Aboriginal Justice Inquiry of Manitoba that Indigenous women "at times lash out against continuing abuse, either in self-defence or as a delayed reaction to being violated," and add that "few lawyers understand that fact well and seldom bring those extenuating circumstances to the attention of the court,"[152] which also implicates lawyering approaches, and the need to deepen them.

Determinative Language: Narrow Agency Within Constrained Options

Judges in my study frequently employ language variously suggesting a kind of predictability or inevitability when referencing Indigenous women's criminalization. I suggest this determinative language reflects judicial recognition of how experiences of victimization constrain Indigenous women's choices within already limited options. For example, Judge Adrian F. Brooks suggests that the "circumstances" of Ernestine Elliott's "upbringing are not adequately captured by the word 'traumatic.'"[153] The judge later questions, "How can those years and years of tragedy not have followed her to who she is today?" and finds that her moral blameworthiness is reduced as a result.[154] In sentencing Jenna McClements, Judge Ruddy references "a distressing history of extensive victimization, beginning with abuse suffered perhaps, not surprisingly, in the very home that was burnt down by Ms. McClements in the offence that is before me," and adds, "This has led to an ongoing struggle with behavioural issues and significant substance abuse issues, including both alcohol and drugs" for her.[155]

Some decisions discussing Indigenous women's experiences of victimization with reference to colonization locate interconnected social problems and the women's criminalization within their communities, articulating a similar sense of predictability. In sentencing a woman from Long Lake 58 First Nation, Justice Dino DiGiuseppe notes that the pre-sentence report "chronicles an all too common experience for many of Canada's indigenous peoples, a lifetime filled with abuse and neglect,"[156] adding that Jessica Bouchard is "a product of her community."[157] The judge also adds about the cyclical effects of intergenerational pains of colonization that "it should be no surprise that Ms. Bouchard's behaviour, which includes substance abuse and violence, reflects the environment she was exposed to as a child, and in some measure, at least within the broader context of her community, continues to be exposed to."[158] Drawing on Georgina McNabb's pre-sentence report, Judge Allen connects the pervasiveness of substance abuse in Moose Lake to violence and especially that within families, finding that "whatever hope she had for a sober life would only have reached fruition in some other location, not within the context of her family, and not within her home community."[159]

Other sentencing judgments reference the constrained agency that Indigenous women with histories of victimization experience along their pathways to criminalization. For example, in sentencing twenty-one-year-old Michelle Arcand from the Muskeg Lake First Nation for possession of cocaine for the purpose of trafficking (her first offence), Judge Felicia M.A.L. Daunt refers to information in the pre-sentence report about her abusive father, parents who abused substances, placement and subsequent escapes from group homes, and teenage pregnancy, finding, "It is not difficult to see why, when faced with financial problems, she might think she had fewer choices than a 21-year-old middle class college graduate who has a family with some financial resources. Ms. Arcand's immediate family is dysfunctional. Many of her peers live on the fringes of society. With that past history and present reality, it is easier to understand how Ms. Arcand might stray into the margins herself."[160] Justice Leigh F. Gower finds that the implicated (and mitigating) *Gladue* factors "have disadvantaged" Jessica Johnson "in many ways beyond her control," accepting the submission by her defence counsel that she "never really had much of a chance to make a success of her life given her upbringing, until now."[161] Judge Robert D. Gorin comments that Melissa Bourke "has had a very difficult background," observing that "it is often far more difficult for people who come from such a background to stay out of trouble with the law all of their lives," and that, against this type of background, "the likelihood of criminal behavior increases."[162] Similarly, Justice G. Bruce Butler affirms the submission by Robyn Hansen's defence counsel that "the circumstances she faced throughout her life made it extremely likely that she would become involved in the criminal justice system."[163]

Several cases feature judicial discourses that address how these Indigenous women's options and choices have been constrained by their experiences of victimization, and how these experiences have accelerated their vulnerability to criminalization. In *R. v. Good*, Judge John Faulkner describes Helen Good's life as the "predictable result of neglect and abuse."[164] Justice DiGiuseppe suggests in *R. v. Tippeneskum* that June Tippeneskum's substance abuse "inevitably led her into the criminal justice system,"[165] and that the abuse and neglect she experienced in her youth "created an unfortunate template for her life,"[166] finding it "not surprising"[167] that her criminalization reflects that template. In *R. v. Gregoire*, Justice William H. Goodridge finds it "not surprising" and "inevitable" that Angela Gregoire's experiences of victimization left her vulnerable to substance abuse and criminalization.[168] In *R. v. Pawis*, Justice Paul H. Reinhardt comments that Nicole Pawis's history of victimization culminated in "a terrible catastrophe just waiting to happen,"[169] an offence that "was almost predictable, in hindsight."[170] These representations of the Indigenous women's histories and criminalization relate to insights conveyed by the victimization-criminalization continuum.

Helen Good

In *R. v. Good*, language suggesting that the trajectory into criminalization predictably flowed from constrained choices is evident. In this case, Judge Faulkner sentences Helen Good to three years' imprisonment for assault causing bodily harm and uttering death threats[171] (the defence had asked for two years less a day), and also designates Good a long-term offender for a ten-year period following her release. After detailing the extensive violence that Good perpetrated, Judge Faulkner poses that "the obvious question is, 'why?'"[172] In response, Judge Faulkner states, "Helen's life is the predictable result of neglect and abuse that she herself has suffered at the hands of her parents, partners, caregivers, and associates. Just as predictably, she has passed on many of those effects to her children: two are dead of drug-related causes and a son has serious psychiatric problems."[173] This demonstrates the judge's understanding that Good's experiences of victimization pervasively reduced her life options and left her vulnerable to criminalization. As the judge recognizes that her victimization has also impacted her options and choices as a mother, this also functions as an oblique reference to the intergenerational effects of colonization. However, the context of colonization is not examined.

Despite judicial recognition that Good's experiences of victimization have impeded her ability to healthily and productively navigate her life, in other respects, Judge Faulkner holds Good accountable to her experiences of victimization. In the context of psychological and psychiatric assessments[174] suggesting that Good presents a high risk to reoffend, Judge Faulkner finds that, "despite years of therapy, the offender fails to take ownership of her violence, but continues to seek refuge in her own victimization as a justification."[175] Judge Faulkner does not expand in detail, but does indicate that, "for instance, she reports and justifies assaulting men because they reminded her of her father. She has never developed any notable empathy for her victims."[176] Drawing from assessments examining Good's mental health, Judge Faulkner notes long-term patterns in Good's more than forty-year record of violence,[177] which often occurred after she drank[178] and was "perpetuated against defenceless victims."[179] It seems the judge describes these victims as defenceless because in an assessment from a previous case, "Helen acknowledged that many of her assaults were premeditated. She would wait until her victim was too drunk to defend himself and then attack."[180] (In a decision I discuss in Chapter 3, having been repeatedly victimized by violent male partners, Helen Smith also waited to assault these men until after they were drunk, because she was not physically capable of assaulting them when the men were sober.) There are also several references to Good having committed violence against other women and her own children.

It seems that the accumulation of serious violence over such a protracted period, her Borderline Personality Disorder and Antisocial Personality Disorder diagnoses,[181] and the assessment ordered for this sentencing that concludes she "remains at high risk of further serious violence if she uses alcohol or other intoxicants"[182] combine to cause her own experiences of victimization to recede into the background. This imbalance becomes problematic in that there are virtually no details offered about Good's personal history apart from the reference to the "neglect and abuse that she herself has suffered at the hands of her parents, partners, caregivers, and associates"[183] and her children's struggles. It is apparent from the number and variety of parties identified who subjected Good to neglect and abuse that her own experiences of victimization were extensive. Even without additional information about her history of victimization, it seems that Good's life reflects how what DeHart calls the "sheer number"[184] of victimizations in women's lives can become "a tangle of barriers"[185] that impede healthier pathways and leave women vulnerable to criminalization.

Judge Faulkner does not properly contextualize Good's violence within these circumstances. The omission of any discussion of her personal history is even starker in the effacement of Good's Indigeneity from the judgment. Judge Faulkner nowhere directly states her Indigenous status. I infer from the text that Good is Indigenous because, when discussing her "significant level of community support,"[186] Judge Faulkner comments that "the Court received a report authored by Mark Stevens, a justice worker with the Carcross Tagish First Nation"[187] and refers to a "support circle"[188] convened for Good. The judge makes reference neither to s. 718.2(e) nor to *Gladue*. The only direct reference to any specific portion of the s. 718.2 sentencing subsections of the Criminal Code is to s. 718.2(a)(ii), as Judge Faulkner finds that this "statutorily aggravating factor"[189] applies because the offences were against her husband. In the Introduction, I registered my discomfort with application of and weighting given to this provision to women with histories of violent victimization in intimate relationships (and maintain that stance for its application in this case), but here I am primarily highlighting how the judge considers this (arguably situationally problematic) sentencing principle, but neglects to include any consideration of another principle, s. 718.2(e).

In *Ipeelee*, Justice LeBel holds that judges in the post-*Gladue* jurisprudence have erroneously interpreted that the *Gladue* analysis does not apply for more serious or violent offences.[190] Additionally, *Ipeelee* deals with two long-term offenders; Justice LeBel finds that because there is a statutory duty requiring judges to apply *Gladue* for any case involving a criminalized Indigenous person, this duty includes cases dealing with a breach of a long-term offender supervision order, and "failure to do so constitutes an error justifying appellate intervention."[191] Judge Faulkner did not have the benefit of the clarity provided by the later-decided *Ipeelee*, but the seriousness and violence inherent in Good's offences and criminal record should not have precluded consideration of *Gladue*, and neither should her ultimate long-term offender designation have obviated the *Gladue* analysis. *Gladue* was implicated, and should have been considered to "provide the necessary *context*"[192] to assist the judge in determining Good's sentence. Because Judge Faulkner does refer to Good's experiences of victimization (albeit without providing a fuller description of her personal history) but fails to engage in a *Gladue* analysis, in this case, judicial recognition of the victimization-criminalization continuum operates without integrating *Gladue* factors into one cohesive analysis.

Like Judge Faulkner, other judges in my research use language of predictability in ways that demonstrate recognition of how experiences of victimization have constrained the available options for Indigenous women, such as where Justice Brenda L. Keyser comments about Vianna Redhead that "tragedy and trauma have led, not surprisingly, to substance abuse."[193] Some judges make the further connection to how limited options leave Indigenous women vulnerable to criminalization. Another such decision is *R. v. Tippeneskum*, where Justice DiGiuseppe comments that "alcohol and drug abuse are key factors that have contributed to Ms. Tippeneskum's behaviour."[194]

June Tippeneskum

In *Tippeneskum*, June Tippeneskum is sentenced to three and a half years' imprisonment for aggravated assault for failing to disclose her HIV positive status to her partner, and other less serious offences. Justice DiGiuseppe identifies Tippeneskum as a "member of the Attawapiskat First Nation," whose pre-sentence report portrays the "all too common picture of a young person raised in difficult circumstances, exposed to violence, abuse, and neglect."[195] (As reported by Kate Rutherford for the CBC, Attawapiskat has suffered ongoing community-wide crises, including those related to housing and suicide.)[196] Through child protection services, Tippeneskum rotated among her mother's residence and foster homes during her childhood, and was "repeatedly traumatized and neglected"[197] throughout. She was expelled from school, and began "abusing alcohol and drugs."[198] Justice DiGiuseppe notes, "This behaviour inevitably led her into the criminal justice system, first as a youth . . . and then into adulthood."[199] Her two children were apprehended and placed in the care of her extended family due to concerns about "parental substance abuse, neglect and lack of care giving skills."[200] Justice DiGiuseppe relates, "The Pre-sentence Report identifies the intergenerational impact that substance abuse had on Ms. Tippeneskum's community and on her in particular. She was exposed to violence and neglect at an early age, and the dysfunction in her family created an unfortunate template for her life. It is not surprising that her behaviour has reflected the environment of abuse and neglect she was exposed to as a child."[201]

Within these references to her trajectory into the justice system, Justice DiGiuseppe comments that Tippeneskum's substance abuse "inevitably" led to her criminalization,[202] and that her experiences of childhood abuse and neglect that further contribute to her later criminalization are "not surprising."[203] Yet, overall, this judgment does not omit the recognition for agency that the victimization-criminalization continuum has been criticized for precluding. Particularly, Justice DiGiuseppe engages in a *Gladue* analysis, situating the "unfortunate template"[204] for Tippeneskum's life within colonization by recognizing the intergenerational impacts of substance abuse on Tippeneskum and her wider community. This recognition also situates Tippeneskum's limited agency within choices constrained by victimization and, more broadly, colonization.

The sense of predictability and inevitability that arises from Justice DiGiuseppe's comments is nuanced by specific acknowledgements of Tippeneskum's agency. Justice DiGiuseppe relates Tippeneskum's own explanation that she "abuses substances to obliterate painful memories related to her upbringing."[205] The picture of the victimization-criminalization continuum that emerges from the case outlines her "pathway" into criminality, allowing for recognition of the circumstances of colonization, and her own agency. Justice DiGiuseppe also specifically determines that Tippeneskum's professed understanding of how her own experiences of victimization have left her vulnerable to criminalization is a mitigating factor. Justice DiGiuseppe states, "Ms. Tippeneskum has some insight into the underlying issues that have contributed to her offending behaviour, and expressed a willingness to address these issues."[206] Combined with other mitigating factors (a guilty plea and expression of remorse),[207] Tippeneskum's ability to identify the victimization-criminalization continuum in her own life intersects with the judge's understanding of her history of victimization through the lens of *Gladue* factors and functions to mitigate her sentence.[208] Justice DiGiuseppe does reference the excerpt from *Gladue* about more violent and more serious offences' producing more similar sanctions for Indigenous and non-Indigenous persons, which *Ipeelee* clarifies has been overemphasized and misunderstood. However, Justice DiGiuseppe leaves the issue in a manner consistent with the general thrust of *Ipeelee* that sanctions for Indigenous persons must be individualized within the context of colonization: "Ultimately, as in all cases, a fit sentence depends on the particular circumstances of the offence, the offender, the victim and the community."[209]

Angela Gregoire

Whereas the causes and intergenerational effects of substance abuse are referenced in *Tippeneskum*, in *R. v. Gregoire,* the relationship with colonization is made more explicit and tied to determinative language. This yields a more integrated picture of the victimization-criminalization continuum and *Gladue* analysis than in *Tippeneskum*. Angela Gregoire, a "Montagnais Innu and a member of the Sheshatshiu First Nation,"[210] is sentenced to a conditional sentence of two years less a day followed by probation for a further two years for impaired driving causing death and that causing bodily harm. Justice Goodridge describes Gregoire as "an alcoholic" who "grew up in a home where multi-generational alcoholism existed."[211] Relying on the pre-sentence report, Justice Goodridge explores the cultural destruction that colonization has induced: "Gone are many of the traditional pursuits which kept people active and in the country in small camps much of the year. Many of the traditional forms of self government which worked well in the past have been displaced. The traditional institution of the family has deteriorated."[212] The judge explains, "While this cultural adjustment does not justify tolerance of criminal activity, it does help me to understand the circumstances which led Ms. Gregoire to a pattern of alcohol abuse."[213] This framework of using *Gladue* factors to contextualize the decision is consistent with *Ipeelee*.

Justice Goodridge discusses the intergenerational effects of colonization through a detailed account of how alcohol abuse has been passed down Gregoire's family and related corrosive effects on family stability and cohesion. Like her grandparents, Gregoire's parents also abused alcohol. The judge comments, "This regularly led to violence in the family home," a "dysfunctional home marked by frequent acts of violence, neglect, physical and emotional abuse."[214] Gregoire "reports that she was a victim of sexual assault" throughout her childhood, and she was often temporarily removed from the home by the director of Child Welfare.[215] Justice Goodridge states, "It is not surprising, considering this background that Ms. Gregoire fell into a pattern of alcohol abuse herself," given that "Ms. Gregoire's social situation growing up inevitably led to her alcohol addiction and was a major factor in these crimes."[216]

This determinative-like language that Gregoire's alcoholism is "not surprising" and "inevitably" a product of her experiences of victimization superficially recalls the criticism of the victimization-criminalization continuum that it precludes depictions of agency. However, it appears that it is precisely this lack of agency that mitigates in the form of *Gladue* factors, because it allows for judicial recognition of how victimization constrained Gregoire's life options. Justice Goodridge states, "The crimes are directly connected to Ms. Gregoire's upbringing and other systemic or background factors,"[217] which "played a substantial role"[218] and "resulted in: dysfunctional family upbringing; victim of physical and sexual abuse as a child; multi generational alcoholism in the family; low education; unemployment; lack of opportunities; depression; low income."[219] Effectively, here, Justice Goodridge lists the various ways in which Gregoire's options have been suppressed due to her experiences of victimization (which the judge contextualizes within

Gladue factors), clearly connecting the victimization-criminalization continuum, through *Gladue* factors, to Gregoire's offending. Justice Goodridge specifically cites as mitigating that Gregoire is an "Aboriginal woman with dysfunctional family background,"[220] and reintroduces recognition of her agency into the judgment with the further mitigating factors that she has the "desire to change her life" and "has discontinued alcohol consumption."[221] The lack of agency conveyed through the determinative language Justice Goodridge employs to describe Gregoire's pathway to her offence also seems to mitigate. That is, by contextualizing Gregoire's experiences of victimization within the systemic and background factors of colonization, Justice Goodridge recognizes how her narrowed options have contributed to her vulnerability to criminalization, and is accordingly able to sentence with sensitivity.

Nicole Pawis

In *R. v. Pawis*, the judge provides a very thoughtful analysis of the relationship between the victimization-criminalization continuum and the *Gladue* analysis, and in even greater depth than in *Gregoire*. Additionally, Justice Reinhardt uses determinative language in relation to Nicole Pawis's victimization and subsequent criminalization, but thoroughly contextualizes this trajectory within constrained choices. Pawis is sentenced to a conditional sentence of two years less a day and three subsequent years of probation for committing aggravated assault on her child after "throwing him around in his stroller" during "an uncontrollable rage at her child for constant crying."[222] Justice Reinhardt draws from both the forensic report and the PSR he refers to as a *Gladue* report because it "addresses those issues mandated by the Supreme Court of Canada when sentencing an Aboriginal offender."[223] From these sources, Justice Reinhardt describes that Pawis is a "status Indian from the Shawanaga First Nation."[224] Alongside her siblings, Pawis "suffered serious abuse at the hands of her father, who she reports sexually abused her until he was forced to leave the reserve."[225] Pawis was raised by her grandmother, a residential school survivor who routinely abused her physically, emotionally, and psychologically for over ten years, kept her socially isolated, and neglected her. Pawis "suffered ostracism and abusive treatment" by classmates and teachers who "ridiculed her for being an aboriginal" and excluded her and other Indigenous students from various activities.[226]

Justice Reinhardt states that Pawis "became pregnant by a partner who was abusive to her,"[227] and "knew she was not ready to care for a child."[228] Pawis failed in her attempt to obtain an abortion because she lacked health insurance coverage, and determined she could not "give him up for adoption . . . because of social pressure."[229] Unable to cope with the strains of motherhood, before "the assault took place she had tried to arrange for the Native Child and Family Services worker to come over and remove Shikhqim [her child] from her care temporarily."[230] With this thorough description of Pawis's struggles through an unwanted pregnancy, endured within an abusive relationship, Justice Reinhardt clearly details how Pawis's experiences of victimization constrained her options, already limited by poverty and marginalization. The judge makes plain that Pawis had made a variety of attempts to exercise her agency in both her pregnancy and motherhood, and each attempt was thwarted for systemic reasons.

Justice Reinhardt also directly connects these restricted choices and resources to Pawis's becoming vulnerable to criminalization. The judge comments that the *Gladue* report demonstrates "that the combination of this child, in the care of this mother, was a terrible catastrophe just waiting to happen,"[231] and that "the resultant assault on Shikhqim by his mother, Nicole, was almost predictable, in hindsight."[232] Here, determinative language appears again, as in previously discussed judgments, but this time thoroughly contextualizing "predictability" within a very clear explanation of how experiences of victimization curtailed Pawis's choices. In making determinations about Pawis's sentence, Justice Reinhardt states, "Ms. Pawis's actions were inexcusable, but they were the result of personal social conditions that were objectively beyond her control."[233] The judge bolsters this understanding with the observation that "she was a young, inexperienced, emotionally damaged and immature mother trying to accomplish a very difficult task, without adequate skills, training or support."[234] This background Justice Reinhardt establishes helpfully sets out the events leading to the offence, including Pawis's personal history and her recognition of her own caregiving limitations in her attempts to navigate pregnancy and motherhood decisions without support.

Within Justice Reinhardt's sensitive exploration of how Pawis's experiences of victimization manifest in the context of colonization, the judge also allows entry points for recognition of her agency. For example, Justice Reinhardt comments, "To her credit, she asked the Native Child and Family Services Worker . . . to intervene and remove the child from her care . . . prior to assaulting her child,"[235] adding that she "knew she was a danger to her totally dependent and helpless son, but could not find the resources either in herself, or in the community, to protect him."[236] These same issues become aggravating. Due to the facts, Justice Reinhardt must consider s. 718.2(a)(ii.1) (evidence that the offender abused someone under eighteen years old in the offence)[237] and s.718.2(a)(iii) (evidence of abuse of trust or authority over the victim in commission of the offence)[238] of the Criminal Code. Justice Reinhardt finds these factors aggravating because Pawis committed "a serious breach of trust" against her "totally dependent and helpless son."[239] The judge notes, "These factors suggest that the appropriate result should be a sentence of incarceration."[240]

However, consistent with the tenor of judicial sensitivity running through the judgment, Justice Reinhardt concludes "after considerable deliberation"[241] that Pawis's history of victimization against the backdrop of colonization sufficiently mitigates to outweigh what would otherwise require a sentence of incarceration, permitting a conditional sentence.[242] Justice Reinhardt references Pawis's lack of family support to assist her parenting, and the long-term impacts of her emotionally isolated and impoverished upbringing, products of her mother's frequent absence and her grandmother's abuse.[243] Justice Reinhardt finds that Pawis's family circumstances "cannot be solely blamed on her."[244] The judge notes that Pawis has been "distraught throughout this [criminal justice] process, and we have had to adjourn the hearing on more than one occasion because she was unable to proceed without completely losing her composure."[245] *Pawis* represents a judgment that not only complies with the judicial duty toward Indigenous persons on sentencing, but also thoughtfully integrates understanding of how victimization constrains Indigenous women's options and foments vulnerability to criminalization within the broader context of colonization.

Decontextualized *Gladue* Analyses

In various cases from my study, judges directly comment upon problems they encounter in obtaining useful *Gladue*-related information pertaining to the Indigenous women they sentence. These judges indicate that some *Gladue* reports and *Gladue*-related information may be inadequate (including those neglecting to offer guidance about meaningful alternative sanctions) or waived entirely; regional variability can hinder the preparation of prompt and fulsome *Gladue* reports; *Gladue* reports and PSRs, when both provided, may present contradictory information; and the quality and reliability of *Gladue* reports remain subject to the limits and biases of their authors.

I begin with *R. v. Whitford* because the presentation of mitigating and aggravating factors in this judgment implicates issues related to experiences of victimization in the life of the woman being sentenced. In this way, it appears that victimization effectively both mitigates and aggravates on sentencing. The *Gladue* analysis is referenced, but it is unclear whether or to what extent this analysis actually guided the determination of sentence. I then turn to *R. v. Killiktee*,[246] in which the judge's reasoning is closely aligned with the victimization-criminalization continuum, but, despite the *Gladue* analysis proceeding through this lens, like in *Whitford*, the victimization history of the woman being sentenced still functions to both mitigate and aggravate. In *R. v. Niganobe*, the judge makes a comment that seems to neutralize the *Gladue* factors of the woman sentenced, to an extent, by abstracting her experience in a universalized reference—although, ultimately, there is clear judicial recognition that systemic factors have constrained her life choices.

In my study, I noticed repeated instances exemplifying the trend highlighted by *Ipeelee* that post-*Gladue* cases have wrongly and inappropriately required criminalized Indigenous persons to demonstrate a causal link showing that their background and systemic factors contributed to their coming before the courts. For example, in an oral judgment sentencing Lucille Littlecrow from the Whitecap Dakota First

Nation, Justice N.G. Gabrielson suggests in reference to what should be s. 718.2(e), but is mistakenly identified in the judgment as s. 718.2(d), and without citing *Gladue* explicitly, that "the pre-sentence report does not indicate that Ms. Littlecrow was disadvantaged in any way that could be related to the offence which she committed."[247] That decision was issued in the year prior to *Ipeelee*'s clarification, but it seems there continue to be instances post-*Ipeelee* that still erroneously indicate requiring a causal connection between Indigenous background and systemic factors and a given offence, and/or that demonstrate some degree of ongoing confusion on that point. In the sentencing decision for Ashley Toews, "a member of the Hagwilget First Nation which is part of the larger Wet'suwet'en First Nation,"[248] Justice Kenneth W. Ball writes, "In order to effect [*sic*] the sentence which the Court might otherwise impose there must be a connection of substance between the Aboriginal circumstances of the offender and the offence."[249] Additionally, despite declaring, "I have also taken into account the *Gladue* factors and fully appreciate that Aboriginal offenders are over-represented in the prison population," Justice Ball continues to conclude that Toews "has minimal, if any, past or present contact with Native culture or heritage,"[250] and comments three times that Toews has never lived on a reserve (her grandmother decided to leave the reserve with her family because she "perceived there was no hope for a future"),[251] without contextualizing any of those life circumstances within an analysis of colonization.

Other post-*Ipeelee* decisions display some level of internal contradictory messages regarding the *Ipeelee* clarification that a causal connection should not be required by the courts. Justice John D. Truscott directly acknowledges in *R. v. Dennis* that "there does not have to be any direct causal connection between the Aboriginal's circumstances and the offence, because *Ipeelee* makes it clear that this sort of connection is not required."[252] However, Justice Truscott later comments that Sunset Dennis committed the aggravated assault for which she is sentenced in conjunction with "attempting to collect a drug debt," adding that this "does not seem to me to have any great connection to her Aboriginal background."[253] In a sentencing decision for Diane Serré, a woman "of Algonquin descent,"[254] Justice Catherine D. Aitken indicates an insufficiency of *Gladue*-related information before the court, despite recognizing her "father's Aboriginal heritage" and its "possible" relationship to his alcohol dependency, determining that while this may have contributed to Serré's having a youth less "stable or secure" than "one would have hoped," she has "not personally suffered from many of the systemic problems that have plagued Aboriginal peoples in Canadian society."[255] Justice Aitken recognizes that "an Aboriginal offender does not have to establish a causal link between the systemic and background factors and his or her commission of the offence,"[256] but adds, "It cannot be said that, due to your Aboriginal heritage and the systemic factors that have hurt Aboriginal people in this country, your education was hampered, your income was negatively impacted, you had periods of unemployment or underemployment, you were susceptible to substance abuse issues, or your mental health suffered. In other words, there is no evidence to suggest that your life experience as an Aboriginal in some way reduces your moral culpability for these offences."[257] When sentencing Eliza Ross, Justice R.D. Maher indicates, "I am satisfied on the evidence that there is a causal link between the background factors of the aboriginal offender and the commission of the current offence."[258] Justice Maher then immediately continues, "This was commented upon in *R v Ipeelee*,"[259] and quotes three paragraphs from *Ipeelee* that elucidate that requiring a causal connection is improper, not required, and perhaps impossible. In *R. v. Hansen*, although not rising to the level of an internal contradiction, Justice Butler also explicitly recognizes that "there is no need for an offender to establish such a connection" in a judgment sentencing Robyn Hansen, but the judge adds that, nonetheless, she "has done so."[260]

The artificial requirement of a causal connection between Indigenous systemic or background factors and a given offence is inimical to the goals and spirit of *Gladue*. *Ipeelee* clarifies how courts must avoid this problem by identifying that it places an unreasonable evidentiary burden on criminalized Indigenous persons whose experiences of colonization are so enmeshed in their lives that it is impossible to disentangle these effects and to distill them into a causal explanation of criminalization.[261] (Indeed, Saskatoon lawyer James T.D. Scott notes that defence lawyers find "establishing such a causal link is close to impossible.")[262] Some cases do properly understand this direction from *Ipeelee*. For example,

Judge Michael J. Brecknell rejects the Crown argument that Theresa McCook's "criminality is more related to greed than her dysfunctional upbringing," concluding that this represents "a far too narrow approach" to the case law and her background.[263] Judge Brecknell instead finds that her "upbringing was chaotic, punctuated with family violence, sexual assault, alcohol abuse, her ostracization due to her mixed family background and the diligent efforts by those who educated her to irradicate her cultural identity. With all of those interrelated factors it is simplistic to suggest that *Gladue* factors do not account, at least in part, for her criminal behaviour."[264] Here, the judge identifies the inseverable nature of McCook's experiences of victimization on her pathway to criminalization and the *Gladue* factors within her life. Moreover, Judge Brecknell then specifically cites *Ipeelee* for its clarification that cases have erroneously indicated a requirement for a causal connection between *Gladue* factors and a given offence before the courts.

For judgments in which this clarification from *Ipeelee* is not heeded, it should still be recognized that sentencing judges are bound by decisions of the appellate courts in their provincial/territorial jurisdiction. For example, in his study of published judgments sentencing Indigenous persons in Saskatchewan between 1996 and 2015, Scott discerns a "resistance to applying *Gladue* principles" on the part of the Saskatchewan Court of Appeal, such that "they now place the onus" on Indigenous persons before them to establish the relevance of "their 'personal circumstances'" to the offence.[265] In this climate, sentencing judges striving to follow the dictates of *Ipeelee* but also having to comply with the guidelines set by the appellate court above them render their decisions with the awareness they could be overturned and that cases only rarely ascend on further appeal to the SCC.

Within the cases I discuss in this section, I present the characterizations of *Gladue* factors that do appear in these cases to emphasize how these histories should, per *Ipeelee*, have simply been used to "provide the necessary context to enable a judge to determine an appropriate sentence."[266] Equally, though still within the individualized sentencing process, these histories must be connected to the larger context and not overly particularized, as *Gladue* factors "need not be tied in some way to the particular offender and offence."[267]

In *R. v. Johnson*,[268] the judge reflects on how variability in information about background and systemic factors received by the courts affects the ability of judges to engage in the *Gladue* analysis, but this framework is problematic against the *Ipeelee* clarification that judges should not require a causal connection between *Gladue* factors and the offence in question. However, *Johnson* also represents judicial engagement with gendered issues in a way that impacts sentencing. Returning to the problem of courts' erroneously requiring causal connections between *Gladue* factors and the offence, *R. v. Jankovic* illustrates one manifestation of this, where the judge attributes this sentenced woman's disadvantages (including experiences of victimization) to her non-Indigenous father, and expressly not to her Indigenous mother. In *R. v. Bluebell*, the judge squarely succumbs to the same causality problem later rejected by *Ipeelee* by finding that the woman being sentenced failed to provide evidence of a connection between her *Gladue* factors and her offence. *R. v. Collins* presents the same problem, but, here, arising from the judge's denial of the relevance of systemic factors and instead relating this woman's criminalization to her individual agency. This formulation is both misaligned with the *Ipeelee* clarification and does not comport with the idea of agency within externally constrained choices from the victimization-criminalization continuum. *Collins* also demonstrates how the *Gladue* analysis should involve contextualization and a shift in conceptual focus (to more restorative-oriented sanctions, where appropriate).

Overall, the cases I discuss in this section implicate problems in the *Gladue* analysis, which involves considerations of victimization through the overlap between *Gladue* factors and experiences of victimization. It should be noted that the problems have been elucidated by *Ipeelee*, which was decided after most of the decisions discussed below transpired, so most of the judges whose reasoning I discuss in greatest depth did not have the benefit of having consulted *Ipeelee*. I focus most directly on the *Gladue* analysis because, in the broader picture, when judges sentence Indigenous women, the most sensitive *Gladue* analyses should be deepened by reference to ideas emergent from the victimization-criminalization continuum. The continuum and *Gladue* analysis have different focuses (and exclusively the latter is legislatively mandated, whereas the former is simply a lens I suggest has purchase): gendered responses to and vulnerabilities from victimization and colonization, and overincarceration, respectively. However, in the sentencing of Indigenous women, both analyses with their respective focuses should be integrated such that the overall analysis is enhanced.

Variability and Inadequacy of Gladue-related Information

In some cases, information about Indigenous systemic or background factors are provided to courts in a separate *Gladue* report with its specific sensitivity and depth (in addition to a distinct PSR), whereas, in other cases, judges simply have a PSR with a "*Gladue* component" (and in still other cases, *Gladue*-related information is altogether absent). *Gladue* reports offer specialized information to assist sentencing judges and appellate review, but, as Tim Quigley notes, "there is currently no explicit legal authority" in the Criminal Code on which judges can rely to order them.[269] Through s. 721 of the Criminal Code,[270] sentencing judges may order probation officers to prepare and file pre-sentence reports, including various stipulated information that might incorporate that related to *Gladue* factors, but differently oriented and authored than *Gladue* reports, and with lesser depth. *Gladue* reports are composed by writers specifically trained to explore issues related to intergenerational and community-wide trauma and the detailed systemic or background factors of the Indigenous person before the court,[271] including information about available community-based restorative justice sentencing alternatives, the related interest of the Indigenous person before the court, and any support by the given Indigenous community or band.[272] By contrast, PSRs with *Gladue*-based information lack this expansiveness and framework, and are prepared by probation officers who operate within the criminal justice system (which may also suppress what Indigenous interviewees are comfortable sharing),[273] are not appropriately qualified, and lack sufficient time.[274] Moreover, as Quigley argues, given the past and ongoing roles of the federal and provincial governments in processes of colonization and systemic discrimination, there is cognitive dissonance and a tarnishing of the appearance of justice in having "an agent of the colonizer prepare a report on the effects of colonialism," and particularly where an Indigenous person may be incarcerated.[275]

Gladue-related information provided in the form of *Gladue* reports may differ meaningfully in both detail and substance from that offered as a subset of a PSR. Such differences may be marked (even involving conflicting evidence) or more nuanced (in that *Gladue* reports and PSRs have different orientations, and *Gladue* reports permit a less constrained narrative format). Indeed, Kelly Hannah-Moffat and Paula Maurutto have explained that PSRs are risk-based instruments that "tend to frame offender risk quite differently from *Gladue* reports, which culturally situate offenders and incorporate racial knowledge to position criminal behaviour holistically within a wider collective history of race relations and colonialism."[276] Hannah-Moffat and Maurutto note that sometimes *Gladue* factors are interpreted as risk factors, producing the effect where Indigenous persons in the system "continue to be characterized as high risk and high need."[277] Milward and Parkes note that this context (in which needs-based *Gladue* factors are appended to risk-oriented PSRs and reformulated through that risk framework) often produces longer sentences.[278]

This slippage between projections/determinations about risk and need signals the necessity for judges to frame and understand *Gladue* factors in a holistic (and not risk-based) manner, underscoring the importance of courts' having access to *Gladue* reports that are directed toward contextualization within past and ongoing individual and collective effects of colonization, as opposed to merely having PSRs with *Gladue* components that remain targeted at an assessment of potential future risk. Benjamin Ralston and Christine Goodwin note that, although the courts of some jurisdictions value the content of available *Gladue* information above whether it appears as a section of a PSR or as a stand-alone *Gladue* report, "form and substance can be so inextricably intertwined that the absence of a full *Gladue* report might be tantamount to the absence of full *Gladue* information."[279] I discuss two decisions below (*R. v. Shore* and *R. v. Audy*) wherein the judicial reasoning demonstrates thoughtful analysis, notwithstanding having access only to PSRs with *Gladue* components, by departing from PSR projections of high risk. Such departures may be anomalous, as Milward and Parkes observe, since "the risk assessment component of a PSR is often determinative of the outcome in a sentencing hearing."[280] To give greatest effect to a fulsome *Gladue* analysis, the provision of *Gladue* reports (as opposed to PSRs with *Gladue* information) should be prioritized and resourced by provincial governments. (Broader accessibility and usage of *Gladue* reports may also have the potential to meaningfully ameliorate the relative punitiveness of carceral sentences. The Correctional Investigator reports in 2016 that one federal men's prison in Alberta "concretely applies the factors found in *Gladue* sentencing reports," using the original reports themselves "to inform decisions regarding the security classification of Indigenous" persons, including to reduce their classification to lower levels.)[281]

There is much regional variability in the method and degree to which *Gladue* reports are made available. For example, as Milward and Parkes note, Yukon judges have registered "[concern] about the lack of *Gladue* reports" available there.[282] Milward and Parkes observe a paucity of *Gladue* reports and consequent frustration articulated by some judges in Manitoba,[283] where the general practice for "a majority of cases" instead involves probation officers appending *Gladue*-related components to PSRs by "'cutting and pasting' generic references" among generalized *Gladue* factors, or adding "descriptions of problems in specific Aboriginal communities, from past report precedents and templates."[284] Milward and Parkes note that defence counsel in Manitoba point to such *Gladue* sections of PSRs "as a significant barrier to their ability to make fulsome *Gladue* submissions."[285] Saskatchewan has "a few" trained *Gladue* report writers, but most *Gladue* reports filed there are completed by those in British Columbia.[286] In British Columbia, a sentencing judge must be satisfied by counsel that any *Gladue* information contained in the PSR, through witness testimony, and/or from expert reports and various other reports, is insufficient before ordering a *Gladue* report.[287] Additionally, Legal Services Society of British Columbia (LSS), which provides legal aid in that province, has indicated that, absent "more stable funding" being allocated, it "may have to cease funding [*Gladue*] reports."[288] The Alberta Court of Appeal has recently pointed to *Ipeelee* to hold that there must be provision of a *Gladue* report for each Indigenous person sentenced.[289]

Quigley notes the tension inherent in the scc's mandating consideration of *Gladue* factors while "the preparation of that information is handled in a [regionally] haphazard fashion that is highly dependent on funding being made available"[290] (and *Gladue* reports are expensive to obtain).[291] To resolve this tension, he suggests broader usage of *R. v. Nasogaluak*, "in which the [scc] held that state misconduct might operate to reduce the sentence that might otherwise be imposed,"[292] and, ideally, that Parliament should authorize judicial ordering of *Gladue* reports by amending s. 721 of the Criminal Code.[293] The jurisdictionally uneven and currently precariously funded provision of *Gladue* reports must be somehow addressed, supported by the finding of lss that its clients who were provided *Gladue* reports "received more probation, suspended sentences, time served sentence[s] and csos, and less actual jail time than those" without *Gladue* reports.[294] For greater accessibility of *Gladue* reports across jurisdictions to be an effective strategy in the implementation of s. 718.2(e), increases in funding and resources should also accelerate the production of these reports, as the period during which they are prepared generally extends custodial time in remand.[295] (lss has also created a template to assist defence counsel or court workers with compiling *Gladue*-related information for the purposes of oral submissions, primarily for clients who may be facing shorter prison terms, suspended sentences, probationary orders, csos, or other such cases in which waiting for the preparation of *Gladue* reports is especially undesirable.)[296]

Beyond the issue of the specific need for *Gladue* reports in that form, the overall inadequacy, and sometimes unavailability, of information related to the systemic or background factors of Indigenous women being sentenced is a theme signalled repeatedly by judges in my research. Justice George observes this recurrent issue when sentencing Tanya Peters (also named Tanya Pitwanakwat), noting that, often, "courts are left to, and indeed are required to take judicial notice"[297] of *Gladue* factors (although in that case, the judge had the benefit of a fulsome *Gladue* report, commenting that "in almost every conceivable way, this report addresses those societal and systemic issues that sentencing courts are required to acknowledge and attempt to address)".[298] This is problematic particularly against the concern identified by Justice LeBel in *Ipeelee* that courts are often hesitant to take judicial notice of Indigenous background and systemic factors,[299] notwithstanding the *Gladue* direction that "in *all instances* it will be *necessary* for the judge to take judicial notice of the systemic or background factors and the approach to sentencing which is relevant to aboriginal offenders,"[300] affirmed by *Ipeelee*.[301] Some judges do take judicial notice in the absence of proper *Gladue* reports and related information. For example, Judge Cozens explains, in sentencing Theresa Samson, that while "there is no stated residential school history and resultant abuse and neglect, I am required to consider her ancestry in a broader context,"[302] and concludes further:

> Although there is not specific evidence before me, such as would be contained in a *Gladue* report regarding the NNDFN [Na-Cho Nyak Dun First Nation], I am prepared to take judicial notice, based upon my experience, that the negative consequences all too often associated with Aboriginal ancestry, flowing from the residential school system and other similarly destructive governmental actions, have impacted many of the members of this First Nation and, as a result, the First Nation's community as a whole. I note that Ms. Samson has numerous extended family members in the community that are or have been involved in the justice system.[303]

However, to give proper effect to s. 718.2(e) and *Ipeelee*, judicial notice should be supplemental to the provision and usage of *Gladue* reports, not rendered necessary due to the dearth or incompleteness of such reports.

In my research, I noticed many instances in which judges reference needing more information to properly engage in the *Gladue* analysis. Judge Heino Lilles indicates in an oral judgment sentencing Tlingit woman Denelle Dickson that he "did not have the benefit of a *Gladue* report and counsel did not provide me with any *Gladue* information."[304] Justice S.H. Smallwood notes having "limited" information about Lillian Kanayok as provided by counsel, "but it is certainly not the extensive information that we sometimes see provided to the Court."[305] When sentencing Bryna Link, Judge M.J. Smith parenthetically states that "(for reasons not known to me, a *Gladue* component was not requested to be included in the PSR)."[306] Judge Robert Higinbotham indicates that "a pre-sentence report was ordered with a *Gladue* component"[307] for Tracy Smith (who appears in this judgment to be Métis), but "very little was forthcoming."[308] This judge "do[es] not find her aboriginal heritage to be of particular significance in this proceeding,"[309] although it is unclear whether this finding is based on the absence of *Gladue* information or the presence of limited information. In the decision for the Crown appeal of the sentence, the court indicates Smith is "a non-status Indian," noting that, "although requested by the [sentencing] court, it appears that a *Gladue* pre-sentence report was not prepared."[310]

Even in cases with more detailed *Gladue* reports or *Gladue*-related information, judges still seek further information. In sentencing Diane Serré, Justice Aitken does have a *Gladue* report, and takes judicial notice "of the history of colonization, displacement, discrimination, deprivation, and hopelessness" that Indigenous communities have suffered for many generations,[311] but notes not having been provided with evidence about "what type of sentencing sanctions would be particularly meaningful" to Serré due to her Indigenous heritage, including that "no alternatives to a custodial sentence were offered."[312] Judge LeGrandeur refers to a PSR with a "*Gladue* component"[313] prepared for Chantelle First Charger, a member of the Blood Reserve, indicating that this pre-sentence report lacks information about which of the identified community-based programs would likely be most helpful to First Charger, and about "the impacts of her actions on the community."[314] Regarding the identification of specific alternatives to incarceration available to a given Indigenous person on sentencing, *Gladue* explicitly directs that "beyond the use of the pre-sentence report, the sentencing judge may and should in appropriate circumstances and where practicable request that witnesses be called who may testify as to reasonable alternatives."[315]

Sometimes, *Gladue* reports or related PSR information are not requested, including when Crown and defence counsel agree to waive them. *Gladue*, and in turn *Ipeelee*, both sanction this form of waiver.[316] However, whereas *Gladue* refers to such a waiver only where the person being sentenced "does not wish such evidence to be adduced,"[317] *Ipeelee* finds more strictly that this waiver must be "expressly"[318] identified. Justice Bishop notes such a waiver agreement when sentencing Janet Masakayash, from "the remote First Nations community of Osnaburgh now known as Mishkeegogamang,"[319] whose "situation demonstrates all of the *Gladue* considerations as she herself has been the victim of both sexual and physical abuse."[320] Both counsel had indicated "no presentence or *Gladue* report is required and they are capable of making and addressing those considerations,"[321] and the judge comments that "both counsel are very experienced and have been involved in defending and prosecuting many Aboriginal offenders."[322] In some cases, counsel may elect to waive the submission of a PSR with a *Gladue* component or a *Gladue* report to accelerate the proceedings (for reasons including the desire to minimize the time their clients are held in remand), as the preparation of *Gladue* reports in particular may prolong the sentencing process. Such waivers of *Gladue* reports may nonetheless remain problematic (particularly where counsel are ill-equipped to address all the issues that should be included in these reports), but at times this instruction may also be unclear or inconsistent. For example, when sentencing C.T., a woman from the Sturgeon Lake Cree First Nation, Judge Brecknell writes, "Her counsel advised the court that she did not wish a presentence report or a *Gladue* report to be prepared prior to sentencing. However, when the defendant came before the court today for to [*sic*] sentencing, she stated that she wished a *Gladue* report to be prepared but then, after further consultation with her counsel, she again confirmed to the court that all the relevant information concerning her aboriginal background and her upbringing had been provided to the court and she wished to proceed to sentencing."[323] The judge indicates having "carefully considered" whether to order a *Gladue* report in this context, but ultimately determines not to do so, given defence counsel's seniority and experience in representing Indigenous persons, and given his having "taken great pains to meet with and confirm and reconfirm the defendant's wishes in this regard."[324]

Other waivers seem to relate to situations in which the woman has multiple heritages, such as where Justice Robin A.M. Baird writes of L.H. that her "father is of Chinese ancestry," "her mother is of mixed Caucasian and aboriginal descent," and she "has no knowledge of aboriginal life or customs and has had no relationship or ties with her mother's ancestral First Nations community," so, "accordingly, the sort of report referred to in" *Gladue* and *Ipeelee* "has been waived."[325] Similarly,

Justice Elizabeth A. Arnold-Bailey notes that Jessica Hanley's "origins are described as half-Vietnamese, a quarter First Nations, and a quarter Scottish,"[326] writing that "both the parties and the Court agree that a *Gladue* report is not necessary in this case given Ms. Hanley's lack of connection with her First Nations' heritage, which makes up one quarter of her racial background."[327] Broadly, Ralston and Goodwin suggest that "courts have arrived at widely varying conclusions as to the relevance of *Gladue* for Aboriginal individuals raised by non-Aboriginal families or those with limited knowledge of their Aboriginal background."[328]

Other judges engage in different reasoning when given background facts in which the woman's connection to her Indigenous heritage is perceived as less direct. Judge P. Ayotte did have access to a *Gladue* report (separate from but alongside a PSR) in sentencing M.A.B., despite both counsels' agreeing that "the usual *Gladue* factors are not present."[329] The judge finds, "I am not satisfied, on further reflection, that the Report should be given little or no weight for that reason alone. Whether or not Ms. M.A.B. was raised in the aboriginal culture which is at least a part of her heritage, that heritage has clearly had an effect on her life, at least indirectly."[330] Judge Ayotte explains she "is a member of the Manitoulin Island First Nation because her father is a member of that First Nation," and adds, "That remains so even though she has had no contact with him since she was three years old and even though her mother is Dutch."[331] Noting that M.A.B. "has had little connection with her aboriginal heritage," the judge suggests that "the question arises whether *Gladue* factors are relevant at all in her case because it might be said that she is only 'technically' aboriginal," but finds that "even if that is true, she is in my view entitled to at least a consideration of what have come to be called '*Gladue* factors'. The Supreme Court of Canada in *Gladue* itself made it clear that s. 718.2(e) applies to *all* aboriginal offenders, regardless of their personal circumstances."[332] Judge Ayotte holds that M.A.B. is "entitled, if appropriate, to the benefit of s. 718.2(e)," analyzes how her heritage did affect her life, and, in part due to these issues, determines "the sentence I impose can justifiably be less than that proposed by Crown counsel,"[333] citing the *Gladue* directive that if there is no available alternative to incarceration, the duration of the prison term must be evaluated.

In other cases, *Gladue* reports are sought, but either through inordinate efforts or to little effect. This signifies broader unevenness in the usage and content of *Gladue* reports, partially due to regional variability in their administration. In *R. v. McCook*, Judge Brecknell examines the process through which *Gladue* reports are ordered, funded, and prepared in British Columbia. Judge Brecknell observes that when a court orders a PSR or psychiatric/psychological report from probation and forensic services, respectively, "there is no question of or interference with the Court's power and authority to order those reports; they are done without question by the appropriate agency,"[334] whereas "the same is not true" for court-ordered *Gladue* reports.[335] While Judge Brecknell acknowledges that the *Gladue* report ultimately produced for the court does detail information about the personal history of Theresa McCook, "a Tahltan woman from the Kwadacha Nation," and amply discusses how her "situation fits into the *Gladue* analysis,"[336] this report was provided only following "several appearances by counsel and some very pointed comments by the Court"[337] directed to LSS. Judge Brecknell itemizes various factors that LSS considers in determining how to prioritize funding for *Gladue* reports; significantly, one such factor is that a given client may receive a sentence of federal incarceration. I highlight this factor because although that administrative reasoning is understandable, given the high stakes involved for persons facing long prison sentences, a further implication may be that Indigenous women likely to receive sentences in the provincial range have diminished access to prompt and full *Gladue* reports.

Judge Brecknell finds that "the present process of having LSS act as a 'gatekeeper' is unacceptable," as it "clearly interferes" with judicial independence on sentencing and further marginalizes Indigenous persons in a criminal justice system within which they are already systemically disadvantaged.[338] The judge concludes, "It is imperative that the Provincial Government give earnest consideration to re-examining the present procedures" in the funding and provision of *Gladue* reports.[339] Interestingly, Judge Brecknell also points to two recent Alberta Court of Appeal cases that suggest the lack of a *Gladue* report may itself be an appealable error, even if the substance of *Gladue* information that might be contained in a report is otherwise before the court.[340]

In a further example of regional variations in access to *Gladue* reports, in a decision sentencing Kathleen Knockwood, an Indigenous woman living at Kahnawake, a reserve in Quebec, Justice S. Casey Hill explains that the Ontario probation services reported to the court that Quebec "was a province where they do not complete *Gladue* reports."[341] Instead, a PSR with "*Gladue* content"[342] became the agreed substitute. However, when ultimately provided, this Quebec report was only four and a half pages and written in French, and therefore inaccessible to English-speaker Knockwood. Although it was translated, she was "devastated by the skimpy and uninformative report" (to the point she independently investigated the issue), and both counsel declared the report "entirely inadequate and non-compliant," with which the judge agrees.[343] Justice Hill records that a separate hearing had found this pre-sentence report "essentially bereft of *Gladue* content and is, accordingly, not only insufficient for sentencing purposes but also in contravention of the spirit of this court's order relating to the preparation of the PSR in this case."[344] In the end, a *Gladue* report was provided at the initiative of the Ontario Ministry through Aboriginal Legal Services of Toronto. Justice Hill discusses the problems encountered in accessing a *Gladue* report at length, characterizing it as "state misconduct,"[345] and declaring, "The outrageousness of this story is self-evident. A shameful wrong. Contempt for the rights of Aboriginal Canadians. A denial of equality."[346] It appears that Justice Hill reduces the sentence as a "*Nasogaluak* remedy"[347] to account for the "extenuating mitigating circumstances"[348] represented by the delay and consequent distress experienced by Knockwood.

In some cases, the relationship between *Gladue* reports and PSRs becomes complicated, such as where evidence contained in each diverges from the other. For example, in sentencing Ashley Toews, Justice Ball refers to instances wherein the PSR and *Gladue* reports provided for Toews document conflicting evidence. Submissions by her counsel clarified some discrepancies, such as those pertaining to her access to her children, who had been removed by the state due to her substance use (usage in part triggered by stress over these legal proceedings). However, Justice Ball indicates that certain "conflicting evidence was not resolved during submissions,"[349] including that the PSR indicated Toews's grandmother went to residential school whereas the *Gladue* report declared the opposite.

As a *Gladue* report or PSR with *Gladue*-related content may be subject to the hidden biases of its writer, a judge's ability to rely on a given report may also depend on the quality of its information, in terms of its reliability and level of neutrality. In a decision sentencing Leah Florence, a member of the Katzie First Nation, Justice Jeanne E. Watchuk explains that the *Gladue* report submitted was problematic for various reasons, including the author's usage of leading questions to obtain information, the incorporation of assumptions undisclosed as such, and the author's overall "unacceptable level of advocacy."[350] To address related concerns presented by the Crown, the author was called as a witness. The judge finds that "it is only because of the cross-examination that serious flaws in the report were exposed and the Court has accurate and sufficient information about Ms. Florence's aboriginal heritage and its effect on her,"[351] later adding that submissions by both counsel were valuable. Justice Watchuk concludes the *Gladue* report in isolation is "of minimal assistance," giving it "little weight," but ultimately determines she is "able to deliver a fit sentence taking into account the individualized *Gladue* factors,"[352] which was upheld following Florence's later appeal.[353] In the sentencing decision, Justice Watchuk finds that the *Gladue* report contained misleading components that were alternately favourable and unfavourable in its representation of Florence. The judge comments that "an objective *Gladue* report is necessary,"[354] given that cross-examining report writers will not be a regular practice in sentencing hearings, emphasizing that it is "therefore imperative" that authors of these reports "strive to present the most accurate picture of the *Gladue* factors and their relationship with a given offender."[355]

In sum, the form, content, and sometimes existence of *Gladue*-related information at the disposal of sentencing judges vary widely. Judges may have such limited information that judicial notice is left to supplant instead of supplement what should be presented by *Gladue* reports (or, at minimum, PSRs with *Gladue*-related content), and judges frequently signal needing additional information even where such reports are sought and provided. *Gladue*-related information is further variable due to uneven regional practices, whether that information manifests in the form of a proper *Gladue* report or a PSR with a *Gladue*-based component, and sometimes due to inconsistencies in the reliability of the content. These challenges and problems in the provision and relative completeness of *Gladue*-related information should be kept in mind, but alongside the judicial duty to actively seek such information. (*Gladue* directs that in cases in which counsel, or unrepresented persons, neglect to provide this information, "it is incumbent upon the sentencing judge to attempt to acquire" it.)[356]

Lisa Whitford

In *R. v. Whitford*, the victimization-criminalization continuum that emerges suggests that experiences of victimization can act to both mitigate and aggravate on sentencing. Justice W. Glen Parrett sentences Lisa Whitford to six years' imprisonment for manslaughter after she pleaded guilty to this included offence of her original charge of second-degree murder. Whitford had what she termed a "difficult relationship"[357] with the deceased, which was dominated by misuse of alcohol and crack cocaine. The judge quotes portions of the pre-sentence report that refer to "collateral sources" reporting the deceased had been violent and abusive toward Whitford.[358] She shot him after he approached her "cursing and swearing"[359] while she was pregnant. Justice Parrett describes that she "is of aboriginal descent, and her mother is a member of the Nak'azdli Band,"[360] with a background that is "horrendous," "one of the bleakest cases I had ever encountered."[361]

   Drawing from the pre-sentence report, Justice Parrett details that Whitford lived with her mother through an "unstable and abusive childhood"[362] in which she was extensively sexually abused by a boyfriend of her mother. Whitford turned to drugs and alcohol, ran away to live on the streets, and had several intimate relationships that were characterized by violence and drinking.[363] She "became so distressed" upon learning that the father of her three children would share custody after "severing the relationship"[364] with him that she dove deeper into substance abuse. Whitford received a federal penitentiary term after an attempted robbery, which later became a "revolving door" of incarceration after repeated parole violations[365] related to her substance abuse issues.[366] Justice Parrett recognizes that the sexual and physical violence

Whitford suffered was continuous,[367] stating that "this is a woman who has made 41 emergency visits to the Prince George Regional Hospital over the years. On no less than five separate occasions, her jaw was broken during altercations with the men she was involved with."[368]

The identified mitigating and aggravating factors are similar, and both reflect the violence Whitford has endured throughout her life. Justice Parrett finds "little in the way of mitigating factors, save and except for the accused's troubled background and the abuse she has suffered over that time,"[369] and "little in the way of aggravating factors, save and except for the sheer and total absence of any social value arising from the accused's lifestyle and actions."[370] It appears that Whitford's experiences of victimization effectively both mitigate and aggravate sentencing. That is, her aggravating "lifestyle and actions" are inevitably connected to her victimization. Justice Parrett clearly recognizes this connection when commenting that her spiral back into substance abuse and criminality from a clean period was triggered after having to share custody with an abusive ex-partner she had cut from her life, and that her "revolving door"[371] parole violations were a product of her substance abuse problems. These issues speak to the "tangle of barriers"[372] that, DeHart explains, frustrate women's ability to healthily and legally navigate their lives. Because Justice Parrett finds that experiences of victimization lie beneath the aggravating factor of the "sheer and total absence of any social value arising from the accused's lifestyle and actions,"[373] and this same victimization also grounds the mitigating factors of her "troubled background and abuse,"[374] a complex portrait of the victimization-criminalization continuum emerges from the judgment. Justice Parrett does articulate, "There is no doubt, in my view, that this is the history of a person with severe substance abuse problems who lacks education, conflict resolution skills, coping skills, and has continuously suffered both sexual and physical abuse,"[375] although some of these issues (particularly "conflict resolution skills" and "coping skills") are individualized.

Justice Parrett does cite s. 718.2(e) of the Criminal Code and highlights aspects of *Gladue*.[376] However, these principles are merely stated without explanation about how this analysis actually impacts the sentence determinations. Justice Parrett merely appends a comment—"after a careful consideration of all the circumstances and the principles to be applied"[377]—to denote consideration of *Gladue*, without explaining what this consideration involved. *Gladue* describes that s. 718.2(e) requires a different "method of analysis,"[378] and *Ipeelee* maintains that this constitutes a distinct "methodology."[379] Justice Parrett does provide this methodology: "Section 718.2(e) directs sentencing judges to sentence aboriginal offenders individually but also differently because the circumstances of aboriginal people are unique. In sentencing an aboriginal offender, the judge must consider: (a) the unique, systemic, or background factors which have played a part in bringing the particular aboriginal offender before the courts; and (b) the types of sentencing procedures and sanctions which may be appropriate in the circumstances for the offender because of his or her particular aboriginal heritage or connection."[380] Despite mentioning having considered this analysis, Justice Parrett does not disclose what, if any, impact it has on the actual determination of sentence. Instead, Justice Parrett determines Whitford must be separated from society for there to be any prospect of rehabilitation,[381] and accepts the Crown's range of sentence from five to eight years' imprisonment, ultimately settling toward the middle of that range at six years. It seems that the pre-sentence report should have provided ample assistance in the performance and representation of the *Gladue* analysis in the judgment, because the judge describes it as "detailed and helpful."[382]

Perhaps a more explicit discussion of the *Gladue* analysis was omitted in favour of the idea of rehabilitation through imprisonment, as Justice Parrett notes that, in her nineteen months of pretrial custody, Whitford "appears to have made progress . . . at least for now on an institutional basis," having "withdrawn from drugs and alcohol abuse," and that the Ministry of Children and Family Development supports her having her young child with her in custody.[383] I discuss the issue of judges using or characterizing prison terms as sources of healing in Chapter 3. For now, it is important to note that the *Gladue* analysis has either been obviated by the portrayal of prison as treatment, or has been undergone but is not made transparent in the judgment. This creates a disjuncture between Justice Parrett's comments about Whitford's experiences of victimization and her *Gladue* factors, as her victimization is discussed but not (at least not expressly) integrated into the *Gladue* analysis.

Louisa Killiktee

The judicial reasoning in *R. v. Killiktee* demonstrates a *Gladue* analysis that is clearly and sensitively filtered through the lens of the victimization-criminalization continuum, although, despite this orientation, similar to *Whitford*, elements of the woman's victimization history still reappear within aggravating factors. Justice Ratushny orders nine years of incarceration (before reducing this sentence by two-for-one credit for pre-sentence custody) for Louisa Killiktee, following her guilty plea to manslaughter. The judge identifies at the outset that Killiktee's "Inuit background and the integration of *Gladue* principles" is a primary issue, given the need "to give appropriate weight to a restorative approach."[384]

Justice Ratushny describes that within the two months preceding the offence in question, Killiktee endured multiple losses while in custody for another sentence (her teenage brother committed suicide and she had a miscarriage in which she lost triplets), none of which she could grieve in accordance with her Inuit culture because she was in prison (she could not attend their funerals and related traditions). Against that background, the judge comments that after her release from that period of custody, Killiktee was "emotionally unstable," and "coped by resuming her abuse of alcohol," which "contributed to her violent reaction to the victim and causing the victim's death" in the current offence.[385] Justice Ratushny outlines the facts for which Killiktee is being sentenced: briefly, she was living at a shelter where the deceased used to visit others, and one night both had been drinking when the deceased called Killiktee a "'whore' and a 'slut'"[386] during a mutual argument, then slapped her head from behind; when the deceased continued walking away, "in a state of rage"[387] Killiktee pulled her down, her head hit the pavement, and Killiktee kicked her four times before there was an intervention. The judge notes from surveillance footage that Killiktee subsequently "cradl[ed] and caress[ed] the victim's head in what appears to be an attempt to assist her,"[388] although the victim later died in hospital.

The judge draws from what she describes as a "careful and balanced presentence report," which appears to have involved a *Gladue* component, including "some historical background" and various descriptions of the challenges and traumas in the lives of "many Inuit today."[389] Justice

Ratushny notes that Killiktee's home community in Nunavut struggles with "high rates of substance abuse" due to the intergenerational effects of processes of colonization, including forced relocations and residential schools,[390] with "inadequate systemic resources to deal with these escalating problems."[391] The judge recognizes that Killiktee "is a product of these complex and serious dynamics," adding that it would be a serious injustice to sentence her "without attempting to stand in her shoes."[392] During her youth, Killiktee witnessed violence against her mother by her father, both of whom were alcoholic, and was physically and sexually abused by various relatives, causing her to live "in a state of sustained fear with nowhere to go and not knowing what to do or how to respond,"[393] and "left traumatized."[394] Killiktee herself says her misuse of alcohol and substances has been "an attempt to hide pain and escape related memories."[395] She has two children, whom the judge describes as "bright stars in her life," "everything to her at the present time."[396] In describing her criminal record (consisting of violent offences and breaches of court orders), Justice Ratushny comments, regarding violence she committed, that Killiktee "had been intoxicated on each occasion."[397]

Considering these experiences of victimization, Justice Ratushny writes, "I accept that for a person with Ms. Killiktee's background . . . the victim's insults and slap to the back of her head were particularly provocative. For a person coming from healthier circumstances, the victim's insults and slap might well not serve to reduce an accused person's moral culpability for a crime such as Ms. Killiktee's. In Ms. Killiktee's circumstances, however, I consider that they do. It is in this way that *Gladue* principles infuse the assessment of a fit sentence in this case."[398] This explanation clearly demonstrates judicial engagement with the *Gladue* analysis through the lens of the victimization-criminalization continuum. However, even *Gladue* analyses well-situated within an understanding of that continuum become complex within the general structure of sentencing. That is, like in *Whitford*, it seems Killiktee's history of victimization operates both to mitigate and to aggravate. Justice Ratushny observes a sustained linkage between Killiktee's past offences and her substance abuse, including her violent offending, recognizing further that her "root issue is the pain of her extensive childhood traumas and her addiction is her attempt to kill that pain."[399] This judicial understanding evokes the underpinnings of the victimization-criminal-ization continuum, but, simultaneously, Justice Ratushny also includes within aggravating factors that "her substance abuse has continued and it is a key contributing cause to her violent offending."[400] Explaining her reasoning, Justice Ratushny writes, "Your abusive childhood and back-ground serve to reduce your moral culpability for your actions in taking her life and, as a consequence, they are able to serve to reduce the length of your sentence. However, because your background also serves to in-crease the risk you present to the safety of the community, that factor counterbalances its mitigating force."[401] Overall, while the judge seems to proceed through the *Gladue* analysis in a delicate manner informed by and contextualized within an understanding of the victimization-criminalization continuum, Killiktee's history of victimization none-theless effectively both mitigates and aggravates her ultimately lengthy prison sentence.[402]

Jeanette Niganobe

In *R. v. Niganobe*, *Gladue* factors also seem to be framed in an almost neutralizing way, similar to how Whitford's and Killiktee's respective experiences of victimization were both mitigating and aggravating. Jea-nette Niganobe is sentenced to five years' imprisonment for impaired driving causing death after she drove through a red light into an inter-section and collided with a police car. Justice W. Larry Whalen finds "little of a mitigating nature,"[403] which seems to relate to the circumstanc-es of the offence. The judge goes into great depth detailing Niganobe's personal history. The judge describes that she "is a full member of the Mississauga First Nation,"[404] with family who are residential school survivors. Niganobe's mother routinely physically abused her and also disbelieved her when she disclosed she had been sexually assaulted. Jus-tice Whalen notes that in Niganobe's youth, "brimming with anger, re-belling and acting out,"[405] and "turning to alcohol," she ran away and was taken into foster care.[406] She came into repeated conflict with the law, including serving time in prison while still in her adolescence. Ni-ganobe had two intimate relationships involving much substance abuse, both resulting in separation after her partners abused her. She has two children from these relationships. Adverting to the intergenerational effects of colonization, Justice Whalen states, "Her ties to family, culture and community have been fractured, and she has had little or no sense of being wanted or belonging,"[407] characterizing Niganobe as caught in a "cycle of dysfunction" within her family and community.[408]

Justice Whalen describes this extensive background replete with violence and substance abuse as "a classic example of the problems discussed by the Supreme Court of Canada in *Gladue*."[409] When considering "the effect of the offender's aboriginal origins on the sentence I otherwise think would be fit," the judge finds "no question that Niganobe's path in life has been affected by" *Gladue* factors.[410] Justice Whalen describes that Niganobe herself is

> a product of the cycle of poverty, lack of opportunity (including education and employment), racism, substance abuse, breakdown of family and community, absence of nurture and disconnectedness characteristic of many of our aboriginal communities because of the generations before her who have suffered residential schools and other racist or paternalistic policies that have created and maintained social cauldrons of dysfunction and despair. I do not doubt that these factors have had great adverse effect in the formation of her character, views and propensities. *Those same antecedents, however,* have made her resistant to many of the ordinary social and regulatory norms that must be respected and maintained for social co-existence, peace and progress in any society, *no matter the race, colour or cultural origin.*[411]

It seems convoluted and contradictory to assert that "those same antecedents"—*Gladue* factors—that are specific to her experience as an Indigenous woman caused Niganobe to stand outside various norms, "no matter" her "race, colour or cultural origin," because her Indigenous experience is intersectional and cannot be bracketed. Niganobe's "resistan[ce] to many of the ordinary social and regulatory norms" should be understood as a component of the disadvantage conveyed by systemic factors (and/or even resistance in the sense of attempting to regain control within experiences of injustice), not as an aspect of her character that can be excised and abstracted "no matter the race, colour or cultural origin." The *Gladue* factors that Justice Whalen describes Niganobe as a "product of" illustrate Justice LeBel's comment in *Ipeelee* that "many Aboriginal offenders find themselves in situations of social and economic deprivation with a lack of opportunities and limited options for positive development."[412] These systemic or background factors also demonstrate how victimization constrains Indigenous women's options. As such, both the victimization-criminalization continuum and *Gladue* factors operate within Justice Whalen's comments, but these understandings are undermined by the judge's suggestion that Niganobe's responses to her constrained options can be separated from these experiences and considered alongside conduct of other people ("no matter the race, colour or cultural origin").[413]

Notwithstanding this problematic peripheral comment that levels Niganobe's unique experience as an Indigenous woman, Justice Whalen decides to order a sentence "at the low end of the range suggested by the crown [*sic*]" because of "the mitigating effect of the offender's aboriginal antecedents, which I recognize and have concluded played a role in her antisocial views and behavior."[414] Justice Whalen explains that Niganobe "did not choose her 'lot in life.'"[415] The judge's reasoning in the end demonstrates that the *Gladue* analysis (including Niganobe's experiences of victimization that inform it) meaningfully shapes the sentence. Further, the judge's comment that Niganobe "did not choose her 'lot in life'" reflects an understanding that the systemic and background factors derived from colonization, including the victimization that Niganobe experienced throughout her life, constrained her options such that her criminalization (and, in turn, her sentencing) should reflect that her life choices have been circumscribed by factors beyond her control.

Juanita Johnson

In *R. v. Johnson*,[416] Judge Cozens comments in an oral judgment on how the variability of information connecting *Gladue* factors to the given offence produces sentencing challenges. The very positioning of a connection between *Gladue* factors and the offence in question as an issue complicating the sentencing of Indigenous persons unhelpfully reinforces the idea that *Ipeelee* later rejects that such persons must establish this connection causally. Judge Cozens sentences Juanita Johnson to serve a ten-month conditional sentence for trafficking. Judge Cozens outlines that Johnson "is a member of the Kwanlin Dun First Nation" whose extended family "have struggled with the fallout of, perhaps, to some extent, the residential school system."[417] Several members of Johnson's family had substance abuse problems, and she herself struggled with addiction for several years.[418] However, Judge Cozens notes that "there is not much in the way of information in this regard," perhaps attributable to the pre-sentence report's having been completed in Alberta and not the Yukon, because "it is not as comprehensive as our pre-sentence reports tend to be. It does not include risk assessments."[419] Without the benefit of the later clarification from *Ipeelee* that a causal connection between *Gladue* factors and the offence must not be required, Judge Cozens outlines how variable information about *Gladue* factors complicates what many judges viewed to be the proper analysis: "Sometimes we are dealing with comprehensive reports that can draw a distinct link between an individual's First Nation status and their offending. Other times, the link is less [*sic*] tenuous, or there is not a link, and in this case, there is not a lot of information, so we do not have a clear, strong link that would lead to Ms. Johnson's First Nation status being a significantly contributing factor to the offence that she has been convicted of committing on this date."[420]

The *Gladue* analysis, done well, should incorporate gendered understandings of criminalized Indigenous women's experiences (such as incorporating analyses of the gendered effects of victimization and colonization)—although, as Balfour has found, the intersection of gender issues and colonization is insufficiently represented in judgments sentencing Indigenous women. While the judge's *Gladue* analysis should not have indicated the need for more information to solidify a causal connection between *Gladue* factors and Johnson's offence, Judge Cozens does seem to use a gendered lens to inform sentencing to achieve a just result. This gendered lens appears in two instances. First, Judge Cozens factors Johnson's fear of being separated from her child into the reasoning that she appreciates that the consequences of her actions may harm others.[421] Second, the judge assigns community service as part of her conditional sentence, acknowledging, "I appreciate that the community service can be more difficult when you have a young child, but there may be viable options there," such as the possibility of "the availability of some programs that involve you and your child assisting other mothers."[422] Perhaps these gendered analyses could have contributed to a richer *Gladue* analysis had Judge Cozens been equipped with a more informative PSR or *Gladue* report, but without also seeking a direct link between Johnson's experience of colonization and her offence. In this decision, the *Gladue* analysis seems somewhat detached from the judge's sensitivity to gendered issues.

Elizabeth Jankovic

Gladue factors are minimized in *R. v. Jankovic* where the judge undermines the relevance of Jankovic's Indigenous connection. Elizabeth Jankovic is sentenced to a total of two years and ten months' imprisonment for robbery, having concealed her face with intent to commit an indictable offence, trafficking, and failing to comply with a probation order. She robbed an inn after assaulting the cashier with bear spray, and "was heavily involved with speed use at the time of these offences."[423] Judge D.C. Norheim writes that she "is of mixed aboriginal and non-aboriginal ancestry" and "holds a treaty card," adding, "I note that her father was not aboriginal."[424] Jankovic was placed into a non-Indigenous foster home at age eight; both her biological parents "regularly abused alcohol and drugs," her father engaged in "inappropriate conduct" with her, and her mother was frequently absent because she feared her father.[425] From this history, the judge finds that "the issues of disadvantage to this accused come from her treatment by her non-aboriginal father, not from her aboriginal mother."[426] I would apply Judge Norheim's usage of "disadvantage" to encompass experiences and effects of victimization.

By locating the "source" of disadvantage (including victimization) in Jankovic's life as stemming from her relationship with her non-Indigenous father (as distinct from any experiences informed by her relationship with her Indigenous mother), Judge Norheim attempts to disentangle issues that are indivisible. Moreover, the judge's line of thinking seems to succumb to the problem later identified and clarified by *Ipeelee* that systemic or background factors are just that, and should be used to contextualize and not to impose an impossible burden on a convicted Indigenous person to demonstrate how colonization has led specifically her to criminalization. Contrary to this subsequent clarification from *Ipeelee*, by defining Jankovic's disadvantages in relation to her non-Indigenous father and expressly not her Indigenous mother, Judge Norheim seems to implicitly seek and deny a causal connection between Jankovic's experience as an Indigenous woman and her offence.

The idea that such issues and experiences can be extricated from one another acts to suppress and deny the multiplicity of Indigenous experiences. Yin C. Paradies, who "identif[ies] racially as an Aboriginal-Anglo-Asian Australian . . . both colonizer and colonized,"[427] discusses how binary, essentialized ideas about Indigenous identities are confining because they assume a uniform experience of Indigeneity and deny "hybrid space[s] of multiplicity."[428] Paradies rejects this problematic, restrictive categorization of Indigenous identities because it creates a "questioning of authenticity" in which some people "who have Indigenous ancestry . . . 'qualify' as Indigenous," and some do not.[429] Paradies points out that this artificial characterization is damaging both on individual and community levels, as it further fragments already fragmented communities into people "who can authentically perform Indigeneity and those who are silenced and/or rendered outside the space of Indigeneity."[430]

Judge Norheim adopts the kind of exclusionary, reductionist characterization of Indigenous identity in *Jankovic* that troubles Paradies. In addition to connecting Jankovic's disadvantage to her relationship with her non-Indigenous father, Judge Norheim states, "This accused, while racially carrying aboriginal blood, has little or no cultural connection with the aboriginal community,"[431] and further abstracts Jankovic from her Indigenous experience with the comment that *"regardless of race,* this accused has had a troubled childhood."[432] Judge Norheim also minimizes the applicability of the *Gladue* analysis to Jankovic's sentencing when responding to a case submitted by defence counsel, a decision that "involved an aboriginal offender," with the comment, "If it is necessary for me to distinguish the *Skani* decision, I do so on the basis that Mr. Skani was an aboriginal offender who was actively involved within the aboriginal community and culture."[433]

Marilyn Brown widens the frame of colonization to *include* experiences of dislocation, explaining that "in the post-colonial context, alienation from indigenous culture and the loss of resources it affords are important, and often unanalyzed factors, in the overrepresentation of native peoples in corrections populations."[434] Perhaps Jankovic's alienation from her Indigenous community is a product of her mother's absences to evade the man she feared and Jankovic's later upbringing in a non-Indigenous foster home (both of which may well relate to colonization). We do not know. But it is artificial and unfair to frame her lack of connection to Indigenous culture and the community as if it somehow depreciates her Indigenous heritage. This reasoning does not comport with the judicial duty to apply the *Gladue* analysis for all Indigenous persons on sentencing.[435]

While Judge Norheim does discuss Jankovic's "mixed aboriginal and non-aboriginal ancestry"[436] within mitigating factors (although without expressly citing *Gladue* in the judgment), it is difficult to understand *how* her experience as an Indigenous woman actually factored into the sentencing process as a mitigating factor. The judge states, "I do give particular attention to her aboriginal bloodline,"[437] although slightly undercuts this comment by adding that "this is not as significant a factor" as "the steps she has taken toward rehabilitation."[438] This attention is also undermined by the comments minimizing the relevance of her Indigenous heritage. Further, because Judge Norheim situates the disadvantages Jankovic has experienced (I again interpret this to include experiences of victimization) with how her non-Indigenous father treated her (and in contradistinction with her Indigenous mother's role in her life), the judge effectively separates such disadvantages from the *Gladue* analysis. As a result, the *Gladue* analysis seems to occupy a different space from the judicial view of how Jankovic's experiences of victimization have impacted her and contributed to her criminalization, which yields an impoverished conception of the victimization-criminalization continuum.

Lisa Bluebell

In *R. v. Bluebell*, the judge determines there is insufficient information connecting *Gladue* factors to Lisa Bluebell's offence, problematically locating that insufficiency in Bluebell's failure to make that connection for the court. After convicting her of attempted murder alongside Bluebell's guilty pleas to lesser charges, Justice Maher sentenced Bluebell to a total of six and a half years of imprisonment. The facts of the case are unclear from the judgment, although Bluebell's personal history is offered in some detail. Justice Maher explains that Bluebell "is a status Indian registered with the Yellow Quill First Nation," who lost connection and involvement with her community when she moved to an urban centre.[439] The pre-sentence report reveals that she "sporadically attended Lestock Residential School"[440] for three years in her adolescence, although there is no further information provided about her residential school experience. Bluebell's father and youngest sister died and her mother raised her; "However her mother was addicted to alcohol and subject to domestic violence."[441] Losing her sister devastated and "impacted the accused's life significantly," and Bluebell "used intravenous drugs and abused alcohol."[442] This substance abuse became a feature of her intimate relationships, including one long-term relationship in which she suffered significant physical abuse. She had four children in that relationship.

It is unclear how any consideration of *Gladue* factors impacted the reasoning behind and quantum of the sentence ordered in *Bluebell*. *Gladue* factors are discussed in the judgment, although this discussion does not appear to meaningfully impact the sentence. Justice Maher comments on Bluebell's detachment from her Indigenous community during the several years that she relocated to an urban centre, writing "There is no evidence that the accused has significant involvement in cultural activities or practices. There was no evidence of the need of the accused to reconcile or re-enter the aboriginal community."[443] This conforms to the part of the *Gladue* analysis where the "particular aboriginal heritage or connection" of the person before the court may help inform what "types of sentencing procedures and sanctions" are appropriate to them.[444] Justice Maher finds that "there is no evidence as to alternatives to incarceration or treatment facility."[445] Perhaps even absent such evidence, other options could still have been considered—though it was decided after *Bluebell*, in *Ipeelee*, Justice LeBel prompts consideration of more radical, innovative alternatives to imprisonment: "To the extent that current sentencing practices do not further these objectives [of deterrence and rehabilitation], those practices must change so as to meet the needs of Aboriginal offenders and their communities," and affirms academic support for more creative sentencing.[446]

In any event, the finding that Bluebell lacked an ongoing connection to her culture and heritage may have influenced the judge in deciding the weighting of the relevant principles, as Justice Maher writes, "I am satisfied that in determining an appropriate sentence I must give primary emphasis to the principles of denunciation and deterrence."[447] It seems that Justice Maher prioritized denunciation and deterrence because of offence seriousness, stating, "I have reviewed several cases that state that the primary factor of denunciation and general deterrence is required in regard to a conviction for attempted murder involving violence of this nature."[448] In *Ipeelee*, Justice LeBel is clear that offence seriousness neither obviates nor diminishes the judicial duty to meaningfully apply *Gladue*, explaining that "numerous courts" have misunderstood the comment in *Gladue* about how more serious and violent offences typically yield more similar sanctions for Indigenous and non-Indigenous persons, and "have erroneously interpreted this generalization as an indication that the *Gladue* principles do not apply to serious offences."[449]

The judicial discussion of the systemic and background factors in *Bluebell* signifies another problem in the reasoning, as *Ipeelee* illuminates. Justice Maher notes the PSR reference to Bluebell's mother's alcoholism and that she abused Bluebell, and makes one explicit reference to Bluebell's experience of racism, where she was "teased that she was native."[450] However, when the judge refers to Bluebell's residential school experience, there is a clear illustration of the misapprehended causality connection later repudiated by *Ipeelee*: Justice Maher writes, "The accused was unable to identify how her experience in the Residential School or being an aboriginal person has impacted her life either as a child or an adult."[451] The judge later reiterates she "has provided no specific or direct evidence about the influence of personal factors specific to herself in relation to systemic issues raised in *Gladue*."[452] Judicial comments to this effect place an unreasonable burden on criminalized Indigenous persons, who should not have to disentangle the impossibly knotted aftermath of colonialism into some elusive explanatory account of causality.[453] *Ipeelee* holds that the frequent, erroneous, judicial requirement for the establishment of a link between the experiences of colonization and criminalization demonstrates "inadequate understanding of the devastating intergenerational effects of the collective experiences of Aboriginal peoples."[454] It should also be noted that within the fairly lengthy list of mitigating factors, *Gladue* factors are not referenced, apart from the decontextualized items relating to substance abuse issues. As such, the *Gladue* analysis seems even further removed from the considerations that were actually brought to bear on the reasoning.

In viewing the judgment as a whole, it appears that Bluebell's Indigenous status and experience are diminished in the judicial narrative. Her history of victimization (within colonization) is identified through details from the pre-sentence report, but undermined by references to an absence of explicit connection between this history and her offending.

Susan Collins

In *R. v. Collins*, agency is depicted as individualized, compartmentalized from systemic factors; *Gladue* is dismissed, and the representation of the victimization-criminalization continuum lies fallow. Justice G. Patrick Smith sentences Susan Collins to sixteen months' imprisonment and a two-year probation order for defrauding the Ontario social assistance program for an amount exceeding $5,000. Collins worked with her co-accuseds on the Fort William First Nation Reserve in the office responsible for administering social assistance to the clients. Together, they fraudulently misallocated funds, and Collins's involvement was attributed to an amount over $68,000. Justice Smith describes from the pre-sentence report that Collins "has lived all of her life on the Fort William First Nation Reserve,"[455] where she "witnessed her father's substance abuse and violence towards her mother."[456] Her "father lost his Aboriginal status through the process of enfranchisement. As a result, Collins was treated poorly, was ostracized," and "regarded as an 'outsider' because . . . she was no longer considered Aboriginal. She only regained this status when she remarried."[457] She has a gambling addiction, which, her family believes, caused her to be susceptible to the fraudulent scheme.[458] Collins is the primary caregiver for her four children.

Justice Smith seems to trivialize her gambling addiction and individualizes her offence to a personal value system where he responds to the defence submission that Collins should receive a conditional sentence in part to allow her to care for her child, who has a disability: "If Angela requires so much of her mother's care that jail would jeopardize her care, one cannot but wonder why the accused spent so many hours gambling away the proceeds of her share of the fraud in the local casino."[459] In conjunction with this comment, while there is much in the pre-sentence report that explores how the community has suffered through the residential school system and its aftermath, including the "dislocation of community members," fragmentation of the family unit, destruction of "any connection to their community or heritage," and escalated unemployment, substance abuse, family violence, and sexual abuse,[460] Justice Smith concludes, "Notwithstanding the evidence that the poverty and suffering on the Fort William First Nation Reserve is considerable and that the residential school experience is in part responsible, I find that the evidence does not support the argument that systemic factors are responsible for bringing the accused before the court."[461]

Justice Smith relates that Collins "described being raised in a strict Catholic home, in which no attention was given to cultural or native traditions since these were viewed as contrary to the Catholic religion."[462] There is no judicial commentary expanding on this, although it is possible this background contributed to Justice Smith's deciding that there is no evidential connection between *Gladue* factors and Collins's offence. This is perhaps an illustration of where, in Toni Williams's words, a judge "did not think that the defendant's Aboriginal ancestry was sufficiently authentic to invoke [section] 718.2(e)."[463] Regardless, while there *does* seem to be ample evidence indicating how *Gladue* factors may have contributed to Collins's criminalization, the issue is moot. Justice Smith's comments invoke the problem later identified by *Ipeelee* that judges in the post-*Gladue* jurisprudence have erroneously required the establishment of a connection between a given offence and systemic and background factors in the lives of Indigenous peoples.[464] Further, Justice Smith perhaps also succumbs to another problem *Ipeelee* clarified, that offence seriousness does not obviate the *Gladue* analysis.[465] Justice Smith decides that *Collins* is a case "where the seriousness of the crime and need for denunciation take precedence over any other considerations,"[466] including that of *Gladue* factors.

It is apparent that Justice Smith focuses upon the issue of individual agency, while systemic factors merely blur into the background: "Each individual must be accountable for their own actions. Blaming others, your upbringing or minimizing one's participation cannot, generally speaking for serious crimes such as large scale fraud, absolve a person from the consequences of their actions."[467] Despite her family's belief that her gambling addiction rendered her vulnerable to the fraudulent plan, Justice Smith concludes, "It is clear that Ms. Collins did not have an easy upbringing however the responsibility for what she has done must be hers. She made a choice to become involved in the fraudulent scheme and she actively became a key player . . . [and] choose [*sic*] to stay involved. Her actions have hurt and divided her community."[468]

It should be noted that the thrust of *Gladue* is not about "blaming" her upbringing or displacing responsibility, but rather understanding how continued effects and processes of colonization contribute to the criminalization of Indigenous peoples and striving to ameliorate the overincarceration of Indigenous peoples where possible through sentencing. In *Ipeelee*, Justice LeBel makes this point clear: "Systemic and background factors do not operate as an excuse or justification for the criminal conduct. Rather, they provide the necessary *context* to enable a judge to determine an appropriate sentence."[469] For a contrasting example of how another judge frames the issue in a way that comports with *Gladue*, in sentencing Constance Stevens, a Mi'kmaq woman, Judge A. Peter Ross declares in *R. v. Stevens* that "this sentence is also informed by *R. v. Gladue*," adding, "I say this not in the sense that her circumstances and background are causal factors for her crime. Rather, it is the shift of emphasis away from deterrence towards the restorative and remedial aspects of sentence that I have in mind."[470] This shift of emphasis is precisely what *Gladue* directs. Without proper acceptance of the contextualization of Collins's criminalization within colonization, the victimization-criminalization continuum discourse of the judgment in *Collins* is similarly impoverished. *Gladue* factors are referenced but their relevance dismissed, and the agency Collins exercised in committing the offence is held as free-standing, disconnected from the systemic factors discussed in the pre-sentence report, instead of enriching the analysis with ideas about how victimization constrains choices.

Where *Gladue* and the Continuum Converge

Two cases are laudable for their strong *Gladue* analyses and productive integration of that analysis with concepts presented by the victimization-criminalization continuum. Both *R. v. Shore* and *R. v. Audy* are sensitive judgments on a variety of levels. Of particular importance, both decisions feature judges looking behind the assessed risk factors for each woman being sentenced, choosing instead to foreground systemic or background factors in a manner consistent with the spirit of *Gladue*. These decisions offer a measure of hope toward the accessibility of s. 718.2(e) for Indigenous women when such factors are invested with gendered understandings of victimization and criminalization; this is significant, given Balfour's finding that "Aboriginal women are disqualified from receiving the full benefits of progressive sentencing reforms as their own violence is not situated in the context of gendered conditions in Aboriginal communities."[471] I also discuss *R. v. Ussak*, primarily for how the judge interprets certain features of the case—such as those relating to ostensible evidentiary discrepancies and whether to apply s. 718.2(a)(ii) to aggravate the sentence—in a manner that strongly resonates with the impulses behind the victimization-criminalization continuum. Although the *Gladue* analysis is more incidental than fully explored in *Ussak*, such as in its treatment of issues relating to abuse, the decision still offers an orientation toward s. 718.2(e) that is expansive in how it is contextualized within broader systemic issues (and not individualized to that specific woman before the court).

Tracey Shore

R. v. Shore is significant for the nuanced judicial treatment of the relationship (or lack thereof) between the victimization-criminalization continuum and risk assessments, and its departure from the inappropriate priority *R. v. Bluebell* placed upon that woman's ability to articulate the effect of *Gladue* factors within her life. In *Shore*, Judge Carol Snell sentences Tracey Shore to a conditional sentence order of two years less a day after her guilty plea to driving while impaired and causing death. Shore was in a relationship with the deceased. After a night of drinking together, they had an argument, and Shore got into their car "to avoid physical confrontation"[472] with him. Shore continued to drive with the deceased on the hood when he jumped on the vehicle, subsequently falling and fatally hitting his head.

The pre-sentence report makes clear that Shore got into the vehicle as an escape from the violent confrontation she feared, as the deceased was both emotionally and physically abusive to her, particularly when he was drinking.[473] Judge Snell effectively adverts to the victimization-criminalization continuum, commenting that "her lifetime experiences with violence . . . no doubt had a significant effect on her decision not to stop once he was on the hood of the vehicle."[474] Describing her personal history, Judge Snell notes that Shore "is a Treaty Indian," who was adopted by her aunt and uncle because her father was incarcerated and her mother was "living a very unstable lifestyle."[475] Shore's aunt had problems with addiction and was later murdered, her uncle was physically abusive, and eventually she moved in with her father. Judge Snell states that "substance abuse and violence typified a succession of relationships."[476] She first lost custody of her children after assaulting them, later regaining their care.

Unlike the judicial reasoning in *Bluebell,* irrespective of Shore's insistence to the writer of the pre-sentence report that she "does not feel her ethnic origin has impacted her life,"[477] Judge Snell infers the opposite. Judge Snell finds, "In my view, the accused's personal history reflects 'the unique systemic or background factors which may have played a part in bringing the particular aboriginal offender before the courts' which so concerned the Supreme Court of Canada in their decision in *R. v. Gladue.* I consider this to be so regardless of the fact that the accused does not attribute any of her life experiences to her ethnic origin."[478] This comment aligns well with the later *Ipeelee* clarification that Indigenous persons must not be required to establish a connection between *Gladue* factors and the given offence on sentencing.[479] Judge Snell expands on this finding: "If I am wrong in that, I still consider the accused's dysfunctional background, particularly her experiences with physical abuse as a child and throughout her common law relationships, to be of great significance in assessing her moral blameworthiness for the offence and in understanding why she committed the offence."[480]

Judge Snell's further comment is significant for its articulation of the relationship between the *Gladue* analysis and the operation of the victimization-criminalization continuum lens in this judgment. That is, Judge Snell describes deciding that, despite Shore's opinion to the contrary, *Gladue* factors are certainly relevant—and that even if they were not, Shore's history of victimization will inform her sentence. Here, the victimization-criminalization continuum is implicated in the *Gladue* analysis, but also stands alone as a tool to sensitively guide sentencing. It is also noteworthy that Judge Snell explicitly states that Shore's experiences of victimization are "of great significance"[481] in the determinations about her sentence. This analysis points to judicial appreciation of the operation of the victimization-criminalization continuum in Shore's life, and directly connects it to what her sentence should be. Additionally, Judge Snell contextualizes and deemphasizes the fact that the victim was Shore's partner, explaining that this statutorily aggravating factor "is tempered greatly by the fact that the accused resorted to the vehicle to avoid a violent confrontation with the victim."[482] This demonstrates a deeper analysis of gendered violence than subsists in many other judgments, and is another instance in which Judge Snell employs reasoning connected to the victimization-criminalization continuum in a way that has meaningful effects on the sentence.

Judge Snell is disinclined to uncritically incorporate the risk assessment from the pre-sentence report, cautioning that "the risk assessment cannot be relied on slavishly to determine whether or not to impose a community-based sentence without regard for the personal circumstances of the offender."[483] Considering her assessed risk factors (such as substance abuse and problems in her family relationships), all of which intersect with *Gladue* factors (including Shore's experiences of victimization), Judge Snell highlights that Shore has managed to be relatively law-abiding *despite* these risk factors, and uses this frame to depart from the risk assessment, concluding that she will "present a low risk to re-offend"[484] with an appropriate sentence. The judge declares, "The length of the conditional sentence will be longer than a jail term would have been, in light of the fact that the accused will be allowed to serve it in the community."[485]

A community sentence can convey its own set of problems for the women serving them. Charalee F. Graydon writes, "Non-custodial penalties such as fines, probation and community service orders, although often seen as lenient sentencing alternatives, may have a disproportionately harsh impact on many female offenders as a result either of the offender's impecuniosity or inability to comply with the Court's direction as a result of competing child care duties."[486] Nonetheless, it is apparent that Judge Snell is motivated to advert to the overrepresentation of Indigenous peoples in prison and to avoid incarceration where appropriate.[487] For example, noting that the pre-sentence report identifies Shore's "minimal education and lack of employment experience"[488] as factors elevating the level of risk she presents, Judge Snell understands that Shore's child-care responsibilities prevent her from improving her education and employment situation, finding that to remove a conditional sentence as an alternative on the basis of such risk factors "would perpetuate the 'systemic' factors which contribute to the over-representation of aboriginal persons in the correctional system."[489] To protect against this consequence, Judge Snell concludes, "In the result, I attribute less importance to those risk factors than the others which the accused could address, and has shown a willingness to address."[490]

Within certain sentence conditions, "which will curtail her freedom and provide her with help in addressing her alcohol and personal problems,"[491] Judge Snell finds Shore to present a low risk of reoffending. Because the judge makes this determination against the high assessed risk, this marks a noteworthy interpretation of the evidence—in other instances, evidence of victimization amplifies the assessed risk to reoffend and may in turn contribute to harsher sentencing. This correlation between victimization and risk is made apparent in such cases as *R. v. S.L.N.,*[492] where Justice James W. Williams writes about the woman before the court that "it was noted that she has been the victim of violence. She has been around violence a great deal of her life and she has grown up in dysfunctional family circumstances. All of those are factors which indicate a higher risk of criminal re-offence."[493] In *Shore,* Judge Snell demonstrates how it is possible to incorporate an understanding of the victimization-criminalization continuum that recognizes how experiences of abuse may contribute to women's later coming before the courts without simultaneously amplifying the projection of a high risk to reoffend from an assessment.

Crystal Audy

R. v. Audy is another decision in which the judge attributes greater weight to factors other than risk assessments to guide the analysis. In *Audy,* there is less explicitly focused discussion about the impact of that woman's experiences of violence than in *Shore*, although the judgment follows similar reasoning, because the judge in *Audy* directs attention broadly to *Gladue* factors (which must be understood as connected to victimization). In *Audy*, Judge Donald R. Slough sentences Crystal Audy to pay a fine and to serve an eighteen-month probation order for impaired driving causing bodily harm. Drawing from the PSR and included *Gladue* report (the judgment refers to these as such, although it is unclear whether the latter refers to simply *Gladue*-related information in the PSR), Judge Slough describes that Audy is a "member of Wuskwi Siphik First Nation,"[494] "the product of a small, remote and impoverished First Nation community," who "frequently saw violence and substance abuse."[495] Her parents are "the product of the residential school system," and Audy "was raised in foster homes and by her grandmother" and "was victimized as a child."[496] The PSR concludes that "victimization issues and her problem with depression" are among the factors that may be relevant to her sentencing.[497]

In crafting an appropriate sentence, Judge Slough declares that a conditional sentence would have been imposed, but is no longer available because the 2007 s. 742.1 amendments removed conditional sentences as an option for serious personal injury offences, which includes impaired driving causing bodily harm.[498] After weighing the remaining alternatives, such as an intermittent sentence (which is unsuitable due to the "logistics and expense"[499] involved in the necessary travel) and various incarnations of probation orders, ultimately Judge Slough settles on a probation order that requires Audy to remain in her residence twenty-four hours per day, seven days per week.[500] Such restrictive conditions are permissible within the "primarily rehabilitative in focus" orientation of probation orders,[501] although it should be noted that this sentence closely resembles the common "house arrest" form of many conditional sentence orders (and also produces pressures that may increase the risk of breaching the order). That is, it appears that this judge has effectively circumvented the amendments to the conditional sentencing regime in an effort to achieve a just sentence.

In fashioning this conditional sentence–like, restrictive probation order, Judge Slough employs an understanding of Audy's Indigenous status that dissociates risk factors from *Gladue* factors and focuses on the larger problem of Indigenous overincarceration:

> In deciding between these alternatives, I must consider
> the finding in the Pre-Sentence Report that the offender
> is a "high risk to re-offend". A number of the factors that
> are delineated in that finding are intrinsic to the offender's
> background over which she has had very limited control,
> for example, being born in a remote, impoverished and
> deprived First Nation community. The Pre-Sentence
> Report indicates Ms. Audy's parents endured residential
> school and the resulting impact, particularly on Ms. Audy's
> mother, caused Ms. Audy to have an unstable upbringing.
> In my view, a more significant factor is that Ms. Audy is
> 29-years-old and has no prior criminal record. While the
> assessment tool utilized in the Pre-Sentence Report has its
> uses I must consider the fact that up to this point in spite
> of the factors considered the offender has been able to stay
> out of trouble. In these circumstances, *I do not regard the
> finding in the Pre-Sentence Report that Ms. Audy is at high
> risk to re-offend as being of great significance. What is of
> significance is the fact that the offender is a member of a First
> Nation.* Manitoba has a very high number of First Nation
> members who are incarcerated. Both the provisions of the
> *Criminal Code* and Supreme Court of Canada decisions
> interpreting those sections are clear that, when possible,
> incarceration should not be imposed where other sanctions

are reasonably available and that this is particularly so with respect to First Nation offenders.[502]

In this respect, Judge Slough chooses to look behind the pre-sentence risk assessment and examines the aspects of Audy's life that emerge from processes of colonization, factors "over which she has had very limited control," and which must be considered with emphasis given to the over-representation of Indigenous peoples in prison. Inherent in this under-standing, is Judge Slough's recognition that colonization has constrained Audy's options such that she became vulnerable to criminalization for the same reasons that have elevated the risk she is projected to present. In-terestingly, Judge Slough focuses not on Audy's assessed, projected risk to reoffend, but instead on the "more significant factor[s]" that she "is 29-years-old and has no prior criminal record," and that she "is a member of a First Nation." This reasoning demonstrates a holistic, contextualized view of her criminalization, particularly against the fact that the PSR does the opposite by acknowledging Audy's lack of a criminal record but ad-vancing her assessed high risk to reoffend in the face of it.

Judge Slough orients the decision around issues consistent with the goals of *Gladue*: the understanding that "risk factors" must be situated within and not subsume or supplant *Gladue* factors, and the broader problem of the overrepresentation of Indigenous peoples in prison. The respective reasoning engaged by the victimization-criminalization con-tinuum and the *Gladue* analysis cannot be interchangeably transposed because they involve different primary focuses (gendered vulnerabili-ties and colonization). However, they certainly implicate shared issues, such as how experiences of victimization inform both the victimization-criminalization continuum and the contextualization of colonization. This overlap means that incorporating the primary focus of the other enriches each analysis, such that the *Gladue* analysis for a criminalized Indigenous woman is understood to have a gendered dimension, and that her experiences of victimization are understood within the context of colonization, with the imperative to reduce overincarceration.

This interplay is evident in Judge Slough's decision to depart from the risk assessment in *Audy*. For example, Judge Slough chooses to look behind the risk assessment put forth by the pre-sentence report, which identifies that (among other factors deemed relevant to Audy's projected risk) her "own victimization issues and her problem with depression"[503] increase her risk level and should impact her sentence. Judge Slough chooses to understand Audy's "victimization issues" in the context of her *Gladue* factors. The judge recognizes that Audy was vulnerable to many of the issues contributing to her elevated risk assessment for systemic reasons beyond her control, and prioritizes the goals of *Gladue* to ameliorate overincarceration above other concerns. While the judgment is concise and only briefly discusses Audy's personal history, through nuanced reasoning, Judge Slough sensitively complies with the later-decided *Ipeelee*.

In terms of the victimization-criminalization continuum, Judge Slough contextualizes Audy's experiences of victimization within colonization, and uses that framework to decide that perfunctory adherence to the pre-sentence report would produce an unjust sentence per *Gladue*. The judge also highlights that Audy has not been criminalized until this offence. Through this reasoning, the judge contextualizes Audy's offence within *Gladue* factors, locating the victimization-criminalization continuum in the macrocosmic cycle of the overrepresentation of Indigenous peoples in prison, and prioritizes the latter. This reflects how the continuum and consideration of *Gladue* factors deepen the overall analysis when read together. Judge Slough's integration of these considerations is particularly significant because the PSR evinces an antithetical view about how *Gladue* factors should inform Audy's sentence, and about her projected trajectory through victimization and criminalization (in the assessment that she presents a high risk to reoffend). This means that the judge had to wade through some conceptual and structural resistance when navigating the decision, making it more noteworthy.

Through this judicial attention to the victimization-criminalization continuum within the context of colonization, the sentence both responds to *Gladue* factors and achieves the necessary "deterrence and denunciation" but "without the use of incarceration."[504] Perhaps this sensitivity was partly inspired (or at least facilitated) by what the judge describes as the "valuable 'Gladue Report'"[505] contained within the pre-sentence report (which must refer to a *Gladue*-related subset of her PSR, not a stand-alone *Gladue* report). It does illustrate the utility (in terms of reaching appropriate sentences in the spirit of *Gladue*) of judicial understanding about how experiences of victimization impact the lives of the Indigenous women appearing before them. Judge Slough's reasoning demonstrates that this understanding must be refracted through a nuanced, contextualized lens that does not pay blind fealty to the trajectory to criminalization mapped by PSRs that overemphasize risk assessments, at the expense of the broader picture.

Shore and *Audy* are particularly significant because the judges in each case were not only able to engage in this nuanced analysis, but did so against the current of pre-sentence reports indicating that the Indigenous women involved presented high risk levels. This is significant for the inherent commitment to *Gladue* and for the judicial willingness to avoid overreliance on PSRs where prioritizing the risk assessments would produce an unjust result. Departing from pre-sentence reports in such cases is also commendable because of the typical judicial tides: Kelly Hannah-Moffat and Paula Maurutto write, "Existing research demonstrates that the PSR plays a central interpretive role in sentencing," and "Canadian studies report an 80 per cent concordance rate between PSR recommendations and dispositions and demonstrate a high level of judicial satisfaction with these reports."[506]

These issues are critical to the problem of Indigenous overrepresentation because the judges in *Shore* and *Audy* primarily decided to depart from the risk assessments as they recognized that the extension of following those assessments would be misaligned from the goals of *Gladue*. As I discussed earlier, Hannah-Moffat and Maurutto differentiate between PSRs and *Gladue* reports primarily on the basis that PSRs are oriented around risk, whereas *Gladue* reports offer information contextualized within colonization. They also find that *Gladue* factors may be reconstructed as risk factors, such that criminalized Indigenous persons are "characterized as high risk and high need."[507] Within this context, the judicial reasoning in *Shore* and *Audy* both signify critical recognition that there must be a shift in emphasis away from the assessed risk factors that often reflect systemic problems and toward responding to the problem of the overincarceration of Indigenous women at sentencing.

Eulalie Ussak

In *R. v. Ussak*, the judge both approaches evidentiary problems in a manner reflecting a delicate understanding of issues navigated by criminalized women who are themselves victims of abuse, and (despite a quite minimal *Gladue* analysis) also appreciates the broader nature of systemic issues experienced by Indigenous persons in the criminal justice system. After a guilty plea to a manslaughter charge, Justice S. Cooper sentences Eulalie Ussak to prison for one year (then reduced by time and a half for pre-sentence custody) and probation for two subsequent years. Ussak had been in a relationship with the deceased for nine years, who verbally and physically abused her throughout (including sexual abuse, although the judgment qualifies this to some degree), intensifying toward the end. She is a mother of two teenage daughters from a previous relationship, and a grandmother to two children. On the date of the offence, Ussak had returned "very tired"[508] from a trip for her work with a youth correctional institution to find her partner again drinking in the shack, and became increasingly frustrated when he refused to stop to spend time with her and the family in their shared house. Justice Cooper notes the "evidence is clear" that Ussak's partner consistently "drank heavily and was abusive when drunk," producing a "constant state of tension" in the family.[509] The judge also indicates that Ussak associated the shack with her partner's drinking and abuse, making it "quite understandable" that Ussak "viewed the shack as being part of the problem."[510] Ultimately, on the offence date, the situation deteriorated; her partner yelled at Ussak in his recurrent accusation that she did not maintain a clean house, and she was overheard yelling both to her partner and a neighbour that she was going to burn the shack down. She then poured gasoline in the driveway to the shack and left with her family while her partner "continued yelling at her, calling her a whore, a slut, and a pig."[511] While driving away minutes after, they saw the shack in flames, but Ussak decided to wait before calling the fire department (her daughter later called). The judge states that there is "no suggestion" of "battered women's syndrome," self-defence, or provocation before the court.[512]

The way in which the judge treats what might otherwise be regarded as problems in the evidence demonstrates an understanding evoking the victimization-criminalization continuum. Justice Cooper notes various inconsistencies or variations in the information in the pre-sentence report, such as among the included reports by the forensic psychologist, evidence provided by Ussak, and other information. The judge describes that certain information "appears contradictory," and other seeming discrepancies involve where Ussak, "over time," describes her relationships with her mother, first husband, and her deceased partner "as more difficult or abusive than she initially did."[513] However, instead of finding that the evidentiary discrepancies undermine Ussak's credibility, the judge accepts that she expressed a greater level of comfort with the forensic psychologist than with the author of the pre-sentence report who interviewed her. Justice Cooper determines that "it is not unusual for women in abusive relationships to hide the abuse, even from those they are close to. It takes time to establish a relationship of trust, such that anyone feels comfortable sharing details of their intimate lives. I accept that this accounts for some of the apparent inconsistencies in the information provided by Ms. Ussak."[514] Moreover, Justice Cooper holds it is "not in dispute" that Ussak experienced abuse from her partner.[515] Expanding the scope of this finding, Justice Cooper cites an Ontario Court of Appeal decision for the principle that, on sentencing, a "judge must assess the mitigating significance of abuse suffered by the offender at the hands of the victim, not by reference to the nature of the abuse but rather, by the impact the abuse has on the offender."[516]

In the Introduction, I register my discomfort with judicial reliance on and usage of s. 718.2(a)(ii) to increase the sentence of Indigenous women whose offences occur in relation to their abusive partners. Justice Cooper says this section "states that evidence that the offender, in committing the offence, abused the offender's spouse or common-law partner, shall be deemed to be an aggravating circumstance on sentence."[517] This provision leaves room for judicial discretion; s. 718.2(a)(ii) directs that a court shall "take into consideration" that a sentence should be increased "for any relevant aggravating circumstances relating to the offence or the offender," including evidence that the person being sentenced abused his or her partner.[518] Justice Cooper correctly exercises this discretion, suggesting, in contrast to the judicial norm, that "the policy reason for the statutory provision may not be as compelling in circumstances where the offender before the court was the victim of abuse throughout the relationship."[519] Given the frequency with which this aggravating factor is uncritically applied and given weight in sentencing determinations, this is a significant judicial statement for Indigenous women whose offences are against their abusive partners. Justice Cooper cites a decision from Justice David Watt of the Ontario Superior Court of Justice, who writes about that case that "the recorded instances of abuse were more directed towards the accused than initiated by her. It seems somewhat incongruous to consider conduct that often results from years of abuse to be aggravated by the simple fact that the deceased-abuser and accused-killer stood in a defined relationship to each other."[520] As such, instead of applying s. 718.2(a)(ii) to aggravate the sentence, given that Ussak committed the manslaughter against her partner, Justice Cooper finds the opposite, writing that "the abusive nature of the relationship played some role in the events of that evening and are mitigating on sentence."[521]

In addition to effectively using the lens of the victimization-criminalization continuum to guide her reasoning, Justice Cooper also takes a broad (though cursory) approach to the *Gladue* analysis. While the judge cites neither *Gladue* nor *Ipeelee*, she references s. 718.2(e) and notes that consideration of Ussak's Indigenous circumstances is her judicial duty. There is only limited discussion of the *Gladue* analysis, and it is unclear whether the judge had been provided with a *Gladue* report, or even a *Gladue*-related component to the pre-sentence report (the judgment itemizes the discrete sources of information considered by the court, and *Gladue* information is not explicitly listed). Justice Cooper refers to an unreported decision to provide some background about systemic factors contributing to high levels of criminalization and incarceration in Nunavut, including the intergenerational effects of residential schools, poverty, the pervasiveness of intimate violence and suicide, and insufficient housing, education, and employment. Significantly, despite the minimal nature of any explicit *Gladue* analysis, Justice Cooper finds, "Although the impact of these systemic factors may not have directly impacted on Ms. Ussak's family home during childhood, she is part of a wider community and population within which *all members are impacted*. The fact that Ms. Ussak has, to a great extent, been able to overcome these influences only speaks to her personal strength."[522] The judge's decision to interpret the ways in which *Gladue* factors did *not* directly affect Ussak's life as being attributed to her own fortitude is compelling in that it arguably turns the problem of individualizing reasoning on its head. Ussak is understood as being inevitably impacted by systemic factors as a member of her community, and to whatever extent her history demonstrates she has been less visibly affected than she might have been, this is to her credit (that is, Justice Cooper particularizes or "individualizes" the way in which she has seemingly managed to evade some of the possible systemic factors in a manner that reinforces the judge's overall contextualized reasoning).

This characterization of and related inference from Ussak's personal background is quite striking, though not entirely isolated. Using related reasoning in another judgment, Justice Butler notes Robyn Hansen was raised at the confluence of "the lives of three generations of women impacted by residential schools, drug addiction, alcoholism, and sexual abuse,"[523] finds various changes she has since made to her own circumstances mitigating, and comments, "These steps towards rehabilitation have *even greater significance in the context of her background circumstances as an Aboriginal. If she can sustain her new lifestyle, she will have broken the pattern of drug abuse, alcoholism, and lack of parental responsibility which has persisted in her family and community for at least three generations. This is significant and worthy of support."[524] Justice Butler determines that this contributes to the need to "reduce the sentence below the usual range."[525] Similarly, when sentencing Samantha Rodrigue, who has "Inuvialuit, of Inuit and Gwich'in heritage" through her mother,[526] Judge Cozens finds mitigating that, "given her background and the negative factors that Ms. Rodrigue has had to deal with in her childhood, she has done remarkably well to achieve the level of success that she has without, other than this offence, becoming involved in the criminal justice system or struggling to overcome long-term substance abuse issues. When I add into this her having to deal with the stress and turmoil associated with living in a situation in which domestic violence has occurred and managing to raise two children, it is all the more remarkable."[527]

Without minimizing the significance of such contextualized judicial reasoning, at times the line between individualized and contextualized thinking may be more narrow than it might initially appear. When sentencing Ernestine Elliott, from the Chemainus (Stz'uminus) band and then the Cowichan Tribes through marriage, Judge Brooks comments that "her absence of criminal record borders on astonishing when her background is taken into account," and that "the only conclusion to draw is that there is at Ms. Elliott's core a person who can be a strong person that can withstand pressures to commit offences."[528] I suggest that although this comment remains within the realm of the examples of contextualized reasoning I provide above from *Ussak*, *Hansen*, and *Rodrigue*, it also implies that its opposite can also be true. That is, it simultaneously implies that if Elliott had a lengthy criminal record, this either would be expected, given her background, or would signify that, at her core, she is a weak person who could not resist pressures to offend; this corollary immediately decontextualizes the analysis in a manner that slides into the individualization of issues that should be understood as systemic. I note this potential narrowness in the distance between contextualized and individualizing reasoning not to problematize or undermine the validity of the above comments from *Ussak*, *Hansen*, *Rodrigue*, and *Elliott*, but rather to observe some inherent fragility in the balance.

This contextualized approach to cases in which criminalized Indigenous women's lives have been seemingly less impacted by certain systemic factors (or cases in which criminalized Indigenous women move through such issues in a positive direction) should be contrasted with other cases in my research. For example, when engaging in the *Gladue* analysis while sentencing Métis woman Danielle Spence, Justice Gabrielson comments about the pre-sentence report that "she reports no adverse experiences related to her cultural heritage," adding, "No other evidence was presented during the sentencing hearing to indicate that any of the '*Gladue* factors' would be mitigating in the circumstances of this case."[529] Similarly, where I discuss above cases that erroneously suggest that a causal connection between Indigenous systemic and background factors and a given offence must be established, I note that Justice Aitken determines that Diane Serré has "not personally suffered from many of the systemic problems,"[530] and comments, "It cannot be said that, due to your Aboriginal heritage and the systemic factors that have hurt Aboriginal people in this country, your education was hampered, your income was negatively impacted, you had periods of unemployment or underemployment, you were susceptible to substance abuse issues, or your mental health suffered. In other words, there is no evidence to suggest that your life experience as an Aboriginal in some way reduces your moral culpability for these offences."[531]

In the discussion above about how such a causal connection is not required, I also note that, when sentencing Lucille Littlecrow, Justice Gabrielson writes in a decision preceding *Ipeelee* that the pre-sentence report "does not indicate" that she had been "disadvantaged in any way that could be related to the offence which she committed."[532] When sentencing Danielle Chamakese, Justice R.S. Smith refers to her being from the Pelican Lake Reserve, and later suggests, "It is interesting to note, however, that the *Gladue* factors that are often invoked are not present in Ms. Chamakese's life. Ms. Chamakese comes from a supportive family. She graduated from Grade 12 and has no previous criminal conviction."[533]

I point to these elements of those decisions here to illustrate the importance of the finding by Justice Cooper that while Ussak may not have been directly impacted by *Gladue* factors, "all members" of her broader community are impacted (thereby including Ussak).[534] As such, while the aspects of the judicial reasoning in *Ussak* that reflect an approach consistent with the victimization-criminalization continuum demonstrate much greater depth of analysis than the comparatively paltry (and not expressly named) *Gladue* analysis, even that brief discussion of issues related to s. 718.2(e) presents a similar (and noteworthy) judicial impulse to contextualize systemic issues, locating them within colonization and its wholesale effects on Indigenous communities.

Different Focuses Sharing the Victimization Overlap

Often engaged by the discussion of *Gladue* factors, the victimization-criminalization continuum frequently appears in some form in the judgments, either implicitly through how the issues from the PSR or *Gladue* report are presented and discussed, or through distinct judicial pronouncements on the variables contributing to the women's offending and any related implications on sentencing. The *Gladue* analysis and the victimization-criminalization continuum contribute different focuses: the former focuses on the reverberating effects of colonization and the need to ameliorate the overrepresentation of Indigenous peoples in prisons, and the latter focuses on gendered responses to experiences of victimization that leave women vulnerable to criminalization. Even more significantly, the continuum has been developed through and with an expressly feminist orientation (and may effectively be incorporated within sentencing decisions by particularly sensitive judges, but is not otherwise provided for through any institutionalized legal structure), whereas the *Gladue* analysis is a construction designed specifically for the sentencing process, which is not inherently a feminist exercise (nor is the criminal justice system a feminist institution). However, while oriented toward different matters, both the *Gladue* analysis and the victimization-criminalization continuum implicate similar considerations and point to a similar need for contextualization. The overlap is victimization issues: the victimization-criminalization continuum has victimization at its core, and the *Gladue* analysis engages judicial consideration of criminalized Indigenous persons' systemic experiences of victimization (which, within my expansive definition of victimization, includes substance abuse, violence, and other forms of abuse/neglect, and alongside oppression/abandonment by the state), as these experiences are often tied to colonization.

Given the manifestation of criminalized Indigenous women's victimization histories in both the victimization-criminalization continuum and the *Gladue* analysis, but due to differences in the orientations of each mode of analysis, the way in which these women's histories of victimization may be interpreted and used by judges may not be compatible (indeed, may be directly contradictory) where elements of each form of analysis converge. At times, the effect of this victimization overlap can involve a doubling, or neutralization, of related issues, such as where experiences of victimization are embedded within and function as both mitigating and aggravating factors. Echoing my discussion regarding *Whitford* above, defence counsel for Leah Florence identifies this issue in her sentencing hearing, submitting that "since one of the systemic factors affecting Ms. Florence as an aboriginal, her exposure to spousal abuse, also forms part of the aggravating factors . . . there is a tension between the *Criminal Code* and *Ipeelee*."[535] Similarly, due to the overlap of Indigenous women's victimization histories in the two (interrelated) modes of analysis (in which these histories may function differently when understood through the lens of the victimization-criminalization continuum versus the *Gladue*—or broader sentencing—analyses), criminalized Indigenous women's experiences of victimization can also simply operate to aggravate, even where it seems such histories should be encompassed within *Gladue* factors, and thereby functioning to mitigate. For example, in sentencing Eliza Ross, Justice Maher includes within her aggravating factors that she, "since she was 13 years of age, has abused alcohol."[536]

Some judgments are quite sensitive about issues related to the victimization-criminalization continuum and its interconnections with the *Gladue* analysis. However, other judgments present problems in one or both of these forms of analyses, such as where the applicability of the *Gladue* analysis is minimized because of inappropriate judicial requirements that *Gladue* factors be directly linked to the offence(s). Andrew Welsh and James R.P. Ogloff find that, even in such cases, Indigenous status "may have an indirect effect" because "prior criminal history, lower socio-economic status, and offence seriousness are more directly associated with sentencing outcome."[537] Some cases within my study that I did not discuss above offer impoverished representations of the issues involved in the *Gladue* analysis, making it difficult to discern *how* the sentencing outcome was achieved vis-à-vis *Gladue* factors. For example, in *R. v. Evaloardjuk,* Justice R. Kilpatrick comments, "It is clear that Suzanne has had a disadvantaged background. The court will not review this in detail, as it was outlined at some length by her counsel in speaking to sentence."[538] Similarly, in *R. v. Elias,*[539] Judge Cozens states, "In sentencing Ms. Elias I must consider her First Nations status. I apologize to Mr. Clarke [defence counsel] who has just recently heard much of this verbatim,"[540] in another case decided proximate to that sentencing.

Equally, in other cases, the judge makes explicit how the *Gladue* analysis has factored into sentencing determinations, even where the judge consciously elects not to detail the personal circumstances giving rise to various *Gladue* factors. For example, in an oral judgment sentencing Jenna McClements, due to the "very personal and sensitive nature" of the information in her *Gladue* report and other submissions, Judge Ruddy determines (presumably with an eye to discretion for her privacy, and perhaps to protect against possible retraumatization) that "it is both unnecessary and, to some extent, inappropriate for me to go into extensive detail in this decision" as a result.[541] Nonetheless, even in the absence of divulging that more comprehensive discussion of her *Gladue* factors, Judge Ruddy both emphasizes having considered all that omitted information and moreover states explicitly that "her history and background, the issues she is struggling with as a result of that history and background, her Aboriginal status, the issues that have arisen in her family flowing back to the residential school system and abuse within that system"[542] (in conjunction with McClements's minimal criminal record) cause the judge to give serious consideration to ordering a conditional sentence order. Similarly, in an oral judgment sentencing Melissa Bourke, Judge Gorin declines to publicly detail her personal history with respect to *Gladue* factors. Nonetheless, Judge Gorin also finds that while s. 718.2(e) "does not apply directly in the sense that I am not being asked to consider imprisonment," the SCC directs that *Gladue* factors may still "lessen the moral blameworthiness."[543] Expressly following *Ipeelee*, the judge consequently decides on a sentence based on "a more restorative approach,"[544] ordering conditional discharges for each offence and probation orders, with the hope of leaving Bourke without a criminal record on successful completion of probation. Judge Gorin also effectively injects an understanding of where the victimization-criminalization continuum intersects with the *Gladue* analysis, observing, "It is often far more difficult for people who come from such a background to stay out of trouble with the law all of their lives. When one comes from a background like that of Ms. Bourke the likelihood of criminal behavior increases."[545]

In other cases, such as *R. v. Keeping*, the judge seems to differentiate between reasoning aligned with the victimization-criminalization continuum and that within a *Gladue* analysis to a degree, but still acknowledges the interrelationship between the two modes of analysis. In sentencing Gail Keeping for theft both under and over $5,000, Justice Robert P. Stack notes having considered "her status as an Inuk woman" as "part of her antecedents," despite neither counsel's having highlighted this.[546] Justice Stack opens the judgment with the comment that "George Keeping takes his surname literally; at least he did regarding his long-suffering wife, Gail,"[547] which both conveys patriarchal stereotypes (suggesting imagery of a husband figure who controls "his woman") and is minimizing (regarding the "long-suffering" characterization), given that Gail Keeping was living in a violent relationship with her spouse whose methods of control included physical, emotional, and financial abuse. Notwithstanding this opening, throughout the rest of the judgment, Justice Stack consistently contextualizes Gail Keeping's offending behaviours (both her limited criminal record, and the offences for which she is being sentenced in this judgment) within her experiences of victimization in that relationship. The judge even goes so far as to suggest the thefts of monies for the current offences are "in the nature of a self-help remedy."[548] Ordering a conditional discharge with two concurrent six-month terms of probation, Justice Stack determines that Keeping's "Inuk heritage appears to play less of a role in her circumstances than does her status as a victim of domestic abuse. Unfortunately the two are related, as are her mental health issues, substance abuse and lack of self-esteem."[549] Including her ostensible "lack of self-esteem" within the various systemic issues that contribute to her criminalization seems extrinsic and unhelpfully individualizing, but, overall, the judge engages in reasoning both consistent with the victimization-criminalization continuum and in a manner that drives the decision, as the *Gladue* analysis is framed as interrelated but otherwise secondary.

Perhaps the jurisprudential landscape that continues to unfold after *Ipeelee* will reflect increasingly thoroughgoing *Gladue* analyses, although the extent to which this follows should be monitored on an ongoing basis, particularly where the shape and movements of judicial reasoning is opaque. As articulated by Justice George in a decision discussed above, "more often than not the principles relevant to the sentencing of aboriginal offenders are spoken of but in the result seem to mean little. Sometimes they're outright ignored."[550] At times, it is challenging to evaluate how *Gladue* and the direction and clarifications in *Ipeelee* are received by judges. For example, in *R. v. SMC*, in sentencing S.M.C. from the James Smith Cree Nation, Judge Garth N. Smith mentions multiple times having considered her *Gladue* factors and ultimately administers a (federal) sentence that falls roughly between the respective sentencing positions of defence and Crown counsel, but also writes, "The sentencing principle s. 718.2(e) of the *Criminal Code* that refers to community based sentencing does not apply to SMC because she is to be sentenced to imprisonment for more than 2 years, and so will not be eligible for a community based sentence. The Supreme Court of Canada has not expressed that the total sentence needs to be different or lowered for *Gladue* factors when an offender is not being considered for a community based sentence. *Ipeelee* did not change what *Gladue* said. There is no reason to discount the sentence for SMC, considering her *Gladue* factors."[551]

As I outlined in the Introduction, *Gladue* requires a change in the "method of analysis" when judges are sentencing Indigenous persons.[552] This specialized mode of analysis is not specific to cases in which community sentences are available, and neither is it exclusive to determinations about the duration of sentence orders, making comments such as those quoted from Judge Smith above difficult to parse when attempting to discern whether judges are properly engaging in that analysis. Taken in isolation, the above comments seem to dangerously approach the error clarified by *Ipeelee* that some judges have wrongly inferred from *Gladue* that *Gladue* principles are inapplicable to serious offences.[553] Even where judges directly state they have considered *Gladue* factors, sometimes it is difficult to determine from the decision how those considerations actually and meaningfully influenced the reasoning and final sentence.

I noted in the Introduction that in *Ipeelee*, Justice LeBel finds that judges must apply *Gladue* principles "in every case" involving the sentencing of an Indigenous person, including those cases that may be considered "serious" (even though offences are not defined as such in the Criminal Code), and that "failure to do so constitutes an error justifying appellate intervention."[554] It seems that this clarification is sometimes lost. For example, in the oral judgment sentencing Aimee McIntyre for second-degree murder, Justice Sosna notes that "defence counsel concedes" that her Indigenous "status as set out in" *Gladue* "should not be considered a mitigating factor, although it may be relevant to McIntyre's future rehabilitation"[555] (the judge's use of the word "concedes" indicates agreement with this conclusion). In another case in which offence seriousness seems to prompt the judge to cast *Gladue* principles aside, when sentencing P.O. and her co-accused for failing in their legal duty to provide the necessaries of life to a child, Justice W.F. Gerein interprets *Ipeelee* to say "*Gladue* does not automatically have application in every case"[556] (rather, *Ipeelee* directs that "application of the *Gladue* principles is required in *every* case involving an Aboriginal offender").[557] It is understandable from the facts that the judge anticipates that "a person looking at the event is bound to feel a sense of horror."[558] However, while Justice Gerein recognizes that the *Gladue* factors experienced by P.O. and her co-accused "flow from their past right into the present," the judge finds that "little or no effect can be given to that,"[559] because "they must know right from wrong,"[560] and "it is not possible to conclude that poverty, abuse, substance abuse or racism contributed to the wrongful treatment of the victim herein. Anyone with even a minimum intelligence knows that it is wrong to mistreat a child, especially a very young one. That knowledge is instinctive and independent of living conditions in either the past or the present."[561] (Although part of the judge's apparent revulsion seems to stem from the differential treatment among their children by P.O. and her co-accused, the substance of the above comments remains antithetical to the spirit and import of *Gladue*.)

Further, in reference to the *Gladue* quote that "generally, the more violent and serious the offence the more likely it is as a practical reality that the terms of imprisonment for aboriginals and non-aboriginals will be close to each other or the same,"[562] *Ipeelee* indicates that this comment has been given "unwarranted emphasis" and has been "erroneously interpreted" by judges to suggest that serious offences are exempt from the application of *Gladue* principles.[563] However, even this clarification seems at times subject to continued misinterpretation. In sentencing Valerie Sack from the Indian Brook First Nation for "a number of property-related and bail-violation charges,"[564] which, Judge Del W. Atwood suggests, occurred within "a fairly extensive enterprise" that constituted "high-dollar-value thefts . . . all intended to support a deep-seated drug habit,"[565] the judge writes, "I recognize, as well, as the Supreme Court of Canada stated in *R. v. Ipeelee,* at para. 84, that as the seriousness and the frequency of crime committed by a First-Nations' offender increase, the sentences a court must consider are those that approximate much more closely those that would be imposed upon a non-aboriginal offender."[566]

Paragraph 84 in *Ipeelee*, quoting and clarifying *Gladue*, does not appear to actively suggest that increased offence seriousness means courts must consider more similar sentences to those of non-Indigenous persons (and it does not even mention offence frequency). Rather, it seems the exclusive purpose and meaning of this passage in *Ipeelee* is to clarify that the related quote from *Gladue* has been erroneously misconstrued to exclude serious offences from consideration of *Gladue* principles. Other cases do properly understand this direction from *Ipeelee*: Justice George sentences Tanya Peters (Pitwanakwat) from the Wikwemikong Reserve and the Munsee-Delaware Nation with an eye to reducing the duration of her sentence where possible, and comments upon the "most common myth" that the more serious the offence, the more similarly Indigenous and non-Indigenous persons should be sentenced, adding that "to suggest, as is often the case, that this is meant to be a rule of general application is inaccurate."[567]

As in *R. v. SMC* above, there continue to be cases post-*Ipeelee* that seem to overemphasize the issue of s. 718.2(e) not functioning to automatically reduce sentences for Indigenous persons at the expense of engaging in the more holistic and specialized changed method of analysis required by *Gladue*. When sentencing Keshia Saskatchewan, a woman "raised on the Hobbema Reserve, now known as Maskwacis,"[568] Judge Bruce R. Fraser asks, "How should the Offender's background as an Aboriginal affect the appropriate sentence?" and then states, "The Supreme Court said protection of the public cannot be automatically considered the paramount goal in sentencing but neither does Section 718.2(e) require an automatic reduction of the sentence simply because the offender is Aboriginal and experienced a very undesirable childhood not uncommon on that reserve. Surely the law is not that everyone from that reserve with a similar background who commits a serious violent offence is entitled to a lighter sentence or reduction in sentence and the purposes and principles of sentencing do not apply."[569]

It is worth noting that a "very undesirable childhood" refers to Saskatchewan's having been abandoned by her father at age eight; her mother's engaging in substance abuse; her removal by the state from her home and reserve, and later living in group homes, shelters, friends' residences, and on the street; having endured childhood physical and sexual abuse; and having been exposed to domestic violence as a child. Moreover, it seems incongruous to the goals and import of *Gladue* and *Ipeelee* to imply that because this background and victimization history are "not uncommon on that reserve," her sentence should not be reduced "simply because" of this context. Rather, it seems the inverse should be true: where a criminalized Indigenous person's victimization history is "not uncommon" on their reserve, this should be understood as an amplified *Gladue* factor, only underscoring the imperative to make determinations within the *Gladue* methodological approach. Further, the judge's characterization of s. 718.2(e) as purely an instrument of sentence reduction does not carry the spirit of the *Ipeelee* direction for restorative-oriented sentencing and greater sentence innovation in the sentencing of Indigenous persons.

The most sensitive judgments I discussed above, such as *Shore*, *Audy*, and *Ussak,* emerge where judges are able to incorporate elements of both the *Gladue* analysis and the victimization-criminalization continuum in the reasoning such that the overall analysis is deepened. I leave this chapter with two quotes, both from cases within my research, but each revealing different conceptions of the meaning of punishment for criminalized women who have experienced victimization. The first quote is taken from a case in which M.A.B., a member of the Manitoulin Island First Nation, pleaded guilty to trafficking in cocaine; in the throes of her own addiction, she had obtained the drug for an undercover police officer asking her where to buy it. Sentencing her to a ninety-day intermittent sentence followed by two years of probation, Judge Ayotte references the frustration of those "attempting to put a stop to this socially destructive conduct," but adds that "the resolution of that problem cannot be achieved by imposing excessive punishments on those who are often, in one sense at least, victims themselves."[570] Offering a different conception of the meaning and import of punishment for those both victimized and criminalized, the second quote emerges from one of the decisions discussed above. In this case, Justice Schuler comments, "If you are serious, Ms. Dennill, about becoming a nurse or about becoming able one day to take over the support and care of your son, then *the sentence can be your chance to get your life in order*, to put some effort into resolving your problems and to get away from your friends in the drug world, because you can be sure that they are not true friends."[571]

The first quote above implies that the experience of punishment can be destructive to those already struggling (or at minimum suggests that punishing those who are victimized is not productive for them or the larger society), whereas the latter quote suggests that punishment can be a juncture for change and healing. In Chapter 3, I explore judicial discourses engaging issues of healing, rehabilitation, and treatment. In reviewing the cases for my study, I noticed a pattern wherein judges ascribe these notions to the sanctions ordered—such as portraying or structuring sentences in ways that suggest imprisonment is an opportunity for healing.

CHAPTER 3

INCARCERATION WOUNDS: JUDICIAL DISCOURSES ABOUT HEALING

In *Ipeelee,* Justice LeBel agrees with the Court of Appeal's finding that the sentencing judge had performed an inadequate *Gladue* analysis, affirming that court's decision that rehabilitation should have been weighted more heavily and with greater transparency to fully conform to s. 718.2(e). Justice LeBel writes that the sentencing judge did describe one of the offender's "history in great detail, but she failed to consider whether and how that history ought to impact on her sentencing decision."[1] In this chapter I look at related impacts on judicial reasoning in terms of sanctions.

Throughout this book, I primarily intend to present conditional sentences in a positive light, in that they confer needed benefits in terms of their restorative orientation and consistency with the *Gladue* goal to ameliorate Indigenous overincarceration. Conditional sentences may also be effectively unavailable for Indigenous women experiencing housing insecurity or instability, or may be actively dangerous for Indigenous women ordered to serve them where that means forced confinement with an abusive partner. These concerns are serious and troubling, and point to the reality that conditional sentences remain prison sentences; more diverse, expansive, and flexible alternatives to incarceration are needed in the community (before and following criminalization) to better support the health and safety of Indigenous women vulnerable to the criminal justice system. Additionally, some features of conditional sentences (such as duration and abstinence conditions) may be challenging for various Indigenous women to complete without breaching. In prison, there is a disparity between treatment services available in provincial and federal institutions, which some judges advert to on sentencing, with various implications for the relative punitiveness of sanctions ordered. Given that some treatment services are provided in carceral settings, it is important to reflect on the securitization of mental health difficulties in prison, and on the inherent conflict within the institutional roles of prison psychologists and correctional officers. Both are part of the prison machinery with its institutional focus of security concerns. That is, structurally, prison staff are first invested in correctional issues, and only subsidiarily in the needs of the prisoners. This is one general example of the securitization of mental health problems in prison, but Ashley Smith's death in custody puts a face to this internal conflict. It is important to keep her institutional story in mind when examining mental health concerns and the experience of women prisoners.

Initially becoming criminalized and imprisoned as a youth and later transferred to adult federal custody, Smith was generally held in segregation,[2] and engaged in self-injurious behaviour, perhaps in an attempt to cope with her isolation.[3] Prison staff responses to her self-harm were security-based, frequently involving uses of force,[4] and the Correctional Investigator reports that her reactions to this intervention often resulted in the accumulation of additional criminal charges.[5] The Correctional Service of Canada (CSC) transferred Smith seventeen times within eleven and a half months[6] (which would have been distressing and destabilizing for anyone), largely for administrative reasons unrelated to her needs,[7] and without a correctional mental health plan.[8] Ultimately, CSC managers made an operational policy decision that frontline CSC staff were not to intervene immediately when Smith self-harmed,[9] "permitting [Smith] to retain ligatures in her possession for extended periods," as Michael Jackson and Graham Stewart describe.[10] On 19 October 2007, nineteen-year-old Smith tied a ligature around her neck in the manner she had many times before, and this time died, after CSC "staff failed to respond immediately to this medical emergency."[11] Following the Ontario coroner's inquest into Smith's death, on 19 December 2013, the jury delivered its verdict and recommendations, finding the cause of her death was homicide.[12]

Resonant with Smith's carceral story, the United Nations Office on Drugs and Crime (UNODC) reports, "Research indicates that female prisoners with mental health care needs are at particular risk of abuse, self-harm and deteriorating mental well-being in prisons."[13] Troublingly, UNODC finds that even "women without any mental health problems prior to imprisonment may develop a range of mental disabilities in prisons."[14] Such issues become further threatening and damaging for Indigenous women. The Canadian Association of Elizabeth Fry Societies (CAEFS) has argued to the Canadian Human Rights Commission that imprisonment "is culturally inappropriate" for Indigenous women, and that such "confinement . . . replicates the control and suppression of Aboriginal people by white colonizers from the time of first contact."[15] In the context of judicial sentencing discourses about Indigenous women's receiving treatment through imprisonment, Smith's tragic story of where institutional security issues systematically and thoroughly trump mental health concerns should be remembered alongside the other research and advocacy work about the detrimental effects of incarceration on women, and specifically Indigenous women. Finally, in moving to discourses about criminal justice responses to the types of narratives discussed in the previous chapter, I structure this chapter differently, no longer using subheadings demarcating specific Indigenous women's (criminal justice–oriented, institutionally constructed) histories of victimization and criminalization. This shift is intended to symbolize that the needs of Indigenous women at the centre of these judgments sometimes recede into the background, such as where incarceration is held out as a place of healing.

From the Victimization Overlap to Prison

In Chapter 2, I discuss what I call the "victimization overlap" between the victimization-criminalization continuum lens and the *Gladue* analysis, in that each form of analysis has a different focus, but both analyses (may, and, as I suggest, should) coincide where the court considers the systemic and background factors of Indigenous women. The extent to which the juncture where these analyses meet actually impacts judicial determinations about the sentence is clear in some decisions and murkier in others. As an example of where the judge makes plain how such analyses affect the final sentence, in a judgment I mention above, Judge Krahn finds that the sentence for Heather McKenzie-Sinclair "should be reduced given some diminishment" in her "moral culpability resulting from her disadvantaged and troubled background and her role in the offence."[16]

In this section, I examine the victimization overlap in terms of how judicial attention to criminalized Indigenous women's experiences of victimization (including where these experiences are implicated in *Gladue* analyses) relates to the discourses about imprisonment as healing. There are several examples of decisions in which judges thoughtfully and appropriately contextualize the Indigenous women's victimization histories within the *Gladue* analysis, such that the sentencing lens is restorative justice–oriented. One such properly contextualized case is *R. v. Pechawis*, because the judge specifically comments that the sentence must respond to the underlying causes of criminalization, ordering a conditional sentence. Using an appropriate contextualizing framework, the judges in *R. v. Fineday, R. v. Pawis*, and *R. v. Woods* also order conditional sentences. These decisions are noteworthy for their reasoning about how community sentences serve the rehabilitation needs of the women, whereas imprisonment would exacerbate their problems. The judge in *R. v. Tippeneskum* also contextualizes that Indigenous woman's victimization and criminalization within systemic factors. Although the judge ultimately orders a federal penitentiary sentence, the sentence may have been substantially longer if not for the contextual analysis. Similarly, the judge in *R. v. Kennedy* orders a federal term of incarceration, but also explicitly comments upon how the interrelationship between the woman's *Gladue* factors and history of victimization produce the need for a lower sentence than would otherwise be appropriate. In *R. v. Chartier*, the judge reduces what would otherwise be the appropriate (provincial) sentence after determining that a very lengthy prison term would be harmful to the woman involved, given her *Gladue* factors.

I turn primarily to three decisions wherein judges individualize and decontextualize the victimization histories and criminalization of the Indigenous women they sentence. In *R. v. Kendi,* the judge orders a conditional sentence, but uses an individualizing analysis of the victimization and criminalization of the woman before the court. In *R. v. Char,*[17] the judge also engages in individualizing logic, decontextualizing the difficulties of the woman being sentenced and offering an impoverished *Gladue* analysis, then assigning a prison sentence. Problematically, the judge defers to prison as the only place where this woman will be able to deal with those difficulties. The decision in *R. v. Diamond* is not entirely aligned with the other individualizing decisions in this section, because, in the end, the judge rejects the PSR's recommendation of a prison sentence for treatment purposes, instead ordering a conditional sentence (albeit a long sentence, and with a long probation order attached). However, it seems there are specific factual reasons motivating this choice (a community treatment centre accepted the woman). Without this support, the individualizing analysis of *Diamond* may have produced a different, more punitive result, particularly given that the judge frames that woman's personal difficulties as aggravating.

Contextualized Judicial Reasoning

In *Pechawis*, Judge Whelan sentences Sharlene Pechawis to an eighteen-month conditional sentence for trafficking in cocaine and Ritalin. Judge Whelan describes the "relatively long sentence" imposed as having conditions "which both restrict personal liberty and endeavor to respond to the underlying causes of the offending, including personal counseling and addictions treatment."[18] The causes Judge Whelan infers contributed to Pechawis's criminalization relate to her experiences of victimization. Pechawis grew up "on the Mistiwasis First Nation Reserve" and has a "very difficult background."[19] She experienced and witnessed extensive abuse within her immediate and extended family, dealt with the suicides of two brothers and her boyfriend, and lived through an abusive intimate relationship.[20] She misused alcohol, although her addiction to cocaine became more pervasive, and Pechawis "was selling small amounts of drugs to feed her addiction" at the time of the offences.[21] (In Chapter 1, I referenced research indicating a correlation between intimate violence and substance abuse, both generally and for marginalized women in particular.)[22]

Judge Whelan's express intention to respond to the causes of Pechawis's offending underscores the importance of thinking about how judges understand and represent women's pathways into criminalization. If sentences are structured in part "to respond to the underlying causes of the offending,"[23] as Judge Whelan writes, judicial understandings of how women are propelled and propel themselves along the continuum directly impact sentencing determinations. In this case, against Pechawis's own assertion in the pre-sentence report "that she needed counseling and believed that she would benefit from the treatment offered by Mistiwasis First Nation,"[24] the judge conveys that such treatment should also be understood as punishment: "I might add that the programming, especially the personal counselling, may, having regard to the unaddressed problems of the Accused, be regarded by the Accused to be punitive as well."[25] This formulation of the purpose of the sentence is consistent with Kent Roach's remark that "although judges may be influenced by restorative justice when crafting conditional sentences and other alternatives to imprisonment, they are still imposing punishment."[26] Equally, Judge Whelan's direction that Pechawis should recognize that the community programming conditions are punitive as well as healing-oriented alludes to the "healing through punishment, punishment through healing" discourses that are the subject of this chapter.

In *Fineday,* the judicial understanding of the background and actions of the woman being sentenced is contextualized instead of offering a purely individualized focus. Crystal Fineday is sentenced to a conditional sentence order of two years less a day followed by three years of probation for impaired driving causing death and that causing bodily harm. Fineday was "raised on the Sweetgrass First Nation," and was removed from her mother's care due to substance abuse issues,[27] having lost her father, who was alcoholic. Judge Mary Ellen Turpel Lafond observes, "Family breakdown and dislocation have impacted her life," but that Fineday "has shown remarkable commitment to overcoming poverty and the education gaps in her community."[28] The judge finds that *Gladue* considerations (including the strong support she has in the community), in addition to her youth and the absence of a criminal record, combine to make her "a suitable candidate for a restorative-based sentence."[29]

Engaging one of the issues Chief Judge Barry Stuart cited in *R. v. Elias* about the conditional sentencing regime post-*Proulx*, Judge Turpel Lafond comments, "The length of the conditional sentence will be longer than a jail term would have been, in light of the fact that the accused will be allowed to serve it in the community."[30] However, while the duration of Fineday's sentence exceeds that of the prison alternative and is more punitive in that sense, Judge Turpel LaFond is mindful of the deleterious risk posed by imprisonment and the more restorative potential of a community sentence. The judge explains:

> Rehabilitative and restorative objectives may be met by
> a community sentence since institutional incarceration
> can sometimes impede the rehabilitation of an offender.
> Conditions of an order might be crafted to respond to the
> offender's specific needs. Since he or she is not imprisoned,
> the offender can, in appropriate cases, also contribute to the
> community by educating others about the perils of drinking
> and driving. Furthermore, the more productive a member of
> the community, especially a young woman, the stronger the
> impulse should be to keep the individual in the community
> given that her life would be permanently altered by exposure to
> prison culture, possibly in the direction of future offending.[31]

Prison is here constructed as inconsistent with rehabilitation, whereas conditional sentences are framed as more conducive to healing. This construction is in large part because of the judge's decision to centrally position *Gladue* factors and their linkage with restorative-oriented sentences, instead of individualizing the factors leading to Fineday's criminalization. Because Judge Turpel LaFond contextualizes Fineday's victimization and criminalization within the *Gladue* analysis, the lens through which she sentences Fineday becomes a restorative lens, producing an outcome consistent with the goals and spirit of *Gladue*.

In *Pawis*, discussed in Chapter 2, the forensic psychologist who prepared a forensic report and testified for the defence at the sentencing hearing juxtaposes how Nicole Pawis would likely experience incarceration against how she would experience a community sentence. He concludes that she is at greatest risk to the community if her sentence perpetuated her "early childhood trauma, her limited education and relative social isolation," leaving her "alienated and isolated without social and economic resources."[32] The psychologist recommends a community sentence "because it would ensure she participates in the needed services and programs," whereas, if incarcerated, "she might not receive the same level of services" and could be victimized and further isolated.[33] Justice Reinhardt constructs a sentence that responds to the psychologist's concerns that "incarceration would seriously harm her, in her path to maturity and full participation in society."[34] The judge orders a conditional sentence including six months of house arrest, noting, "More than six months would not be an appropriate requirement of her conditional sentence, because social isolation has been singled out by Dr. Haley as one of the determinative causes of her limited cognitive and social development. One of the most important goals for this sentence over the next five years should be to help her develop her social skills and to find ways to give her opportunities to improve her self [*sic*] by continuing education and employment training."[35] The psychologist's and in turn the judge's concentration on how her past experiences of victimization have isolated Pawis point toward a community sanction, yielding the image that imprisonment is not a place that cultivates the connectedness and support that are critical to most people's healing (and general well-being). This orientation, broadened past a purely individualistic focus, is facilitated by the extensive discussion of *Gladue* factors, drawn from the *Gladue* report filed.

Similarly, in *Woods*, also discussed in Chapter 2, Judge Whelan finds the pre-sentence report to be "of considerable assistance,"[36] and is "satisfied based on the advice of" its author that Candace Woods's "risk is manageable in the community, provided she is supervised under strict conditions."[37] The judge explains, "A period of incarceration at this stage, I fear, would be counter-productive to the very significant gains by Ms. Woods."[38] She has already "started down the road to rehabilitation" and "is highly motivated to maintain her status as a responsible contributing member of our community," having successfully complied with her restrictive bail conditions, "despite many changes and stressors in her living circumstances."[39] The objective of rehabilitation is foregrounded, and Judge Whelan omits certain conditions that would be more coercive, by declining to extend the electronic monitoring aspect of her bail conditions into those attached to her conditional sentence, in keeping with the recommendation by her bail supervisor. The list of optional conditions remains extensive, including a term of house arrest followed by a term of strict curfews that may undermine her ability to continue sex work to support herself, and, as directed by her probation officer/ conditional sentence supervisor, conditions requiring general forms of counselling or programming and participation in a program specifically for addressing substance abuse. Julian V. Roberts and Thomas Gabor caution that "increasing the number of conditions generally increases the likelihood that an offender will violate a condition."[40] However, due to the seriousness of the offence (robbery), Judge Whelan acknowledges that "a conditional sentence is exceptional in these circumstances."[41] In this light, it is significant that Judge Whelan emphasizes Woods's rehabilitative efforts and the continuation of that rehabilitation.

In *Tippeneskum*, Justice DiGiuseppe comments that, in addition to June Tippeneskum's youth and guilty plea, "the systemic factors that may have contributed to her offending behaviour require that due consideration be given to the sentencing objective of rehabilitation."[42] Justice DiGiuseppe contextualizes Tippeneskum's criminalization within her experiences of victimization, and the inherent interconnections with colonization, resonating with the victimization-criminalization continuum. There is tension in the judgment between the sentencing objective of rehabilitation and the judge's assessment from the case law provided by counsel that for this type of aggravated assault, the overriding objectives are denunciation and deterrence. It seems perhaps Justice DiGiuseppe assigns a lesser sentence than may have been ordered absent the considerations within victimization and colonization, although this is nowhere stated directly. Justice DiGiuseppe orders a three-and-a-half-year prison term. This sentence is not expressly oriented toward rehabilitation (and neither is it the "reformatory jail sentence" followed by a probationary term "to provide the structure and support needed to address rehabilitation"[43] sought by the defence), but is significantly less than the five- to seven-year range requested by the Crown. As such, it seems that while the aggravating factors "cry out for a significant jail term,"[44] the judicial reasoning connecting systemic factors along her pathway to criminalization contributes to a potential reduction in sentence duration, despite not being otherwise geared toward rehabilitation. While, again, the reasoning culminating in the three-and-a-half-year determination is not definitively clear, it appears that judicial understanding of systemic factors does impact the final sentence.

In *Kennedy*, Judge Christine Harapiak sentences Shanna Murdock alongside one of her two co-accuseds for robbery during a home invasion, breaching her recognizance, and theft under $5,000. Murdock is a young woman from the Valley River First Nation whose mother went to residential school, and Murdock became a mother herself at age fifteen. The judge reports that Murdock has retained strong relationships with her family, although her parents both dealt with alcoholism during her upbringing, her father was abusive, and she spent a year in foster care. The father of her two children was violent with Murdock, and served a prison term for assaulting her. She was in a relationship with one of her co-accuseds, and the judge accepts her mother's suggestion to the writer of the pre-sentence report that Murdock often strived to appease him.

Judge Harapiak specifically refers to the paragraph from *Ipeelee* that finds that the socio-economic deprivations and limitations experienced by many criminalized Indigenous persons may diminish their moral culpability, and also cites an Alberta Court of Queen's Bench decision for its comment that "few mortals could withstand such a childhood and youth without becoming seriously troubled,"[45] connecting this to proportionality. Ordering a three-and-a-half-year federal term of incarceration, Judge Harapiak expressly indicates having considered her *Gladue* factors, the limited relevance of her minimal criminal record, her "strong need to please" her co-accused, and "the pull of that desire to please in the context of her background of having been a victim of domestic violence and having been raised with violence."[46] Having contextualized Murdock's offences within both her victimization history and *Gladue* factors, the judge concludes that "her penalty should fall quite far below the usual range for this type of case"[47] (although, while the sentence ordered may be below that typically issued in similar cases, it is not a departure from the respective positions of counsel, remaining between the three to three-and-a-half years of imprisonment sought by the defence, and the four-year term sought by the Crown).

In *Chartier*, the judge finds that the experience of incarceration would be actively damaging for the specific woman being sentenced, given how *Gladue* factors have impacted her life, and reduces her sentence as a result. In sentencing Shelly Chartier from Chemawawin Cree Nation for extortion, uttering threats to cause bodily harm, fraud under $5,000, and personation, Judge Rolston finds from her pre-sentence report that her home community "epitomizes the impact of colonization," including issues of "substance abuse, family violence, high unemployment, low incomes, lack of educational opportunities, limited social supports and cultural loss."[48] The judge observes that Chartier "was not immune to her community's issues."[49] In a manner aligned with the victimization-criminalization continuum, Judge Rolston concludes that her creation of "an alternative fantasy existence on the internet," the domain of her offences, is a coping mechanism.[50] Given the direction from *Ipeelee* that the constrained circumstances of many criminalized Indigenous persons may function to reduce their moral culpability, the judge accordingly decides Chartier's "moral blameworthiness is diminished."[51] Judge Rolston finds that a conditional sentence would not be appropriate to the principles of sentencing, and identifies that a global sentence of "23 months of real jail" would be fit, before taking a "last look" to evaluate whether that initial sentence determination should be reduced for the principle of totality.[52] The judge concludes that, given her "lesser moral culpability due to the circumstances related to her background" (essentially, where the victimization-criminalization continuum and *Ipeelee* meet), and given that "she has lived a reclusive lifestyle," sentencing her to "real jail" would be "more difficult [for her] than [for] a typical first time offender."[53] As such, finding that, "based upon these factors, a 23 month sentence would be crushing to her,"[54] Judge Rolston reduces her sentences for each count, producing a cumulative sentence of eighteen months in prison followed by a probationary order of two years. Thus, in this decision, incarceration is deemed to be particularly oppressive for this specific woman, given her

Gladue factors and the way in which those systemic factors have shaped how she conducts her life, and that, together with her diminished moral culpability resultant from those same factors, produces a demonstrably and meaningfully lowered sentence.

Individualizing Judicial Reasoning

Gladue factors should immediately situate systemic issues in the centre of the judicial frame. Judge Anderson makes an almost explicit statement to this effect when sentencing L.M.L. from the Saddle Creek Nation, suggesting about her mental health concerns (which other cases often pathologize and individualize) that "life has taken a toll on" her,[55] and that her "general psychiatric condition is the product of a background that epitomizes the type of background circumstances identified in *Gladue* and which must be taken into account in attempting to arrive at a just sentence."[56] This type of contexualization is aligned with Renée Linklater's comment that individualizing lenses (those of psychiatry, in her discussion) frequently "[result] in pathologizing the experiences of Indigenous peoples who may be responding to colonization."[57] Because the relevance of *Gladue* may be variously undercut within judicial reasoning, when thinking about the operation of the victimization-criminalization continuum, it is useful to reflect on whether Indigenous women's pathways to offending are properly contextualized within systemic factors or are unhelpfully and inappropriately individualized. In their analysis of federally sentenced women eligible for parole, Sarah Turnbull and Kelly Hannah-Moffat find that "women's criminal histories were used as evidence of bad choices. . . . Through the decision narratives, the paroled subject is variously positioned as a victim, a follower, a recovering addict, someone who lacks sufficient impulse control and makes poor choices, and/or someone who suffers from low self-esteem. Her law-breaking is understood not in relation to larger social and material conditions, but as a consequence of her personal failures, which are considered to be her gendered 'risk factors.'"[58] These forms of the individualization of criminalized women's difficulties (abstracted from systemic factors) also feature in some cases I have consulted.

Individualizing judicial discourses can be particularly problematic where Indigenous women's offences involve resisting violence. CAEFS and NWAC have written that such resistance may lead to criminalization, as "the state has effectively trained many Aboriginal women to believe they are on their own in circumstances where they face violence,"[59] so they become structurally displaced and respond to violence in ways that seem/are necessary in the absence of support, which may produce criminal charges. The facts of *Kahypeasewat*, discussed in Chapter 2, seem to conform to this analysis. Largely, that decision does contextualize Kahypeasewat's violence within her own experiences of victimization (and particularly within her abusive relationship with the deceased). Individualizing victimization discourses may inadvertently reinforce the CAEFS and NWAC comment that the state has taught Indigenous women that they are isolated, alone to confront problems they experience.

Shoshana Pollack describes the way in which individualistic thinking obfuscates how social forces affect women's choices and offending: "Structural factors such as poverty, systemic racism and violence against women" become "reconstructed as being a result of individual psychological and cognitive deficits."[60] For example, when sentencing Carmine Nayneecassum from the Ahtahkakoop Cree Nation (who witnessed violence in her family as a youth, whose parents were both alcoholic, whose mother is a residential school survivor, and Nayneecassum herself later "struggled as a single parent"),[61] Judge Daunt notes that Nayneecassum "left her daughter with her parents"[62] to live on the streets, where the "winos and junkies . . . stole from her and . . . in turn, taught her how to steal."[63] Although the judge acknowledges that leaving her daughter with her parents was safe, in response to defence counsel submissions that Nayneecassum's *Gladue* factors reduce her moral blameworthiness, Judge Daunt concludes she "had choices," and "she chose the drugs over her daughter. She had options. It's not like she had nowhere to turn. If she wanted it, she knew where to get help, having accessed it before."[64]

Similarly recharacterizing systemic factors as individualized difficulties, in an oral judgment sentencing Teri Schinkel for offences including impaired driving causing bodily harm, Judge E. Dennis Schmidt notes that Schinkel's ex-boyfriend assaulted her twice that night (before she got into the car and then again inside the car), upon which, Schinkel reports, she was "traumatized by that event and out of her mind because of it and took off in the car."[65] (In the Crown appeal, which was dismissed apart from an amendment to the driving prohibition order, these assaults are further described as violent and by choking—the latter is one of the most dangerous forms of intimate partner violence—and that Schinkel "was being assaulted at the time that some of the poor driving was observed.")[66] Schinkel was "in such a state that she was very difficult to deal with for the paramedics,"[67] which the sentencing judge also describes as her "present[ing] herself as the victim in all of this to all and sundry."[68] In reference to various intergenerational issues connected to the residential schools in Schinkel's family history, Judge Schmidt comments that "now she is a mother herself and she is really carrying on with the same alcoholic and drug-addicted lifestyle that she saw and says that has traumatized her so badly. *Nobody knows why that happens.*"[69] Some decisions, such as *Schinkel*, are difficult to parse, because some of the thinking in the judgment is individualizing in the terms described by Pollack above, but yet still produces a sentence that seems properly adjusted due to *Gladue* principles (sixty days' incarceration served intermittently alongside two years of probation).

Pollack's comments about how systemic factors are recharacterized as individual failings can be telescoped to the particularization of mental health difficulties. Erin Dej argues about the pathologization and labelling of mental health problems (specifically, Fetal Alcohol Spectrum Disorder [FASD] diagnoses) that "psy-diagnoses reduce complex individual problems rather than seeing them as part of the social and structural inequalities facing Aboriginal communities."[70] In the decisions I discuss in this section, the thrust of the judicial discourses is that criminalized Indigenous women's difficulties are similarly attributed to how they choose to orient themselves in the world, and decontextualized from *Gladue* factors.

Within the overarching paradigm in which, as cited in *R. v. M(CA)*, "sentencing is an inherently individualized process,"[71] judicial understandings of the victimization-criminalization continuum can also relegate systemic issues contributing to offending to the periphery of the judicial reasoning. Focusing on the individualization of problems Indigenous women experience instead of contextualizing those issues within structural entanglements does not reflect the actual challenges that women experience in the community (where they grow up, where they live, where they raise their children, and where criminalized Indigenous women are serving conditional sentence orders, serving the balance of their sentences on probation, or upon reintegration). Judith Rumgay writes, "The stresses associated with poverty, residence in disadvantaged, possibly dangerous neighbourhoods, parenthood and problematic interpersonal relationships, are unlikely to disappear merely because the offender has committed herself to a pro-social identity."[72] Criminalized Indigenous women often contend with many structural barriers (and other obstacles/struggles derived from colonization and other forms of victimization) that must be addressed at the societal level, in the absence of which these women may become recriminalized.

In *Kendi*, Judge Bernadette E. Schmaltz orders Deborah Kendi to a fifteen-month conditional sentence followed by one year of probation for breaking and entering, mischief, and breaches of probation. This judgment references a previous proceeding at which Crown and defence entered a joint submission recommending a prison sentence of four months followed by probation, but the judge had concerns about the appropriateness of this sentence and reserved, directing the preparation of a pre-sentence report. Judge Schmaltz sought the PSR "to allow me to more fully consider Ms. Kendi's personal circumstances."[73] Having reviewed the PSR for this decision, Judge Schmaltz concludes that she has struggled through a difficult life. The fact that Kendi is an Indigenous woman is not mentioned in the judgment, *Gladue* factors are not discussed, and neither that decision nor s. 718.2(e) is cited. Notwithstanding these omissions, from the judgment it is at least probable that Kendi is Indigenous, although the cues are subtle: she committed the offences in Fort McPherson (a predominantly Indigenous community in the Northwest Territories where she has always lived), and she broke into the home of the then chief of the community, now an Elder. This is one of the judgments I identified that required me to carefully examine the text to discern whether the woman being sentenced was Indigenous. (I have since confirmed that Kendi is an Indigenous woman through a lawyer who told me she is from a Gwitch'in family.) There is no elucidated understanding of the victimization-criminalization continuum in the judgment, only allusions to Kendi's intoxication during the offences and comments that "her motivation was for the 'pure excitement'"[74] and "I do not know why Ms. Kendi continues to drink."[75] Her criminal history is detailed in an outline of her lengthy record.

Without any discussion of (or clear reference to) her life and *Gladue* factors, it seems plain that the judge did not incorporate these considerations into the reasoning for the sentence. Judge Schmaltz expresses apprehension that Kendi would regard another community-based sanction as an insubstantial consequence that would only amplify her "contempt for the criminal justice system,"[76] finding that the need to protect the public supersedes rehabilitative goals, because the rehabilitation-oriented sentences Kendi received in the past "have failed."[77] Nonetheless, the judge still concludes that a conditional sentence is most appropriate, drawing in part on Kendi's support system in the community and PSR assertions that she would abide by community-based conditions as ordered.

In absence of discussion about Kendi's life, there are few indications in the judgment about her vulnerabilities. Judge Schmaltz highlights only a few items from the overall "positive"[78] pre-sentence report, including its assertion that "jail is not a place she would like to come back to, and it is not like her to be in a place like this."[79] The judge does not expand further on Kendi's experience of imprisonment, except to emphasize that her community sentence order "is a jail sentence and it is not a lenient sentence."[80] The judge acknowledges that Kendi "may still have issues to deal with,"[81] but neither imprisonment nor a rehabilitative sanction is portrayed as an automatic salve to those issues: "The Court cannot force Ms. Kendi to change; a rehabilitative sentence can provide the tools, but it is up to Ms. Kendi to use them. To date Ms. Kendi has not taken the steps to change her behaviour."[82] Her rehabilitation is left to her to "[make] the choices she has to make to deal with her issues."[83]

The omission of any discussion of *Gladue* factors in the decision is glaring, perhaps even further highlighted by Judge Schmaltz's specific attention to the pre-sentence report (having reserved to allow for its preparation). The decision reveals little about Kendi as a person, including her trajectory into criminalization. Her criminal history is presented, but only itemized. Any narrative behind it is missing, despite the grip her repeated and ongoing criminalization has had on her life, given that she first entered the criminal justice system as a youth. Judge Schmaltz repeats the refrain "yet she continues to drink"[84] twice in the judgment—three times including the judge's reflection that "I do not know why Ms. Kendi continues to drink."[85] The judge does not address what difficulties may underlie her substance abuse. Instead, Judge Schmaltz comments, "I do not see that Ms. Kendi has much insight into the repercussions of her behaviour."[86] Overall, the judge does not contextualize Kendi's criminalization within systemic factors (neglecting to engage in any *Gladue* analysis entirely) and frames Kendi's difficulties as her own choices in the abstract (repeating that she persists in her decision to drink, and suggesting that rehabilitation is contingent on her making different choices).

Noting that Kendi must take responsibility for her own rehabilitation is not itself problematic, particularly against the backdrop where Judge Schmaltz observes that her previous rehabilitative-oriented sentences "have failed."[87] However, it becomes problematic to explain Kendi's criminalization and attempts to rehabilitate purely in these particularizing terms, absent contextualization within the *Gladue* analysis. It is additionally problematic in practical terms that the judge ultimately assigns a sentence of far greater duration than was requested in the joint submission between Crown and defence. It appears that Judge Schmaltz strives for a rehabilitative sentence. However, this becomes less apparent, given the sentence duration, in two respects. First, Judge Schmaltz finds that "a global sentence longer than 4 months is necessary to reflect the seriousness of these offences, to achieve the goals of deterrence and parity, and to hold Ms. Kendi accountable for the harm done."[88] Here, given the wide disparity between the requested four months plus "a period of probation"[89] and the imposed fifteen months plus one year of probation, it seems that these other considerations outweighed rehabilitation in the end. The second reason that the sentence is less rehabilitative than it may otherwise appear (given that it is to be served conditionally) is that Judge Schmaltz notes, "I do not know whether Ms. Kendi would take any conditions seriously," registers uncertainty about whether she "really has learned anything while awaiting sentencing, and really does want to make changes in her life," and questions "whether Ms. Kendi's attitude has changed."[90]

Moreover, Judge Schmaltz directly states, "If Ms. Kendi does not take the conditions seriously, as has been the case in the past, then I expect that she will end up serving her sentence in jail. I do not say this as a threat to Ms. Kendi, but simply stating the seriousness of and the reality of Ms. Kendi's situation."[91] It appears the judge lacks confidence that Kendi will be able to comply with the terms of her conditional sentence, which would mean that in the event of a breach, Kendi would likely end up serving the remainder of her sentence in prison—and, due to the disparity in duration between the joint submission and the sentence ordered, any remainder could well be longer than the four months requested in that submission.

Additionally, there are conditions attached to Kendi's conditional sentence that depend on her remaining sober. Given her entrenched substance abuse problem, these conditions may set Kendi up for failure. Because of the duration of her sentence, in the event of a breach, Kendi's likely effective sentence (serving the balance of her conditional sentence in prison) would be quite punitive. This result would be antithetical to both Judge Schmaltz's attempts to integrate rehabilitative concerns into her sentence and the *Gladue* analysis that should have been considered. In sum, while the judge's decision to order a conditional sentence may at first glance appear consistent with the more restorative goals of *Gladue* than a straight imprisonment term, there are other problems with the final sentence, mostly connected to the duration of the sentence and its conditions. Research from Juristat has shown that Indigenous women are much more susceptible to breaching conditions than non-Indigenous women, with a "breach rate" that is "almost triple" that for non-Indigenous women.[92] The edges of these problems may have been dulled had Judge Schmaltz engaged in an analysis of systemic factors contributing to Kendi's criminalization.

In *R. v. Char*, the issue of judges individualizing problems that should be contextualized against systemic dynamics is stark. Judge Elizabeth L. Bayliff sentences Noreen Char to a global sentence of imprisonment for fifteen month on "a series of shoplifting and breach of court order charges"[93] after she accumulated an extensive shoplifting record with escalating sanctions. Judge Bayliff identifies that Char is an Indigenous woman from the Redstone community.[94] (At Char's appeal from sentence, Justice Kenneth J. Smith for the Court of Appeal of British Columbia identifies her as of the Alexis Creek Band, living on the Redstone Reserve.)[95] This sentencing decision marks the second legal proceeding for which Char appeared before Judge Bayliff, who notes having presided over Char's family law matter in the past. In this sentencing decision, the judge comments that in the previous family law proceeding, she discerned that both Char and her partner "just could not say no to drugs particularly, but also alcohol."[96] At that time, Char and her partner asked his parents to take care of their two children for a period, recognizing that they were struggling with substance abuse issues. The grandparents then refused to return the children (resulting in what Justice Smith on appeal refers to as an "emotional custody dispute,"[97] through which Char was unsuccessful in having her children returned to her). Judge Bayliff finds during sentencing that Char and her partner remain "not capable of raising their children at present."[98]

Judge Bayliff acknowledges Ms. Char's "explanation" that her offending stems from "her sense of depression over the loss of her children . . . [which] is a factor."[99] (At her appeal, Justice Smith observes Char's explanation that "the loss of her children triggered a downward spiral in her life.")[100] This kind of criminalization trajectory, stemming from child custody issues, is consistent with other women's offending patterns.[101] However, Judge Bayliff also comments, "We also have to be realistic about how that situation has come about."[102] Judge Bayliff states, "I do not think that the fact that the children are with the grandparents is actually the problem here," explaining that "the problem is *something in what Ms. Char is bringing to the world, her way of looking at the world*, and her severe difficulties with addictions, and there may well be psychiatric issues here."[103] For the judge, the critical question is, "What is it that leads her to be so unable to exist out in the community without abusing substances and without stealing things that do not belong to her?"[104] The judge positions treatment with "psychiatric attention" as the mode to answer that question, "to try to understand what the root of the addictions and psychiatric difficulties are."[105]

For Judge Bayliff, the necessary treatment must occur in prison, "because I think it is only in jail that Ms. Char will be held in place long enough, away hopefully from substances long enough, that she can actually try to address the psychiatric issues and addictions underlying her actions and her problems."[106] The problems the judge identifies "include problems with the men in her life, the problem of children not being with her, depression and anger and disregard for the rights of others that flows from that and from other issues."[107] There is no description of Char's personal background in the judgment, so "problems with the men in her life" are ambiguous—conceivably, this might be a reference to abuse, but this is speculative. It is difficult to discern anything approximating an understanding of the victimization-criminalization continuum in the absence of this background, although it is revealing that the judge comments, "I have to believe that these issues flow from the root problems of how she is looking at the world, controlling impulses, dealing with addictions."[108] Judge Bayliff seems to place considerable confidence in the rehabilitative possibilities of a prison sentence for Char.

According to Françoise Bouchard, research has shown that, "in women, substance abuse does not occur in isolation of other needs,"[109] and it is reductionist to identify "how she is looking at the world" as one of the principal destructive issues in Char's life without reference to what systemic factors are refracted through that world view. Moreover, Char's perspective and way of thinking may have no corrective bearing on the external stresses that have rendered her vulnerable to criminalization.

There is no explicit reference to *Gladue* apart from a nod to the contents of s. 718.2(e), which "is of course a crucial issue here because Ms. Char is aboriginal."[110] It must be acknowledged that, on appeal, Justice Smith notes that Judge Bayliff did not have access to a PSR (to say nothing of *Gladue* information in a subsection of a PSR or a distinct *Gladue* report), despite having made an inquiry of counsel about this, and was told "there would be no utility" in ordering one.[111] Although Judge Bayliff has "given it my anxious consideration," she "simply feel[s] unable to contemplate anything other than a substantial sentence of jail."[112] In this way, systemic factors recede into the background, in place of individualized difficulties the judge, lacking further information, considers to predominate. This individualization of Char's difficulties also shapes the judge's conception and representation of imprisonment itself. Addressing s. 718.2(f) of the Criminal Code, the sentencing objective to promote a sense of responsibility and acknowledgement of the harm done, Judge Bayliff finds that "I have, I suppose, a slight sliver of hope that perhaps a lengthy jail sentence with the right kind of psychiatric attention, counselling attention, might allow Ms. Char to feel a sense of responsibility, to *choose* not to steal, because until she does that, *until she is able to think in that way*, we really are simply going to be continuing to go through this process every year or so as the charges accumulate."[113] Here, Judge Bayliff constructs prison as a place where Char can deal with her individualized problems by changing her thought patterns.

Of the various sentencing principles, "deterrence" is dismissed on the expectation that Char is unlikely to be deterred, and "separating the offender from society" is foregrounded as the "largest sentencing principle here."[114] "Rehabilitation" seems to dominate much of the discussion, but is expressly weighted only as being "an element" in the considerations.[115] Judge Bayliff seems to struggle with how best to approach this sentencing task, commenting, "I ask myself, what could be done here to rehabilitate and reintegrate Ms. Char? What could be done? Is there some other option to custody here? Is there something that the court should be doing differently here?"[116] However, because systemic forces are not meaningfully discussed in the judgment, even these questions about the sentencing process are not contextualized. Equally, the ability of Judge Bayliff to engage in such contextualization is severely hindered by the lack of detailed *Gladue*-related information, as becomes clear on appeal, where Justice Smith admits a *Gladue* report as fresh evidence, and suggests that "this information would likely have had an effect on the disposition"[117] at sentencing. Justice Smith explains, "I think it is clear that the sentencing judge was looking for information such as this when she asked, at the commencement of the sentencing hearing, 'Were any reports ordered, or anything of that sort?'"[118] and that she posed misgivings about whether there were available alternatives to prison. (With the finding that rehabilitation was given insufficient weight in light of the new *Gladue* report disclosing her background "involv[ing] violence, sexual abuse, and abuse of alcohol and drugs in her family and surrounding community"[119] and identifying supports and treatment services in her community, Char's sentence appeal is granted, with a six-month sentence followed by one year's probation supplanting her original sentence.)

At sentencing, in an exchange with Judge Bayliff before the delivery of the decision, Char herself comments, "I'm seeking treatment, I know I need treatment, and that's the first step to getting my kids back."[120] A more contextualized understanding of Char's offending, situated within her experience as an Indigenous woman and any related *Gladue* factors, does not preclude a finding that—consistent with her own expressed wishes—treatment should form a component of the sentence. There is some research suggesting that for some women who experience difficulty accessing and receiving help for their addictions within their own communities, prison offers the possibility of otherwise elusive help.[121] However, former Correctional Investigator Howard Sapers has problematized the idea of treatment in prison, noting that the physical conditions of imprisonment represent deprivation, isolation, and alienation from society, all of which are damaging to people's mental health.[122] Sapers explains that because prisons are based on control, mental health struggles often receive security-driven responses. Sapers is specifically talking about mental health concerns in federal prisons, but his comments about how securitization and the fundamental punishment philosophy underpinning imprisonment are antithetical to prisoners' mental health needs are also salient to the issue of substance abuse treatment in prisons generally. Further, beyond the inherent tension between any form of healing/treatment and imprisonment, it is also problematic to suggest that because there is some programming in prisons, prisoners will receive it; Sapers emphasizes that there are long waiting lists for prisoners trying to obtain federal programming, and that prisoners are gaining access to programs later in their sentences.[123] (Indeed, Ivan Zinger, the current Correctional Investigator, reports in 2017 that often after waiting several months to access programming, merely about 20 percent of Indigenous federal prisoners could complete their programming before their first release eligibility date).[124] At the provincial level, Canadian prisons are widely known to lack programming entirely.[125]

In *R. v. Diamond*, Judge Bonin sentences Elaine Diamond to a conditional sentence of two years less a day followed by a two-year probation order for the aggravated assault of her then common-law spouse. Diamond had learned he was the father of a friend's baby, and stabbed him several times while he was visiting the friend, while "under the influence of alcohol," and, the judge states, "out of jealousy."[126] Judge Bonin concluded that Diamond had not "grown up in a dysfunctional milieu"[127] and had parents who were "positive role models."[128] There is no sustained discussion of her personal background, so any emergent understanding of the victimization-criminalization continuum is thin, although, in reflecting on her criminal record, the probation officer reports "that alcohol consumption has always been linked to her delinquency."[129] Diamond's alcohol misuse features prominently in the decision. She began drinking when she was fifteen years old, at the same time her relationship with the deceased began, and the heavy use of alcohol suffused their relationship within a "history of violence" that was "just as pervasive."[130] Two years before sentencing, she also began using cocaine.

The principles involved in sentencing Indigenous persons are discussed in the judgment, and *Gladue* is quoted extensively, although how these considerations actually impact Judge Bonin's reasoning is not made explicit. The pre-sentence report may have lacked detail, because although it "mentions that her consumption was mainly to deal with her problems and forget painful memories,"[131] Judge Bonin comments that "she has never mentioned what are these painful memories."[132] The judge finds that "an accumulation of frustration and unresolved issues are the basic causes of her crime."[133] This view presents another example of how the difficulties related to Indigenous women's offending (including experiences of victimization) may be individualized on sentencing at the expense of having regard to systemic factors. This in turn has potential deleterious penal consequences for women—Judge Bonin writes that these "causes" of Diamond's crime become "aggravating since the accused had known for years that she had those issues to work with and had done nothing about it."[134] It seems inimical to the sentencing objective of rehabilitation, and to the principle of proportionality more broadly, to formulate intractable issues (which are often connected to systemic dynamics) as aggravating in this manner. Diamond may have had enough self-awareness to recognize her reliance on substances was problematic, but perhaps she lacked the support, resources, services, or financial ability to address it, and she should not be further penalized on that basis.

Judge Bonin asserts about her use of drugs and alcohol that "it is only today when she now faces jail that she says she would accept to receive help about it."[135] The author of the pre-sentence report recommends a prison sentence for treatment reasons. Judge Bonin ultimately rejects this recommendation and concludes that a conditional sentence is appropriate. The factors most persuasive for Judge Bonin seem to be that a treatment centre will accept Diamond in the community, and that she is the primary caregiver of her three children. The latter is cited within mitigating factors and constructed as such, although the judge also writes that "it is not a mitigating factor in itself."[136] Judge Bonin earlier references that "although Ms. Diamond has not resolved many issues, she is described as a person who puts in priority her children and who is a good mother for them."[137] Moreover, her children are characterized as the route to her addressing her issues, as "they would be her main source of motivation for change."[138] This frame seems to be the corresponding side to the assertion of CAEFS and NWAC that the state positions Indigenous mothers to "correct the systemic conditions of poverty and violence affecting Aboriginal families and punish[es] her with the loss of her children if she fails."[139] That is, because the judge understands Diamond to be a "good mother" and the primary caregiver of her children, her relationship to them is then constructed as a means to resolve her own difficulties, which the probation officer and the judge both reduce to individualized factors.

Undoubtedly, as Judge Bonin comments, "her children will be happy to see their mother getting back control over her life,"[140] and the conditional sentence ordered should allow them to be part of that process in a way that imprisonment in a correctional institution would not. This aspect of Candace Woods's release conditions was beneficial: in *Woods*, Judge Whelan notes that while on release on an undertaking before sentencing, Woods was "confined to her residence much of the time," during which she "developed a close bond with her son and she is the primary caregiver."[141] Regardless, it would be helpful if the judgment in *Diamond* reflected more thoroughly on the systemic factors pertaining to Diamond's life instead of providing an almost exclusive focus on her need "to find other solutions to solve conflicts, increase her self-esteem, [and to] learn to talk about her problems."[142]

There is a risk inherent in an overly individualized focus on criminalized Indigenous women's lives such that—as demonstrated in *Char*—the judge may conclude that only treatment in prison is sufficient to respond to those highly specialized needs, and without the counterbalance that *Gladue* requires a shift in focus to restorative alternatives. In Diamond's case, a community treatment centre accepted her for a period, making this an option the judge deems appropriate—but these resources are not always available, often due to issues stemming from colonization such as poverty and the isolation of Indigenous communities.[143] As a result, it is important to take a broader view encompassing the systemic factors within Indigenous women's lives to protect against the concern that their difficulties will be interpreted as so particularized and complex that they can be adequately dealt with only in prison. As participants expressed to Department of Justice Canada in its review of the criminal justice system, in the context of sentencing, regarding challenges such as addictions and mental illness and related needs for decriminalization, "Indigenous women are particularly vulnerable, and this is an area where we must therefore make a special effort to address their needs."[144]

The Nexus Between Judicial Understandings of Victimization Histories and Imprisonment

In *Char*, it is troubling that the individualized account of Char's offending, without a representation of the victimization-criminalization continuum, seems connected to the determination that rehabilitation can be achieved only through treatment in prison. Judge Bayliff believes Char's "situation may be so complex that she needs professional expert attention here," instead of the "sort of well-intentioned but not effective sort of miscellaneous kind of sympathy and vague support" that she might receive if "some sort of conference" was convened with her family and community.[145] There seems to be a correlation between the individualization and concurrent decontextualization of Char's problems and the deemed necessity for professional treatment in prison. In *Diamond*, the author of the pre-sentence report makes a similar recommendation to the judge that Diamond's difficulties necessitate imprisonment.

Judge Bonin relays this recommendation: "To come to a point where she would present no risk, the probation officer is of the opinion that she needs specialised help offered in a structured environment. The probation officer says that considering the extent and the depth of her problems, she would need to work on her issues in an intensive manner and therefore would need to be in a confined environement [*sic*] with treatment for at least three months."[146] While Judge Bonin departs from the probation officer's view that prison is necessary to Diamond's rehabilitation, such PSR recommendations remain disconcerting. As I discuss in Chapter 2, research has shown that judges rely heavily on pre-sentence reports, with, according to Hannah-Moffat and Maurutto, an "80 per cent concordance rate" between these recommendations and judicial decisions.[147]

Many decisions I examined funnel discussions about women's experiences of victimization into the idea that specialized treatment in a custodial setting is necessary, and/or that a lengthier carceral sentence is necessary to best effect treatment. For example, in sentencing Cheyann Peeteetuce for two counts of criminal negligence causing death and one count of criminal negligence causing bodily harm and impaired driving, among related offences, Justice T.C. Zarzeczny finds from her *Gladue* report that "she is an archetypical example of a person who has been subjected to all of the '*Gladue* factors' recognized by the Supreme Court of Canada,"[148] and determines that her sentence must recognize her "need for counselling and programming," to address "the negative risk factors which the PSR has identified."[149] Justice Zarzeczny continues, "The counselling and programs provided by Corrections Canada, specifically targeted at First Nations individuals and, in your case, the needs of women, can only be successful if the time required to deliver them to you is realistically reflected in the court's sentence."[150] The judge includes these programs in the court's recommendations to CSC, noting that "they are intended to reflect the court's recognition of its appropriate response" to s. 718.2(e).[151]

Of course, such pronouncements about the specialized need for lengthy treatment in prison may be combined with other sentencing considerations, such as public safety. For example, in *Killiktee*, while Justice Ratushny acknowledges that "treatment has been minimally effective in the past"[152] for Louisa Killiktee, "sustained treatment in a controlled setting"[153] is necessary both "in the interests of public safety and, additionally, so that she can receive the supervised treatment she wants and needs."[154] Justice Ratushny suggests that "it will not be a quick process for treatment to succeed," and, to address public safety concerns and to promote specific deterrence and rehabilitation needs, "a substantial period of incarceration" is warranted.[155] The judge emphasizes the intended dual nature of the duration of the sentence regarding treatment, suggesting to Killiktee that "the longer you are able to be treated while you are supervised and controlled and the longer you are able to work hard at treatment while you are supervised and controlled, the safer the public will be at the time of your release."[156]

Similarly, in *R. v. Shecapio*, Judge Gilles Cadieux sentences Lindy Shecapio to eight years' imprisonment for manslaughter[157] following her guilty plea, commenting that, given her "serious alcohol abuse and addiction problem which she never tried to resolve up to now," a "term of imprisonment in a penitentiary will provide the accused with the professional and specialized assistance that she needs to solve this problem and minimize the effects of her alcoholism on her life and that of the people around her."[158] Shecapio is a "member of the Cree nation."[159] She was exposed to her parents' alcohol abuse and violence, and her four children were removed from her care because of her own substance abuse. Two psychiatric medical reports and an "evaluation summary" from a psychotherapist "confirm that the alcohol abuse and addiction by the accused was an important factor in the offence," although one psychiatrist adds that "this alcohol abuse was not exceptional whether as to its quantity or its nature."[160] The probation officer notes that Shecapio's "alcohol abuse and addiction has exacerbated the accused's personal and psychological problems and impaired her social functioning."[161]

The Crown and defence agreed that federal imprisonment is warranted "even though the accused is an aboriginal offender."[162] Judge Cadieux follows this, declaring that "it has been clearly established"[163] that more serious and violent offences will likely produce similar sentences for Indigenous and non-Indigenous persons (the *Gladue* reference that *Ipeelee* later finds has been erroneously emphasized). As Shecapio's personal history is sparse in the judgment, it is difficult to interpret how the judge understands and frames her experiences of victimization. Nonetheless, incarceration is favoured for its treatment options. Given that Shecapio is sentenced to eight years' incarceration, there was no (community) alternative for rehabilitative services. However, the concept of prison rehabilitative services offering "specialized assistance" may be particularly problematic in the context of more borderline decisions (hovering around the two-year range), because that concept of "specialized" services may militate toward more punitive sanctions (such as a federal term at the lower end as opposed to a provincial term at the higher end, or a term of incarceration instead of a conditional sentence order).

The idea that prison is a healing place, offering specialized mental health services to criminalized persons with challenging problems, is also evident in *R. v. Waskewitch.* Judge David Arnot sentences Deborah Lee Waskewitch to four years in a federal penitentiary after she pleaded guilty to manslaughter. A member of Onion Lake First Nation, Waskewitch was in a relationship with the deceased, with whom she has three children. He told her he no longer loved her (amid a recurrent argument about alleged infidelities), pushed her, started to choke her, and threatened to hit her, until Waskewitch told him she intended to stab him. He responded in a "taunting and threatening manner," approaching her and "inviting her to stab him," and "she complied."[164] (As mentioned above, choking is a particularly dangerous form of intimate partner violence even beyond the immediate risk of death; research, by Nancy Glass et al., for example, finds "non-lethal strangulation is an important predictor for future lethal violence" against women.)[165] Judge Arnot discusses her personal history, including Waskewitch's having rotated through over twenty foster homes during childhood, wherein she was "the victim of child abuse consisting of neglect, physical, verbal abuse by her mother and sexual abuse by a cousin" and developed substance abuse issues.[166] Her substance abuse persisted into adulthood, and she "was the victim of much physical abuse and violence at the hands of [the deceased] in their domestic situation."[167] (Absent further information and on the facts presented, as in *Kahypeasewat* and *Simms,* this is another decision over which an unsettling air of self-defence seems to hover.) Judge Arnot describes that this personal background "help[s] to explain the circumstances of the offence and her personal situation," but these circumstances "cannot excuse" that she took a life.[168]

After discussing various sentencing directives per *Gladue*, Judge Arnot determines that a conditional sentence is not appropriate, citing inadequate resources in her community and that "much more in-depth counseling is required for Ms. Waskewitch before she can be reintegrated safely into the community."[169] It is somewhat surprising that the judge finds the available community resources insufficient. Defence counsel suggests Waskewitch has already made "positive steps" in that context.[170] The judge later declares that "the resources available to her at her home community made a praiseworthy effort in working with her for the past sixteen months," which must have been effective, as the judge continues, "I commend the dedicated people with whom she has been working for the progress they have produced."[171] Judge Arnot again intimates that the community resources are worthwhile, adding that she will benefit from them on release because they will remain "available," offering "strong follow-up counseling and programming to her. They will no doubt augment the success we hope Ms. Waskewitch will achieve in an institutional setting."[172] While Judge Arnot lacks confidence the community could manage the risk she has been assessed to present,[173] the judge also finds that, while Waskewitch was on bail in the community, "she abided by the conditions and availed herself of the counseling and support proffered to her by the resources in the community. She did not breach any of the conditions."[174] It should also be noted (particularly given that defence counsel seeks a conditional sentence) that, before trial, Waskewitch abided by these conditions and underwent counselling within "restrictive terms" that the judge indicates "were quite harsh, more so than some conditional sentences."[175]

Despite these cumulative indications that the resources in the community are both valuable and have been well-utilized by Waskewitch, Judge Arnot finds that "the nature, quality, and severity of Ms. Waskewitch's psychological, and other significant issues require very experienced counselors working in a structured institution to create the best chance for long term success,"[176] in a "specialized individualized, clinically based, therapeutic treatment plan."[177] The judge finds that these resources "are not realistically available" in her community or provincial institutions.[178] Research notes the disparity between federal and provincial programming; Jennifer Bernier writes that there are "relatively consistent services at the federal level and non-standardized policies, procedures, practices, and programming at the provincial level."[179] The "in-depth counseling and programming" the judge finds necessary for Waskewitch "to truly begin a successful path of rehabilitation" are framed as "opportunities to obtain the help she needs" and as best available "in the federal female correction institution system."[180]

It is clear that Judge Arnot centres much of the sentencing reasoning on this perception of Waskewitch's rehabilitative needs. While the judge registers concern about how the community would manage the risk she is assessed to present, Judge Arnot simultaneously clarifies that she "has high risk needs, but she is not necessarily a high risk offender."[181] The basis for this finding is the pre-sentence report, which "classifies Ms. Waskewitch as a 'high risk to re-offend' unless a variety of factors are addressed."[182] Hannah-Moffat and Maurutto explain that, increasingly, PSR policy has shifted toward an actuarial risk-based model "in which assessments and recommendations are primarily based on criminogenic risk/need," and "Gladue factors are positioned and itemized alongside (and sometimes interpreted as) risk factors."[183] They suggest that within this paradigm of amplified risk-related assessments and recommendations in pre-sentence reports, "an offender's problems are no longer situated within a broader social context."[184] Moreover, Hannah-Moffat and Maurutto observe that this risk-based policy shift does not offer much direction to probation officers about how they should "reconcile their holistic culturally situated assessments of the offender with the policy's emphasis on criminogenic risk/need. The result is Aboriginal offenders continue to be characterized as high risk and high need."[185] Hannah-Moffat and Maurutto extrapolate that this PSR policy shift "reflect[s] a shift in emphasis from rehabilitation (understood within an individualized treatment model) to risk of re-offending and risk-informed rehabilitation (for which non-criminogenic factors such as remorse, future plans and physical and emotional health are no longer considered relevant and are considered difficult to target in treatment)."[186] They point out that, generally, these policy changes pass unknown by judges.[187] Against the individualizing logic of risk-based pre-sentence reports, Hannah-Moffat and Maurutto suggest, "sentence recommendations and, ultimately, sentences become a mechanism to regulate offender risk through treatment interventions as determined through actuarial techniques."[188]

These problems with the individualizing framework and recommendations of pre-sentence reports may also be exacerbated for women. Kim Pate has identified that often PSRs are inaccurate, misleading, and unfair, presenting gendered views of women's difficulties (for example, past abusive relationships may be depicted as evaded responsibilities and risk factors).[189] Some judges do recognize the ways in which such information in pre-sentence reports are problematic for women, such as where Judge Cozens observes the "medium level of criminogenic need" assessed for Samantha Rodrigue in her PSR, but suggests it seems "the rating of medium as compared to low is primarily based upon the static factors of her childhood circumstances, her having been assaulted by her domestic partner and the involvement of her parents and ex-partner in the criminal justice system."[190] Judge Cozens explains that static factors beyond a person's control may have the capacity to produce a higher needs rating, but "I am just being careful not to assume that these factors will necessarily do so in any particular case, and in particular in the case of Ms. Rodrigue."[191] However, it seems this degree of judicial sensitization to gendered and individualizing PSR information is uncommon, as is consistent with research that indicates strong levels of consonance between pre-sentence reports and judicial determinations on sentence, and overall high judicial contentment with PSR content. In *Waskewitch*, while Judge Arnot makes the slippery distinction that Waskewitch "is not necessarily a high risk offender" but has "high risk needs,"[192] the implication is the same: the judge concludes that it is necessary for Waskewitch to be "in an institutional setting . . . to properly address the issues identified in the Pre-sentence Report," because she "will continue to be a high risk if these factors are not dealt with effectively."[193]

The sentencing judge in *Waskewitch* specifically alludes to s. 718.2(e) and relevant case law when she notes, "I have considered the principles" directed by a few decisions on sentencing Indigenous peoples (*Gladue*, *R. v. John*, and *R. v. Laliberte*), and finds that "a sentence of two years less a day or shorter would not serve the rehabilitation needs of the accused or properly reflect the gravity of the offence."[194] The latter concern may be a related function of the problem identified by Justice LeBel in *Ipeelee* that sentencing judges have oversubscribed to the comment in *Gladue* that more violent and serious offences will likely produce more similar sentences for Indigenous and non-Indigenous persons.

Judge Arnot recommends to correctional authorities that Waskewitch be transferred to the Okimaw Ohci Healing Lodge,[195] a prison for Indigenous women located on a reserve in Saskatchewan, but this remains a federal institution. Additionally, Waskewitch receives the Crown sentence recommendation of four years, far in excess of the defence submission for a conditional sentence. Altogether, it seems there is a risk that attention to *Gladue* factors, including histories of victimization, may be retranslated as specialized needs that judges determine require rehabilitative services that are exclusively available in the prison setting. Andrew Welsh and James R.P. Ogloff write:

> Judicial consideration of these systemic factors, as prescribed by section 718.2(e), may pose indirect problems for Aboriginal offenders. Simply put, given the significant problems experienced by a number of Aboriginal offenders and the more serious nature of their criminal history, judges may deem community-based dispositions, such as probation, to be an inappropriate means of supervision. Despite the general finding that the likelihood of a non-custodial disposition increased when judges cited rehabilitation as an important sentencing objective, in cases involving Aboriginal offenders, judges may consider the level of supervision and access to rehabilitative programs available in correctional facilities to be necessary for the successful rehabilitation.[196]

The dynamic outlined by Welsh and Ogloff seems to manifest in a decision sentencing Donalda Sinclair for a "serious home invasion,"[197] including aggravated assault and assault with a weapon, in which Judge Cynthia A. Devine portrays prison as a place of healing for her, and repeatedly suggests "she is not ready for the community."[198] Sinclair is a Cree woman whose upbringing the judge describes as "tragic,"[199] and finds that it reduces her moral culpability. Judge Devine suggests her "prospects for rehabilitation look good, while she is in the highly-structured, *protective* environment of the women's jail."[200]

The intersection of (or tension between) prison and healing is difficult to navigate in this judgment. The concept of prison's constituting a "protective environment" for women is antithetical to the belief underlying much feminist work on women and imprisonment that prison is generally actively harmful to women. Where this belief converges with conceptualizations of risk, Hannah-Moffat suggests some prison reform efforts and those seeking expansion of community-based programming derive from the view that women prisoners "*do not* represent a substantial risk to the public," and indicates various feminist research based in the idea that women are instead "*at risk*" of victimization while incarcerated, including engaging in self-harm.[201] UNODC finds that "research is unanimous in underlining the particularly detrimental effects of prison on women."[202] Many women suffer in prison specifically due to the experience of incarceration, and it can exacerbate or trigger mental health difficulties, while simultaneously removing women from their families and the communities that could truly act as a source of healing through connection to loved ones and outside resources. One of the problems inherent in this separation from women's real lives and sources of family and community support (and thereby complicating the idea that prison can be a source of "healing") is visible in Sinclair's own articulation of her experience in detention. Judge Devine quotes her pre-sentence report in which Sinclair expressed to its author that while "it is wonderful that she is learning all of these skills" in custody, "she has yet to put it into practise [*sic*] for reality and it sometimes makes her question her abilities."[203] Judge Devine has underlined this comment, presumably emphasizing the judge's determination that Sinclair is not ready to be returned to the community, although I would emphasize it for the inverse: irrespective of any readiness, she has been barred (literally and figuratively) from implementing any newly acquired "skills" because she has remained in custody (and this causes her self-doubt, "mak[ing] her question her abilities"). As Comack writes, "women's troubles have their source and basis *outside* the prison walls," difficulties they "do not have the power or autonomy to attend to" in prison.[204]

Equally, in this judgment, Judge Devine finds that "all of the restorative goals and progress that Ms. Sinclair has made have been achieved in the Women's Correctional Centre"[205] (where she had been detained for nearly a year), noting, for example, that "she has been able to abstain from alcohol and drugs in the confines of the jail for the longest time in her life," and adding that "her knowledge of community resources was not enough for her to quit in the past."[206] The judge determines that Sinclair "does well in a closely-monitored, structured environment," suggesting that, "for now, that is the Women's Correctional Centre."[207] Judge Devine cites *Gladue* for its direction that sentencing judges do have (limited) power to ameliorate the overincarceration of Indigenous peoples through restorative sentences, and references *Ipeelee* for its implication that innovative sentences are available and should be considered for Indigenous persons who might otherwise face a prison term. Against this framing, the judge orders the maximum provincial sentence available (prison for two years less a day followed by probation for three years), and characterizes it as a "restorative sentence."[208]

Judicial concerns that criminalized Indigenous women need intensive treatment, and that this treatment is best administered in prison, become particularly complicated where women's past experiences of incarceration have demonstrated that imprisonment exacerbates their problems and that programming has not proven to be healing/rehabilitative. These complexities are evident in *R. v. Pelletier*[209] and *R. v. Redhead*.

Josephine Pelletier is sentenced for robbery, arson, and assault, receiving three years and three months' imprisonment (after the reduction for remand custody), followed by a seven-year supervision order. The judge also grants the Crown application that she be declared a long-term offender. Justice C.L. Dawson recounts her personal history, which is replete with violence and its after-effects. Pelletier's father was repeatedly incarcerated, and her mother had entrenched substance abuse issues and abused Pelletier's stepfather. In her childhood, Pelletier was physically, sexually, and emotionally abused, suffering in isolation when her mother refused to believe the sexual abuse. Her mother routinely evicted her unless she brought home drugs. She "turned to stealing and prostitution,"[210] was first criminalized in her youth, and later amassed a serious criminal record. She cycled through foster homes. In adulthood, she endured relationships marred by substance abuse and physical abuse. Justice Dawson cites her "very troubled upbringing and background" as a mitigating factor that "contributed to her conduct," noting the clear application of *Gladue* factors to her sentencing.[211]

The portrait of imprisonment that emerges from the judgment is very complex, simultaneously holding prison out as a place of treatment and the site of the acceleration of Pelletier's anti-social issues. Justice Dawson relates, "The author of the Pre-Disposition report indicated that Ms. Pelletier had numerous issues that probably could only be addressed while she was in closed custody."[212] The forensic psychologist testified at the sentencing hearing that "she would need a sentence of at least two years, as Correction Services of Canada ('CSC') [*sic*] has an 18 month rotation, so she would need a minimum of two years in a federal institution to go through the programming,"[213] and recommended that for the length of post-incarceration community supervision, "the longer the better."[214] Justice Dawson agrees that "in the context of a long-term offender, it is important to provide sufficient time to allow for appropriate treatment regimes," and that Pelletier "needs extensive, intensive treatment if she is ever to live a pro-social life."[215] Although Pelletier had spent years in remand, the judge determines that to give her the then "standard two for one credit" for this time "would be inimical to any future rehabilitation prospects," and on this basis only counts her time in remand at a ratio of one to one.[216] Justice Dawson makes treatment-related recommendations to correctional authorities about the administration of her sentence: "I would also recommend to the federal authorities that Ms. Pelletier be incarcerated in an institution which will ensure that she receives meaningful and intensive assistance in terms of psychological and sexual abuse counselling, substance abuse therapy, counselling which integrates her aboriginal heritage, life skills training, and occupational or vocational training."[217]

Given this representation of a woman with deeply entrenched personal challenges who must be subjected to extensive treatment in prison, and its corollary, the representation of prison as a place of treatment, a complicating factor emerges: imprisonment seems to exacerbate Pelletier's issues. Her past conduct in prison becomes aggravating on sentencing because the judge notes that she "has conducted herself in a similar fashion [to her conduct in the predicate offences] on previous occasions while incarcerated."[218] The forensic psychologist who conducted her assessment reported, "Pine Grove Correctional Facility staff portray Ms. Pelletier as a very hard individual to manage and a person who has great difficulty complying with the institutional regime," and whose "abilities to comply with remediation attempts, while incarcerated, were spotty at best."[219] Additionally, the Deputy Director of Programs at that correctional facility testified that prisoners in segregation or classified to maximum security do not have access to programming,[220] and that any available programs were not "high enough intensity" for Pelletier.[221] It seems that Pelletier has various treatment needs arising from poverty and a chaotic, violent upbringing; prison programming is insufficient but will be relied on; she must be separated from society; and imprisonment triggers Pelletier's challenging behaviours. None of these factors are easily reconcilable. (Appealing the length of her determinate sentences, Pelletier sought to introduce new evidence in the form of an assessment by a forensic psychologist regarding "why she offends" and has "performed poorly while in custody."[222] This evidence is not admitted, as Justice Georgina Jackson for the Saskatchewan Court of Appeal finds that while, at times, new evidence pertaining to rehabilitation after the imposition of sentence is permissible, Pelletier has "struggled to maintain acceptable behaviour while incarcerated,"[223] and her sentences are not demonstrably unfit.)

In *Redhead*, Vianna Redhead is sentenced to ten years' incarceration for the attempted murder of a police officer. Redhead is "a member of the Shamattawa First Nation,"[224] and a *Gladue* report is referenced in the judgment. Justice Brenda L. Keyser describes that Redhead "has lived a horrific existence,"[225] and details the unrelenting violence she has witnessed and experienced. The judge declares, "I appreciate that some of the *Gladue* factors in her background have contributed to her problems, sometimes significantly."[226] However, despite this recognition of the systemic dynamics within her impoverished community and the effects on her personally, Justice Keyser finds that her risk to the public is paramount.

In one of the filed reports, Redhead is assessed as needing "long-term substance abuse treatment."[227] Justice Keyser notes that during her pretrial custody, Redhead has had "multiple problems with authority and instances of aggression," attributed to attitudinal issues.[228] Justice Keyser comments, "Unless there is significant change in attitude, she remains a very high risk to reoffend violently. If she cannot control her violent impulses while incarcerated, what chance does she have to successfully reintegrate into society without putting members of the public at considerable risk?"[229]

It is problematic to equate institutional behaviour with that in the outside world, because these environments are completely dissimilar with different stressors, and, as Hannah-Moffat notes, "some researchers argue that there is little relationship between behaviour in prison and that outside."[230] In a correctional report commissioned about federally sentenced women, Margaret Shaw observes that it seems there is "no direct relationship" between criminal histories and institutional behaviour.[231] Shaw finds that women prisoners' institutional violence and disruption (including self-harming behaviour) often relate to women's difficulties coping in an oppressive regime based on punitiveness and isolation, which actually *engenders* women's institutional violence/disruption.[232] Moreover, Shaw suggests that women's institutional violence and disruptiveness "may well provide a *better measure of institutional characteristics* than of individual risk."[233] I would add that such disruption or violence might also tell us more about the general experience of incarceration itself. Hannah-Moffat writes, "The assumption that these behaviours are linked often obscures other significant issues such as the relationship of the prison environment to the production and provocation of 'risky behaviours.'"[234] Further, Indigenous women's behaviour in prison may not be reflective of how they will relate to people beyond the walls. *Gladue* recognizes this broadly, explaining that systemic and background factors cause Indigenous persons to be "more adversely affected by incarceration and less likely to be 'rehabilitated' thereby, because the internment milieu is often culturally inappropriate and regrettably discrimination towards them is so often rampant in penal institutions."[235]

Monture-Angus explains that "dislocation and disconnection" are "predominate experiences of those who live within correctional institutions in Canada," and that colonization has produced these feelings for Indigenous peoples.[236] As such, Indigenous prisoners experience a distinct sort of isolation and alienation. Further, Monture-Angus writes that Indigenous women who reported their experiences of imprisonment to the Task Force on Federally Sentenced Women[237] did not experience prison itself as a healing place: "Almost all the healing experiences that the Aboriginal women who have been in prison reported lie outside the conventional prison order. They come through the bonds formed with other women in prison, through the support of people on the outside, and from the activities of the Native Sisterhood."[238] Additionally, programming that women may (or may not) receive in prison may be ineffective outside the walls due to the same idea that life in prison cannot be related to or instructive of life outside. As one former prisoner illustrates (and recalling the related discussion in *Sinclair* above, in which the judge underlines that Donalda Sinclair had not yet put her prison-acquired skills into practice): "All they really do here is teach you how to be in jail. They don't teach you how to survive on the outside."[239] In sum, as Shaw describes, many feminist writers have argued that "violence and disorder in prisons must be seen not as the result of individual pathology but as social and situational events [because] violence is gendered,"[240] and "the experience of imprisonment is both gendered and racialized."[241] For these reasons, Justice Keyser's suggestion that Redhead's institutional violence indicates she presents a risk to public safety is problematic for implying equivalence between life behind and outside the walls.

Justice Keyser concludes, "Redhead needs significant rehabilitative work in a secure facility" to deal with her "aggression" and "limited insight into the triggers for violent behavior," both for her own well-being and to reduce her risk to others.[242] This suggests a view of incarceration that prison has the capacity to modify behaviour, and convicted individuals with complex behavioural difficulties must be sent there to address those difficulties. However, even this picture of the rehabilitative power and efficacy of prison is complicated by its failure to heal and change Redhead's conduct in past periods of incarceration: the judge comments that "it is clear that her aggressive behaviour has not been curbed by the fact of incarceration at all."[243]

A different picture of the role and impact of imprisonment emerges from *Chouinard*, wherein the community is identified as the better place for rehabilitation. I discussed Justice Ratushny's sensitivity to Josée Chouinard's experiences of victimization in Chapter 2. Justice Ratushny imposes a three-year sentence of imprisonment followed by two years of probation, but because Chouinard spent seven months in remand, the judge credits her with two-for-one custodial time (reducing her effective sentence to the remaining twenty-two months). As the remaining time is under two years, Justice Ratushny decides a conditional sentence is available, ordering that Chouinard serve the rest of her sentence of imprisonment in the community. Justice Ratushny concludes a community sentence is appropriate because of her understanding of how Chouinard's "lifetime of abuse"[244] impacted her behaviour regarding her offence. This understanding prompts the judge to develop a restorative-oriented sentence "to try to assist in her rehabilitation."[245] Justice Ratushny concentrates on "treatment and counselling" as the "primary focus" of Chouinard's sentence of imprisonment and the following probation order.[246]

The overall duration of Chouinard's sentence is long and onerous: Justice Ratushny explains that she "will be supervised for almost a four-year period,"[247] and the terms of Chouinard's probation order "are basically the same as those for [her] conditional sentence"[248] (although the repercussions in the event of a breach would differ, as a breach of her conditional sentence order would likely result in Chouinard's serving the rest of her sentence in prison, whereas she could be newly charged for a breach of her probation order). However, it is clear that the judge was motivated to avoid sending Chouinard to prison. Justice Ratushny finds that "a focus on specific deterrence through rehabilitation, in this way, I think, will better achieve specific deterrence than a real jail term, because Ms. Chouinard is not a person who needs to learn her lesson by being incarcerated any further. She has already served a period of pre-sentence incarceration and now, in my view, she is a person in need of highly structured, mandatory and controlled help."[249] In other decisions I have discussed above, some judges decide that when Indigenous women they sentence are "in need of highly structured, mandatory and controlled help," they locate the source of that structure and control in the prison setting. Justice Ratushny's comments demonstrate another, less coercive way of thinking about and imposing structure and control—in the community.

Other decisions also suggest that the community meets treatment needs better than does prison, such as where Judge Smith comments in the sentencing of Bryna Link that, in this case, "the protection of the public is best served by emphasizing rehabilitation, in particular addressing the alcohol and drug risk factors. Those factors are being addressed now effectively—and likely even more effectively—in the community than in jail."[250] Similarly, in sentencing Theresa McCook for theft over $5,000, Judge Brecknell orders a conditional sentence order of two years less a day followed by probation for three years and a substantial restitution order, commenting that the "restorative aspects of the sentence are more appropriately addressed in a Conditional Sentence Order as opposed to incarceration," and "addressing the underlying reasons for the criminal behaviour such as addiction is better accomplished in the community."[251]

In *R. v. Redies*, Judge Barnett delivers a nuanced oral judgment that suggests prison is not an institution where healing happens. Judge Barnett sentences Vanessa Redies to a global period of twelve months' imprisonment and six months' probation following her release (including conditional sentence-like probationary terms of house arrest for the first three months) for impaired driving causing bodily harm, amongst other offences. Judge Barnett conveys distaste that, as a judge, "there are times when you just cannot feel happy about what you have to do, and this is one of those times."[252] This sentiment seems related to having to order imprisonment for an Indigenous woman from a community that the judge understands is troubled and where many people are "traumatized," having *Gladue* "pretty firmly in my mind."[253]

Although Judge Barnett optimistically comments, "I do hope that something good may be able to happen while you are at the correctional centre,"[254] prison is not understood as a healing place in this judgment. Instead, the judge tells Redies, "I have never told anybody that they were going to jail because it would be a good and useful experience for them. I think in your case a term of imprisonment is necessary."[255] Within the probation component of her sentence, Judge Barnett assigns house arrest for a shorter duration than "it might otherwise be,"[256] due to dissatisfaction with how such orders are administered. Judge Barnett is sensitive to how Redies will experience her sentence, adding that if she would prefer her sentence structured differently, the probation order could be revised and she could spend a longer period of imprisonment in Whitehorse.[257] This judicial flexibility represents an instance where "what the system hears" is heard in a reflexive way, engaging the woman being sentenced in a dialogue about her own experience and needs.

Reaffirming that prison is not a place of healing, the judge comments, "I think that the probation order is a more effective way of accomplishing some useful things,"[258] which is consistent with the legislative intent for probation orders to function as primarily rehabilitative instruments.[259] Judge Barnett leaves this rehabilitative function for Redies to determine vis-à-vis her own needs: "Without ordering Ms. Redies to get out of town to go to a treatment centre or to go for some specialized counselling, this I think may encourage her to do that."[260] In this way, Redies's sentence supports her ability to attend a treatment program or counselling in Whitehorse without implementing that as a punitive component of her sentence (upon which a breach of that term would perhaps produce an additional charge and sanction). Judge Barnett describes this formulation as "a better way to do things, I hope,"[261] than a greater period of imprisonment. This decision is noteworthy for foregrounding the need for treatment, but without importing this need into the sentence in a punitive fashion.

Despite the prevalence of the concept that prison is a healing place in the judgments, there are other decisions that communicate the inverse— that prison either fails to promote rehabilitation or is actively harmful to the women ordered there. For example, in sentencing Michelle Arcand from the Muskeg Lake First Nation for possession of cocaine for the purposes of trafficking, Judge Daunt finds that "some jail is warranted" to promote denunciation and deterrence, but adds that "it should be short enough that it does not interfere with the goals of rehabilitation, reparation to the community, and promoting a sense of responsibility in the offender."[262] Similarly, in a decision for another woman sentenced for trafficking in cocaine, M.A.B. from the Manitoulin Island First Nation, Judge Ayotte expresses that a lengthy carceral sentence duration would be damaging. Judge Ayotte finds this woman's moral culpability "relatively low," but that her offence necessitates "a significant deterrent element."[263] The judge determines that this requirement can be satisfied through an intermittent sentence involving "numerous weekends in custody," as "a longer sentence which destroys all that and drives her back to the lifestyle which brought her here does not benefit anyone."[264] The judge writes that this intermittent prison sentence "has the added advantage of allowing her to retain both her home and her employment and to build on the strides she has made in dealing with her history and her addiction."[265]

When sentencing Bryna Link for various offences including robbery, Judge Smith finds that "even a short period in a custodial institution would risk disrupting the road to rehabilitation that Ms. Link has now taken."[266] The judge comments, "Fortunately for our community and for Ms. Link, as she is eligible for a CSO, I can fashion a sentence that will not disrupt her rehabilitation."[267] (However, Judge Smith also adds that her CSO "will be lengthier in duration than would a jail sentence required to be served in an institution,"[268] and orders an eight-month CSO followed by two years of probation, which introduces the risk that she, like other criminalized Indigenous women, may then breach and be ordered to serve the remainder of her sentence in prison, and for longer than she would otherwise have been incarcerated.) In sentencing Tracy Smith, who seems to be Métis, for impaired driving causing death, Judge Higinbotham orders a prison sentence of one day followed by a probationary term of three years, explaining that rehabilitation and reformation must prevail. The judge states that, "in light of the clear evidence that any significant prison sentence will, at minimum, render meaningless and useless all of the progress to date, no half way measures are fit,"[269] and that public safety is best achieved through Smith's remaining a "ward" at an addictions treatment centre in the community, "not a prison inmate."[270] (After the Crown appeal of this sentence, the British Columbia Court of Appeal set aside this sentence, finding it overly focused on rehabilitation and failing to account for deterrence, and substituted a prison term of two years, reduced by one day to account for the day she had already served,[271] and by fourteen additional days for her time in custody on remand,[272] retaining the three-year probation order.)

The Availability of Community Resources

Sentencing is an inherently difficult process, often engaging competing issues and principles. There are challenges regarding the availability of community resources, as well as some features of conditional sentences that may contribute to Indigenous women's vulnerabilities to breach. There is also a fraught relationship between incarceration and rehabilitation, and the gap between provincial and federal treatment services further complicates the judicial task.

While it is problematic that some women may be sentenced to prison for rehabilitative services despite the availability and otherwise appropriateness of a community sentence, sometimes any given community resources are simply insufficient and judges lack options on sentencing. In *R. v. Petawabano,* although Judge Lucille Chabot orders a penitentiary sentence of five years for manslaughter and does not discuss the prospect of a conditional sentence, the judge nonetheless comments upon the isolation of that community, and other remote communities: "Whenever more specialized services are required or must be given more frequently than the visits of the traveling professionals coming to the community, people have no choice but to go out of the community to get the services."[273] Judge Chabot presents rehabilitation through imprisonment as a priority, commenting that it is "necessary for the accused to get involved in therapy and to receive the professional services needed for her condition, both psychological and psychiatric."[274] The final sentence falls within the four years submitted by defence counsel and the six presented by the Crown (so imprisonment at the provincial level is excluded in the judgment). In another decision producing a federal sentence but nonetheless pointing to the dearth of community resources, Justice Heather J. Holmes sentences Destiny Fields for manslaughter, and indicates having been "advised that with your transgender identity, health and community supports specific to your complex of specific needs are not available to you in your community of origin, which is the Saddle Lake Cree First Nation."[275] Ultimately, Justice Holmes orders the seven-year prison sentence put forth in the joint submission by counsel (reduced to five years and sixty-six days for pre-sentence custody). The judge recommends Fields be referred to a certain program in the federal correctional system, although it appears this program is simply geared toward risk management and is still not tailored to the "complex of specific needs" related to her transgender identity that the judge finds unavailable in her community.

For cases where conditional sentences are considered, the availability of community resources becomes critical. In sentencing Jenna McClements, a member of the Teslin Tlingit Council, for a number of offences including arson and various breaches of release conditions, Judge Ruddy comments that "the lack of a clear indication of the likelihood of her being able to access appropriate treatment and programming"[276] hindered the judge's ability to order a conditional sentence order. The judge notes this issue remains "not completely answered," which "is unfortunately a result of the practical realities we deal with when trying to access treatment outside of the Territory."[277] Nonetheless, Judge Ruddy orders a conditional sentence order of two years less a day plus three years' probation for the arson offence, and concurrent sentences for the breaches, "because if I go over that two year mark I cannot do a conditional" sentence.[278] It seems that Judge Ruddy is motivated to order a conditional sentence due to the rehabilitative efforts McClements had begun, as the judge determines she "is in fact now treatment ready"[279] regarding her substance abuse, and because McClements might be accepted into one of two community treatment programs. At times, such community treatment options will be even fewer or more tenuous. As Timothy F. Hartnagel explains in the context of youth sentencing, where a judge decides "some type of community-based treatment program" is the most appropriate sanction as an alternative to incarceration, "if such a program is not available in the province the judge might then have little option but to impose a term of custody."[280]

In other decisions, the community resources are considered inadequate to the deemed treatment needs of the Indigenous woman being sentenced, and prison is found to be the only remaining option for rehabilitation. This is evident in *R. v. Waskewitch,* where the judge delivers a four-year imprisonment term against the submission of defence counsel for a conditional sentence. The judge rejected this submission after finding that the community (and provincial institutions) lacks proper rehabilitation-oriented resources and that Deborah Lee Waskewitch requires specialized treatment in a prison setting. Similarly, in *R. v. Smith*,[281] Judge Lilles finds that the treatment resources in the community are insufficient, and sentences Helen Smith to thirty-one months' imprisonment to be followed by a further three years of probation for assault causing bodily harm.

Helen Smith had been "partying into the early morning hours" with her husband, and punched and kicked his head after he made derogatory comments to her.[282] Smith is a survivor of the residential school system, and her psychological assessment reports that, in her childhood, she experienced "emotional, spiritual, physical, sexual abuse and neglect at home."[283] She began her involvement with alcohol as a child, which developed into an addiction. Smith's substance abuse extended to heroin and cocaine several years before this sentencing (at which she was fifty-one years old), and her addictions have compromised her memory from when she was a sex worker "living in skid row in Vancouver."[284] In terms of the pattern of Smith's offending, the RCMP report filed suggests that her past assaultive behaviour has generally escalated in tandem with her drinking, and mostly involves aggression against men. The judge states that, despite her recognizing the nexus between her drinking and these assaults, "it has not resulted in a change in her behaviour."[285] Her psychological assessment notes that "violence has been part of all her relationships."[286] It seems that she was the victim of much partner violence, and was also abusive to her partners—but, presumably due to a strength and power imbalance, she "often wait[ed] until they were drunk before assaulting them, since she could not successfully assault them when the men were sober."[287] (In Chapter 2, I note that Helen Good also resorted to this assaultive pattern.)

The depiction of her violence within the psychological assessment is troubling, as her assessor finds vis-à-vis her abusive relationships that "her expectations of her partners were often not met in that she believed the men should work and not stay at home and drink and abuse her (generally they were chronic alcoholics as well). As a result of her partners not meeting her idealistic expectations, she would build up resentment and eventually attack them when they were drunk."[288]

It is problematic for the author of the report to suggest that Smith's expectation that her partners work, strive to take responsibility for managing their addictions, and refrain from abusing her is "idealistic." It is inconceivable that a similar report for a criminalized urban, white, middle-class woman would suggest these expectations are unreasonable or idealistic. Or, removing criminalization entirely: it is even more inconceivable that anyone would make such a comment about an urban, white, middle-class woman's relationships. I mention above that Pate has found that criminalized women's pre-sentence reports offer gendered perspectives of women's struggles; this example from Smith's psychological report is a similarly gendered, raced, and classed representation of her pathway to criminalization. Further, as most judges rely heavily on recommendations from pre-sentence reports, Smith's psychological assessment is a primary source of information for the sentencing judge. It is clear that Judge Lilles, too, relies on Smith's psychological assessment: the doctor's "report and oral evidence were extremely helpful in understanding Mrs. Smith's issues and the nature of treatment or programming that may be of assistance to her."[289] Nonetheless, despite reliance on a report that contains the above problematic comments, Judge Lilles does find in mitigation that Smith was exposed to violence in her childhood, and, "as an offender, she has also been a victim."[290]

There are several aggravating factors, including Smith's past assault(s) upon her husband, offence seriousness, and her extensive, lengthy criminal record of other serious assaults. Judge Lilles does refer to Smith's being an Indigenous woman with "a most unfortunate childhood where she was exposed to violence"[291] within mitigating factors, but the judgment does not directly mention *Gladue*, and neither does it cite s. 718.2(e). This is insufficient to discharge the judicial duty in *Gladue*,[292] as affirmed by *Ipeelee*.[293]

Against the backdrop of the violence in Smith's life, the author of her psychological assessment determines that she presents a "substantial level of risk to the public that cannot be moderated without significant treatment interventions that should be delivered in a secure setting in my opinion."[294] The doctor evaluates her as presenting a high risk to reoffend (and violently), with a low projected level of manageability in the community, and as having extensive treatment needs for addictions and the abuse she has experienced. The author of this report also "concludes that the mix of counseling and treatment programs available in the Yukon are insufficient to reduce her risk to her current husband or future partners to a level manageable in the community."[295] Judge Lilles affirms this conclusion, stating, "I agree. On the other hand, there are a variety of programs available in the federal system, including several which accommodate traditional aboriginal values and customs."[296] As Smith has been "diagnosed with Anti-social and Borderline Personality Disorders," the judge finds that "she requires a lengthy period of intensive and structured treatment, which is not available in the Yukon or in the community, in order that her risk factors can be managed in the community."[297] Judge Lilles reiterates that "protection of the public can best be achieved by 'rehabilitation', meaning intensive treatment in a structured setting. Such programs are only available in or through the Federal system."[298] After examining the options canvassed by the author of the psychological assessment, Judge Lilles concurs with the recommendation for the program for violent women at Fraser Valley Institute,[299] adding that while there may be additional suitable programs, they appear to be "very few in number."[300]

This judgment is complex in terms of how it deals with treatment issues, as there is tension in the decision regarding rehabilitation. The author of her psychological assessment describes Smith's "unresponsiveness to treatment,"[301] and, in response to being "specifically asked" whether the programming Smith completed while awaiting sentencing was sufficient to reduce her assessed risk, the doctor "advised that they have not."[302] Similarly, Judge Lilles comments that Smith's prior sentences from previous offences (including long prison sentences and community sanctions) "have not been effective in deterring her offending."[303] The judge considers this an aggravating factor. However, among mitigating factors, Judge Lilles includes that Smith "has taken and successfully completed all the programming that was available to her during her detention"[304] (which included both remand at the Whitehorse Correctional Centre and time in the community at the Yukon Adult Residential Centre, where "she was essentially under house arrest").[305] The judge adds that Smith "is clearly motivated to deal with her issues," although qualifies that with an underlined "at this time."[306] Judge Lilles lists the "numerous" counselling options that Smith "has taken advantage of"

during both her imprisonment and community detention while awaiting sentencing:

> She has made contact with and received counseling from
> Alcohol and Drug Services, the Family Violence Prevention
> Unit, CAIRS (a programme for residential school survivors),
> and a variety of support people in her home community of
> Carcross. She has been seeing Dr. Hutsul on a regular basis.
> Dr. Hutsul is a psychologist funded by the Carcross/Tagish
> First Nation. Mrs. Smith completed a three-week substance
> abuse program, the SAM program, while in detention. She
> completed a 15-hour Suicide Intervention Skills Program
> in October 2003. During the latter part of 2003, she was
> released on bail to complete a four-week Women's Residential
> Treatment Program for alcohol and drug addictions. She has
> also contacted Hospice Yukon. Throughout this period, she
> has maintained contact with various religious organizations,
> from which she receives support.[307]

Further, Judge Lilles states that Smith's "attendance and participation in
all the programs were reported as excellent,"[308] and the doctor who performed her psychological assessment communicates that Smith's level
of engagement in these programs "indicate[s] a high level of motivation
which is a positive sign."[309]

Ultimately, Judge Lilles decides that the need to protect the public,
"and in particular, those individuals who may in the future enter into a
relationship with her,"[310] supersedes other considerations. This concern
is reasonably based in her history of assaultive behaviour against men.
However, it (like the doctor's comments that Smith's expectations of her
abusive partners were idealistic) also fails to recognize the context of
those relationships. I again note that there is no *Gladue* analysis, apart
from one offhand reference within mitigating factors recognizing that
Smith is an Indigenous woman, so it appears that the judge decided protection of the public is the "paramount principle in this sentencing"[311]
without properly balancing that against s. 718.2(e).

Nonetheless, it appears that Judge Lilles largely decides Smith's sentence should be a term of federal imprisonment so that Smith can receive treatment services. It is slightly unclear from the above list of programming that Smith completed during her pre-sentence detention which programs she underwent during that period in the correctional institution, and which she participated in while on release in the community. It does appear that while there was some programming that she made use of in the institution, there were other programs within the community, too. For example, Judge Lilles notes in the above list that Smith "was released on bail to complete a four-week Women's Residential Treatment Program for alcohol and drug addictions."[312] There may have been other reasons motivating her judicial interim release, but from this it does appear that Smith had to leave the correctional institution and return to the community to receive that specialized treatment programming. This, in tandem with the diligence, willingness, and success that Smith demonstrated in her pre-sentence treatment, renders it unclear why Judge Lilles determines that only federal prison programs are sufficiently intensive to suit her needs.

It would be instructive to know whether this reasoning would have been altered had the judge engaged in a proper, robust *Gladue* analysis, including its shift in focus toward restorative alternatives to incarceration. Additionally, it is interesting that Judge Lilles comments, as above, that "protection of the public can best be achieved by 'rehabilitation', meaning intensive treatment in a structured setting,"[313] and locates that in the federal penitentiary. Here, the judge defines that "rehabilitation" *means* "intensive treatment" in prison, instead of defining rehabilitation in a more restorative-oriented way, consistent with the need and duty to look to alternatives for criminalized Indigenous persons. Although the issues are entangled within offence seriousness and Smith's lengthy history of criminalization, these complications should not preclude a *Gladue* analysis (as I have referenced throughout this book, *Ipeelee* has clarified that the judicial duty remains in such cases). In sum, *Smith* represents a clear instance in which a judge orders federal incarceration specifically for treatment reasons, and holds out programming in prison as being necessary for the specialized needs of that woman being sentenced.

Sometimes, judges prioritize rehabilitation and find there are sufficient resources in the community to provide treatment services. Indeed, in the judgment sentencing Jasmine Aisaican, Judge M.J. Hinds determines from a Saskatchewan Court of Appeal decision that "this Court is entitled to assume that adequate facilities exist"[314] in the community (although, while perhaps this judicial entitlement should be extended across reasoning regarding other sanctions, this case specifically makes this finding in reference to curative discharges). In *R. v. Isaac*, the judge finds adequate community treatment resources and orders Michelle Isaac to a conditional sentence of sixteen months for defrauding the Ministry of Social Services of over $5,000. Judge R. Green makes efforts to fashion a sentence that responds to Isaac's history of victimization, and notes that she has "ties to Ochapowace First Nation."[315] The presentence report outlines Isaac's childhood, which Judge Green describes as "shocking by any measure"[316] and includes sexual abuse by her grandfather, abuse by her father, and foster care. Isaac became involved with "excessive substance abuse" and multiple relationships that produced seven children, all removed into foster care.[317] While addicted to cocaine, Isaac has sold drugs and attempted suicide by overdose. Ultimately, the judge finds that, "given these unique circumstances, and the resources available for her supervision and treatment in the community,"[318] a conditional sentence is appropriate. Judge Green is clear about how *Gladue* factors and Isaac's history of victimization cumulatively bolster the need to prioritize the principle of rehabilitation, writing,

> I find the reality of her mental illness and her addiction
> to cocaine during the commission of this offence, the fact
> she was sexually abused for six years in foster care as a child,
> and the other *Gladue* factors listed above, to be compelling
> factors in her sentencing. While not in any way negating the
> principles of denunciation and deterrence, in my view these
> factors make clear the importance in this sentencing of the
> principles of rehabilitation and of seeking an alternative
> to incarceration that is reasonable in the circumstances,
> especially considering her circumstances as an Aboriginal
> offender. Taken together with her recent stability, addictions

treatment and her ability to access mental health and other services in the community, I find a conditional sentence to be a reasonable alternative to sending her to the Pinegrove Correctional Centre.[319]

Thus, the judge uses the *Gladue* analysis to discern that Isaac's vulnerabilities and past victimization require a more restorative-oriented sentence. Perhaps it should be noted that Isaac's offence was non-violent, as this may also have more readily allowed the judge to prioritize the principle of rehabilitation.

In *R. v. C.G.O.*, the judge uses the goal of healing to orient and structure a sentence that relies on community resources (as noted by Justice Elizabeth A. Bennett at the British Columbia Court of Appeal in the reasons for the Crown's unsuccessful appeal of C.G.O.'s sentence, "the sentencing judge concluded that the best way society could be served was by rehabilitating Ms. O").[320] In a judgment from First Nations Court, Judge Marion Buller Bennett[321] sentences C.O. to a conditional sentence order of two years less a day followed by a three-year probation order for the aggravated assault of a child and failure to provide the necessaries of life that permanently affected the health of the child. C.O. bathed her sister's three-and-a-half-year-old daughter in hot water that badly burned her skin. Her partner administered traditional first aid, but he refused to take her to the hospital because he "did not trust doctors" and feared that their own children would be removed from their care.[322] After a few days, C.O. insisted they go to the hospital, where examining doctors also found marks on the child's body consistent with "inflicted trauma and severe neglect."[323] The child is now quadriplegic, with brain damage, among other permanent afflictions, and is entirely dependent on a caretaker.

Judge Bennett provides extensive details about C.O.'s personal history: C.O. is Cree, and grew up on a reserve afflicted with poverty, addictions, and abuse, among other "inter-generational impacts of the residential school system."[324] She experienced unrelenting abuse in her life, including long-term sexual abuse by her father and almost continual abuse by her partner, with whom she has several children. Their children have been in and out of state care "voluntarily and by removal," due to social workers' concerns about "parental neglect, insufficient health care and unhealthy living conditions as well as Ms. C.O.'s mental health."[325] Her uncle, an Elder, reported to the sentencing court that C.O. is isolated, having "been away from her family support and traditional life skills."[326]

The judge contemplates her *Gladue* factors, finding from the constellation of systemic factors that victimization has constrained her options, as C.O. "has had few realistic opportunities to change. In my view, the poverty, isolation and violence are precisely what brought Ms. C.O. to court."[327] Judge Bennett extends this understanding of the factors that contributed to her criminalization; although the offences are serious, "in my view, Ms. C.O.'s unique circumstances are inextricably interwoven with the offences."[328] This demonstrates a clear judicial recognition of how the victimization-criminalization continuum, contextualized within *Gladue* factors, has operated in C.O.'s life.

Rooting the understanding of her criminalization in this interplay of systemic factors allows for a solutions-based approach to sentencing wherein the judge states that restitution can be approached only through rehabilitation: "In my view, 'making it right' in this case means two things: providing Ms. C.O. with aboriginal-based services and resources so that she can address her mental health issues: [*sic*] and, ensuring that she addresses her mental health issues in a meaningful way."[329] Judge Bennett fashions a conditional sentence specifically to support C.O., with conditions "aimed at providing the necessary resources for her"[330] and a probationary term "aimed at providing resources for healing."[331] As such, these sanctions are structured and represented as healing instruments. This orientation is consistent with the opinion that C.O.'s uncle (who works in prisons in his capacity as an Elder) expressed at the sentencing hearing: rehabilitation must occur at home because "rehabilitation does not and cannot happen in jail."[332] Broadly, I support this formulation of imprisonment and its limits.

It must be remembered that this sentencing judgment issues from First Nations Court, as it seems that the sentencing paradigm is different in its explicit and sustained focus on rehabilitation from the outset: a "fit sentence" is referred to as "the healing plan."[333] Chris Andersen writes that "for Aboriginal communities interested in taking control of their own justice processes, 'healing is justice,' and 'justice is healing'"[334] (although, of course, First Nations Court remains a government initiative and is not itself representative of Indigenous control over their own justice processes). As described by Robert McFatter, the significance of a given sentencing paradigm has been elucidated by studies demonstrating that a determinative factor in sentencing practices is "penal philosophy," or "the decision-making rules or strategies" judges use in sentencing (such as whether the primary orientation is guided by rehabilitation or deterrence).[335]

The representation of imprisonment that emerges from *C.G.O.* is complicated. It seems that the judge shares the view of C.O.'s uncle, the Elder, that rehabilitation will not happen in prison, because the judge references his opinion and ultimately administers a rehabilitative-oriented community-based sentence, against the Crown's submission that incarceration is required. At the same time, Judge Bennett suggests that imprisonment would not deter C.O., because she "has been imprisoned for most of her life by these very same [systemic] factors," and imprisonment "in some respects, means an improvement in her quality of life."[336] By portraying C.O. as imprisoned by *Gladue* factors, Judge Bennett characterizes imprisonment as a potential respite; that is, prison is not expressly presented as a place of active healing, but at least "healing" in the sense of providing a reprieve from the abuse, poverty, and other challenges in her life. Nonetheless, by ordering a conditional sentence to promote healing, Judge Bennett recognizes that straight incarceration would not be conducive to C.O.'s healing needs.

I suggest that the relationship between punishment and healing is inherently fraught. In several cases in my research, it becomes apparent that the Indigenous women before the courts not only do *not* experience prison as a place where healing is possible, but also have past negative experiences and anticipatory fears about the criminal justice system generally and imprisonment in particular. Periodic moments in certain judgments make visible how Indigenous women experience the spectre of prison as a source of threat. Many (and perhaps all) criminalized Indigenous women may experience the prospect of incarceration, and imprisonment itself, as threatening and damaging (and an extension of oppression through colonization), but these feelings and experiences likely often reside outside the text of a given judgment.

The Spectre of Prison

Much research documents the inherent pains of imprisonment for women, and particularly for Indigenous women. As a visceral contrast to the concept of prison as a place for healing, the spectre of prison for the women being sentenced is a source of fear, anxiety, and anger. Several decisions also suggest that the Indigenous women being sentenced mistrust the criminal justice system as a whole, and specifically the correctional system. The entire experience of moving through (or being processed through) the criminal justice system is often stressful and upsetting, sometimes to the point of undermining the women's progress or destabilizing their lives. As quoted above in relation to the constrained choices available to Nicole Pawis in her mothering, leaving her vulnerable to the offence for which she is sentenced, Justice Reinhardt observes that she was continually "distraught" throughout her proceedings, and comments that multiple adjournments were necessary "because she was unable to proceed without completely losing her composure."[337] I also refer to *Knockwood* above for its discussion of regional variations in the standards and provision of *Gladue* reports, where I mention the distress Kathleen Knockwood experienced through the process of obtaining her (wholly inadequate) pre-sentence report with *Gladue* content. Justice Hill notes that in violation of her bail conditions, she used substances just days before her sentencing, and her counsel submitted to the court that Knockwood "has struggled over the past few months with the stress of the sentence proceeding."[338] I also briefly discuss *Toews* above with reference to courts erroneously requiring a causal connection between systemic factors and the given offence, and regarding conflicting evidence between her PSR and *Gladue* report. The *Gladue* report provided for Ashley Toews indicates that she had used cocaine in the months before her sentencing (upon which both of her children were apprehended), and in her interview with its author, she "said she 'slipped,'" and "attribut[ed] this to the stress of her impending legal matters and the 'hopelessness' she felt regarding her children's and her own prospects for the future."[339] In sentencing Jasmine Aisaican for driving while impaired and while disqualified, Judge Hinds writes that she testified at her sentencing hearing "quite candidly that she is very frightened of going to jail," and is "scared that jail will affect her ability to care for her own children and to keep the home which she has resided at for many years with her children."[340] Aisaican lived on the Sakimay First Nation and the Sakimay Reserve in her youth, and is also a member of Cowessess First Nation. She "does not feel that she is entirely done treatment for her alcoholism," and testified that she was so "stressed out and scared of being away (jailed) from her family and her children" that she consumed alcohol in the days before her sentencing hearing.[341]

Across the judgments, there are many instances revealing the anxieties Indigenous women experience as a direct product of facing the power and stakes of the criminal justice system. Indigenous women's fears about the experience (and after-effects) of incarceration are eminently reasonable and well-founded, realized in their own lives across various stages of the sentencing process. For example, Eulalie Ussak struggled through her pre-sentence custody, and then suffered subsequent challenges directly due to her involvement in the criminal justice system. Justice Cooper writes that she "was remanded into custody at the Baffin Correctional Centre. At that time there was no separate unit or facility for women. Her time in custody was extremely difficult. Because of the lack of facilities for women, she was in her cell 23 hours a day. She lost 30 lbs. during the 40 days she was in Remand and the authorities had serious concerns for her health."[342] Justice Cooper notes that, even following her release on bail, Ussak "has continued to experience loss by her inability to gain employment and the loss of her home."[343]

Another example of where prison represents a source of anxiety is a decision in which a Métis woman, R.C.L., has made what the judge describes as a "heartfelt"[344] statement to the court near the end of her sentencing hearing for improper or indecent interference with a dead body. Judge Michael B. Hicks conveys about her emotional response to spending forty-four days in pre-sentence custody that "it had a profound affect [sic] on her," and "if I could summarize her words, I would say that she does not want to be part of or influenced by that jail culture."[345] This issue, and "the implications of R.C.L.'s upbringing as an Aboriginal woman in chaotic circumstances,"[346] prompt the judge's reasoning that the sentence must engage "remedial, restorative and rehabilitative factors."[347] Due to the circumstances of the offence, Judge Hicks decides a conditional sentence order is inappropriate and prison is necessary, and, after crediting double her time in remand, orders a sentence of an additional twenty-one months, and attaches three further years of probation (the Crown had asked for a federal sentence).

Similarly, in *R. v. Gambler*, the prospect of prison produces stress and fear, and prison is also portrayed as an ineffective place for healing when contrasted with a community treatment centre. In the decision sentencing Bonnie Gambler for driving while disqualified and with a blood-alcohol level over the legal limit, Judge Green references the distinction Gambler makes in her own prior experiences in prison as compared with those in a treatment centre. Gambler testified at her sentencing hearing, and "questioned the quality and effectiveness of any treatment or programming she received when previously incarcerated at the Pine Grove Correctional Centre," elaborating that this institution "was a very stressful place to be."[348] A member of the Cote First Nation, Gambler directly contrasts this with her experience when voluntarily attending a treatment centre through the Métis Addiction Council of Saskatchewan, Inc. between the date of her offences and her sentencing. She voices that this treatment centre gives her greater ongoing access to counsellors, provides access to a twenty-four-hour help line, and overall "has worked for her."[349] Judge Green notes that during cross-examination, Gambler was questioned about "whether the fear of being incarcerated again was overwhelming," and "she agreed that it was."[350] A counsellor at the treatment centre, who was qualified as an expert in the sentencing hearing, testified that the treatment program offered at the centre surpassed any available treatment in prison primarily because the former is "based on the importance of the therapeutic relationship," and "was more extensive and went further than anything attempted at Pine Grove."[351] Judge Green ultimately orders a curative discharge and probation for three years, alongside a concurrent eighteen-month CSO.

Other judgments reveal some of the specific oppressiveness of the experience of incarceration for Indigenous women, such as in *R. v. Johnson*. Jessica Johnson pleaded guilty to robbery, discharging a firearm with intent to prevent arrest, aggravated assault of a peace officer, and using a firearm during flight from a robbery (her co-accused, with whom she was in a relationship, went to trial). Johnson's mother is a member of the Little Salmon Carmacks First Nation, and her father is a member of the Kluane First Nation. Justice Gower reviews her *Gladue* report and finds mitigating that *Gladue* factors "have disadvantaged Ms. Johnson in many ways beyond her control," and thereby accepts her defence counsel's submission that she "never really had much of a chance to make a success of her life given her upbringing, *until now*."[352] In this respect, through the phrase "until now," it seems her sentence is framed as an opportunity for positive change, although the judgment suggests a complex image of the meaning of prison, in general and for Johnson in particular.

Justice Gower quotes from the psychologist's report that Johnson "becomes discouraged easily and she appears to benefit from having a sense of hope. A lengthy incarceration may further entrench her resentment towards *what she perceives as an unjust system*."[353] (As an aside, it is worth noting that all people, and certainly those facing a prison sentence, benefit from being able to retain a sense of hope.) Johnson's understanding that the overarching system(s) in which she is being sentenced is unjust is profoundly significant. In their report for the TFFSW, Sugar and Fox, themselves Indigenous women and former federal prisoners, differentiate the experience of imprisonment for Indigenous women for reasons including their fraught relationship with settler law, as prison rules echo colonial rules, and, "for us, prison rules have the same illegitimacy as the oppressive rules under which we grew up."[354] Sugar and Fox elucidate that "our understandings of law, of courts, of police, of the judicial system, and of prisons are all set by lifetimes defined by racism," extending to cultural and economic oppression and marginalization and producing "oppressive regimes whose authority we resent and deny."[355]

This context is alluded to by the psychologist's observation that a long period of incarceration could amplify Johnson's resentment toward what she experiences and understands to be an unjust system, but it becomes effectively individualized in how it is translated in the judgment. That is, Justice Gower decides that the relevant aggravating factors include Johnson's "apparent disregard for authority, as evidenced by her criminal record for process offences, the WCC [Whitehorse Correctional Centre] reports of internal disciplinary offences," and her "psychological report."[356] The judge endeavours to contextualize Johnson's behaviours while in custody by suggesting that she "is suffering from significant psychological challenges, which to a large extent are beyond her control," as "she has been diagnosed with post-traumatic stress disorder and a personality disorder with borderline antisocial features."[357] Drawing on related comments from the psychologist, Justice Gower posits, "In that context it is perhaps not surprising that Ms. Johnson would be reported to have exhibited the type of rude and disrespectful behaviours described in the WCC reports."[358] However, while compassionate, this frame still individualizes what are likely much deeper, more systemic concerns. Against the psychologist's observations that Johnson resents the system, finding it unjust, it would be helpful to further contextualize Johnson's process and disciplinary offences within her experience as an Indigenous woman living in an unjust political and criminal justice system, which, in practical terms, could mean the judge's deciding that these process and disciplinary offences do not constitute aggravating circumstances.

Members of the Kluane First Nation Elders Council submitted a letter for Johnson's sentencing, in which they write, in terms evoking the victimization-criminalization continuum, that "trauma . . . has put her there,"[359] in the system. The judge relates that they suggest that "some of the British Columbia penitentiaries have a healing component" and put this forward for sentencing consideration.[360] Justice Gower makes a recommendation that CSC consider Johnson for the Tsow-Tun Le Lum Substance Abuse Treatment Centre in British Columbia and the Okimaw Ohci Healing Lodge for Indigenous women in Saskatchewan, and, heeding the Elders Council request, lists a few correctional programs for Indigenous prisoners. The judgment does demonstrate judicial recognition that prison is not inherently a healing place, such as where Justice Gower writes in reference to the attempt to "incorporat[e] a healing component to this sentence, *to the extent that that can be done in a penitentiary* in British Columbia."[361]

The issue of "healing" is effectively discarded in *R. v. Papin*, but, like *Johnson*, this decision engages issues that recall Sugar and Fox's comments about Indigenous women's experience of the criminal justice (and certainly correctional) system(s) as fundamentally unjust. In a judgment determining a dangerous offender hearing and sentencing

(connected to the predicate offences of aggravated assault and possession of a weapon for a dangerous purpose), Justice John T. Henderson
finds that "even though many significant Gladue factors are present in
this case, the actual impact that those factors will have on the ultimate
sentence is slight."[362] In part due to the conclusion that her "behavior . . .
will not improve with further treatment,"[363] the judge sentences Papin
to a total of five years' incarceration for the predicate offences and a ten-
year long-term supervision order (the maximum duration). Justice Henderson notes Tammy Papin's "persistent involvement with the criminal
justice system,"[364] observing that she "has been in custody in both the
federal and the provincial correctional systems for the majority of her
adult life."[365] Papin is a member of the Enoch Cree Nation, and was embroiled in various institutions (including residential treatment facilities)
in her earlier life, too, after a childhood "characterized by domestic violence, alcoholism, drug addiction and sexual abuse."[366] The judge writes
that she "endured horrific conditions as a child during which she was
in and out of foster care and also, at various times, was housed in institutional settings."[367] It seems Papin has been institutionalized in some
form throughout her life. As Comack observes, "For some [women], incarceration is part of a long line of state intervention into their lives."[368]

Referring to one of Papin's previous periods of incarceration, Justice
Henderson indicates that she expressed to the psychologist of the secure
unit that "the correctional system was unjust,"[369] and that psychologist
testified that Papin "did not trust the custodial system."[370] Incidentally, from my comparison of the dates provided within the judgment, it
seems Papin made these comments to the psychologist during the same
period of incarceration at Nova Institution in which she "filed a griev-
ance regarding her lack of access to Aboriginal services, particularly
sweats."[371] (The judge acknowledges that "not all federal inmates have
access to a full range of Aboriginal programming.")[372] Papin's mistrust-
ful perception of the system as unjust should perhaps also be understood
with reference to her having been "convicted of a number of additional
offences which extended her period of incarceration"[373] while she served
sentences in federal institutions in the past, although the judge does not
explicitly connect these experiences in the decision.

As this decision deals with a dangerous offender hearing, the Crown argues that Papin's past offences demonstrate a pattern of violence. In response, the judge contextualizes her violence, including finding it to be as generally "low level violence which resulted in little, if any, injury."[374] Justice Henderson concludes, "In most instances the Offender was reacting to circumstances that were presented to her."[375] The judge finds that "very often she was responding violently to police officers or security guards who were attempting to arrest her. . . . In other situations she was responding violently when she was being moved or otherwise dealt with by correctional officers while in custody. . . . In most situations the Offender's violence was directed to persons who were lawfully trying to physically control her. None of the violence was directed against victims who were randomly targeted."[376]

Justice Henderson further infers that "the prevalence of assaults against persons in authority such as police officers, security guards and correctional officers suggests that the Offender has little, if any, respect for persons in authority."[377] The judge does not directly connect her mistrust in what she experiences as an unjust correctional system and her seeming lack of respect for authority figures with her *Gladue* factors and related history of institutionalization, although, given the insights of Sugar and Fox about the invalidity and oppressiveness of the prison system for Indigenous women, I suggest these issues should be understood as interrelated. I pointed earlier to research finding that institutional violence (including self-directed) and disruptiveness of women prisoners do not directly correlate to their conduct outside of prison walls, and that such behaviours within prison should be understood as products of the experience of incarceration itself, and not indicative of the level of risk the women may present in the community. The ways in which Papin acted out violently while in prison (against authorities trying to control her) should also be read through this framework, coupled with Sugar and Fox's understanding of what prison signifies for Indigenous women.

Although these cases point to the issue of Indigenous women's fearing and mistrusting the criminal justice system and finding it and its prison system oppressive and illegitimate, it should also be recognized that processes of colonization and related ongoing torment and pain for Indigenous individuals, families, communities, and nations simultaneously produce similar fears and perceptions of other (sometimes intersecting or interdependent) government systems. The UN Committee connects the overrepresentation of Indigenous children removed into the state welfare system with amplified vulnerability of Indigenous women to experiencing violence, given that mothers "are reluctant to seek help from authorities for fear that their children will be taken away."[378] This relationship between the disproportionate state removal of Indigenous children and the victimization of Indigenous women can also be extended to the criminalization of Indigenous women, as a related broader personal and collective sense of apprehension toward and distrust in government systems surfaces in moments in the cases. For example, in *R.C.L.*, Judge Hicks suggests that R.C.L. acted "for selfish motives" in failing to contact authorities about the death of a man in her home (she was sentenced for improper or indecent interference with a dead body, which she had attempted to dispose of herself); her "stated reason for failing to alert police was to prevent child welfare staff from stepping in to apprehend the children and carry out their responsibilities."[379] The degree to which R.C.L.'s decision was a "selfish" act should be challenged. As Randi Cull indicates, many years of "unjustified state intervention" into Indigenous mothers' lives demonstrate "how the state has done an appallingly bad job when acting as the parent or guardian" of Indigenous children, and that the focus must be shifted from surveilling and evaluating Indigenous mothering and instead redirected toward "the state's continued negligence"[380] on this issue. Cull notes that across various historical and ongoing forms of state intervention into Indigenous families, Indigenous peoples "have always strongly resisted the removal of their children," but that the vast power imbalance between the state and Indigenous peoples obstructs such efforts.[381] Toward the end of her sentencing hearing, R.C.L. delivered a statement to the court, and the judge writes that "she referred to her own experience in foster care and in her family of origin and the impact that has had on her own dealings with Ministry officials in regard to her own children."[382] Her *Gladue* report indicates that her mother was abused in foster care, and, during R.C.L.'s own childhood, she "experience[ed] systemic inequality . . . including dislocation, poverty, substance abuse and family breakdown."[383] All of R.C.L.'s youngest children were apprehended by the state.

This judgment also discloses that during the period in which her pre-sentence report was being prepared, R.C.L. was pregnant, but denied this to her social worker and gave the hospital an assumed name when giving birth (her reasons for denying her pregnancy and providing a false name to the hospital are not identified in the judgment, although it seems reasonable to infer she was afraid her children would be removed from her care). She could not pick up her baby from the hospital to which he was transferred because she was detained in advance of her court date for the final sentencing submissions. As R.C.L. was in custody and unable to receive her baby, and because he was not linked in hospital records to her real identity, her baby was apprehended. Her fears about the child welfare system intersect powerfully with her experience of the criminal justice system in this case, effectively coming full circle: she reports that her offence was motivated by her fears about her children being appre-hended, and her newborn baby was apprehended while she was detained awaiting her consequent sentencing. Indeed, in outlining the breadth of its mandate, the MMIWG Inquiry indicates its purview encompasses "other forms of *institutionalized violence* beyond the justice system," not-ing that such institutionalized violence includes the child welfare system and incarceration.[384] Gordana Eljdupovic, Terry Mitchell, Lori Curtis, et al., note that the residential school system, "child welfare practices," and the overincarceration of Indigenous peoples all (each and together) produce "ongoing separation" of Indigenous children "from their fami-lies, communities, and culture," which replicates the isolation, familial and cultural alienation, and vulnerabilities their parents may have expe-rienced in their own childhoods, and reproduces the same intergenera-tional "cycles of poverty and violence," increasing the likelihood of their own later criminalization and incarceration.[385]

In another case where an Indigenous woman's fears about losing her children to one state system contributes to her criminalization in an-other, Charissma McDonald pleaded guilty to criminal negligence caus-ing the death of her baby by not ensuring the child received medical care. When born, that baby had been initially apprehended and placed into foster care after testing positive for opiates, and McDonald's other chil-dren were also removed and placed with other family members. All her children were later returned to her care. At one point, a doctor making a home visit when McDonald was not present told another family member that McDonald should immediately take her baby to the pediatric emergency for an infection. McDonald did not seek further medical attention until she called an ambulance two weeks later to report her child had stopped breathing. In her statements to police, McDonald indicated that she had not taken her baby "to a doctor because she was scared that, due to the bruises on" the baby's body, "she and the other children would be apprehended by Social Services."[386] Additionally, there are other women who also lose their children because of their general involvement in the system, and/or through their actual incapacitation through incarceration. For example, in *R. v. C.T.*, in a decision referenced in Chapter 2 regarding waivers of *Gladue* reports, Judge Brecknell writes that C.T. "was pregnant when she went into custody and gave birth to what is now her third child who is now under the care of the Ministry of Children and Family Development," noting that this woman from the Sturgeon Lake Cree First Nation "was not permitted to care for her child after its birth while in custody up to this point."[387]

Indigenous women incarcerated in a provincial prison told Justices Hamilton and Sinclair for the Aboriginal Justice Inquiry of Manitoba that they were concerned about their children having "been taken away from them and that their criminal involvement had led to questions being raised about their competency as parents," and many of the women explained having committed their offences "in order to feed and provide for their children."[388] It must be remembered that many (probably most) of Indigenous women's concerns about the system are never fully articulated to actors within the system, and/or are never received (or "heard") by those administering the system. These women's perceptions (and the realities) of the systems that control them, at least as "heard" or recorded in the judgments, should be kept in view in the consideration of the tension between punishment and healing. That is, it is the Indigenous women being sentenced in the judgments who live the tension between punishment and healing, and it is these women (along with their families and communities) who are pulled within and feel the pressures and strains of this tension.

Punishment, Dispersed

My own mother told me a story I want to share here, about the bonds of motherhood weaving together Indigenous and non-Indigenous women and their daughters inside, through, and outside the criminal justice system. In 1985, my mother was junior counsel representing a woman who was convicted of second-degree murder for shooting her husband (that woman lost her appeal with different representation, and then my mother sought and was denied leave to appeal before the SCC). My mother kept in touch with her through much of her imprisonment, and one day her former client mailed her little moccasins, for me. My mother's former client was a mother herself, to two daughters. The moccasins have magenta suede and cranberry and soft pink beaded flowers, and were special to me. In 2015, now a judge, my mother rediscovered the moccasins, had them repaired, and gave them to me again. Fran Sugar and Lana Fox made them for me while in prison, at the request of my mother's former client. (Inevitably, it would have been difficult to make the moccasins while the women were incarcerated.) Incidentally, Sugar and Fox are the authors of the above report about Indigenous women's experiences within the oppressive, colonizing structure of federal prison. I tell this story about the prison moccasins to highlight the family relationships grounding many criminalized Indigenous women's lives, and connecting all of us, across different positioning within and beyond the system.

As I noted in Chapter 1, the vast majority of criminalized Indigenous women are mothers, which was starkly evident on review of the cases in my research. Approximately 80 percent of the women in my research are positively identified as mothers in the judgments. Specifically, there are 175 decisions in my study, in which 177 Indigenous women are sentenced (two of the decisions involve the sentencing of two Indigenous women co-accuseds). Of the 177 Indigenous women sentenced, the judges include information explicitly establishing that 141 have children. (Given that judgments vary in the level of detail about the lives of those sentenced, and that PSRs or other sentencing instruments may be similarly variable, it is possible that additional women are also mothers but not indicated as such.)

For some women, their role as mothers is a factor influencing their pathways to criminalization. In certain decisions, judges point to this trajectory. I discuss one such judgment in Chapter 2, in which Justice George delineates a clear line from Summur George's experiences of victimization (including that at the hands of the state, in terms of child apprehension) to her becoming criminalized, inferring that the removal of her two children into state care prompted the onset of her "serious problems which has ultimately led to this offending behavior."[389] In another decision from that chapter, Justice Ratushny identifies traumas that Louisa Killiktee suffered, including miscarrying her triplets and being prevented from participating in traditional Inuit grieving practices because she was in prison at the time, and connects this to her later recriminalization, suggesting that Killiktee coped with her losses on release through drinking, which "contributed to her violent reaction" in the offence for which she is sentenced.[390] I briefly refer to the sentencing of L.M.L. earlier in this chapter, a decision in which Judge Anderson notes that "her children were taken into care for a period of time while she struggled with her addictions," and she later "regained care of her children,"[391] but then all her children were again apprehended by the state. The judge observes that in the years between this removal of her children and the offences for which she is sentenced, L.M.L. had no contact with them, and that her "personal circumstances deteriorated even further following the loss of her children."[392]

When Indigenous women navigate and are moved through the criminal justice system, at every stage (from becoming criminalized to undergoing punishment), while they are the direct, intended objects of the processes of punishment, their families suffer, too. Behind criminalized Indigenous mothers' pathways through the system—including their arrests, struggles with how to manage domestic and other responsibilities when they are denied bail, decisions about whether to proceed to trial or to plead guilty, and the ways in which they cope with their own experience of incarceration and the fact of being removed from their families and communities (or with other sanctions and supervisory orders), among other junctures—are their children. In various decisions, judges recognize this context and meaningfully consider how the punishment they order will impact the families of the Indigenous women they sentence. It seems that, in these cases, judges regard the women's children as not simply part of their lives and responsibilities outside of their assigned place in the system, but as an active dimension of the women's rehabilitation while they remain under the system's control. I observed this dynamic operating in two primary modes in the cases in which motherhood is persuasive for the judge: in some cases, judges determine that mothering responsibilities function to mitigate the sentence; in others, judges specifically consider how a prison sentence might affect the children involved.

As I discuss in Chapter 2, Juanita Johnson's fear about being separated from her young daughter (she is also pregnant at sentencing) is not expressly framed as mitigating, but functions similarly. Judge Cozens comments that this is "not a determinative factor by any means, because offenders that go to jail will be separated from their children, but it can be a factor in a person realizing the extent to which the consequences of their actions may harm other people,"[393] and ultimately orders a conditional sentence. Earlier in this chapter, I discuss *Diamond*, in which mothering is constructed as mitigating. In other examples of where mothering becomes mitigating, when sentencing Janet Masakayash (referenced in Chapter 2) for manslaughter, Justice Bishop writes that she "immediately after the stabbing thought of her circumstances relating to her unborn child and made efforts to phone Ester Bottle to take care of that child as she knew that she would be incarcerated."[394] Masakayash "gave birth to that child while in custody," and the judge finds this "is another mitigating factor and Gladue consideration which this court experiences from time to time."[395] In a decision sentencing Kimberly Spencer, who has connections to Carry the Kettle First Nation, Ochapowace First Nation, and Cowessess First Nation, Justice Ellen J. Gunn includes among the factors mitigating her sentence that she "has had the primary responsibility to raise her six children, largely without the assistance of the fathers of the children—both of whom have been abusive to her. The children, some of whom are now adults, are also productive members of society."[396] The judge notes that two of her children are young and remain under her care. For her charge of impaired driving causing bodily harm, Justice Gunn orders a ten-month sentence plus probation for one year, "declin[ing] to order a victim fine surcharge" because the judge finds it would cause her or her children undue hardship.[397] Similarly, in sentencing Ivy Pijogge, Justice Stack includes within her mitigating factors that this woman of Innu and Inuit descent "is the mother of 5 (and is still breastfeeding her youngest)."[398] The judge references her role as a mother multiple times in the decision, including noting within the *Gladue* analysis that her "personal circumstances require her, if possible, to remain available for her children, especially her youngest."[399] Considering her combined mitigating factors, Justice Stack finds, "I should strive to find a sentence that will avoid imprisonment,"[400] and sentences her to a conditional sentence order of six months for leaving an accident scene knowing bodily harm had been caused.

Pijogge's mothering role also seems to function in a punitive manner in her ultimate sentence. Justice Stack includes within the conditions attached to Pijogge's conditional sentence order that she must "provide for the support and care of her children" for the duration of her sentence,[401] which leaves her open to being found to violate this condition if she is perceived as failing to comply. (Justice Stack does note that Pijogge "has indicated a willingness to comply with conditions of sentence,"[402] although it appears this is a generalized, anticipatory willingness expressed without reference to the specific terms of her ultimate sentence order.) As well, Justice Stack indicates, "I have not made an exception to the order for house arrest permitting Ms. Pijogge to shop for groceries and other supplies for her family. That task will have to be undertaken by someone else for the period of her sentence unless her circumstances change and an application for a variance is made pursuant to s. 742.4. The restrictions on Ms. Pijogge's freedom must be meaningful and must come at a price."[403]

The judgment indicates that Pijogge "has strong family support,"[404] and "has been in a stable relationship for seven years,"[405] so it seems she does have others on whom she can rely to obtain domestic supplies and the like while she is confined (the judge also makes certain other exceptions to the house arrest component of her conditional sentence order, such as permitting her to attend her place of employment and any medical appointments for her family). Nonetheless, restricting Pijogge from purchasing necessities does mean that these responsibilities shift to her family, which arguably transfers some of the experience of "punishment" to them. It is, of course, unknown how she may have been impacted on sentencing had she lacked that base of family support and not had a committed partner.

Like Pijogge, Schinkel's abilities to fulfill both the requirements of her sentence and her child-care responsibilities depend upon family support. Other criminalized Indigenous mothers may not be in a position to rely on such support to assist with their abilities to complete their sentences and simultaneously care for their children or other dependents. As I briefly discuss in Chapter 2, Judge Schmidt orders concurrent intermittent sentences of sixty days and attaches two years of probation for Teri Schinkel's offences of impaired driving causing bodily harm, dangerous driving causing bodily harm, and refusing a breathalyzer. The judge notes that Schinkel reports "that this accident brought her to a different way of thinking, and that she now wants to care for her child properly," and has the support of her family.[406] Judge Schmidt expects this sentence should "assist you in your healing; it will not detract from it,"[407] and explicitly adds, "The reason it is intermittent is to—and I should state this on the record—is so that it allows you to carry on with your healing and look after your child. I have heard from a number of people that seem responsible. I am certain that they can be part of your child's care while you are doing your intermittent time."[408] Judge Schmidt comments, after delivering the sentence order for Schinkel, "I also am very encouraged by the way that your child is coming first in your thinking and is encouraging you to be strong."[409] The Crown appealed the sentence; in upholding the sentence (but amending the driving prohibition), the Court of Appeal for Yukon notes that the sentencing judge "recognized and gave significant weight to Ms. Schinkel's healing and rehabilitation," and "identified the importance of her role in healing her family, which for generations had experienced systemic Aboriginal suffering."[410]

When sentencing Keshia Key from the Key First Nation for a summary charge of assault with a weapon, Judge D.J. Kovatch orders a conditional sentence order of six months followed by one year of probation, with both sanctions sharing the same conditions, and conditions partially selected to facilitate her mothering. Key's daughter was apprehended and placed in foster care after Key was taken into custody for this offence, although later returned to her care. It seems her defence counsel emphasized the intergenerational effects of colonization processes in submissions, submitting that "this offence is directly related to the accused being a native person," because Key's mother and grandmother had attended residential schools and "did not learn how to be a mom, and were not able to pass this on" to her.[411] Key's defence counsel suggested that Key "saw alcohol and drug abuse and physical abuse, and began to participate in that kind of life," and argued that the judge should use a rehabilitative and restorative approach[412] to further support rehabilitative steps Key had begun. Citing *Gladue* and *Ipeelee*, Judge Kovatch adopts defence counsel's reasoning and approach regarding Key's pathways from victimization to criminalization, commenting, "It seems to me and I would conclude that defence counsel has very nicely made the case that a number of these historical factors and this accused's particular upbringing are very significant and influential, thus bringing her to this point in life when she came into conflict with the law. Ms. Key had an unfortunate upbringing and received little guidance or support from her parents. In addition, she witnessed physical abuse, and alcohol and drug abuse. There was family breakdown. Ms. Key began to be involved in some of the same lifestyle."[413] Judge Kovatch suggests that Key's motherhood influences the sentence determinations, noting having "decline[d] to put her on the electronic monitoring system and to make her subject to house arrest" to support her ongoing education pursuits and because she "is a young mother."[414]

In another decision in which the judge finds counsel submissions compelling, when sentencing Chantal Tizya of the Vuntut Gwitchin First Nation, Chief Judge Michael Cozens follows the joint submission by counsel and orders sixty days' time served for assault causing bodily harm, concurrent three-month conditional sentence orders for two counts of assault, and probation for nine months for failing to comply with conditions of her undertaking. Tizya is a mother to a young son, and Judge Cozens includes within the details supporting the judge's acceptance of the joint submission that she has made a commitment "to try to be a mother for her four-year-old son, who is currently with her sister and will be living with her" during her community sentence.[415]

When making sentencing determinations, some judges consider Indigenous women's role as mothers and their relationships with their children with respect to the objective of rehabilitation. In these decisions, the women's mothering is associated with healing (in terms of both their own rehabilitation and the health and well-being needs of their children), which is often framed as incompatible with carceral sentences. In some decisions, this reasoning is connected to judges' looking to criminalized Indigenous women's needs and desires to care for their children as a source of personal motivation toward their own rehabilitation. For example, the judge sentencing Janine Firth finds that her children are a motivating force in her healing. I discuss aspects of Firth's sentencing above, particularly with reference to the perception shared among the judge and other actors (including Firth herself) that the federal correctional system is best equipped to support her needs. For her various offences including robbery, Judge Ruddy ultimately orders a global sentence of thirty-six months, then reduced by her five months in pre-sentence custody. After referencing Firth's "history of victimization," and her consequent "lengthy history of self-medication" through substance abuse and how that features into her offending behaviours in the matters before the court and on her criminal record, Judge Ruddy comments that she does "appear to have a real desire to address her issues, and has a certain degree of motivation in the fact that she has three young daughters between the ages of five and ten, whom I accept she loves dearly and wants to be in a position to play a role in their lives. They are currently in care, but it appears that they are in a good placement and they are currently together, which is important to her."[416]

In sentencing Ernestine Elliott, Judge Brooks similarly finds that her family provides motivation for her own rehabilitation. Judge Brooks also reflects on the import of punishment itself. Concluding that Elliott's offence of theft over $5,000 warrants a prison sentence (whether in the community or in an institution), Judge Brooks examines the likely impact of a carceral term on her and her family, including her children:

> If Ms. Elliott is sent to jail she will serve that sentence on
> the lower mainland. There is no jail for women to serve
> their sentence on Vancouver Island. If jailed, she would be

taken from where she has lived virtually all her life to a place
where it will be extremely difficult for her family to visit her.
Such a visit would likely require more than one day of travel
for her family. Ms. Elliott would be separated from all those
ties which support her in her pro-social lifestyle. She would
be denied the motivation to rehabilitation which comes
from the love and support of family members. *Every day
would be an excruciating punishment for Ms. Elliott above
and beyond that which would be faced by any male sentenced
to jail or any female sentenced in the lower mainland.* I am
satisfied that, as a matter of law, I am entitled to take this
factor into account. . . . I am also satisfied that this is a
significant factor in determining the appropriate sentence
for Ms. Elliott.[417]

In this light, "punishment" does not simply refer to an entity uniformly
imposed on and felt equally by any party to whom it is administered;
instead, Judge Brooks suggests that the meaning of "punishment" is differential and contingent both upon institutional limitations and the
specificities of the identity and circumstances of a given person being
sentenced. Sentencing is an individualized process, and articulating that
the consequent punishment itself is felt differently by different individuals is an important further consideration. For Elliott's sentencing,
Judge Brooks indicates that a form of punishment (incarceration) that
deprives her of family support signifies a deeper, more oppressive punishment that would detrimentally affect her rehabilitation by compro-
mising her own motivation toward that objective. Judge Brooks rejects
the Crown assertion that the offence seriousness requires "an actual jail
sentence."[418] The judge finds such a sentence focused on general deterrence and denunciation would both neutralize "the forceful language of
Ipeelee," and, moreover, represent punishment that "would extend beyond what was fit if Ms. Elliott were incarcerated on the lower mainland
so far from family and friends who would assist in her rehabilitation."[419]
Judge Brooks settles upon a conditional sentence of eighteen months
followed by probation for two years.

In other decisions, judges focus upon both the criminalized Indigenous women's role as mothers as well as the potential (likely) impacts of incarceration upon their children. The persuasiveness of mothering responsibilities and the extended impacts of prison upon children are distinct and unambiguous in the reasoning of Justice Bonnie L. Croll when determining T.A.P.'s sentence. Sentenced for possession of a loaded prohibited firearm and for knowing that its serial number had been modified, T.A.P. pleaded guilty on facts indicating police attended her home after being notified of "a violent domestic occurrence."[420] The facts detail that police arrested T.A.P.'s partner once her daughter told them he had threatened her, and then arrested T.A.P. when her partner informed them of the gun in T.A.P.'s possession. The judge accepts T.A.P.'s evidence that she "simply accepted possession" of the gun from someone due to fears about safety related to a former partner and nearby drug dealers.[421]

It is clear from the decision that T.A.P.'s role as a mother is more persuasive for the judge than any *Gladue* considerations. Although T.A.P. believes her grandfather is Mi'kmaq and testified to this effect at the sentencing hearing, Aboriginal Legal Services of Toronto was unable to verify this and thus did not produce a *Gladue* report. Justice Croll accepts T.A.P.'s evidence, but finds "any nexus between her Aboriginality and her criminal behaviour would be remote at best," adding that "there are no unique systemic or background factors that have influenced or impacted T.A.P.'s coming before this court and which would influence her sentence."[422] Instead, Justice Croll appears guided by the needs of T.A.P.'s children.

She has five children, two of whom have developmental and mental health issues, and one of whom was born after T.A.P. was raped. In accordance with a letter filed as an exhibit by a doctor overseeing her two children with greater needs, Justice Croll finds that T.A.P. "is trying her best to be a good mother to her two younger children."[423] Drawing on this doctor's letter, the judge notes that "these children have come to rely on her for their sense of security and wellbeing," and that her incarceration would "be nothing short of devastating to her girls."[424] Justice Croll finds that a community prison sentence is precluded by conditional sentencing amendments and a suspended sentence with probation is inappropriate, but a sentence of provincial incarceration would not promote T.A.P.'s rehabilitation, societal reintegration, and her acceptance of responsibility, and would actively "be harmful to her and to her children."[425] The judge comments that a prison sentence in the provincial range might be otherwise appropriate to the objectives of deterrence and denunciation, but reiterates that imprisonment "would remove T.A.P. from her very vulnerable daughters who need her."[426] Justice Croll writes that if T.A.P. is incapacitated in prison, "it would prevent her from participating in their ongoing therapy," and "would be very damaging to their development and would destabilize the progress they have made, progress which is linked to their mother's involvement and support."[427] The judge suggests that "separation from her children due to a determinate jail sentence would also serve to undermine T.A.P.'s self-improvement," finding that "her personal recovery is inexorably connected to her involvement with her children, and a determinate custodial sentence would jeopardize the significant advancements she has made, both with respect to her children and her own personal healing."[428] As a result of this reasoning, Justice Croll decides that a ninety-day intermittent prison sentence followed by a three-year probation order is most appropriate, given that this sentence "will allow T.A.P. to care for her two younger children during the week and to continue to participate in their therapy, and when T.A.P. is in custody on the weekends, the children can remain in the care of her eldest daughter M. A sentence of this nature will not disrupt the girls' routine or their wellbeing and security, and will also protect and encourage the tremendous rehabilitative progress T.A.P. has made to date."[429]

Justice Croll concludes that this penalty supports multiple sentencing objectives while also "allow[ing] for and support[ing] her ongoing personal progress and parental obligations."[430] (Following the Crown appeal of this sentence, the Ontario Court of Appeal supplanted a conditional sentence order of two years less a day, finding it available on one count, and maintained the three years of probation.)[431]

The degree to which T.A.P.'s role as a mother and her children's needs influenced her ultimate sentence is evident, although there are other decisions demonstrating judicial attentiveness to and consideration of how incarcerating a criminalized Indigenous mother would impact her children. For example, Justice David Harris discusses inter-generational impacts of the residential school system when sentencing Deborah Hill, and evaluates how a sentence of incarceration would af-fect the lives of her own four children and her niece's child over whom Hill has legal custody (her niece is among several of Hill's family mem-bers who have attempted or committed suicide). Hill is a "Haudeno-saunee woman of Mohawk and Tuscarora ancestry, a member of the Bear Clan,"[432] and several of her family members went to residential school. Justice Harris observes that "the damage done by these insti-tutions is now well documented," including the corrosive effects upon the children's sense of culture and identity, producing intergenerational "internalized rage, alcohol and drug abuse, family and community vio-lence and a lack of or poor social skills."[433] The judge suggests that Hill, sentenced for impaired driving, drinks as a "coping mechanism and a stress reliever."[434] Justice Harris notes that Hill is the sole caregiver for five children, expressing concern that "they could well end up in the care of the Children's Aid Society if I send her to jail."[435] The Children's Aid Society "looked into her situation after she was charged with this offence," but returned her children to her care, and the judge finds that "she works hard for these children."[436] Acknowledging that "it would be easy to say that hers was a very serious offence and that she should go to jail for a long time,"[437] Justice Harris instead emphasizes restorative jus-tice objectives (primarily rehabilitation) and orders a conditional sen-tence for nine months, followed by three years of probation, and waives the victim fine surcharge, "in light of her family obligations."[438]

Whereas both T.A.P. and Hill were primary caregivers for their children, and this is significant to the respective judges' reasoning on sentencing, another case illustrates an instance in which the judge also considers the needs of the children against the prospect of their moth-er's incarceration even where they are not under her immediate care. In sentencing Tiffany Sowden from the Six Nations Reserve for dangerous driving (for which the Crown proceeded summarily) and two offences under provincial statutes, Justice Harris concludes, based on *Gladue* principles (particularly the need to consider a shorter prison sentence), the totality of her sentences, and "the impact that her continued deten-tion would have on her child,"[439] that the Crown's position of four to six months' incarceration on the dangerous driving charge would be inappropriate. Further, Justice Harris is influenced by how Sowden's seven-month-old baby would be affected by her ongoing detention, despite his remaining in a paternal family member's custody, which points to the judge's recognition of the significance of the mother-child relationship in itself and not simply necessitated by immediate child-care needs. (Similarly, as above, Judge Ruddy frames Firth's relationship with her daughters, who were not in her care, as a motivating force in her rehabilitation.) Additionally, Justice Harris cites the detrimental impact of Sowden's remaining in custody on her child even though he was in the car during her offences and therefore "put at risk,"[440] recognizing that she has exhibited a "marked change" across various dimensions of her life and "has been attentive and caring as a mother."[441] Justice Harris orders time served for the provincial offences, and an intermittent prison sentence of ninety days for dangerous driving, followed by a three-year probationary term.

Motherhood may be identified as an issue on sentencing, but without actually producing a reduced or different form of sanction, due to other considerations. In sentencing Métis woman Danielle Spence for trafficking in marijuana and possession for the purposes of trafficking in cocaine and marijuana, Justice Gabrielson notes she is still breastfeeding her baby, and "is virtually her child's sole caregiver," despite having a partner.[442] The judge writes, "The child could be significantly impacted if Ms. Spence is not allowed to serve her sentence in the community."[443] Her pre-sentence report indicates that she "seek[s] a community based sentence in order to continue her parenting and be least disruptive to her parent/child attachment" and "presents with a positive family support system within the community," but still suggests the court may choose to focus on denunciation, due to the seriousness of the offence.[444] Spence herself communicates to the court in a personal statement that she "is asking for compassion" because she "rarely leaves the house as she is caring for her daughter while her husband works," "is still breastfeeding and hopes to do so until her child reaches 18 months of age," and "has never been apart from her daughter for more than three hours, and her daughter needs her."[445] Justice Gabrielson does include within mitigating factors that she "has a young child for whom she is the major caregiver," and continues to breastfeed.[446] The judge cites another case for its review of how courts respond to the impacts of incarceration on children of the person being sentenced, including that that case resulted in a carceral term, due to the need to emphasize denunciation and deterrence, but notes this was the sentencing of a man with children older than Spence's baby. Ultimately, Justice Gabrielson determines that denunciation and general deterrence prevail (primarily because her drug offences were committed in a penitentiary in which she had been employed), and, despite "the significant mitigating factors,"[447] orders a prison term of eighteen months.

Where judges consider criminalized Indigenous women's mothering and their children's needs within the context of their histories of victimization and the related experiences of colonization, a broader vision emerges regarding the meaning of sanctions and what sentencing should address. For example, in sentencing Robyn Hansen for aggravated assault, assault with a weapon, and uttering a threat, Justice Butler specifically comments upon the intergenerational effects of processes of colonization, particularly the residential school system and foster care system. The judge finds mitigating that Hansen "is the third generation of women in her family to suffer the effects of systemic and background factors which have torn her family structure apart. Like her mother, she was raised in foster homes and subjected to sexual abuse and introduced to drugs and alcohol at a young age."[448] Multiple times in the judgment, Justice Butler highlights the ways in which her family has been torn apart by colonization through generations. The judge also notes that Hansen "is living in a positive supportive housing environment" with her three children,[449] and that "she says she is committed to providing a home for her children as their mother."[450]

Hansen's defence counsel submits that a ninety-day intermittent prison sentence followed by probation for three years would allow Hansen "to remain in her current housing with her children and would allow her to continue her successful efforts towards rehabilitation."[451] By contrast, the Crown seeks a prison term of twenty-six to thirty months. Justice Butler notes that the defence concedes that a longer period of incarceration might be otherwise suitable, but also contends that "a custodial sentence of that length would have the effect of, once again, removing an Aboriginal mother from the lives of her children."[452] It seems the judge finds the imperative to break this intergenerational cycle of forcibly separating Indigenous families compelling, as Justice Butler orders the sentence requested by Hansen's counsel, responding to the latter's submission that an innovative sentence is needed.

In another decision wherein the judge actively considers the expanded effects of incarceration upon Indigenous families within the context of colonization, Judge Daunt examines the anticipated impact of the symbolic meaning of incarceration on the child of the woman being sentenced. As mentioned earlier in this chapter, Michelle Arcand is sentenced for possession of cocaine for the purposes of trafficking, and the judge finds that deterrence and denunciation require "some jail," but that the duration should be "short enough" so as not to compromise other sentencing objectives, including rehabilitation.[453] Judge Daunt reflects on how seeing her mother in prison would likely impact Arcand's child in a manner that could normalize and perpetuate the intergenerational effects of colonization:

> In considering *Gladue* factors, I must also be mindful of the next generation. Ms. Arcand has a daughter who is 4½ years old. If I sentence Ms. Arcand to a lengthy prison term, what effect will that have on her daughter? Visiting her mother in jail may well reinforce the notion that it is normal for aboriginals to live in prison. Will that make it easier for her daughter to stray down a similar path later in life? Or perhaps the goal of a just, safe, and peaceful society is better achieved by Ms. Arcand continuing with her education, raising her daughter, and becoming a role model for others in her community.[454]

Importantly, Judge Daunt includes these considerations about the projected impacts of a carceral sanction on Arcand's daughter within the *Gladue* analysis, thereby expanding the frame of the analysis to contemplate how Arcand's daughter (and, by extension, Indigenous communities in a broader sense) would be affected by this sentencing. This widened frame is critical to goals of decolonizing, including those targeted by s. 718.2(e). Like Justice Butler in *Hansen*, Judge Daunt orders an intermittent sentence of ninety days, combined with probation for two years (the Crown had asked for a fifteen- to eighteen-month prison sentence, whereas Arcand's defence counsel had requested a lengthy probationary term).

Judicial consideration of how incarceration could affect a woman's children is appropriate simply within the context of individualized sentencing, as her child-care responsibilities are part of her personal circumstances and can be understood as connected to sentencing objectives including rehabilitation. However, another case presents an opportunity to reflect further on the basis for judicial contemplation of how children will experience the imprisonment of their mothers. In a decision sentencing Theresa Samson, the judge orders a conditional discharge with a probationary term of one year after she pleaded guilty to theft over $5,000. To arrive at this decision, Judge Cozens highlights Samson's hope to run for a governance position with her First Nation, and considers that if she were to emerge from this sentencing with a criminal record, she would be precluded from eligibility as a candidate for council, according to Na-Cho Nyak Dun First Nation legislation. The judge concludes that a conditional discharge would permit her "the fullest opportunity to contribute" to her community, adding, "Whether she does so from a leadership position or not is something for her community to decide, should Ms. Samson choose to pursue that path."[455] Dismissing the Crown appeal of this sentence on grounds unrelated to this reasoning, Chief Justice Robert James Bauman for the Court of Appeal of Yukon states, "I note that I do not agree with the Crown's submission that it was improper for the sentencing judge to consider this fact," because "collateral consequences can be taken into account when crafting a sentence."[456] Justice Bauman cites the Supreme Court of Canada decision *R. v. Pham*[457] for this principle.

I suggest that judges should also be able to rely on this direction that collateral consequences can be considered in determinations about sanctions with respect to the sentencing of criminalized Indigenous mothers (even criminalized mothers more broadly, especially where they are primary caregivers) and the likely impacts of their incarceration on their children. Although both *Samson* and *Pham* address collateral consequences that are attached to the persons being sentenced (and not to external parties), the same reasoning can still be extended to consequences that affect children whose mothers face imprisonment. I contend this reasoning can be extended past the woman being sentenced to her children on two primary grounds, both connected to the sentiment in the judgments that the relationship between criminalized Indigenous mothers and their children is connected to their healing (both the rehabilitation of the mothers, and healing from a decolonizing perspective by striving to keep families intact). First, the comments above by the sentencing judge in *Samson* and supported by the Court of Appeal can (and, I suggest, should) be understood to indicate that issuing a conditional discharge in part to enable Samson to participate in Na-Cho Nyak Dun First Nation governance is not simply of benefit to her, but also to her community (that is, the "collateral consequences" of this sentencing consideration attach not simply to Samson, but also to the Na-Cho Nyak Dun First Nation). Second, given that the children of a primary caregiver mother will be directly and profoundly impacted by her incarceration as they need immediate care, it becomes difficult to draw a bright line demarcating to whom the "collateral consequences" of sentencing refer, suggesting what I will term the concept of "dispersed punishment." This demands deeper reflection on the meaning of "punishment," in terms of to whom it is directed and who experiences it. Who are we punishing when we send a primary caregiver to prison, and why are "indirect" effects/implications of punishment not held to be of equal importance as its explicit objectives, particularly in the decolonizing context of attempting to ameliorate the overincarceration of Indigenous peoples (and the related fracturing of their families and communities)?

Contemplating the question of the proper and acceptable object of punishment, and specifically imprisonment, introduces a morass of entwined problems. Not least of those problems is that if criminalized Indigenous women's children are truly recognized as inevitably, intimately, and irreversibly impacted by the incarceration of their mothers (and in a manner that perpetuates processes of colonization), and if it is determined that the direct and indirect "recipients" of punishment may be different from the intended objects of punishment, but that this distinction is not ethically defensible (particularly given the intergenerational impacts of various modes of state control over Indigenous peoples), then this has substantial implications about the use of prison as a sanction in this context. Prison abolitionism, either as a broad belief and movement or applied to certain contexts, demands serious thought, given the ways in which the experience of incarceration is damaging to prisoners and fragments families and communities. (Davis suggests that simply "dismantling" physical prisons "is not the project of abolition," but that "the economic, social, and political conditions" that structure the prison "will also have to be dismantled,"[458] requiring strategies dealing with "the connections between institutions," then "re-imagining" and ultimately "creating new institutions.")[459]

Punitive Aspects of the Restorative-Oriented Conditional Sentence Order

Given the criminal justice system in its current iteration, conditional sentence orders (as alternatives to imprisonment) remain challenging for Indigenous women to navigate and comply with. Conditional sentence orders are designed to be more restorative than prison sanctions, but if women receive conditional sentences that they are susceptible to breaching, this may still land them in prison. Moreover, statistics about the recidivism of Indigenous women suggest that imprisonment is not a healing force in these women's lives. Multiple judges in my research decide to extend the duration of a conditional sentence order past the length of the carceral sentence that might otherwise be appropriate. Judge Brooks observes in *Elliott*, "An actual jail sentence will only partially be served in jail," whereas "a conditional sentence, every day of which will be served, can result in a much longer oversight," and explains that denunciation and general deterrence can be effected using a conditional sentence order "by extending the length of a sentence beyond what would otherwise be imposed," and through "careful use of stringent conditions."[460] In sentencing Bryna Link, as mentioned earlier in this chapter, Judge Smith suggests, "Generally, a conditional sentence is somewhat longer than a sentence that would be required to be served in an institution,"[461] and determines that "in accordance with the case law, Ms Link's CSO will be lengthier" than what would otherwise be the institutional prison sentence.[462]

Judicial reasoning for these longer community sentences may be variously attached to rehabilitative goals or objectives of denunciation and deterrence. Where the reasoning is oriented toward rehabilitation, that purpose becomes more complicated, given the punitive elements of conditional sentence orders and the implications of breaching. Judge Ruddy explains when sentencing Jenna McClements that "for rehabilitation, sometimes it is harder to [*sic*], if not impossible, to achieve rehabilitative objectives with jail terms," but for cases necessitating rehabilitative objectives alongside those of denunciation and deterrence, a "significantly restrictive" conditional sentence order may be appropriate.[463] The judge comments, "If I was going to send Ms. McClements to jail directly, I likely would have done 18 months. For a conditional sentence, I think two years less a day is appropriate because the focus of this is rehabilitative in nature, and this is not a short-term prospect."[464] As such, McClements's sentence is made longer to promote healing, but this also extends the period of supervision, within which she might violate her conditions.

I return here to *Isaac* to introduce the issue of the tension between punishment and rehabilitation and to identify some of the less visible ways that this tension may play out in conditional sentence orders. I want to emphasize that, ultimately, the decision in *Isaac* is appropriately restorative-oriented, and I do not intend to obscure this message with my discussion. I aim to merely highlight some of these problems, without undercutting the sensitivity of the overall judgment in *Isaac*. I use this decision only as a vehicle, and alongside other decisions, because the issues it introduces (duration and specific conditions) are representative of those in many other judgments ordering conditional sentences. I believe conditional sentence orders are an important sentencing tool (absent wider measures to reduce incarceration), but also want to offer some nuance because they still present challenges for Indigenous women.

In *Isaac*, in addition to various "strict and restrictive conditions," Judge Green explains that the sentence quantum "will be longer than the term of imprisonment she would have otherwise received if she had been sentenced to the Correctional Centre."[465] Implementing a longer conditional sentence than the imprisonment alternative may be something of a judicial norm, but seems misaligned with the assertion by Judge Stuart in *Elias* that "to be successful, conditional sentences must focus on healing, not punishment."[466] It could be argued that longer sentences are consistent with greater involvement in whatever rehabilitative features are attached (and sometimes this is the case, particularly where the alternative is straight incarceration). For example, in sentencing Ernestine Elliott to an eighteen-month conditional sentence order followed by two years of probation, Judge Brooks determines, "The sentence of imprisonment to be served in the community must be longer than that suggested by Crown or defence"[467] (the Crown position was for eight to twelve months' incarceration in an institution followed by probation, and the defence had asked for a sentence of the same duration but served in the community). However, the judge is motivated to keep Elliott close to her family as an important component in her rehabilitative needs and to give effect to *Ipeelee*. Further, it is consistent with the direction in *Proulx* that sentencing judges may decide to order longer conditional sentences than the prison term may otherwise have been, to ensure proportionality to the gravity of the offence and to reflect the responsibility of the person before the court, "since a conditional sentence will generally be more lenient than a jail term of equivalent duration."[468] Equally, however, often even a "healing" approach to a longer, more restorative-oriented conditional sentence can slide into greater punitiveness (additionally, as a further mode of increased criminalization, the Criminal Code was amended in 2015 with the addition of s. 718.2(a) (vi),[469] which now makes any new offences committed while serving a conditional sentence order deemed statutorily aggravating).

Longer community sentences mean lengthier periods during which women can breach their conditions and face consequent penalties, including incarceration. Criminalized Indigenous women themselves indicate concerns related to this risk. For example, Tiffany Sowden disclosed to the author of her pre-sentence report that "she did not find rehabilitation to be beneficial long term for her as she relapsed after each program" attempted in the past.[470] In a judgment dealing with a sentencing for trafficking in marijuana and centring on whether the prison sentence should be served in an institution or in the community, Justice

DiGiuseppe suggests Jessica Bouchard shows "progress in . . . addressing her issues" because she "continues to resist a lengthy and restrictive community supervision order."[471] Her "extensive criminal record" includes "breaches of court orders," and the judge notes "four separate breaches of conditional sentence orders . . . resulting in the termination of that order."[472] Justice DiGiuseppe explains that Bouchard "is fearful that she may be unable to comply with conditions, and find herself continuously stuck in the quagmire of the justice system,"[473] and ultimately orders imprisonment for four months, followed by a probationary term of twelve months. The judge comments that such "struggles with compliance" are "unfortunate," suggesting that "community based dispositions, coupled with her insight and commitment," offer her "the best opportunity through counselling to address those factors that contribute to her offending behavior."[474]

In certain transcribed oral decisions, judges effectively ask the women about their concerns about the risk of breaching their conditions (although the effectiveness of such queries is, of course, at best uncertain, given the power differential involved in judicial questions to accused persons, and the lived complexities of Indigenous women's circumstances). For example, in ordering conditional discharges and probation for Melissa Bourke's offences of assault of a peace officer and a breach of an abstinence condition, Judge Gorin asks Bourke about her probation requirement to stay within the Northwest Territories, "Is that going to present any difficulty?"; and, about a treatment-related condition, "Does she have any difficulty with treatment?"[475]; and, about her community service requirements, "Any reason why you cannot do that?"[476] Similarly, in another transcribed judgment, Justice Harris sentences Deborah Hill for impaired driving and repeatedly asks her whether she understands and can comply with the terms of her nine-month conditional sentence order and subsequent three years of probation. Justice Harris also asks Hill, of her probation, "Do you understand that if you breach the terms of any of those orders you can be charged with various offences?"[477] and whether she understands that breaching the conditions attached to her conditional sentence could mean she is incarcerated for the remainder of her term.

Other judges try to attend to the concern about breaches, such as where Judge Anderson orders L.M.L. to various sentences including a conditional sentence order of nine months for an offence of sexual touching, and writes, "This sentence is longer than it would have been if it were not to be served in the community but not so long that it would result in an unduly long jail sentence if Ms. L. cannot follow the conditions."[478] Similarly, in consultation with counsel about expanding the house arrest component of Jenna McClements's conditional sentence order, Judge Ruddy comments, "What I am also worried about, and mindful of, is that two years less a day is a long sentence, and I want there to be some light at the end of the tunnel such that she does not feel unduly discouraged when she is going through the sentence," adding, "I do not want it to feel so overwhelming that I prevent her from being successful, I guess, is what I am saying."[479] Nonetheless, the duration of many other conditional sentences is not attenuated to minimize the concern about breaching, and criminalized Indigenous women are particularly vulnerable when facing conditions over long periods.

Research has shown that Indigenous women breach their conditions at almost three times the rate as non-Indigenous women.[480] In conjunction with this higher breach rate, because longer conditional sentences mean more time during which breaches are possible, those sentences may be particularly difficult for Indigenous women. This is significant in terms of the goals of *Gladue* because the presumptive penalty (barring reasonable excuse) for breaching a conditional sentence is for the remainder of her sentence to be ordered served in prison.[481] Roach writes, "Healing conditions when administered through the coercive apparatus of the state may start out with the best of intentions but result in imprisonment."[482] Some judges demonstrate a great deal of sensitivity to these issues. In *Elias*, Judge Stuart agrees with the defence submission that the probation order "should be as minimally intrusive as possible and should be designed to make it as clear as possible so that Ms. Elias, who does not have a good track record of following any kind of court order, can do the best she can to follow this one. I do not wish to set her up for further failures or breaches, recognizing the limitations that are clearly indicated in the pre-sentence report. This is designed for one primary purpose, which is the rehabilitation of Ms. Elias, which will, ultimately, best protect society and anyone close to Ms. Elias."[483]

In *Isaac*, Judge Green attaches special conditions that relate to treatment needs, including that Isaac must participate in a substance abuse program and attend counselling for "personal, psychological and psychiatric" issues as arranged by her supervisor.[484] (Such conditions are common; Shawn Bayes states, "conditional sentences have also been widely used to help offenders begin to tackle issues, like addictions, underlying many crimes.")[485] Judge Green also imposes a condition prohibiting Isaac from consuming any alcohol or other substances. Abstinence conditions are frequently imposed for those with substance abuse problems.[486] Nonetheless, Sarah Turnbull and Kelly Hannah-Moffat have observed, "Despite the widespread use of conditions in various phases of the criminal justice system, their purposes and the implications associated with their use remain under-theorized."[487] Roach outlines that abstinence conditions in a conditional sentence order may be implemented for the person's "own good," but render those who have addictions to substances immediately vulnerable to breaching, and "the catch is that any breach may well result in imprisonment for the duration of a sentence that may have been extended for rehabilitative reasons."[488]

The concern about criminalized Indigenous women's breaching abstinence conditions also extends beyond conditional sentences to other forms of restrictions and sanctions. For example, one of the offences for which Melissa Bourke is sentenced is a breach of a condition of an undertaking requiring she not consume alcohol.[489] Such breaches can cause women to become further entrapped and entrenched in the criminal justice system, including where the oppressiveness of their experience of the system is amplified as a result of a breach, such as where a woman's judicial interim release is revoked. Among Lori Abraham's offences is a failure to comply with her recognizance; she was released on bail and then rearrested and detained after breaching two conditions, including that prohibiting her from drinking. Judge Robert Heinrichs directly connects this to victimization, writing that her breaches were triggered by her "being sexually abused by an extended family member" and consequently resuming "her alcohol and drug addictions."[490]

Some judges have recognized this vulnerability in individuals they sentence who struggle with addiction. For example, in the probation variation judgment *R. v. Coombs*, Justice Joanne B. Veit explains:

> Ms. Coombs' re-integration into society will be facilitated if she remains in the community while acquiring the means of coping with her drug addiction through counselling and treatment and also the means of understanding her self-destructive behaviour through psychological and psychiatric counselling and treatment. Such provisions are already contained in her probation order and Ms. Coombs consents to take such counselling and treatment. Imposing an absolute prohibition on some addicts, including alcoholics, may only set them up for failure and ensure that they will be jailed. Ms. Coombs became an addict during her formative years; her medical and emotional rehabilitation is likely to include slips. Her re-integration into society will not be assisted by being jailed for every slip along the difficult road ahead.[491]

I allude to these problems in my discussion of *Kendi* earlier in this chapter. Here, Justice Veit demonstrates one way for judges to administer conditions that promote treatment in the community, but without amplifying the punitive features of the sentence in a way that could result in incarceration. Also recognizing this issue of particular vulnerability to abstinence conditions, Justice Stack directly connects Elizabeth Merkuratsuk's experiences of victimization with her *Gladue* factors in a judgment sentencing her to prison for forty-five days followed by probation for thirty months for sexual interference. The judge orders this duration of imprisonment because it is the mandatory minimum, and Justice Stack notes that her offence "arises directly from Ms. Merkuratsuk's abuse of alcohol and a lifetime of despair and hopelessness," and that she, "as an Inuk woman who has personally witnessed and suffered the debilitating troubles faced by her people, should be subject only to the minimum period of incarceration" to service general and specific deterrence.[492] Justice Stack further declares, "I have not ordered as a condition of probation that she abstain from alcohol. Ms. Merkuratsuk has no previous *Criminal Code* conviction and, given her chronic alcohol abuse, it is not helpful to her to impose a condition that she may not be able to comply with. If her alcohol abuse leads to her committing a subsequent offense, then she will be accountable for that."[493]

The problem of sentenced persons' (and particularly those struggling with substance abuse) becoming vulnerable to breaching conditions of their community sanctions is a challenging issue for judges. In the face of these complexities, in *Isaac*, Judge Green strives to impose a restorative-oriented sentence that is consistent with *Gladue,* recognizing and responding to Isaac's experiences of victimization. The conditional sentence the judge orders for Isaac remains much better aligned with the goals of *Gladue* than the sentence of incarceration that would have otherwise been imposed.

Other judges are also sensitized to issues related to some women's vulnerability to breaching abstinence conditions. Contrary to the Crown position that Bryna Link contends with unresolved substance abuse and should not be given a conditional sentence order because of her failures to comply with court orders, Judge Smith finds that "while the breaches are clearly troubling and have not been overlooked, it is understandable that addressing a serious drug addiction issue is difficult, and there can be missteps," pointing to progress she has made since her last breach and noting that "all of the breaches occurred prior to the significant steps taken on the road to rehabilitation."[494] As I discuss earlier, Judge Smith orders a conditional sentence order. For Lillian Kanayok's offence of fraud over $5,000, Justice Smallwood orders a conditional sentence of two years less a day plus probation for one year. In the transcribed discussion with counsel, the judge comments, in response to a Crown query about whether there will be an abstention condition attached to Kanayok's conditional sentence order, "There is no indication that the offence involved alcohol, so I did not see the need to include that."[495] Justice Smallwood adds that the pre-sentence report indicates "there was previously an alcohol problem but that is no longer the case. So, in the circumstances, I did not feel that it was necessary."[496]

I discuss the sentencing decision for Jenna McClements earlier in this chapter, in which Judge Ruddy orders a conditional sentence of two years less a day and an additional probationary term of three years for her most serious offence, arson. The judge assigns concurrent sentences for her remaining offences, including various breaches of her release conditions. For violating the abstinence condition, Judge Ruddy comments that the "Crown had suggested 30 days, and for that one, I think 15 days is appropriate, particularly in light of the fact that she has serious substance abuse problems which make compliance with that type of condition particularly difficult."[497] In a decision in which the judge exercises some creativity to minimize the potential of a breach, Judge Donald S. Luther imposes abstinence conditions but only within certain parameters. Judge Luther orders an intermittent sentence of sixty days and one year of probation for Roxanne Simms's conviction for aggravated assault, with staggered, non-absolute abstention conditions such that she must not have any alcohol on weekends and Mondays throughout her intermittent sentence, which "will ensure that there will be no alcohol in her body when she shows up to serve her sentence."[498] It should also be recalled from the earlier discussion about the anxieties and mistrust criminalized Indigenous women may face specifically due to their experience of (including a sense of alienation from, and oppression within) the criminal justice system that they may become vulnerable to consuming substances as a coping mechanism. Thus, even the staggered abstinence conditions Judge Luther constructs for Simms may render her vulnerable to breach due to stress triggered by the onset of those periods of intermittent custody.

In the context of undertakings, in *R. v. Omeasoo*, Judge B.D. Rosborough asks, "Under what circumstances should alcoholics be prohibited from consuming alcohol as a condition of their release from custody?" and the further question, "What is a fit sentence for those alcoholics who breach that condition?"[499] In this decision addressing two independent cases in which two Indigenous persons were released on abstinence undertakings, notwithstanding their alcoholism, the judge sentences Jennifer Omeasoo to one day's imprisonment for two counts of failing to comply with her abstention undertaking. She had been subject to this undertaking after her release from custody for a minor offence, and was again arrested and charged for breaching it when she was found intoxicated when police attended a domestic assault complaint of which she was the victim. She was again released, but police found her intoxicated a month later, charging her with the second violation of her undertaking. She was detained until she pleaded guilty to both breaches several days after this arrest. Her parents both dealt with alcoholism, and Judge Rosborough notes that, "unsurprisingly, Omeasoo became an alcoholic at an early age," although, once pregnant, she refrained from drinking until her children were older, and then "fell back into what she had known throughout her childhood and started drinking" again.[500]

Judge Rosborough suggests, "It is trite to say that conditions in an undertaking which the accused cannot or almost certainly will not comply with cannot be reasonable" per the objectives of such undertakings, elaborating that "requiring the accused to perform the impossible is simply another means of denying judicial interim release."[501] This carries increased significance for criminalized Indigenous persons, given that they are already denied bail more frequently than non-Indigenous persons. Judge Rosborough cites various cases in which courts have found that abstention conditions are both "not entirely realistic," and "set the accused up for failure."[502] Following an Alberta Court of Queen's Bench case that cites *Gladue* and *Ipeelee* in this context, Judge Rosborough finds that "special considerations apply when ordering abstinence in the case of a detainee who is both an alcoholic and aboriginal," given that holding Indigenous persons denied bail in custody contributes to their overrepresentation in prison.[503]

Judge Rosborough is careful to differentiate between conditions attached to judicial interim release orders and those connected to sentencing orders such as probation and conditional sentence orders, observing that bail and sentencing proceedings and orders "are authorized by different statutory provisions and serve different purposes."[504] For example, the judge indicates that the objective of rehabilitation that guides probation orders might mean that breaches of abstinence conditions attached to probation orders are "tolerate[d]," whereas similar such relapses and consequent breaches of conditions attached to judicial interim release would be considered unacceptable.[505] Judge Rosborough also cites another Alberta Court of Queen's Bench case, declaring that "the authorities are clear then that, on appropriate evidence touching on the accused's individual circumstances, an abstinence provision in a probation order may be inappropriate."[506]

Regardless of the differences in objectives among conditions attached to bail, probation, and conditional sentence orders, breaches of abstinence clauses attached to each of those forms of orders may be nearly inevitable for those who deal with alcoholism or addictions to other substances. Moreover, in each context (judicial interim release, probation, or conditional sentence orders), such breaches immediately engage the risk of deepened criminalization, including additional or lengthened periods of incarceration. Again, remembering the fears and mistrust that criminalized Indigenous women may hold in relation to the criminal justice system, alongside how substance use functions as a coping mechanism for some women, such abstinence conditions become further problematic for these women, irrespective of the type of proceeding or sanction involved.

I use the decisions presented in this section as an opportunity to discuss how conditional sentences can be challenging for some criminalized Indigenous women to comply with, because the stakes are high, given that the presumptive result of a breach is for them to serve the remainder of their sentences in prison (the precise penalty conditional sentences are designed to avoid). For this reason, even elements of conditional sentence orders may engage the tension between punishment and rehabilitation. For more pronounced iterations of this tension, I turn to sentences of incarceration.

The Revolving Door of Prison

The ways in which Indigenous women experience attempting to navigate the intersection of their histories of victimization and becoming criminalized (both including how their lives have been impacted by *Gladue* factors) may also translate into their struggling to comply with conditions (those attached to bail, probation, conditional sentence orders, etc.) that can cause them to be steadily more deeply entrenched in the criminal justice system. For example, in Janine Firth's sentencing, Judge Ruddy suggests her experiences of victimization have prompted her extensive self-medication, and that her substance abuse features heavily into her offending behaviours. Judge Ruddy observes that, among other entries on her criminal record, she has "numerous offences for failing to comply with court orders,"[507] and that Firth "has significant difficulty right now complying with conditions, and that has landed her continually back in custody," adding, "She has numerous issues relating to past trauma that need to be addressed."[508]

Milward and Parkes write that, contrary to the formulation of individualized risk pervading the criminal justice process, "for many Aboriginal people prison is actually a 'risk factor' that increases their likelihood of further engagement with the criminal justice system."[509] Statistics about recidivism provide some information about the (in)effectiveness of imprisonment, in terms of its revolving door. Reporting the results of a five-year study (1999 to 2004) of the reinvolvement of Indigenous and non-Indigenous individuals in the Saskatchewan provincial correctional system, Sara Johnson notes significantly different statistics for their respective rates of reinvolvement. For this study, "reinvolvement" means returning to correctional services after sentence completion, and relates exclusively to Saskatchewan provincial correctional services (including incarceration, conditional sentences, and probation). The disparities between the reinvolvement of Indigenous and non-Indigenous individuals are stark: after release, 57 percent of Indigenous persons became reinvolved in the system, compared with 28 percent of non-Indigenous persons.[510]

Indigenous persons were particularly vulnerable within the first year following their release, with 29 percent returning to the correctional system within that period, compared with 13 percent for non-Indigenous persons. Johnson attributes this vulnerability to the complex and higher needs of Indigenous persons post-release.[511] Johnson reports that people sentenced to the community (such as those serving conditional sentences or probationary orders) demonstrated the lowest likelihood for reinvolvement in correctional services.[512] For Indigenous persons, of those who were sentenced to the community, 43 percent returned to correctional services post-release, which is substantially less than the 65 percent figure for Indigenous persons who became reinvolved after serving custodial terms.[513] For non-Indigenous persons, 20 percent became reinvolved in correctional services after release from community sentences, versus the 33 percent who returned to corrections after completing a sentence of incarceration.[514] Johnson suggests, "It is possible that community supervision contributes to more successful treatment and thus reintegration, and that those offenders released following a period of community supervision are less likely to become re-involved in the system,"[515] and calls for further research to substantiate this theory.

In a more recent study of the Saskatchewan criminal justice system spanning 2009 to 2012, Shannon Brennan and Anthony Matarazzo examine issues relating to the degree to which previously criminalized persons were again charged with a subsequent offence after the completion of the process for their initial/prior contact with the system. Brennan and Matarazzo report that Indigenous persons "were significantly more likely" (at 80 percent) to again come into contact with police "following their correctional involvement" than non-Indigenous individuals (at 57 percent), with even greater disparity for Indigenous youth.[516]

Neither of these reports disaggregate their respective results into statistics about Indigenous women specifically.[517] However, Johnson does note that her study comprises data for the over 2,700 Indigenous women who were involved in Saskatchewan provincial corrections for that period, and indicates that of the total number of Indigenous persons (male and female) in her study, Indigenous women constitute 19 percent of that total.[518] She also observes that Indigenous women become reinvolved in the system at higher rates than both non-Indigenous women and non-Indigenous men (41 percent of Indigenous women were returned to correctional services within four years of their initial release).[519] In a broader sense of the overrepresentation of Indigenous women in Saskatchewan provincial corrections, Tina Hotton Mahony's report for Statistics Canada states that in 2008–09, "Aboriginal women comprised more than 85 percent of admissions of women to adult provincial sentenced custody in Saskatchewan and Manitoba and just over half in Alberta."[520]

As these statistics apply only to Saskatchewan correctional services, results from other provinces and territories may differ. But, using the above data in an illustrative manner, it is apparent that Indigenous women are overrepresented in prison, significantly more likely to return to the correctional system post-release, and, although they become reinvolved at lower rates after community sentences than after periods of incarceration, their rates of reinvolvement still far exceed those of non-Indigenous persons. I have provided information for these provincial statistics because I have tried to focus on provincial-level sentences where possible, to foreground conditional sentences, given the importance of conditional sentences to respond to the goals of *Gladue* to reduce overincarceration.

Despite my intended focus on provincial-level sentences, federal statistics remain relevant, given my methodological decision (as explained in the Introduction) to include decisions in which exclusively federal sentences were contemplated, or were ultimately ordered. In their report about the recidivism of federally sentenced women, Renée Gobeil and Meredith Robeson Barrett find that Indigenous women are significantly more likely to have their conditional release revoked and to be reconvicted than non-Indigenous women.[521] (The Correctional Investigator also reports in 2016 that Indigenous persons in federal prison "are still being released later and revoked much more often than their counterparts.")[522] Gobeil and Robeson Barrett studied the recidivism rates (where "recidivism" means any revocation of conditional release or any new conviction within two years) of "all federally sentenced adult women released on day parole, full parole, statutory release, or sentence expiration/warrant expiry during the study period,"[523] from 2002 to 2004. Gobeil and Robeson Barrett calculated these rates for each year within the two-year period separately. For the 2002–03 period, they report, 50 percent of Indigenous women returned to the system after a revocation of their conditional release, compared with 33.1 percent of non-Indigenous women.[524] This is similar to the 2003–04 data, which show that 47.3 percent of Indigenous women had a revocation of their conditional release, and 34.5 percent of non-Indigenous women.[525] For 2002–03, 43.9 percent of Indigenous women received a reconviction during that period, compared with 23.1 percent of non-Indigenous women.[526] The 2003–04 results show that 38.5 percent of Indigenous women received a reconviction, compared with 25.1 percent of non-Indigenous women.[527] Taken as a whole and echoing the provincial data from Saskatchewan, the federal figures demonstrate that, relative to non-Indigenous women, Indigenous women are more likely to return to the correctional system post-release.

Mandy Wesley writes in a report about the marginalization of Indigenous women in the federal correctional system that to reduce recidivism and to help Indigenous women reintegrate more successfully into the community after their release, they require greater resources and support.[528] Laura Shantz, Jennifer M. Kilty, and Sylvie Frigon note that "because women leaving prison lack basic resources, they are often forced to rebuild their lives on the margins of society."[529] As the above statistics about correctional reinvolvement suggest, Indigenous women pass through (or, are processed through) the revolving door of prisons too often. The reasons for this phenomenon are complex (and rooted in colonization), but gesture to the inherent tension in the conception of prison as a place of both punishment and healing.

Prison Treatment Services

Prison existence is defined by control and exclusion, which permeate the structure and delivery of programming. Women in prison have reported finding the inherently punitive prison environment antithetical to the implementation and effectiveness of rehabilitative and therapeutic programming.[530] This discordance may be particularly felt where the role of prison psychologists is predominantly to assess prisoners' risk level (both regarding recidivism and institutional security) and to make recommendations for security classification, but also to provide counselling services.[531] Some scholars and advocates have flagged this dual securitization/therapeutic role for its inappropriateness.[532] These two roles establish a conflict of interest for the psychologist, because, as Andrew Haag explains, "when a psychologist is performing risk assessment, or is involved in rehabilitative programming addressing risk, the government is typically the client."[533] This form of conflict is not just embodied in institutional psychologists, but also applies to correctional officers. The intrinsic conflict within the role(s) of correctional officers is recognized in a decision dealing with a dangerous offender application for Marlene Carter, related to two predicate offences of assault with a weapon, both committed while this woman from the Onion Lake First Nation and Saulteaux First Nation was in custody at the Regional Psychiatric Centre. Judge Whelan finds that "there has at times been conflict between the 'correctional' side and the 'clinical' side of the operation."[534] The judge details that while detained at this institution, Carter "has been cared for by a good number of dedicated thoughtful individuals: psychiatrists, psychologists, nurses, and corrections staff, including those in a social work or supervising capacity, as well as guards. But she has also been caught up in a system which seems to lack the will or ability to make available a setting which appropriately addresses her mental health needs. Despite repeated recommendations that she be placed in a mental health facility where guards are not the first responders to self-harming behaviour, [such as] a hospital in Brockville Ontario; the system has proven unable to act upon this sensible solution."[535]

Justice Arbour notes in her report for the Commission of Inquiry into Certain Events at the Prison for Women in Kingston that "the inherent conflict between the role of correctional officers as security guards and their roles as supporters and counselors is sharpened"[536] for women prisoners who have histories of victimization. She quotes a prisoner who told the commission, "'The CX staff, in particular, you hear that term: Well, he's a nice guy. Well, you've got the nice guy/bad guy syndrome because he's a nice guy when everything is going okay, but all of a sudden, if something happens in the institution, and there's a male that's needed, he becomes the bad guy, he becomes the aggressor, he becomes the intimidator, he becomes the force, he becomes the muscle.'"[537] According to Sugar and Fox, this dichotomization within the role of correctional officers is further exacerbated for Indigenous women who often "have histories that have led them to mistrust white authority."[538]

Wesley notes "the lack of gender appropriate programming in an Aboriginal cultural context"[539] at the federal level, which complicates correctional rehabilitative efforts for Indigenous women and contributes to their already challenging prison experience. Wesley also highlights that the general type of correctional programming offered at the federal level may not be effective because of its traditional concentration on substance abuse and violence prevention strategies instead of other aspects such as employment skills.[540] More pointedly, Sugar and Fox find that treatment services in prison are "culturally inappropriate to us as women and as Aboriginal people," adding that prison doctors "are typically white and male," and asking, "How can we be healed by those who symbolize the worst experiences of our past?"[541]

All these barriers to effective programming are compounded, as Cindy Peternelj-Taylor describes, by the "diversity [across] the health care challenges experienced by the correctional population and the marginalized status of offenders in general."[542] There may be greater provision for programming options at the federal level in part because, according to a Statistics Canada report by Gannon et al., "research has suggested that federal inmates have substantially higher levels of needs and therefore, may require greater attention and programming,"[543] and also because, as Bernier notes, it is simply easier to offer consistency across "policies, procedures, practices, and programming" within "a single governing body."[544] Provincially, there is some provision for correctional programming. For example, the British Columbia Corrections website indicates it "delivers programs designed to reduce the risk factors that contribute to crime,"[545] including cognitive behavioural programs for persons assessed as high-risk that attempt to change "thinking and behavior" (which is, of course, an individualized framework) related to substance abuse, violence, and "difficulties with spousal relationships," with the suggestion that these programs will help people "make better choices."[546] However, as Marnie Norwich writes, Betty Krawczyk and Phyllis Iverson (a former prisoner and a member active in a prisoner-support group, respectively) have commented that there is a paucity of programming to which provincially-sentenced women in British Columbia have access.[547] Krawczyk comments, "Any kind of rehabilitation is not taken seriously by this government for the women in the provincial prisons."[548] This problem can be extended across Canadian provinces, where "provincial jails are infamous for their lack of programming and support, they tend to function primarily as warehouses" and federal prisons "appear to be better options"[549] by contrast. As provincial sentences are necessarily for less than two years, rehabilitative prison services are often unavailable at the provincial level; where services are available, their effectivity may be hampered, as professionals have less time to administer their services.[550] Moreover, as per discussions above, I suggest the experience of imprisonment is inherently incompatible with rehabilitation, and particularly for Indigenous women. Sugar and Fox, themselves former prisoners, explain that for Indigenous women, "prison is an extension of life on the outside, and because of this it is impossible for us to heal there."[551]

In a clear instance of counsel's submitting that federal institutions offer greater rehabilitative services than provincial, Justice Smith notes when sentencing Danielle Chamakese that her defence counsel seeks a twenty-four-month prison term, adding that her counsel "opts for the full 24 months rather than two years less a day so that Ms. Chamakese might benefit from some of the programs available in the federal penitentiary system"[552] (the judge sentences her to twenty-six months of federal imprisonment for dangerous driving causing death and nine months concurrent for leaving the scene of the accident). *Toews*, discussed variously in Chapter 2, yields a sentence that is just barely a federal sentence, with federal programming seeming persuasive for the judge. Justice Ball sentences Ashley Toews for various robberies, finding that neither a suspended sentence nor a community sentence (as sought by defence counsel) is appropriate, due to the nature and repetition of the offences, and that a sentence "in the low end of the federal range" is most fit.[553] Having already assessed about her home reserve on the Hagwilget First Nation that "any resources this community might offer to Ms. Toews appear illusory,"[554] Justice Ball was provided by the *Gladue* report writer with information about rehabilitative programs in federal and provincial institutions available to Indigenous women prisoners, and about the Tsow-Tun Le Lum Aboriginal Treatment Centre, which the judge describes as "appear[ing] to be an excellent rehabilitative program."[555] The judge writes, "I note that the federal system provides a possibility for the accused to become involved in an Integrated Correctional Program Model, an innovative and holistic approach that includes an Aboriginal specific multi-target program to address the needs and risks of this specific offender group. *Therefore*, the sentence that I impose today is a sentence of two years' incarceration followed by three years of probation."[556] (The probationary order also includes among its conditions that she must attend the treatment centre.)

Firth also demonstrates a shared belief among the various actors that the federal system provides better programming than the provincial system. Judge Ruddy recognizes that Janine Firth's unresolved experiences of trauma and resultant substance abuse problems have impeded her ability to comply with conditions, causing her continual reinvolvement in the system. She had entered guilty pleas to a number of offences, the most serious of which is robbery (the others are mostly charges of theft under $5,000), and on facts suggesting she was in sustained and acute distress, given that she attempted to strangle herself on two separate occasions when arrested by police. Judge Ruddy recognizes, in part due to these attempts at self-strangulation, that "there are clearly mental health issues," but suggests, "The difficulty is we do not have a diagnosis as to what those are or how best to treat them."[557] Both counsel suggest a federal term of incarceration, which, the judge comments, "quite frankly, is probably appropriate when I consider the number and nature of the charges before me."[558] It seems that all involved parties (including Firth herself) are in agreement that federal incarceration presents the greatest resources for her, and that the provincial system is inadequately equipped. Judge Ruddy discloses that Firth "appears to have spent some time trying to decide, from her own perspective, where she feels that she can get assistance, and is satisfied that the federal system would have more at this time to offer her to meet her needs than we have here in the Territory," adding that her *Gladue* report includes "that the numerous individuals spoken to all appear to believe that, at this point in time, she may find more assistance within the federal system."[559] The judge finds, "I do not have any difficulty in this case, particularly when I note the extensive history of struggling with complying with conditions, in determining that placing Ms. Firth within *the federal system is probably in her best interests* at this point in time."[560]

In *R. v. Good*, Judge Faulkner draws a distinction between provincial and federal imprisonment, ultimately representing federal prison as a place of treatment (in contrast to provincial prison) and highlighting its programming options. The judge sentences Helen Good to three years' imprisonment followed by supervision per a long-term offender designation for assault causing bodily harm and uttering death threats to her husband. I discuss this decision in Chapter 2, with reference to the judicial recognition that victimization has constrained her choices, but without contextualizing this victimization within a *Gladue* analysis. One of her several psychological and psychiatric assessments reports that Helen Good had already "undergone extensive and repeated counselling and therapy to no obvious effect."[561] The judge agrees that these sessions have "been ineffective at best and, more likely, counterproductive. It has allowed Helen to see herself only as a victim and to blame her violence on her own abuse."[562] Judge Faulkner comments that Good "continues to seek refuge in her own victimization as a justification"[563] for her offending.

When considering whether to designate Good a long-term offender and with regard to constraining Good's violence, Judge Faulkner lauds a "particularly intensive form" of the Dialectic Behaviour Therapy (DBT) program, which is available only to women serving federal terms.[564] The judge dismisses a related DBT program available at the territorial level at the Whitehorse Correctional Centre, explaining that "the availability of appropriate treatment is a powerful argument in favour of a federal sentence."[565] Although Good participated in treatment and counselling at the Whitehorse Correctional Centre while she was in remand, Judge Faulkner accedes to the Crown argument that she "has always participated in treatment while incarcerated but always repeats the pattern of offending once released."[566] Against this backdrop, and also considering public safety, the judge decides, "In my view, it is time to try a different approach. That approach requires a penitentiary sentence."[567]

As Good has undergone significant periods of treatment while she was incarcerated in the past without a subsequent change in behaviour, a different type of program in a different context of incarceration may not offer much of a "different approach" to her rehabilitation. It does, however, signify a transition in how healing through imprisonment is represented within the judgment. That is, with respect to Good's former periods of incarceration, during which she underwent treatment and then continued to offend upon release, the judge conveys a construction of prison that suggests it is either ineffective or counterproductive (at least for Good) in terms of any healing capacities. However, by stating "it is time to try a different approach" and identifying that this different approach will be found in the federal correctional system, Judge Faulkner suggests another representation of the experience of imprisonment, wherein healing (perhaps generally, but at least for Good) is possible.

Judicial awareness of the disparity between federal and provincial programming options emerges in a number of other cases I have considered and discussed above, including *R. v. Waskewitch*, *R. v. Pelletier*,[568] and *R .v. Smith*.[569] Even in the sensitive decision *R. v. Connors*, where the judge grapples with the 2007 amendments to the conditional sentencing regime and concludes that the changes preclude that otherwise appropriate sentencing option, in the end, the judge decides that "a two year sentence in a federal penitentiary, as Crown is seeking, would not only give appropriate recognition to denunciation and deterrence, but also suit the needs of the offender better than a lengthy term in a provincial jail."[570] Judge A.P. Ross does not elaborate on the substance of these needs, and the reason(s) why the judge considers a federal penitentiary better suited to Shayla Connors's needs are not specified, but it is likely this refers to the dearth of programming in provincial institutions.

Provincial correctional institutions are widely known to lack programming services, but there were instances in the cases I examined that provided a slightly different picture. In sentencing Lori Abraham from the Sagkeeng First Nation for assault connected to a break and enter offence, aggravated assault, and assault with a weapon (all part of a home invasion Abraham committed with her co-accused, in which the victim was her abusive former partner, who refused to accept that she wanted to end the relationship), Judge Heinrichs finds that her *Gladue* factors "must temper the need for a lengthy denunciatory and deterrent sentence," and below that of her co-accused.[571] The judge finds that the least restrictive and most appropriate sentence is time served (fifteen months and eight days) "plus the maximum provincial sentence of 2 years less one day," followed by the maximum (three-year) probation order with "somewhat onerous" conditions attached.[572] Judge Heinrichs comments that this sentence will enable her "to continue with the programming and education already started in the provincial jail and will, in all likelihood not be moved elsewhere."[573] As her global sentence (before reducing it for pre-sentence custody) would be in the range of a federal term of incarceration, it seems the judge made a deliberate decision to order her remaining sentence in the provincial range, both to maintain stability and continuity with the provincial programming she had already begun, and to permit extended community supervision (although the latter also extends the time during which Abraham could breach her probationary conditions and be charged).

As a further example, in *Woods*, discussed above and in Chapter 2, an almost inverse representation of imprisonment emerges from that in

Redhead, in which the experience of incarceration seems to have triggered her institutional violence instead of being rehabilitating. Judge Whelan sentences Candace Woods to a conditional sentence of two years less a day, concluding that the circumstances of her offence (robbery) did not necessitate incarceration.[574] A community sentence is additionally appropriate because of her family commitments. She was released on bail under strict conditions; Judge Whelan observes that "because she has been confined to her residence much of the time, she has developed a close bond with her son and she is the primary caregiver."[575] In terms of her experience of (pre-sentencing) imprisonment, it seems that Woods made some progress while in custody on remand. Woods's mother conveys to the judge that remand was "an 'eye opener'" for Woods, "who is motivated to avoid drugs and criminal activity so as not to jeopardize her being able to care for her infant son."[576] Judge Whelan reports that Woods's addictions motivated her offending, but that, while in remand, Woods completed the Women's Substance Abuse Program and remained in the Methadone Program, maintaining her sobriety, after her release.[577]

There are some apparent positive impacts from Woods's time in pre-sentence custody, but Woods's experience of remand was relatively brief (two months), so it may not be representative of the damaging effects of imprisonment for longer periods. As well, this seemingly positive experience of incarceration appears to be an anomaly in the cases I studied. I present it as a counterbalance to the idea that imprisonment (and at provincial institutions in particular) is always and necessarily detrimental. However, benefiting from programming in (remand or sentenced) prison certainly does not preclude the idea that the same (or greater) benefits could be derived from similar programming delivered in a community setting. If Indigenous women like Woods *do* receive some benefit from their time in remand, this benefit has the potential to be eroded during sentence determinations: Judge Whelan writes, "The availability of programming is one factor taken into account when determining the credit to be given for remand."[578] Judge Whelan nonetheless decides to credit Woods for her remand time at a ratio of two to one. It should be noted that recent legislation[579] constrains judicial discretion regarding sentence reduction by restricting the ratios that judges can use to credit persons being sentenced with remand custody.[580]

As Milward and Parkes find, "Sentencing judges are often under the impression that Aboriginal people will have access to culturally appropriate and much needed programs, therapies, and resources for healing if they are sentenced to federal prison time."[581] All these issues are complex, particularly for Indigenous women on the borderline of provincial and federal time for whom judges (and/or amendments to the legislation) have eliminated conditional sentences—if judges decide incarceration is necessary for an Indigenous woman, it seems to make intuitive sense that "while she is there anyway," she be placed where (federally or provincially) she is most likely to receive rehabilitative services. It becomes more problematic where, as in *Pelletier*, it appears that prison sentences longer in duration are being considered specifically to prolong involvement in prison rehabilitative services. Such instances suggest that prison is being promoted as a rehabilitative sanction, whereas much evidence demonstrates that the experience of imprisonment (including its isolation, coerciveness, oppressiveness, and bleakness) causes people's mental health to worsen.

Imprison with Great Caution

Women's victimizations impact how they experience imprisonment, which emphasizes the importance of thinking about how victimization is understood and incorporated into sentencing. The stresses of incarceration often retrigger post-traumatic stress disorder[582] or other mental health problems arising from past violence, often because the powerlessness, vulnerability, and fundamentally unequal power dynamics characterizing women's prison lives replicate patterns of abuse they have experienced.[583] The reactivation of past experiences of victimization has prompted many incarcerated women to engage in self-injurious behaviour, become (sometimes suicidally) depressed, and suffer further detrimental mental health effects.[584] In another iteration of the problem of individualizing structural factors, these reactions may be formulated as pathological by correctional systems instead of being understood as coping mechanisms derived from past traumatic experiences.[585] This understanding sometimes results in increased punitive measures such as institutional charges or intensified isolation through segregation.[586]

Simply being severed from society, their children, and loved ones/support networks often causes the erosion of women's self-conception and mental health[587] (and, of course, erodes family and community cohesion). These painful processes underscore how imprisonment is incompatible with any kind of healing process for Indigenous women because it often aggravates pre-existing trauma and engenders additional trauma. As such, judges must take great care and caution before concluding that it is the best sentencing option.

Additional research finds that women have difficulty reintegrating into the community after serving carceral sentences because of the way the experience of imprisonment indelibly marks their lives. Laura Shantz, Jennifer M. Kilty, and Sylvie Frigon are careful to identify that "reintegration" itself is a problematic concept, because structural inequalities that contribute to women's imprisonment also signify that "women who are subject to imprisonment are never fully *of* the community."[588] I understand this to mean that criminalized women ordered to terms of incarceration are often already so marginalized that they were never fully integrated into the functioning core of the community to begin with, so that post-release, when they are being "reintegrated," they are really just being thrust back to those same margins. Women adjusting from living within the (oppressive) structure of imprisonment may feel anxious, stigmatized, and further marginalized, often returning to the isolation of poverty and having to renavigate their lives with inadequate resources in the community.[589]

In these and related ways, prison should not be regarded as a place of healing—quite the opposite. It has been widely documented that prison amplifies and foments pain and struggles instead of offering a salve. Additionally, Michael Jackson observes that what many "official reports suggest is that the experience of imprisonment, as a response to crime, is itself criminogenic: it actually produces and reproduces the very behaviour it seeks to control"[590] (and particularly for incarcerated women, this phenomenon can also be internalized, manifesting as self-harm). Because of the ways incarceration exacerbates criminalized Indigenous women's struggles, judges should not understand prison as a place of healing, and should exercise great caution when considering appropriate sanctions.

REFRACTED THROUGH INSTITUTIONAL LENSES

In the Introduction to this book, I related that the program coordinator for Kindred House, Shawna Hohendorff, had told a parliamentary subcommittee on sex work that her clients (of whom about 80 percent were Indigenous women) felt systemically unheard. Hohendorff told the subcommittee that her clients "don't feel listened to," feeling that bureaucracies are "not open" to "their particular life stories."[1] She explained to the subcommittee that she "[does not] know all of the answers," and that she "think[s] it's a complex set of problems," but that, above all, what "we need to do is to listen, so that it is holistic, and so that they are part of our community, not separate."[2]

I use Hohendorff's words to frame this book both because I want to foreground the criminalized Indigenous women at the centre of my work, and because I have sought to understand how aspects of their (institutionally penned) "life stories" are heard by the criminal justice system, with respect to experiences of victimization. The sentencing discourses relating to the Indigenous women discussed above are sometimes decontextualized, but the judicial frame must be refocused and widened to respond to the (individual and collective) histories, needs, and humanity of the women at the centre, and particularly those needs relating to victimization and colonization.

Processes within the criminal justice system (sentencing and corrections) have a limited focus (due to their internal structures, mandates/objectives, etc.), and the victimization narratives I discuss in this book are refracted through these institutional lenses. The narratives about criminalized Indigenous women's lives that are filtered through, presented to, and heard by the criminal justice system certainly do not (and cannot) define or encapsulate their lives, but these accounts are significant to how these women are understood and treated in the system. Razack points to the relative positioning of dominant and oppressed groups in critiques of narratives, posing the questions, "Who is describing and assessing the realities of whom, how do we hear these descriptions and what relations do they secure?"[3] For the discourses in this book, the judges are (primarily) the storytellers, but situated within a web of narratives. The victimization narratives I explore in Chapter 2 are the stories written by many actors in the criminal justice system (particularly police officers, probation officers, psychiatrists and psychologists, lawyers, and judges), and constructed within certain parameters defined by the system, such as in the format of pre-sentence reports and counsel submissions, to service the goals of the system. As the narratives conform to these parameters, and are then told through judges' words in sentencing decisions, the "listening" that I perform (and in which the reader participates) in this book is an act of critically listening to both the elements of life stories that legal officials relate about the victimization histories of these criminalized Indigenous women, and also the institutional response, in terms of how sentencing judges, the gatekeepers to prison, develop corresponding discourses about imprisonment.

Regarding the overrepresentation of Indigenous women in prisons, I pay particular attention to conditional sentence orders in this book because this sanction most readily replaces what would otherwise be a term of institutional incarceration (within the confines of the criminal justice system in its current form). To fully respond to the directives in *Gladue*, as reinforced by *Ipeelee*, conditional sentences must remain central within available sentencing options. As Judge Ross notes in *Stevens*, "*Gladue* arises most often, it seems, when a court is considering whether a custodial sentence ought to be imposed on an aboriginal offender."[4] This observation is salient to my choice to focus (at least where possible) on sentencing judgments where conditional sentences could have been, or were once, available. Equally, I choose this focus due to the predominant position that imprisonment occupies within our criminal justice system (as a spectre and in its reality/institutional form), but I suggest that particularly for criminalized Indigenous women, expanded usage of alternative, non-carceral sanctions within better resourced communities would be most preferable. The UN Committee indicates that Indigenous women "are less likely to be sentenced to alternative measures to incarceration"[5] in Canada. This *must* be changed. In 2015, the TRC called "upon federal, provincial, and territorial governments to commit to eliminating the overrepresentation of Aboriginal people in custody over the next decade,"[6] and to be accountable to this through ongoing annual progress reports.

The (institutionally structured) personal histories of criminalized Indigenous women as related in this book often involve extensive experiences of victimization. This underscores the importance of my use of the feminist theory of the victimization-criminalization continuum to inform this book. NWAC emphasizes, "It is essential that those in the criminal justice field recognize . . . that there is a link between victimization and criminalization which occurs at both an individual and a collective level. Aboriginal women/girls suffer additional gender specific forms of collective discrimination within the victim to criminal cycle, and attention must be paid to this."[7] Such attention must run through the criminal justice process, including through lawyering approaches. Justices Hamilton and Sinclair report for the Aboriginal Justice Inquiry of Manitoba that Indigenous women "told us that lawyers do not understand the problems" they experience, and "lawyers do not understand the Aboriginal community or how the forces within it affect women."[8] Justices Hamilton and Sinclair state that Indigenous women "who have experienced long-term abuse, leading up to the offence with which they are charged, feel they should be presented to the court as victims and not simply as offenders," and suggest that Indigenous women are overrepresented in Manitoba's provincial correctional system "because of problems they experience with the courts."[9]

I have sought to make this link between victimization and criminalization visible by drawing out judicial discourses about how it relates to the sentencing process. Indigenous women's experiences of victimization impact their lives before, during, and after the sentencing process (including victimization inflicted *by* sentencing, imprisonment, related criminal justice processes, and intersecting processes by adjacent state institutions). This impact is potentially complicated by impediments to access community resources (including the dearth of such resources, particularly in isolated, impoverished communities). Kelly Hannah-Moffat writes about the security classification process for federally sentenced women that "victimization becomes an informal measure of risk."[10] This observation sometimes extends to judicial understandings of Indigenous women's histories of victimization at sentencing, particularly where judges fail to engage in a thorough *Gladue* analysis and instead use decontextualized reasoning.

Often, these histories of victimization contribute to or are translated into the idea that Indigenous women require therapeutic intervention in some form (through prison programs or treatment conditions in the community) to minimize risk and promote rehabilitation. Some judges consequently portray imprisonment as offering a specialized mode of treatment. The appropriateness of treatment through imprisonment is complicated. For example, sometimes communities lack the internal support to manage community sentences safely and effectively, and incarceration therefore becomes the foremost remaining option. Judicial conceptions of how victimization histories contribute to the need for treatment give rise to sentencing challenges in cases where the judge finds that community resources are insufficient. Judicial perceptions that federal incarceration does offer adequate treatment services are similarly troubling because of the deleterious effects of the experience of imprisonment. As Pollack writes, "That women are willing to serve longer prison sentences in order to get help that is often unavailable in their communities, and that judges are willing to sentence them in this way, is quite disturbing."[11] This outcome is disturbing because, fundamentally, prisons are not structured to provide treatment, but are instead oriented toward security concerns.[12]

Many actors in the criminal justice system advance the suggestion that imprisonment provides access to treatment programs that are necessary to rehabilitation—not only judges, but also defence and Crown counsel, and probation officers, among others. The multiple sources of the idea that prison is a place of treatment were evident in my research. In *Diamond,* the author of the pre-sentence report suggests that Diamond must address her difficulties with specialized professionals in a confined setting.[13] Defence counsel in *Whitford* acknowledges (alongside the related Crown submission) that Whitford "needs a longer period of time in a structured setting to allow her to continue her rehabilitation and to permit her access to the programs that are offered."[14] The judge in *Whitford* adopts the same view: "I am satisfied that a significant period is needed to allow her to complete that [rehabilitative] process as far as possible and to avail herself of the programs, counseling, and other factors that are available."[15]

While I am critical of these views in this book, I acknowledge that, when effectively administered, and *only* where there are no available community-based alternatives, prison programming may be helpful for some prisoners.[16] However, at the federal level, the Correctional Investigator reported in 2011 that the Correctional Service "has not done enough to ensure Aboriginal offenders are given sufficient access to culturally sensitive programming and services."[17] The Correctional Investigator continues, "The areas of concern associated with Aboriginal corrections go far beyond the issue of over-representation and require focusing on what happens to this group of offenders while in the care and custody of the Correctional Service."[18] In the Correctional Investigator's 2014–15 annual report, Howard Sapers acknowledges that, at the federal level, csc recently internally produced research into how *Gladue* factors are used and affect correctional decisions pertaining to Indigenous offenders.[19] The Correctional Investigator's 2015–16 annual report finds that, at a policy level, "csc has extended the application of *Gladue* factors to correctional decision-making which means that the social history of an Aboriginal offender must be considered in security classification, penitentiary placement, institutional transfer and administrative segregation decisions," but adds that "there remains insufficient and uneven application of *Gladue* social history considerations in correctional decision-making."[20] For my purposes in this book, it is sufficient to identify and challenge discourses in the criminal justice system that suggest criminalized Indigenous women's victimization experiences precipitate a need for treatment in prison.

Both *Gladue* and *Ipeelee* have held that incarceration is particularly problematic for Indigenous persons (and Sugar and Fox have presented experiences of Indigenous women prisoners that explain this), so all actors in the system must be very cautious before holding out imprisonment as a source of healing. Additionally, Judge Stuart's more general comments in *Elias* are instructive and should be understood by all actors in the criminal justice system: "I do not suggest that there is no place for punitive responses, but it must now be recognized that jail as the sentencing tool of choice has never lived up to its claims—and has enormously damaging side effects."[21] For Indigenous women, these side effects become writ large, appearing on both the collective level in the form of overrepresentation, and at the individual level in terms of the deleterious impacts on their own lives and well-being (and on both levels together, due to how the incarceration of Indigenous women and mothers fractures and devastates families and communities). Given these problems inherent in imprisonment, sentencing judges have a challenging, complicated task.

The Role of the Sentencing Judge

In *Gladue*, Justices Cory and Iacobucci acknowledge that sentencing judges have a "limited role" "in remedying injustice against aboriginal peoples in Canada."[22] The ongoing processes of colonization behind that injustice are long-standing and complex, so sentencing initiatives are just one aspect of the many issues that must be addressed and redressed. Justices Cory and Iacobucci write that "sentencing innovation by itself cannot remove the causes of aboriginal offending and the greater problem of aboriginal alienation from the criminal justice system."[23] In *Ipeelee*, Justice LeBel echoes that "it would have been naive to suggest that sentencing Aboriginal persons differently, without addressing the root causes of criminality, would eliminate their overrepresentation in the criminal justice system entirely."[24] There is a spectrum of approaches and reforms needed to respond to the overincarceration of Indigenous peoples. However, notwithstanding the "admittedly limited"[25] role of sentencing judges in this broader task, sentencing remains a necessary and important role. Justice LeBel states that despite the need for other approaches, "that does not detract from a judge's fundamental duty" to arrive at an appropriate sentence, and "nor does it turn s. 718.2(e) into an empty promise."[26]

In *Ipeelee*, Justice LeBel describes the responsibility and pivotal role played by sentencing judges: "Sentencing judges are among those decision-makers who have the power to influence the treatment of aboriginal offenders in the justice system. *They determine most directly whether an aboriginal offender will go to jail*, or whether other sentencing options may be employed which will play perhaps a stronger role in restoring a sense of balance to the offender, victim, and community, and in preventing future crime."[27] *Gladue* identifies sentencing as a "critical juncture" at which the overincarceration of Indigenous peoples can be meaningfully addressed because judges set in motion the way in which Indigenous peoples are processed through the system. The trajectory of this motion is often cyclical: I discuss in Chapter 3 that, according to Juristat, "research has found that Aboriginal persons are more likely than their non-Aboriginal counterparts to be re-admitted to the correctional system after being released."[28] The revolving door swings with particular force for Indigenous women. Both *Gladue*[29] and *Ipeelee*[30] emphasize that Indigenous peoples experience imprisonment differently,[31] often making it a less appropriate sanction. Specifically, Hannah-Moffat says, "The experiences of Aboriginal women prisoners are different from those of non-Aboriginal women prisoners."[32] Additionally, as I address in Chapter 2, criminalized Indigenous women are especially vulnerable to pleading guilty. In this context, the legislative and community provision of availability of alternatives to imprisonment, and judicial consideration of those alternatives, becomes vital.

Some judges were attuned to such issues prior to *Ipeelee*. In sentencing Deborah Hill before *Ipeelee* was decided, Justice Harris anticipates the *Ipeelee* clarification that courts have erroneously held that serious offences render *Gladue* principles inapplicable:

I am also mindful of the fact that more than 10 years
after the Supreme Court of Canada released *Gladue*, the
proportion of aboriginal offenders incarcerated in Canada's
prisons and reformatories has increased. Clearly that is not
going to change if we simply pay lip service to the principles
of *Gladue* and then point to the Supreme Court of Canada's
comments to the effect that generally, the more serious and
violent the crime, the more likely it will be as a practical
matter that the terms of imprisonment will be the same
for similar offences and offenders, whether aboriginal or
non-aboriginal.[33]

As such, Justice Harris concludes, "The new method of analysis which
Gladue mandates that I as a sentencing judge must use in determining a
fit sentence for aboriginal offenders will only have real meaning if, in appropriate cases, I choose not to send someone to jail for a serious crime."[34]
Justice Harris considers Hill's circumstances as "a Haudenosaunee woman of Mohawk and Tuscarora ancestry, a member of the Bear Clan,"[35]
and orders a nine-month conditional sentence followed by three years
of probation for impaired driving. In a later decision, post-*Ipeelee* but
seemingly issued by the same judge (discussed in Chapter 3 regarding
judicial consideration of Tiffany Sowden's relationship with her child),
Justice Harris again comments that incarceration of Indigenous persons
has continued to increase "more than 14 years after" *Gladue*, reiterating
that, "clearly, that is not going to change if we simply pay lip service to
the principles of *Gladue* and then look for reasons not to apply them."[36]
In this judgment, Justice Harris finds, "*Gladue* also requires that as the
sentencing judge, I must consider a shorter period of imprisonment in
appropriate cases for an aboriginal offender,"[37] ordering the intermittent
prison sentence and probation discussed in reference to judicial attention to mothering needs in Chapter 3.

Ipeelee describes that sentencing judges are best positioned "as frontline workers in the criminal justice system" to be critical about how systemic factors can permeate the sentencing framework, and "re-evaluate
these [sentencing] criteria to ensure that they are not contributing to

ongoing systemic racial discrimination."[38] In this critical approach, judges benefit from the information in *Gladue* reports and pre-sentence reports with *Gladue* components, so both types of reports should be informed by a deep understanding of what is involved in the *Gladue* analysis (implicating the roles of other actors in the system, of course, and ideally meaning the provision of *Gladue* reports instead of relying on pre-sentence reports with *Gladue* sections). As I explain in Chapter 3, I am critical of the decontextualized judicial reasoning in *Char*. However, Judge Bayliff's comments do reflect the challenges inherent in the sentencing process, and the need for guidance about (and the availability of) alternatives to incarceration: "I ask myself, what could be done here to rehabilitate and reintegrate Ms. Char? What could be done? Is there some other option to custody here? Is there something that the court should be doing differently here?"[39]

In Chapter 2, I discuss various decisions indicating that information about *Gladue* factors presented to sentencing judges varies in its adequacy, with resultant challenges for judges engaging in a *Gladue* analysis. Many judges in my research reference the information provided related to *Gladue* factors is lacking. Other research has found that Manitoba judges have expressed concern and frustration at the insufficiency (or absence) of *Gladue* reports in their experience, and have identified the need for greater information and guidance to support a proper *Gladue* analysis.[40] As mentioned in Chapter 2, LSS of BC has created a comprehensive resource (essentially a workbook to complete) for accused or convicted Indigenous persons, their lawyers, Indigenous court workers, or advocates, to assist with the preparation of *Gladue* submissions.[41] Increased usage of such resources should assist judges in their capacity to ameliorate the overincarceration of Indigenous peoples.

The sufficiency of information made available to judges about Indigenous systemic and background factors (particularly in the form of *Gladue* reports and counsel submissions) is intrinsically useful to the purposes of sentencing Indigenous persons, but has added significance in the context of the concern identified by Justice LeBel in *Ipeelee* about judicial hesitance to take related judicial notice.[42] I observed some of this hesitancy in certain cases in my own research. For example, in sentencing the Tlingit woman Denelle Dickson without the assistance of either a *Gladue* report or any counsel submissions about her background and systemic factors, Judge Lilles writes, "I must be cautious about taking judicial notice of the broad systemic and background factors," although he adds, "I am very familiar with the Teslin community as a result of almost 20 years of presiding there as a judge," including his awareness of "the impact of residential schools on generations of Teslin citizens."[43] This combination of a dearth of *Gladue*-related information and judicial cautiousness in taking judicial notice could even more strongly substantiate the concern identified in *Ipeelee* in cases where the judge has less direct and long-term familiarity with the community (perhaps including newer judges, those less generally familiar with the *Gladue* analysis, and circuit judges).

Creative Sentencing and Judicial Discretion

Those who participated in the Department of Justice Canada review of the criminal justice system (including lawyers, judges, Indigenous leaders and communities, and representatives from non-governmental organizations that support persons in the system) indicate among their suggestions for reform that judges must be given "the discretion they need to make decisions based on a person's circumstances."[44] Reporting that "the system does not currently leave enough room for judicial discretion," they contend that "real change would require an approach that allows the court to take an accused person's history into account," and that "the courts should be free to apply the principles that the Supreme Court of Canada outlined" in *Gladue* and *Ipeelee*.[45] These suggestions for reform are sobering in reflecting that judges operate within legislative constraints that limit their ability to give full effect to *Gladue* and *Ipeelee*. (Perhaps there is hope for expanded judicial discretion: on 29 May 2018, Independent Senator Kim Pate introduced a bill permitting judicial discretion to decline to impose mandatory minimum sentences where appropriate.[46] If passed, this would also have the effect of relieving some of the current restrictions on the availability of conditional sentences.)

Ipeelee holds that, "as the statistics indicate, section 718.2(e) of the *Criminal Code* has not had a discernible impact on the overrepresentation of Aboriginal people in the criminal justice system."[47] The decision indicates that this failure may not be a problem within the provision itself, but instead a reflection that "the *Gladue* principles were never expected to provide a panacea," and that sentencing decisions demonstrate a "fundamental misunderstanding and misapplication of both s. 718.2(e) and this Court's decision in *Gladue*."[48] It is to be hoped that, on an ongoing basis, the clarifications provided by *Ipeelee* will be increasingly meaningfully incorporated into sentencing decisions, facilitating the combined ability of s. 718.2(e) and its interpretation in *Gladue* to better realize their mutual goal to reduce the overincarceration of Indigenous peoples. Additionally, as Scott argues regarding Saskatchewan, but expanded to other provinces/territories, too, due to "the principles of judicial independence and *stare decisis*" structuring the Canadian justice system, appellate courts should perform a "leadership role" here.[49] In their report for the Aboriginal Justice Inquiry of Manitoba, which preceded the 1996 sentencing amendments and *Gladue* and *Ipeelee*, Justices Hamilton and Sinclair already foresaw the need for appellate courts to "encourage more latitude and more creativity in sentencing."[50] Justices Hamilton and Sinclair write that appellate courts should embolden sentencing judges to "depart from such a rigid approach" as occurs where courts simply impose the same sentence for the same offence, and recommend expanded reliance on alternatives to incarceration.[51] Justices Hamilton and Sinclair find that where appellate courts overturn and effectively subvert innovative sentencing decisions, consequently there is a continued "standardization of particular sentences for particular crimes, without much concern for unique circumstances," and that future "initiative" by sentencing judges "is discouraged."[52]

In *Ipeelee*, Justice LeBel comments on the legislated objectives of sentencing, but adds the direction that "to the extent that current sentencing practices do not further these objectives, those practices must change so as to meet the needs of Aboriginal offenders and their communities."[53] There is no explicit directive that judges look to more radical sentencing alternatives, but it does seem that *Ipeelee* at minimum encourages creative sentencing. For example, this implicit support for more creative sentencing outcomes appears where Justice LeBel quotes academics Jonathan Rudin and Kent Roach: "[If an innovative] sentence can serve to actually assist a person in taking responsibility for his or her actions and lead to a reduction in the probability of subsequent re-offending, why should such a sentence be precluded just because other people who commit the same offence go to jail?"[54] This too reflects the view of Justices Hamilton and Sinclair, who emphasize the need for sentencing judges to "be more creative," meaning that "existing sentencing options must be utilized more fully, and the courts should encourage the establishment of other options and solutions that are tailored to particular offenders and particular communities."[55] (Of course, these recommendations emerge from their report published in 1991, nearly thirty years ago, and the urgency for this approach to sentencing Indigenous persons has only intensified since).

Additionally, Justice LeBel summarizes the purpose of sentencing: "To promote a just, peaceful and safe society through the imposition of just sanctions that, among other things, deter criminality and rehabilitate offenders, all in accordance with the fundamental principle of proportionality."[56] Importantly, Justice LeBel continues, "Just sanctions are those that do not operate in a discriminatory manner,"[57] and combines this with Parliament's direction in s. 718.2(e), noting that this legislative direction was "to ensure that judges undertook their duties properly."[58] From these comments, it seems that *Ipeelee* stands for the idea that part of the duty of a judge sentencing Indigenous persons includes the need to step outside the box and develop more innovative, creative sanctions where such outcomes contribute to rehabilitation and minimize the risk of reinvolvement in the system. Also, the Convention on the Elimination of All Forms of Discrimination against Women requires that for Indigenous women "to enjoy their human rights and fundamental freedoms," Canadian state actors "at all levels, including police *and the judicial system*," must comply with certain "due diligence obligations in order to put them into effect."[59] Among other state/judicial responsibilities, these "due diligence obligations" include "to prevent" and "protect from" gender-based violence against Indigenous women, and compel the state to have "systematically strengthened its institutional response to be commensurate with the vulnerabilities identified and the seriousness of the situation."[60] While the UN Committee identifies these state responsibilities in relation to victimized Indigenous women, given the prevalence of victimization histories among criminalized

Indigenous women, I suggest Canada's institutional responsibilities under this international convention should be read broadly to encompass its obligations to Indigenous women in the criminal justice system, which should then implicate the government and the judicial system in securing and preserving the safety of Indigenous women at sentencing, including through crafting innovative sanctions.

Certain other decisions from lower courts but preceding *Ipeelee* also point to the need for creativity and flexibility in the sentencing of Indigenous persons. For example, in *George*, Justice George quotes a 2001 Manitoba Court of Appeal decision that states that s. 718.2(e) provides "recognition that the sentence must be individualized and that there are serious social problems with respect to aboriginals that require more creative and innovative solutions," and that this provision "is an acknowledgment that to achieve real equity, sometimes different people must be treated differently."[61] Regarding "the potential for decolonizing legal practice," Balfour suggests that, on sentencing, the "blameworthiness" of Indigenous persons should be "locate[d] . . . as relational to conditions of endangerment . . . as well as the lack of resources within their communities."[62] In this reframing, for example, any unavailability of community resources could more reliably function as mitigating as opposed to a reason to order prison terms for Indigenous women as a partial means of attempting to secure those otherwise inaccessible resources.

Regarding alternatives to incarceration per s. 718.2(e), Murdocca writes, "The transfer of responsibility for incarceration rates to Aboriginal and Inuit communities, with the intent of having a community 'deal with its own problems,' highlights the manner in which government responses to overincarceration continue to rely upon the notion that 'social problems' are somehow both the ontological property of indigenous people and the collective responsibility of those communities."[63] Much as in this expanded frame, where responsibility is located in the state, judicial creativity on sentencing should involve deepened institutional recognition of the ways in which the criminal justice system is itself implicated and culpable in the lives and systemic experiences of victimization of the Indigenous peoples it processes and controls, and this system and its institutions must interrogate and challenge their own foundations. As Walter Benjamin declares, "When the consciousness of the latent presence of violence in a legal institution disappears, the institution falls into decay."[64] Razack suggests while a "culturally sensitive judge might understand that colonization has wreaked havoc on Aboriginal communities," this understanding may not be extended to "an understanding of the current workings of white supremacy," in that colonization is represented in terms of "involving only Aboriginal people, not white colonizers."[65]

Indicating some hope for the justice system reflexively examining its own role in oppression and striving for a measure of institutional accountability, some judges do seek to identify the institutions and forces perpetuating colonization. In a decision sentencing Valerie Sack from the Indian Brook First Nation, Judge Atwood points to the complicity and responsibility of the institutions of which all judges are primary (and powerful) actors, referring to *the offences that have been committed against First-Nations' communities* throughout Canada—and those offences have *implicated the justice system* of this province and other provinces."[66] Judge Atwood writes that, "in many respects," Sack's "life is a result of that tragic past" as she and other members of Indigenous communities contend with systemic "repression" and "overwhelming social, familial, and health and wellness-related tensions," and "have been deprived unjustly of the resources needed to cope with them."[67] In a context in which the judge's function is to determine an appropriate sentence for a given offence, this obviously presents a very different conception of what constitutes an "offence" (as contrasted with those defined in the Criminal Code), situates related problems within Indigenous community needs (and rights), and calls justice systems to account. In this characterization, the concept of "victimization" is effectively expanded to include experiences of victimization engendered *by the criminal justice system itself*, and within the context (and as an extension) of colonization. This refers back to the discussion in Chapter 1 about criminalization as a strategy of (or complicit with) colonization, and involves issues discussed in Chapter 3 with respect to criminalized Indigenous women's various apprehensions about and mistrust of the criminal justice system (and other intersecting systems such as child welfare) and the ways in which state sanctioning of mothers can effectively extend that punishment through their families.

I discuss the sentencing of Robyn Hansen variously above, particularly with regard to judicial consideration of issues connected to mothering, family structures, and colonization. For Hansen's offences of aggravated assault, assault with a weapon, and uttering a threat, Justice Butler orders an intermittent prison sentence of ninety days followed by three years of probation, in part to keep Hansen's family intact against the corrosive intergenerational effect of colonization on Indigenous families. Justice Butler finds that this "intermittent custodial sentence gives a measure of denunciation which will be understood by the community," and that her probationary term aligns with the objectives of individual and general deterrence.[68] Moreover, Justice Butler writes that these "sanctions will impress upon the community and bring home to Ms. Hansen the value the justice system places on breaking the pattern of family dysfunction caused by parental neglect and substance abuse. This is deterrence in action by way of an innovative sanction."[69] To support this finding, Justice Butler cites *Ipeelee*, suggesting the Supreme Court of Canada here "approved the use of innovative sentences to assist in reducing recidivism and promoting safe communities."[70]

Hansen indicates that some judges are receiving the *Ipeelee* impulse and direction that they should seek to craft innovative sentences for Indigenous persons. Further, Justice Butler's suggestion that Hansen's sanctions communicate to the community that the justice system is invested in disrupting family patterns derived from colonization is significant. This judicial statement situates the criminal justice system not as an external body, responding to individual offences, but instead as an active participant in the healing of families and communities devastated by colonization. By implication, it also indirectly suggests that the justice system is complicit in the continued fracturing of Indigenous families and communities, which places accountability and an imperative on the system to confront this complicity and this fracturing (involving the related need for trust-building). These moments in *Sack* and *Hansen* suggest the potential for further development of such consciousness within the system. If this consciousness of systemic complicity in colonization accumulates in the jurisprudence, perhaps judicial reasoning could supply greater capacity to respond to Murdocca's concern about s. 718.2(e), where she asks, "What is it in this provision that demands a focus on the 'characteristics' of cultural difference (the degree of cultural difference) rather than a focus on the 'circumstances' that could lead to a focus on the systems that sustain Aboriginal subjugation in Canada?"[71]

In a judgment sentencing Tanya Peters (Pitwanakwat) mere months after *Ipeelee* was decided, Justice George gestures toward the appropriateness of innovative sanctions, writing that courts "can, however, deviate from what might be a typical sentence for a particular offence, if there is a reason to do it and if it is done with a view to achieve the purposes contemplated by section 718.2(e) and *Gladue*."[72] However, judicial creativity is hampered by encroachments on judicial discretion, and particularly where those encroachments impinge on the availability of community-based sanctions. In the Introduction, I introduce the problem of incursions into judicial discretion vis-à-vis conditional sentence orders through the respective passage of Bill C-9 in 2007 and Bill C-10 in 2012. With the depletion of conditional sentences as a sanction available to judges, it is uncertain how much real scope and impact the clarifications in *Ipeelee* will have on the overrepresentation of Indigenous peoples in the system, and particularly its prisons. For example, while *Connors* was decided before *Ipeelee* and the further restrictions on conditional sentences after Bill C-10 entered into force, Judge Ross signalled that the 2007 amendments to the conditional sentencing regime already problematically trenched on judicial discretion. Judge Ross found that the amendments "preclude[d]" him from considering a conditional sentence order for that young Indigenous woman, and sentenced her to federal custody.[73] In reaching that conclusion, Judge Ross cites another case that refers to the effect of the amendments on the "reduction of judicial discretion [as] an 'undesired result.'"[74]

Other decisions also demonstrate problematic impacts of the reduced availability of conditional sentences. In Chapter 2, I note that Justice George sentences Summur George to thirty days in prison followed by a probationary term of two years for robbery, and I allude to the unavailability of a conditional sentence order, given amendments to the regime. This robbery is her first offence, notwithstanding an unrelated breach that the judge discounts. Justice George explicitly writes that counsel presented the court with "a half-hearted joint submission," noting, "Notwithstanding this joint proposal, all seemed to agree that were it available as a sentencing option, Ms. George would have been a suitable candidate for a conditional sentence. It's hard to imagine a case better suited for that type of disposition. With that recognition, and accepting that it is not available, both counsel did wonder aloud whether or not there were alternative, more creative ways to address all of the sentencing principles, including denunciation, deterrence, and rehabilitation and doing so within the framework set out by the Supreme Court"[75] in *Gladue*, *Wells*, and *Ipeelee*. There were many other decisions from my research in which sentencing judges directly comment that conditional sentence orders are now precluded due to amendments to the regime.[76]

Some judges do strive to navigate the restrictions on judicial discretion imposed by the two waves of conditional sentencing amendments through innovative sentencing attempts. For example, I return here to the sentencing of Ivy Pijogge to highlight the creativity of the judge in determining the appropriate sanction. Justice Stack seeks an alternative to incarceration and orders Pijogge to a six-month conditional sentence. At the date of Pijogge's offence of leaving an accident scene knowing bodily harm had been caused, the 2007 conditional sentencing amendments constituted the regime in force, but the law changed again through the 2012 amendments by the time of Pijogge's sentencing. Justice Stack observes that Pijogge's offence would have eliminated a conditional sentence order as an option under the law active on her offence date, and instead chooses to apply the law as set through the 2012 amendments. The judge decides the 2012 conditional sentencing regime applies by finding that s. 11(i) of the Canadian Charter of Rights and Freedoms, part of the Constitution Act, 1982, is engaged, which stipulates that if the punishment for the offence has been amended between the offence date and sentencing, the person charged is entitled to the lesser punishment. Here, Justice Stack was motivated to find an alternative to incarceration for Pijogge, and achieved this through the operation of the Charter.

The problem of incursions into judicial discretion may also dilute sentences in some cases. In the Introduction I reference *Audy*, in which Judge Slough orders probation (with conditional sentence–like conditions including an absolute curfew of twenty-four hours a day, seven days a week for the first nine months of the order), but notes that before the 2007 amendments, a conditional sentence would have been the outcome.[77] *Smith* is another case in which these restrictions on judicial discretion produce a diluted sentence, which is then overturned on appeal when found unfit. In Chapter 3, I note that Judge Higinbotham sentences Tracy Smith to prison for one day followed by probation for three years, due to her rehabilitative needs. After a successful Crown appeal, the British Columbia Court of Appeal supplanted a prison sentence of two years (reduced by one day for time served), maintaining the subsequent three-year probationary term. In the sentencing decision, Judge Higinbotham writes that Smith attended a "very secure," prison-like residential treatment facility to assist with her substance abuse upon her release on bail,[78] and that in this "semi-custodial setting"[79] she made significant progress. Judge Higinbotham suggests that "in such circumstances," a community prison sentence might be appropriate if she could continue treatment there, but that "a conditional sentence order is not open to me as a result of amendments to the *Criminal Code* that preclude it where the index offence is a 'serious personal injury offence' as defined in s. 752,"[80] which encompasses Smith's offence of impaired driving causing death.

Regarding *Smith*, there is some dissension in the Court of Appeal judgment regarding the implications of the sentencing judge's attempt to contend with the conditional sentencing amendments. Writing the majority judgment for the Court of Appeal, Justice Bennett comments that Judge Higinbotham was merely trying to construct a sentence that would still promote Smith's rehabilitation, given the unavailability of a conditional sentence order, and "was not trying to perform an 'end-run' around Parliament's intentions,"[81] despite finding Judge Higinbotham's sentence order unfit. In a brief minority judgment for the Court of Appeal concurring in the result, Justice Edward C. Chiasson suggests that "often in these cases two lives are lost: the victim and the offender," writing, "I understand the judge's desire to attempt to save the respondent, but it was not open to him to do so by circumventing Parliament's express intention that such offenders be incarcerated."[82] In either event, however the sentencing judge's aims are framed, it appears that a conditional sentence order premised on Smith's remaining at the treatment facility would have been imposed if available, and either not appealed or upheld, given the attention to deterrence and denunciation such a sentence would have communicated. At sentencing, Judge Higinbotham writes explicitly, "A conditional sentence of maximum length would be most fit, but it is not open to me to pass that sentence. Neither would a suspended sentence be legal. The only option that is effectively open to me in order to meet the sentencing goal identified earlier is the shortest possible jail sentence with the longest possible probation period containing provision for continued treatment in the place she is now residing."[83] In the result, it seems a watered-down sentence was ordered by the sentencing judge, then replaced by a more punitive sentence on appeal, each as compared with what would likely have been a conditional sentence order before the amendments.

Some judges reject or are otherwise uncomfortable with the prospect of imposing a diluted sentence in place of an unavailable conditional sentence order. Amendments to this regime preclude a conditional sentence order for Roxanne Simms's offence of aggravated assault, but, in response to the submission by defence counsel "to consider a tightly crafted probation order via a suspended sentence to achieve the same result," Judge Luther comments, "I do not agree with that approach in this case."[84] The judge instead orders an intermittent prison sentence of sixty days (then reduced for pre-sentence custody) followed by one year of probation. In another case, defence counsel for M.A.B. is confronted with the removal of a conditional sentence order as an option for her offence of trafficking in cocaine, and submits to Judge Ayotte that the judge could instead impose a lengthy probationary term and include house arrest among the attached conditions. Judge Ayotte finds, "I do not feel that it is open to me to impose that sort of sentence,"[85] and explains:

> Even if one is dismayed, as many judges are, by the current legislative trend toward reducing the discretion of sentencing judges, Parliament is given the constitutional mandate to make criminal law. Judges must attempt to give effect to the will of Parliament as expressed in the *Criminal Code* and related legislation. That body, by the amendments it made in 2012, has clearly indicated its position that conditional sentences should not be imposed for offences

involving trafficking in cocaine and other 'hard' drugs . . . no matter how small the amount and no matter the personal circumstances of the accused. To do as defence counsel has invited me to do, sympathetic as I might be to his position, would be nothing more than a transparent and inappropriate attempt to flout the will of Parliament by attempting to do indirectly what I clearly cannot do directly.[86]

The judge instead orders a prison sentence of ninety days, served intermittently, and followed by two years of probation. By contrast, other judges do not characterize other sentencing options as "diluted," finding non-custodial options still available despite restrictions on the conditional sentencing regime. For example, in sentencing Michelle Arcand for possession of cocaine for the purposes of trafficking, Judge Daunt disagrees with the Crown contention that "because a conditional sentence is proscribed for this offence, Parliament must have intended that nothing short of incarceration could be a fit sentence."[87] Instead, the judge comments, "It does not appear that, in enacting section 742.1(c), Parliament turned its mind to any specific offence. Section 742.1(c) is drafted in general language. The purpose is to foreclose a conditional sentence order for the most serious offences, including manslaughter, aggravated assault, attempted murder, terrorism offences, and others. . . . I cannot find that Parliament intended that for any specific offence—such as breaking and entering a dwelling house—other penalties, such as fines, fines plus probation, or suspended sentences are similarly no longer available."[88] Judge Daunt imposes a ninety-day intermittent prison term, and two years of probation.

A fuller examination of the impacts of the 2007 and 2012 conditional sentencing amendments on judicial discretion exceeds the parameters of this book. Nonetheless, it remains important to highlight that within my research I found decisions in which the judges specifically flag that these sets of amendments have reduced their ability to construct just and appropriate sentences. Further, it is also critical to underscore that incursions into judicial discretion in this area impair the capacity of s. 718.2(e) to ameliorate Indigenous overincarceration and are thus hugely problematic for criminalized Indigenous persons and women in particular. In *Pijogge*, Justice Stack cites a Supreme Court of Canada decision from 2000 in which Justice Lamer writes, "In circumstances where either a sentence of incarceration or a conditional sentence would be appropriate, a conditional sentence should generally be imposed. This follows from s. 718.2(*e*) of the *Criminal Code*, which provides that all available sanctions other than imprisonment that are reasonable in the circumstances should be considered for all offenders. I would note, however, that there may be circumstances in which a short, sharp sentence of incarceration may be preferable to a lengthy conditional sentence."[89]

Given this directive, issued before the two waves of amendments to the conditional sentencing regime, clearly, further legislative restrictions on the availability of conditional sentences compromise the purpose and effectiveness of s. 718.2(e). (The latter qualification about certain circumstances benefiting from a brief prison term instead of a lengthy conditional sentence is consistent with the discussion in Chapter 3 about the punitiveness of conditional sentences, particularly regarding the risk of breaches.)

To illustrate the scope of the problem wherein judges have lesser manoeuvrability to effect s. 718.2(e), given amendments to the conditional sentencing regime, I have identified which offences in the judgments I reviewed for this book would no longer be eligible for conditional sentence orders after the passage of Bill C-10, now the 2012 conditional sentencing amendments. I first looked up the most serious offence in the Criminal Code (or the Controlled Drugs and Substances Act, for possession/trafficking offences), and evaluated it against the current (2012) version of s. 742.1. Many offences were eliminated exclusively after this step, based entirely on the law. In some cases, where the offence was hybrid and the judgment was issued by a provincial court equivalent (as opposed to a superior entry-level court), it required determining whether the Crown proceeded by indictment.

I want to highlight how the 2012 conditional sentencing amendments would have radically changed the sanctions ordered for those cases that actually resulted in a conditional sentence order. Of the 175 decisions I considered for this book (sentencing 177 Indigenous women, given two sets of Indigenous women co-accuseds), conditional sentence orders were either raised by defence counsel or considered to some degree (actively, or only peripherally) by judges in 104 of the total number of cases, and 44 of the Indigenous women sentenced were given conditional sentence orders. Those sentences were ordered between 1999 and 2015 (and spanned the years after the 2007 amendments). Following the 2012 s. 742.1 amendments, thirty-six of those forty-four conditional sentence orders would no longer be possible (two additional cases are inconclusive). That bears repeating: either immediately on the law, or because on the facts the Crown proceeded by indictment for a hybrid offence now excluded by s. 742.1, thirty-six of the forty-four Indigenous women who received conditional sentence orders would no longer be eligible for conditional sentences for the same offences/facts today. For two further cases,[90] I was unable to determine whether the women would remain eligible for a conditional sentence, because that hinges on whether the Crown proceeded by indictment or summarily, which seems unclear in the judgments. I found only six decisions of the forty-four that actually resulted in a conditional sentence order that would continue to be eligible for a conditional sentence order after the 2012 amendments. To be clear, that means that those thirty-six (possibly thirty-eight, depending on the two judgments I could not definitively settle) criminalized Indigenous women would likely have been sent to prison instead under the current 2012 law (although perhaps, in limited cases, a strict probationary term may have been ordered). This regressive turn in sentencing law is deeply troubling, and threatens to further exacerbate the ongoing problem of overrepresentation.

As I suggest in this book, maintaining the availability of conditional sentence orders is critical (alongside other alternatives) to serve the goal of s. 718.2(e) to reduce the overrepresentation of Indigenous peoples in prisons. The TRC includes in its recommendations that "we call upon the federal government to amend the *Criminal Code* to allow trial judges, upon giving reasons, to depart from mandatory minimum sentences and restrictions on the use of conditional sentences."[91] This call to action must be accompanied by greater provision and support for Indigenous community involvement in the sentencing process. Balfour suggests, from her study of the sentencing of Indigenous men and women for serious personal injury offences, that "little if any consultation is conducted with Aboriginal community agencies to develop effective and meaningful sentencing alternatives."[92] She relates this lack of inclusion to Indigenous communities' being under-resourced to propose alternatives and provide "supervision and treatment," given "community infrastructures ravaged by colonialism."[93]

In the brief the Assembly of First Nations provided to the Standing Committee on Justice and Human Rights during the Bill C-9 debates, the Teslin Tlingit Council explains that, in the Yukon, conditional sentences have been "proven to be an effective instrument utilized by the Territorial Courts working with First Nation community processes, such as the Teslin Tlingit Peacemaker Sentencing Panel."[94] It is noteworthy that the Teslin Tlingit Nation here supports conditional sentences as a sentencing option consistent with their own concept of justice, and that they are actively involved in the sentencing process through their own sentencing panel. The Teslin Tlingit Council continues, "Conditional sentences have contributed towards the promotion and exercise of community accountability and support of offenders to achieve the successful completion of their conditions, while also acknowledging and responding to the interest of those who have been victimized by a crime. The result is that families are kept together with a focus on balancing retribution and rehabilitation of the individual, which provides for the benefit of the overall community."[95]

This example is instructive, because it illustrates both the consonance of conditional sentences with some understandings of Indigenous justice, and, moreover, it demonstrates the need to consult and include Indigenous groups throughout criminal justice policy and legislative changes. This level of engagement necessarily involves the need to develop more complex and deeper relationships between the justice system and Indigenous women. Justices Hamilton and Sinclair, commissioners for the Aboriginal Justice Inquiry of Manitoba, emphasize that "we are convinced that Aboriginal women must be fully involved in the design and delivery" of alternatives to incarceration, within and beyond the justice system.[96] Given the power relationships underpinning prisons, Monture-Angus suggests this amplifies the government's fiduciary duty toward Indigenous peoples, and that this expanded fiduciary duty "provides a unique opportunity to challenge the colonial underpinnings of the relationship between the criminal justice system and First Peoples"[97] (she also notes this is "an imposed criminal justice system").[98] Debra Parkes and Kim Pate agree that the "undeveloped legal terrain" of the federal "government's fiduciary duties to criminalized Aboriginal women"[99] should be mapped out and navigated in this context. The issue of such fiduciary duties exceeds the scope of this book, but would be a valuable area for further research.

In *R. v. M.(C.A.)*, Justice Lamer comments regarding retribution and denunciation that "our criminal law is also a system of values. . . . In short, in addition to attaching negative consequences to undesirable behaviour, judicial sentences should also be imposed in a manner which positively instills the basic set of communal values shared by all Canadians as expressed by the *Criminal Code*."[100] Inside and outside the system, we must consider deeply and honestly what (and whose) system of values our current criminal justice law and institutions communicate to those vulnerable to and ensnared within this system. Given that the crisis of the overincarceration of Indigenous peoples (and particularly women) persists and intensifies, which communities and whose "communal values" are truly reflected within this system? How can we shift and reorient this value system, this criminal justice system, to actually function as a decolonizing force (to whatever limited extent that may be possible through the system)? Or rather, given that the criminal justice system (and particularly its prisons) *actively* functions as a *colonizing* force as a system of control over Indigenous peoples (and therefore inherently cannot be a decolonizing institution), how might we push the justice system to reflexively see itself and its harms more clearly, and then to see outside of itself, by minimizing its own interventions and harmful impacts, and diverting more criminalized Indigenous persons out of the system? Sheehy cautions that the ongoing role of criminal law in colonization must itself be "interrogate[d] . . . before we can confront the task of reforming criminal law so that it does not perpetuate Aboriginal exclusion."[101] To further widen the frame, as Davis suggests, instead of seeking "prisonlike substitutes for the prison," perhaps ultimately a system might be conceived "in which punishment itself is no longer the central concern in the making of justice."[102]

Listening, but Alongside Voice and Action in Communities

In *Elias*, Judge Stuart holds that "our inmate populations stand as stark reminders of our failed investments in punishment."[103] I would extend that sentiment specifically to the gross overrepresentation of Indigenous peoples in prison, which exponentially compounds this failure. In this book, against this backdrop of overrepresentation, I have focused on criminalized Indigenous women. Murdocca indicates that "very little has been written about the impact of the *Gladue* decision on Aboriginal women's experience of violence."[104] Balfour suggests that "the relationship between Aboriginal women's own use of violence and their victimization" is under-theorized,[105] finding it "difficult to surmise how often section 718.2(e) is applied on behalf of women with regards to the prevalence of gendered violence."[106] Similarly, CAEFS and NWAC find, "What is not known is the degree to which the *Criminal Code* and the *Gladue* decision are of assistance to women. This is an area where further research is recommended to determine if women receive access to the *Gladue* provisions and the degree to which the court's analysis of race that *Gladue* demands is coupled with a gendered analysis."[107] This book offers a contribution that strives to respond to this recommendation, as it explores where judicial discourses about the victimization of criminalized Indigenous women intersect with the *Gladue* analysis.

Gladue and *Ipeelee* hold that sentencing initiatives to respond to overrepresentation offer an important but limited role in the broader need to ameliorate the overincarceration of Indigenous peoples. Similarly, I believe that work analyzing sentencing discourses offers an important but limited role. Reading the judgments that form the backbone of this book brings into relief that real change must occur at the ground level, in communities. (Indeed, even the very concept of the "overrepresentation" of Indigenous women in prison almost implicitly suggests that a more "proportionate" number might be acceptable, yielding the impossible question: How many Indigenous women *should* be in prison?) The UN Committee emphasizes the need for thoroughgoing reforms, given that to address access to justice issues encountered by Indigenous women and discrimination against them within the justice system, "the magnitude of the required changes cannot be achieved by piecemeal reforms of existing programmes and services."[108] The safety of Indigenous women has not been governmentally prioritized. The UN Committee determines that the Canadian federal government "has failed" to address violence against Indigenous women "as a serious and large-scale problem requiring a comprehensive and coordinated response."[109] Additionally, the MMIWG Inquiry states that "efforts to address the root causes of disproportionate violence against Indigenous women and girls have been stunted for decades by budget cuts and funding caps."[110] It is troubling that the previous Conservative government under Prime Minister Steven Harper budgeted $2.1 billion for prison expansion[111] when this money could have been directed, as Shawn Bayes notes, "to health, education, housing, welfare, employment programs, addictions and sexual-abuse treatment,"[112] and other healing-oriented and community-building reforms. Although budgetary decisions change over time and across different governments, this type of allocation recalls a comment by a criminal lawyer to the TFFSW: "If you build more prisons, you will find more women to fill them."[113] As Carlen writes, most imprisoned women need help of various sorts, but *always of a kind that no prison can provide.*"[114] Ideally, this needed assistance would come in the form of better funded, resourced, and supported communities; Balfour observes, "The limits of law reforms are revealed here in the spaces of profound deprivation."[115] This has particular resonance for Indigenous women who want to stay in or be returned to their home communities, and feel unable to make that choice (or, in certain cases, are unable to present that option to the sentencing court and/or are precluded from that option). In the decision sentencing Tanya Peters (Pitwanakwat), whose mother is from the Munsee-Delaware Nation and father is from the Wikwemikong Reserve, Justice George notes that her cousin described for the *Gladue* report author "how alcohol, drugs, housing shortages and lack of employment opportunities are some of the community's most pressing concerns and as a result, most feel that they have no choice but to leave the reserve and re-locate to other towns, or cities" (Peters agreed and "indicated that she does not believe she can return as there are insufficient resources available").[116]

Before criminalization, research has shown that, as Pollack notes, women have "identified obstacles to receiving drug or alcohol treatment in the community, such as long waiting lists, programs that are not culturally relevant for Aboriginal people or responsive to women's needs, and expensive fees."[117] For community sentence orders and post-release after imprisonment but within the sentence remaining (such as during probation orders), criminalized women may also be prevented access to community treatment resources at the outset. The administration of these resources may restrict access based on what Shantz, Kilty, and Frigon have described as "exclusionary factors,"[118] which, ironically, can include factors such as criminalization and mental health issues. This latter barrier may contribute to problems discussed in this book, such as cases in which judges order incarceration because community resources are insufficient to meet treatment needs. Even access barriers that seem smaller may further alienate women who lack community resources. For example, in sentencing Jasmine Aisaican, who has roots in the Sakimay First Nation and is a member of the Cowessess First Nation, Judge Hinds notes that she was connected with "services which could help her connect to her culture" through a previous probationary order, and "she called them a few times, but did not receive a reply and gave up."[119]

Danielle Dirks suggests that "if we understand that women's criminality is inextricably linked to their victimization and traumatization, we also need to then examine the structural changes that must occur to disrupt the current cycles of victimization in the lives of girls and women."[120] These structural changes precede and extend far beyond sentencing, and beyond the criminal justice system entirely. As Pate stresses, "It seems ludicrous that we continue to pretend that telling women and girls not to take drugs to dull the pain of abuse, hunger or other devastation, or tell them that they must stop the behaviour that allowed them to survive poverty, abuse, disabilities, et cetera, [will be effective] in the face of no current or prospect of any income, housing, medical, educational or other supports."[121] In this light, Indigenous women may be criminalized for coping mechanisms developed in reaction to victimization and related disadvantages stemming from colonization. Instead, the focus should be on expanding the availability of and access to community resources.

Alongside these reforms at the community level, it remains helpful to analyze how sentencing judges respond to issues presented by criminalized Indigenous women. As part of this practice, I suggest that it is important to critically listen to and reflect on what the criminal justice system "hears," through how this is recorded in sentencing judgments. "Listening" to institutional accounts of women's lives may assist judges in the challenging task of finding just and appropriate sanctions for criminalized Indigenous women. Perhaps the greater direction and clarity offered by *Ipeelee* will have further meaningful effects on how sentencing judges hear and respond to the narratives of criminalized Indigenous women, particularly if its support for innovative sentencing is expanded. In this book, my goal has been to amplify the judgments that "hear" and respond in a way consistent with the *Gladue* analysis and through the lens of the victimization-criminalization continuum, and to offer some thoughts about others that could "hear" and respond more effectively. The ultimate goal (among other related goals, including and particularly those defined and implemented by Indigenous peoples and their communities, with greater internal control and self-determination) should be that Indigenous women and their communities become better resourced, and that Indigenous women have the security and support they need to thrive in all areas of their lives.

In late May of 2015, I travelled with regional representatives of CAEFS to the Okimaw Ohci Healing Lodge in Maple Creek, Saskatchewan, to visit with the Indigenous women prisoners there while then Executive Director Kim Pate led their Human Rights in Action workshop with the women. On our first evening there, the women drummed and sang for us. I found it almost overwhelming, just listening to the power of their voices, and watching the fire between where I sat and where the women filled the air. Amid the drumming, the volume of their collective voices seemed to represent both how many Indigenous women are in prison (in terms of their overrepresentation) and their profound strength and resilience through it all. These are the voices that all agents of the criminal justice system, and those positioned outside who seek to dismantle/reconstruct it, must hear, and must engage in active efforts to amplify. Moreover, these voices have the capacity to be loudest when unconfined—when Indigenous women remain safely in, and are returned to, their communities.

ACKNOWLEDGEMENTS

After extensive expansion and rewriting, this book emerged from my LL.M. thesis, which was completed at the Peter A. Allard School of Law at the University of British Columbia. My work has been financially supported variously through a Four-Year Fellowship from the University of British Columbia, a SSHRC Doctoral Fellowship, and a SSHRC Impact Grant held by Dr. Emma Cunliffe.

I am profoundly grateful to and for my supervisor, Dr. Emma Cunliffe. Beyond her brilliance and invaluable feedback, she is always in my corner, and with gentleness. I could not have taken the space to write this book without knowing that. I extend heartfelt appreciation to Michael Jackson, the second reader for my LL.M. and now a part of my doctoral committee, who also first provided the opportunity and inspiration for my incorporating art into law, and my first linocut. Thanks to Kim Pate, now on my doctoral committee too, whose lifetime of work with women in the system has been a beacon, and whose support for my LL.M. thesis and then this book has been sustaining on a number of levels.

This book would not have happened without Debra Parkes having believed in it from the beginning and first connecting me to the University of Manitoba Press through Karen Busby, whose patience and help was also instrumental in getting this off the ground. I hold deep gratitude for all at and associated with the University of Manitoba Press, particularly for their thoroughgoing investment in ensuring the integrity of this work and consistent guidance through the editorial and production processes with true respect and care, especially Glenn Bergen, Jill McConkey, David Larsen, Pat Sanders, and Jess Koroscil. I also acknowledge the anonymous peer reviewers, whose reports were thoughtful, insightful, and meaningfully assisted my revisions.

Finally and always, loving thanks to my parents, Archie Kaiser and Anne Derrick, and two sisters, Catriona and Freya, who kept consistent faith that I could write a book even when I faltered.

NOTES

INTRODUCTION: LISTENING TO WHAT THE CRIMINAL JUSTICE SYSTEM HEARS

1   The coordinator described the centre's harm-reduction philosophy in these terms to me when I first attended Kindred House, although this direct quote is from her submission to a parliamentary body: Ottawa, House of Commons, *Subcommittee on Solicitation Laws*, 31.

2   Initially, I had used the word "Aboriginal," largely to retain consistency with its usage in many cases, and also because it comports with the legal term. However, I have since changed it to "Indigenous," largely for this same reasoning. I felt disquieted, given that I had elected to primarily use "Aboriginal" to correspond with its usage in s. 718.2(e) and the cases, but the law itself may signify an oppressive, alienating, untrustworthy force within an imposed/illegitimate legal system for Indigenous peoples generally, particularly those criminalized, and specifically Indigenous women. "Indigenous" connects to global Indigenous communities, and "includes First Nations, Inuit, and Métis peoples" (Vowel, *Indigenous Writes,* 10). The term "Aboriginal 'has been broadly criticized both in Canada and internationally as yet another colonial construct that promotes divisiveness and 'Pan-Indianism'" without respecting individual nations, diversity among them, and their autonomy in naming themselves (Native Women's Association of Canada [NWAC], "Culturally Relevant Gender Based Models," 3). The term "Aboriginal" has been problematized for "originat[ing] from 'outside-naming'" because it is a settler term for Indigenous peoples (Martel and Brassard, "Painting the Prison," 358). Writers have responded to this issue in various ways, including by referring to each nation by its Indigenous name to avoid essentializing. In the spirit of the latter approach, when discussing the cases, I endeavour to identify the nation to which each woman being sentenced is connected (where judges specify the nation). "Aboriginal cultures in Canada are extremely diverse and complex in their values, beliefs, customs and traditions" (Andersen, "Governing Aboriginal Justice," 308). I am non-Indigenous; for thoughtful comments about non-Indigenous scholars writing about Indigenous issues, but striving to do so with sensitivity and a view to assist decolonizing efforts, see Martel and Brassard, "Painting the Prison," 341–42.

3   Ottawa, House of Commons, *Subcommittee on Solicitation Laws*, 33.

4   For the Crossroads outreaches, part of my role was to record information about the women who approached; the vast majority of the approximately thirty women using the van resources each night self-identified as Indigenous, which the staff member drivers affirmed was representative of a typical night's demographics.

5   Royal Commission on Aboriginal Peoples [RCAP], Bridging the Cultural Divide, 46.

6   Ibid., 47.

7   Ottawa, House of Commons, Subcommittee on Solicitation Laws, 31.

8   Ibid., 32.

9   Canada, Department of Justice, What We Heard, 9.

10 Ibid.

11 Ibid., 11.

12 Razack, Looking White People, 37.

13 Ibid., 40.

14 Criminal Code, s. 718.2(e).

15 Balfour, "Falling Between the Cracks," 102.

16 Ibid., 103.

17 Ibid., 116.

18 Balfour, "Do Law Reforms Matter?" 90.

19 Statistics Canada, Hotton Mahony, Jacob, and Hobson, Women and the Criminal Justice System, 39.

20 Murdocca, To Right Historical Wrongs: Race, Gender, and Sentencing in Canada, 62.

21 Statistics Canada, Women in Canada, 3.

22 Office of the Correctional Investigator, Annual Report of the Office of the Correctional Investigator 2016–2017, 59.

23 Ibid., 48.

24 Juristat, Adult Correctional Statistics in Canada, 5.

25 Statistics Canada, Aboriginal Statistics, 31.

26 Ibid.

27 Ibid.

28 Statistics Canada, Dauvergne, Adult Correctional Statistics in Canada, 2010/2011.

29 Juristat, Perreault, Criminal Victimization, 2014, 16.

30 Ibid., 17.

31 United Nations Committee on the Elimination of Discrimination against Women, Report, 53.

32 Juristat, Boyce, Victimization of Aboriginal People, 13.

33 Juristat, Brennan, Violent Victimization of Aboriginal Women, 7.

34 Ibid., 11.

35 Data from the Northwest Territories, Yukon, and Nunavut are excluded from these figures. For information and statistics about victimization

in the territories, see Juristat, Perreault, and Hotton Mahony, *Criminal Victimization in the Territories*. For information and statistics about victimization and offending in the territories, for Indigenous peoples, see Statistics Canada, Canadian Centre for Justice Statistics, de Léséleuc and Brzozowski, *Victimization and Offending*, 12.

36   Monture-Angus, *Thunder in My Soul*, 171.

37   Juristat, Perreault, *Criminal Victimization, 2014*, 17.

38   Ibid., 27.

39   Green, "Balancing Strategies," 143.

40   Tuhiwai Smith, *Decolonizing Methodologies*, 21.

41   Ibid., 28.

42   Ibid.

43   Ibid., 97.

44   Ibid.

45   Ibid., 69.

46   Bracken, Deane, and Morrissette, "Desistance and Social Marginalization," 66.

47   Tuhiwai Smith, *Decolonizing Methodologies*, 69.

48   RCAP, *Report, Looking Forward*.

49   Tuhiwai Smith, *Decolonizing Methodologies*, 69.

50   Ibid., 148.

51   O'Neil, "Editorial," 4.

52   See generally RCAP, *Report, Looking Forward*.

53   For a thorough and troubling article about the poverty and lack of infrastructure and resources on Indigenous reserves, see Stastna, "Shacks and Slop Pails."

54   For a complex exploration of living in Canadian cities by Indigenous peoples themselves (including challenges they experience, and how they challenge stereotypes), see CBC Doc Zone, "Indigenous in the City." For essays on Indigenous peoples reclaiming spaces, cultures, and collective identities in Canadian cities, see also Howard and Proulx, *Aboriginal Peoples in Canadian Cities*.

55   Green, "Balancing Strategies," 144.

56   Juristat, Brzozowski, Taylor-Butts, and Johnson, *Victimization and Offending*, 20n5.

57   Martel and Brassard, "Painting the Prison," 341.

58   Balfour, "Re-Imagining a Feminist Criminology," 742.

59   Tyagi, "Victimization, Adversity," 134.

60   Adjin-Tettey, "Sentencing Aboriginal Offenders," 192.

61   Kirmayer, Brass, and Tait, "Mental Health of Aboriginal Peoples," 609.

62   Tuhiwai Smith, *Decolonizing Methodologies*, 5.

63   "Not all trial and sentencing decisions are reported. For example, a judge will write a decision if he or she believes that the case is significant or will

contribute in an important way to case law." Balfour, "Falling Between the Cracks," 111.

64 Welsh and Ogloff, "Progressive Reforms," 511.

65 Scott, "Reforming Saskatchewan's Biased Sentencing," 9.

66 For the parliamentary stages of Bill C-9, see Canada, Bill C-9.

67 For the stages of Bill C-10, see Canada, Bill C-10.

68 Commission of Inquiry into Certain Events, Arbour, *Report*, 220.

69 United Nations Committee on the Elimination of Discrimination against Women, *Report*, 40.

70 See Dell and Boe, "Research Reports," 10. See also Juristat, Brzozowski, Taylor-Butts, and Johnson, *Victimization and Offending*, 13.

71 See more generally Brave Heart, "The Historical Trauma Response."

72 Poole, "Integrating Trauma," 42.

73 Monture-Angus, *Thunder in My Soul*, 171.

74 Ibid.

75 Ibid.

76 Ibid.

77 Ibid., 172.

78 Ross quoted in Linklater, *Decolonizing Trauma Work*, 26.

79 Brave Heart and DeBruyn, "The American Indian Holocaust," 60–61.

80 Gone, "Reconsidering American Indian Historical Trauma," 403.

81 Denham, "Rethinking Historical Trauma," 398.

82 Gone, "Reconsidering American Indian Historical Trauma," 390.

83 Manson et al., *Sentencing and Penal Policy*, 481.

84 *R. v. Gladue*, para. 39.

85 Code, s. 718.2(d).

86 Ibid., s. 718.2(e).

87 Bill C-32. An Act to Enact the Canadian Victims Bill of Rights and to amend certain Acts (Victims Bill of Rights Act).

88 Two of the cases in my research involved offences committed after the amended version of s. 718.2(e) entered into force, although neither case cites or explicitly deals with the amended text of s. 718.2(e). See *R. v. Nayneecassum*, 2015 SKPC 172, and *R. v. Saskatchewan*, 2015 ABPC 252, para 11.

89 Code, s. 718.

90 Ibid., ss. 718(a)–(f).

91 *R. v. Proulx*, para. 102.

92 Ibid., para. 107.

93 *R. v Gladue*, para. 43.

94 Ibid.

95 Ibid., para. 42.

96 Zehr, *Little Book of Restorative Justice*, 59.

97   Doob and Webster, "Countering Punitiveness," 338.

98   For example, the Saskatchewan Court of Appeal has been found to prioritize retribution over restorative justice and public safety over proportionality, at the expense of seeking to ameliorate Indigenous overrepresentation. See, e.g., Scott, "Reforming Saskatchewan's Biased Sentencing," 10.

99   *R. v. M(CA)*, para. 92.

100   See, for example, *R. v. Gladue*, para. 43, where a substantial component of restorative justice is described as the attempt "to rehabilitate or heal the offender."

101   Canada, Department of Justice, *What We Heard*, 12.

102   Ibid., 14.

103   Code, s. 718.1.

104   *R. v. Ipeelee*, para. 37. See also *R. v. Arcand*, 2010, paras. 47–49.

105   *R. v. Nasogaluak*, para. 41.

106   *R. v. Arcand*, 2010, para. 53.

107   Ibid., para. 54.

108   Ibid., para. 56.

109   Ibid., para. 61.

110   Code, s. 718.2(b).

111   *R. v. Arcand*, 2010, para. 62.

112   Code, ss. 718.2(d), (e).

113   *R. v. Arcand*, 2010, para. 62.

114   Ibid., para. 63.

115   Code, s. 718.3.

116   *R. v. Arcand*, 2010, para. 56.

117   Ibid., para. 64.

118   Ibid.

119   Ibid., para. 65.

120   Code, s. 718.2(a).

121   Manson et al., *Sentencing and Penal Policy*, 117. Allan Manson identifies various factors that frequently operate to mitigate, including being a first-time offender, pleading guilty and demonstrating remorse, and engaging in rehabilitative efforts after the offence. See also pp. 120–30.

122   *R. v. Wells*, para. 38.

123   See *R. v. Ipeelee*, para. 73.

124   *R. v. Gladue*, para. 115.

125   Milward and Parkes, "Colonialism, Systemic Discrimination," 129.

126   Ruby, Chan, and Hasan, *Sentencing*, 28.

127   Code, s. 718.2(a)(ii); emphasis added. The government has just proposed Bill C-75, which if passed into law would amend this section by supplanting "intimate partner" for "spouse or common-law partner." See Canada Bill

C-75, An Act to amend the Criminal Code, the Youth Criminal Justice Act and other Acts.

128 Ruby, Chan, and Hasan, *Sentencing*, 26.

129 *R. v. McIntyre*, para. 7.

130 Women's violence often transpires within the domestic context; see Pollock and Davis, "Continuing Myth," 22. Additionally, Indigenous women are at a higher risk of violent victimization than non-Indigenous women, including the most severe forms of intimate violence. See Juristat, Brzozowski, Taylor-Butts, and Johnson, *Victimization and Offending*, 5–6.

131 Offending within a spousal relationship is found to be aggravating in the following judgments from my research: *R. v. Gilpin*, para. 11; *R. v. Fisher*, para. 18; *R. v. Asp (R. v. CMA)*, para. 45; *R. v. Kahypeasewat (R. v. VK)*, para. 72; *R. v. Heavenfire*, para. 19; *R. v. Diamond*, para. 10; *R. v. SCM*, para. 12; *R. v. Neshinapaise*, para. 18; *R. v. Petawabano*, para. 31; *R. v. Small Eyes and Hunt*, para. 25; *R. v. Tippeneskum*, para. 21; *R. v. Florence*, 2013, paras. 31, 101; and *R. v. McIntyre*, para. 7.

132 *R. v. Ussak*.

133 See generally Juristat, Brennan, *Violent Victimization of Aboriginal Women*, 7.

134 *R. v. Gladue*, para. 64.

135 Ibid., para. 48.

136 Ibid., para. 70.

137 Tuhiwai Smith, *Decolonizing Methodologies*, 155.

138 Whether the period after the 1996 sentencing amendments constituted a wholesale "paradigm shift from punitive to restorative justice" has been disputed, although the 1996 amendments certainly substantially amplify the role of restorative justice in sentencing. Roach, "Changing Punishment," 251–52.

139 *R. v. Gladue*, para. 71. This process, of attempting to repair the harmony that crime ruptures, engages consideration of the factors contributing to the offence and the harms experienced by the victim(s), requiring the offender to demonstrate a sense of responsibility (Zehr, *Little Book*, 59) and to make reparations to the victim(s) and the community (*R. v. Proulx*), para. 18.

140 Linklater, *Decolonizing Trauma Work*, 135.

141 *R. v. Gladue*, para. 43.

142 Ibid., para. 74.

143 Murdocca, *To Right Historical Wrongs*, 65.

144 See, e.g., Cameron, "Stopping the Violence." See also Cunliffe and Cameron, "Writing the Circle."

145 *R. v. Gladue*, para. 33.

146 Ibid.

147 Ibid., para. 37.

148 Ibid., para. 68.

149 Ibid., para. 84.

150 See, e.g., Juristat, Perreault, *Incarceration of Aboriginal People*, 15–16.

151 As a microcosm of the overrepresentation of Indigenous peoples in the system, Indigenous peoples are disproportionately designated within the maximum-security classification level. Monture-Angus, "Women and Risk," 26.

152 For a thorough discussion of how assessed needs are transmuted into indicators of risk, see generally Maurutto and Hannah-Moffat, "Assembling Risk."

153 *R. v. Gladue*, para. 92.

154 Ibid., para. 66.

155 Ibid., para. 69.

156 Ibid., para. 73.

157 Ibid., para. 74.

158 Ibid., paras. 78–79.

159 Ibid., para. 81.

160 Ibid., para. 80.

161 Ibid., paras. 83–84.

162 Ibid., para. 87.

163 *R. v. Ipeelee*, para. 62.

164 Ibid.

165 Ibid., para. 60.

166 Ibid., para. 80.

167 Ibid., para. 81.

168 Ibid., para. 82.

169 *R. v. Gladue*, para. 69.

170 *R. v. Ipeelee*, para. 83.

171 Ibid.

172 Ibid., para. 84.

173 Ibid.

174 Ibid., para. 86.

175 Ibid., para. 85.

176 Ibid.

177 Ibid., para. 87.

178 Ibid., para. 95.

179 Ibid., para. 73; emphasis added.

180 For a discussion of how judicial overreliance on deterrence in Saskatchewan may be inappropriate to the sentencing of Indigenous persons who are generally "not rational actors" at the time of offence commission and instead "are the victims of the legacy of colonization," see Scott, "Reforming Saskatchewan's Biased Sentencing," 28, and, generally, 27–33.

181 *R. v. Ipeelee*, para. 73.

182 Ibid.

183 Ibid., para. 74.

184 Ibid., para. 75.

185 Ibid.

186 Ibid.

187 Ibid.

188 Scott, "Reforming Saskatchewan's Biased Sentencing," 10.

189 Ibid., 12.

190 Ralston and Goodwin, "*R v Drysdale*," 117.

191 Justice Derrick, Address.

192 *R. v. Gladue*, para. 65.

193 Ibid., para. 67.

194 Williams, "Punishing Women," 277n43.

195 *R. v. Ipeelee*, para. 77.

196 *R. v. Gladue*, para. 70.

197 Ibid., para. 40.

198 *R. v. Proulx*, para. 21.

199 Ibid., para. 46.

200 See ibid., paras. 21–22.

201 See, e.g., ibid., para. 23.

202 Ibid., para. 32.

203 Ibid., para. 25.

204 Juristat, Reitano, *Adult Correctional Statistics in Canada, 2015/2016,* 4.

205 *R. v. Proulx*, para. 36.

206 Ibid., para. 105.

207 Ibid., para. 41.

208 Ibid., para. 44. See also Roberts and Gabor, "Living in the Shadow," 108.

209 Roach, "Changing Punishment," 261.

210 Carlen, *Sledgehammer,* 5.

211 Adjin-Tettey, "Sentencing Aboriginal Offenders," 183.

212 Truth and Reconciliation Commission of Canada [TRC], *Honouring the Truth, Summary,* 174.

213 Juristat, Perreault, *Incarceration of Aboriginal People,* 9.

214 *R. v. Ipeelee*, para. 57.

215 Commission of Inquiry into Certain Events, Arbour, *Report,* 219.

216 Canadian Association of Elizabeth Fry Societies [CAEFS] and Native Women's Association of Canada [CWAC], "Women and the Canadian Legal System," 382, 385.

217 Juristat, Reitano, *Adult Correctional Statistics, 2015/2016,* 5.

218 Commission of Inquiry into Certain Events, Arbour, *Report,* 199.

219 Chewter, "Book Review of *In Conflict,*" 216.

220 See *R. v. Arcand*, 2010, para. 43.

221 Juristat, *Adult Correctional Services in Canada 2008/2009.*

222 For the text of the passed Bill C-9, see Canada, Bill C-9.

223 For the parliamentary stages of Bill C-9, see Canada, Bill C-9.

224 For the text of Bill C-10, see Canada, Bill C-10.

225 For the parliamentary stages of Bill C-10, see Canada, Bill C-10.

226 Code, s. 742.

227 Ibid., s. 752.

228 Ibid.

229 Commission of Inquiry into Certain Events, Arbour, *Report*, 221.

230 Faith and Near, *13 Women*, 294.

231 Office of the Correctional Investigator (OCI), *Annual Report 2016–2017*, 59.

232 OCI, *Annual Report 2015–2016*, 62.

233 OCI, *Annual Report 2014-2015*, 51.

234 Campbell, "Federally Sentenced Women," 5.

235 See, e.g., Balfour, "Falling Between the Cracks," 105.

236 Maynard, "Criminal (in)justice," 33.

237 This list consists of the following offences: prison breach, criminal harassment, sexual assault, kidnapping, human trafficking, abduction of those under fourteen, motor vehicle theft, theft over $5,000, breaking and entering a place other than a home, being unlawfully in a home, and arson for fraudulent purpose. See Canada, Bill C-10, Text.

238 Canada, Department of Justice, *What We Heard*, 11.

239 *R. v. Ipeelee*, paras. 84–86.

240 Canadian Bar Association, National Criminal Justice Section, "Bill C-9."

241 Ibid., 5.

242 Ibid., 1.

243 Ibid., 5.

244 Parliament of Canada, Law and Government Division, *Legislative Summary: Bill C-9*, 1, 17. I also note anecdotally that I read the entirety of the Bill C-9 debates, and although the passed version of Bill C-9 was different from the form in which it was proposed, it appears that the 2012 s. 742.1 amendments signify a complete reversion to the conditional sentencing regime that the Conservatives initially proposed (and which received much backlash by other parties) in Bill C-9. That is, it seems that the current s. 742.1 (as enacted in 2012) is essentially a reproduction of the vision of s. 742.1 that the Conservatives proposed in Bill C-9 and which was amended after much pushback.

245 See, for example, *R. v. Audy*, para. 5, in which Judge Slough states that "prior to the amendments to the Criminal Code, a Conditional Sentence Order would have been imposed."

246 See, for example, *R. v. Connors*, para. 18, in which Judge Ross seems inclined toward a conditional sentence order, given the "strong support" for the defence position advocating such, and the comments that "however, amendments to the Criminal Code effective December 1, 2007, appear

to preclude me from even considering the possibility of a conditional sentence of imprisonment." After concluding the amendments do indeed preclude a conditional sentence order, the judge imposes a two-year term of incarceration in a federal penitentiary for robbery.

247 *R. v. Arcand*, 2010, para. 84.

248 Ibid., para. 85.

249 Ibid., para. 85ncxxxi.

250 See, for example, *R. v. McDonald*, 2012, and R. v. Flett, 2012.

251 The judge does not specify the conditional sentencing regime engaged in *R. v. Morgan*, but this case involves the sentencing of a woman whose offence date was in 2006, preceding both sets of amendments to this regime.

252 See *R. v. Michelle*, 2008

253 See *R. v. Chartier*, 2015.

254 See *R. v. Arcand*, 2014.

255 Cover, "Violence and the Word," 1601.

256 Ibid., 1613.

257 Ibid., 1611.

258 Ibid., 1608.

259 Sugar and Fox, "Nistum Peyako Séht'wawin Iskwewak," 470.

260 Simon, "Vicissitudes of Law's Violence," 41.

261 Ibid., 38.

262 Ibid.

263 Constable, "Silence of the Law," 96.

264 Davis, *Abolition Democracy,* 42.

265 Ibid., 94.

266 Milward and Parkes, "Colonialism, Systemic Discrimination," 123.

267 Golder and Fitzpatrick, *Foucault's Law,* 71.

268 Ibid.

269 Ibid., 110.

270 Murdocca, *To Right Historical Wrongs*, 172.

271 Sugar and Fox, "Nistum Peyako Séht'wawin Iskwewak," 475.

CHAPTER 1: PATHWAYS THROUGH FEMINIST THEORIES, INTO THE SYSTEM

1 Public Inquiry into the Administration of Justice and Aboriginal People, *Report*, Volume I, Chapter 13, "The Sentencing of Aboriginal Women."

2 Ibid.

3 Ibid.

4 Pollock and Davis, "The Continuing Myth," 19.

5 Sugar and Fox, "Nistum Peyako Séht'wawin Iskwewak," 473.

6   In this book, I strive to refer to the Indigenous women being sentenced
     in terms that foreground their humanity and the systemic processes that
     produce their position in the criminal justice system, instead of using the
     word "offender." I want to acknowledge, and seek to align this book with,
     other feminist work that endeavours to use the term "criminalized" "to
     signal processes and practices rather than a reified identity" (Pollack, "I'm
     Just Not Good," 172), "to bring attention to the social, political, economic,
     cultural, and psychological processes that influence crime and criminality"
     instead of "individualiz[ing] and pathologiz[ing]" terms (Bernier,
     "Breaking Down the Walls," 14). Based on this reasoning, and bolstering
     my support for the "victimization-criminalization continuum" above other
     theories expressing similar ideas, I frequently use the term "criminalization"
     to describe the confluence of factors intersecting to bring Indigenous
     women in conflict with the law. While I try to avoid the term "offender"
     wherever possible, at times (and particularly where explaining elements
     of the law) I do use it for clarity, to most accurately denote the stage
     of proceedings.

7   Tyagi, "Victimization, Adversity," 134.

8   Muftic, Bouffard, and Bouffard, "Exploratory Study," 771–72.

9   Pollock and Davis, "Continuing Myth," 19.

10   Muftic, Bouffard, and Bouffard, "Exploratory Study," 757.

11   Raeder, "Domestic Violence," 92.

12   Comack, "Introduction," 64.

13   Ibid., 72.

14   Public Inquiry into the Administration of Justice and Aboriginal People,
     Report, Volume I, Chapter 13.

15   Raeder, "Domestic Violence," 91.

16   Ibid.

17   Ibid., 92.

18   Ibid.

19   Tuhiwai Smith, *Decolonizing Methodologies,* 153.

20   Chan and Chunn, *Racialization, Crime, and Criminal Justice in Canada*, 33.

21   Presser, "Narratives of Offenders," 191.

22   Belknap, "'Offending Women,'" 1080.

23   Chesney-Lind, "Patriarchy, Crime, and Justice," 8.

24   Pollock and Davis, "Continuing Myth," 19.

25   Burgess-Proctor, "Intersections of Race," 44n2.

26   Britton, "Feminism in Criminology," 72.

27   Ibid.

28   Comack, "New Possibilities," 165.

29   Chan and Chunn, *Racialization, Crime, and Criminal Justice in Canada*, 34.

30   Balfour, "Re-Imagining a Feminist Criminology," 742.

31   Ibid.

32   Balfour, "Falling Between the Cracks," 110.

33   See, generally, Balfour, "Re-Imagining a Feminist Criminology."

34   Ibid., 743.

35   Ibid.

36   Hannah-Moffat, "Re-Forming the Prison," 39n4.

37   Balfour, "Re-Imagining a Feminist Criminology," 743.

38   Tyagi, "Victimization, Adversity," 134.

39   Comack, "New Possibilities," 164.

40   Ibid., 165.

41   Ibid., 166–67.

42   LaRocque, "Métis and Feminist," 61.

43   Ibid.

44   Ibid.

45   Britton, "Feminism in Criminology," 62.

46   DeHart, "Pathways to Prison," 1378.

47   Ibid., 1376.

48   Tyagi, "Victimization, Adversity,"134.

49   Ferraro and Moe, "Mothering, Crime, and Incarceration," 23.

50   Ibid., 25.

51   Ibid., 30.

52   Ibid., 36.

53   See, e.g., Jackson, *Justice Behind the Walls*, 18.

54   OCI, *Annual Report, 2013–2014*, 46.

55   I had difficulty finding information about provincially sentenced
      women in my own research. Jennifer Bernier, too, notes that compared
      with the federal level, there is a dearth of information about provincial
      correctional systems and the women within them. See Bernier, "Breaking
      Down the Walls."

56   See, e.g., Jennifer Bernier's study of thirty-two women who were in
      provincial correctional institutions or who had previously spent time in
      provincial custody across Atlantic Canada. Ibid.

57   Ferraro and Moe, "Mothering, Crime, and Incarceration," 36.

58   Ibid., 26.

59   Ibid., 27, 33.

60   Ibid., 30.

61   Faith, *Unruly Women*, 108.

62   Ibid.

63   Ibid.

64   Conaghan, "Intersectionality and the Feminist Project," 21.

65   Ibid.

66   Ibid., 36.

67   Public Inquiry into the Administration of Justice and Aboriginal People,
      Report, Volume I, Chapter 13.

68 Cited in St. Denis, "Feminism Is for Everybody," 40.

69 Kuokkanen, "Myths and Realities," 81.

70 United Nations Committee on the Elimination of Discrimination against Women, *Report*, 50.

71 Faith, *Unruly Women,* 108.

72 Ibid., 109.

73 Dirks, "Sexual Revictimization," 108.

74 Kim Pate in CAEFS, *CAEFS' Oral Submission to the Canadian Human Rights Commission 2003 [Part 1]*, 16:50.

75 *R. v. Ipeelee*, para. 73.

76 DeHart, "Pathways to Prison," 1362.

77 Ibid., 1365.

78 Ibid., 1363.

79 Ibid.

80 Ibid.

81 Ibid., 1370.

82 Ibid., 1371.

83 Ibid., 1366.

84 Ibid., 1371.

85 Ibid., 1368.

86 Ibid., 1371.

87 Native Women's Association of Canada [NWAC], "What Their Stories Tell Us," 13.

88 Tyagi, "Victimization, Adversity," 134.

89 Statistics Canada, Gannon et al., *Criminal Justice Indicators: 2005*, 171.

90 Ibid.

91 NWAC, "What Their Stories Tell Us," 12.

92 Peternelj-Taylor, "Conceptualizing Nursing Research," 350.

93 DeHart, "Pathways to Prison," 1374; emphasis added.

94 Ibid.

95 See, e.g., Juristat, Brennan, *Violent Victimization of Aboriginal Women*.

96 DeHart, "Pathways to Prison," 1374.

97 Ibid., 1375.

98 Ibid.

99 Brave Heart, "The Historical Trauma Response," 7.

100 DeHart, "Pathways to Prison," 1378.

101 Ibid., 1377.

102 Tusher and Cook, "Comparing Revictimization," 1906.

103 Ibid., 1907.

104 DeHart, "Pathways to Prison," 1378.

105 Statistics Canada, Hotton Mahony, Jacob, and Hobson, *Women and the Criminal Justice System*, 7.

106 Ibid., 16.

107 Juristat, Boyce, *Victimization of Aboriginal People*, 13.

108 DeHart, "Pathways to Prison," 1374.

109 Ibid., 1375.

110 Brave Heart, "The Historical Trauma Response," 7.

111 Some other Saskatchewan Indigenous women attending this conference expressed reservations about Blaney's statement. See Provincial Association of Transitional Houses and Services of Saskatchewan [PATHS], *Restorative Justice*, 27.

112 Green, "Taking Account," 22.

113 Ibid.

114 Ibid., 22–23.

115 Brownridge, "Understanding the Elevated Risk," 366.

116 See, especially, Smith, "Native American Feminism"; 116, and 126-27.

117 Juristat, Brennan, *Violent Victimization of Aboriginal Women*, 9.

118 Pate, "Advocacy, Activism," 82.

119 United Nations Committee on the Elimination of Discrimination against Women, *Report*, 41.

120 Ibid., 52.

121 Ibid., 3.

122 Ibid., 53.

123 Ibid., 44.

124 Government of Canada, News Release, "Government of Canada Launches Inquiry." Also, in the way I have presented the background of the UN Committee and the Canadian government decision to hold a national inquiry, I do not intend to suggest a direct causal relationship between these two processes, in the sense that I cannot determine the degree to which the UN Committee report and recommendation prompted the government to take this initiative, given other pressures and needs that simultaneously existed.

125 Macdonald and Campbell, "Lost and Broken."

126 Canada, The National Inquiry into Missing and Murdered Indigenous Women and Girls, *Interim Report*, 73.

127 Ibid., 57.

128 Ibid., 3.

129 Ibid., 19.

130 Royal Canadian Mounted Police [RCMP], *Missing and Murdered*, 7.

131 Ibid., 8.

132 RCMP, *Missing and Murdered: 2015 Update*, 12.

133 Blaze Baum and Grant, "Missing and Murdered."

134 Tasker, "Confusion Reigns."

135 Blaze Baum and Grant, "Missing and Murdered."

136 Canada, Special Committee on Violence Against Indigenous Women, *Invisible Women*, 35.

137 Canada, The National Inquiry into Missing and Murdered Indigenous Women and Girls, *Interim Report*, 3.

138 Ibid., 7.

139 RCMP, *Missing and Murdered*, 13.

140 RCMP, *Missing and Murdered: 2015 Update*, 3.

141 NWAC, "What Their Stories Tell Us," 31.

142 RCMP, *Missing and Murdered*, 17.

143 NWAC, "What Their Stories Tell Us," 31.

144 Campbell, Boyd, and Culbert, *A Thousand Dreams*, 142.

145 DeHart, "Pathways to Prison," 1370.

146 NWAC, "What Their Stories Tell Us," 33.

147 Ibid., 24.

148 Truth and Reconciliation Commission of Canada [TRC], *Honouring the Truth, Summary*, 180.

149 Conaghan, "Intersectionality," 29.

150 Ibid., 41.

151 Razack, *Looking White People*, 159.

152 Smith and Ross, "Introduction," 1.

153 Balfour, "Do Law Reforms Matter?" 98.

154 Balfour, "Falling Between the Cracks," 115.

155 Ibid., 102.

156 Ibid., 103. For a study of how mandatory charging policies for domestic violence police calls in the United States have had similar deleterious impacts on women, see, e.g., Muftic, Bouffard, and Bouffard, "An Exploratory Study."

157 Balfour, "Falling Between the Cracks," 103.

158 Ibid., 104.

159 Ibid., 115.

160 Ibid., 104.

161 Ibid., 105.

162 Ibid., 102.

163 Ibid., 116.

164 Ibid., 114.

165 Ibid., 113.

166 Ibid.

167 Balfour, "Do Law Reforms Matter?" 90.

168 Ibid., 114.

169 Ibid., 115.

170 Brownridge, "Understanding the Elevated Risk," 355.

171 TRC, *Honouring the Truth, Summary*, 1.

172 Juristat, Brzozowski, Taylor-Butts, and Johnson, *Victimization and Offending*, 20n5.

173 Brownridge, "Understanding the Elevated Risk," 365.

174 *R. v. Gladue*, para. 84.

175 Ibid., para. 91.

176 Statistics Canada, *Aboriginal Peoples in Canada,* 3.

177 Blackstock et al., *Keeping the Promise*, 44.

178 Ibid., 49.

179 Howard and Proulx, "Transformations and Continuities," 4.

180 For a discussion of community-building through Indigenous friendship centres in cities, see Howard, "The Friendship Centre," 87.

181 Howard and Proulx, "Transformations and Continuities," 8.

182 Ibid., 15.

183 TRC, *Honouring the Truth, Summary*, 133.

184 Ibid., 1.

185 Ibid.

186 Ibid.

187 Ibid.

188 Ibid., 1–2.

189 Royal Commission on Aboriginal Peoples [RCAP], *Report, Looking Forward, Looking Back*.

190 Ibid.

191 Ibid.

192 TRC, *Honouring the Truth, Summary*, 3.

193 Ibid.

194 Blackstock et al., *Keeping the Promise,* 153.

195 TRC, *Honouring the Truth, Summary*, 3.

196 NWAC, "What Their Stories Tell Us," 7.

197 Flynn, "Plains Indian Ways," 228.

198 TRC, *Honouring the Truth, Summary*, 40–41.

199 Ibid., 3.

200 Ibid., 41.

201 Ibid., 43.

202 Ibid., 2.

203 Although these abuses resist categorization because they are interrelated, for a list of such abuses, see, for example, Chrisjohn, Young, and Maraun, *Circle Game,* 49–51.

204 TRC, *Honouring the Truth, Summary*, 43.

205 Blackstock et al., *Keeping the Promise,* 153.

206 Ibid., 154.

207 NWAC, "What Their Stories Tell Us," 7.

208 Smith, *Conquest*, 52.

209 Ibid., 51.

210 Ibid., 44.

211 Chrisjohn, Young, and Maraun, *Circle Game*, 63.

212 Ibid., 60–63.

213 Ibid., 61.

214 Ibid., 51.

215 TRC, *Honouring the Truth, Summary*, 54–55; emphasis added.

216 Ibid., 133.

217 Ibid., 3.

218 NWAC, "What Their Stories Tell Us," 8.

219 TRC, *Honouring the Truth, Summary*, 183.

220 Flynn, "Plains Indian Ways," 228.

221 Donovan, "Challenges and Successes," 126.

222 Howard and Proulx, "Transformations and Continuities," 6.

223 TRC, *Honouring the Truth, Summary*, 55.

224 Ibid., 229.

225 Ibid., 55.

226 Flynn, "Plains Indian Ways," 229.

227 Ignass, "'Why Is My People Sleeping?'" 204.

228 Darnell, "Nomadic Legacies," 41–42. See also the recent Supreme Court
    of Canada decision finding that Métis and non-status persons are "Indians"
    under s. 91(24) of the Constitution Act, 1867, *Daniels v. Canada*.

229 Green, "Taking Account of Aboriginal Feminism," 23.

230 Ibid., 22.

231 See, e.g., St. Denis, "Feminism Is for Everybody," 37–38. However, there
    is some debate about whether traditional Aboriginal societies actually
    represented gender equality. See, e.g., LaRocque, "Métis and Feminist," 55.

232 For example, David R. Newhouse writes, "My mother was born a status
    Indian, became a non-status Indian upon enfranchisement, and became a
    status Indian again upon marriage to my father, a status Indian." He also
    describes how he continues to be affected, because "as a result of the arcane
    membership rules of the Indian Act, I am considered to have 50% Indian
    blood, 50% non-Indian blood." See Newhouse, "Urban Life," 29.

233 Darnell, "Nomadic Legacies," 45.

234 Howard, "Friendship Centre," 102.

235 *Descheneaux c. Canada (Procureur Général)*.

236 Bill S-3. An Act to amend the Indian Act in response to the Superior Court
    of Quebec decision in *Descheneaux c. Canada (Procureur Général)*.

237 Galloway, "Senate Backs Down."

238 NWAC, "What Their Stories Tell Us," 8.

239 Ibid.

240 Ibid.

241 Ibid.

242 Canada, The National Inquiry into Missing and Murdered Indigenous Women and Girls, *Interim Report*, 48.

243 *First Nations Child and Family Caring Society of Canada et al v. Attorney General of Canada*, para 473.

244 NWAC, "What Their Stories Tell Us," 8.

245 TRC, *Honouring the Truth, Summary*, 139.

246 Blackstock et al., *Keeping the Promise*, 159.

247 Ibid., 155.

248 NWAC, "What Their Stories Tell Us," 10.

249 Ibid.

250 TRC, *Honouring the Truth, Summary*, 182.

251 Monture, "Confronting Power," 26; emphasis added.

252 Patricia A. Monture-Okanee, cited in Murdocca, *To Right Historical Wrongs*, 38.

253 See http://dictionary.reference.com/., s.v. "strategy."

254 TRC, *Honouring the Truth, Summary*, 3; emphasis added.

255 NWAC, "Arrest the Legacy," 4 (in Insert 1).

256 TRC, *Honouring the Truth, Summary*, 3.

257 NWAC, "Arrest the Legacy," 4 (in Insert 1).

258 Murdocca, *To Right Historical Wrongs*, 63.

259 Canada, Bill C-9, 19 September 2006, 1600.

260 Ibid., 1 November 2006, 1645; emphasis added.

261 Bill C-32. An Act to enact the Canadian Victims Bill of Rights and to amend certain Acts (Victims Bill of Rights Act).

262 Ibid, 9 April 2014, 1615.

263 Code, s. 718(f).

264 NWAC, "What Their Stories Tell Us," 9.

265 Duff and Garland, "Introduction," 4.

266 *R. v. Gladue*, para. 37.

267 Ibid., para. 64.

268 Monture, "Confronting Power," 28.

269 Crenshaw, "A Tale of Two Movements."

270 Davis, *Abolition Democracy*, 35.

271 Alexander, *New Jim Crow*, 2.

272 Ibid., 22.

273 Ibid., 219.

274 Cited in ibid., 22.

275 Ibid., 184.

276 Davis, *Are Prisons Obsolete?* 103.

277 Ibid., 26.

278 Ibid., 73.

279 Balfour, "Do Law Reforms Matter?" 86.

280 Flynn, "Plains Indian Ways," 229.

281 TRC, *Honouring the Truth, Summary*, 186.

282 Public Inquiry into the Administration of Justice and Aboriginal People, *Report*, Volume I, Chapter 14, "Aboriginal Peoples and the Child Welfare System in Manitoba."

283 United Nations Committee on the Elimination of Discrimination against Women, *Report*, 28.

284 Ibid.

285 Ibid., 137–38.

286 Ibid., 209.

287 Canada, The National Inquiry into Missing and Murdered Indigenous Women and Girls, *Interim Report*, 31.

288 Ibid., 45.

289 Sugar and Fox, "Nistum Peyako Séht'wawin Iskwewak," 476.

290 The Aboriginal Healing Foundation, *Reclaiming Connections*, 61–62.

291 Mirchandani and Chan, "From Race and Crime," 14–15.

292 Chrisjohn, Young, and Maraun, *Circle Game*, 30.

293 Alexander, *New Jim Crow*, 183.

294 Smith, *Conquest*, 154.

295 Murdocca, *To Right Historical Wrongs*, 53.

296 Blackstock et al., *Keeping the Promise*, 154.

297 NWAC, "What Their Stories Tell Us," 8. See also TRC, *Honouring the Truth, Summary*, 138.

298 The federal government has reached a preliminary settlement with survivors of the Sixties Scoop totalling $800 million. See Tasker, "Ottawa Announces $800M."

299 Representative for Children and Youth for BC, "Delegated Aboriginal Agencies; How Resourcing Affects Service Delivery," 11.

300 Cited in Marchetti, "Intersectional Race."

301 See the discussion in Marchetti, "Deep Colonizing Practices," 461–62.

302 Ibid., 462.

303 I have used the word "engagement" here (instead of "consultation") for resonance with its usage by the MMIWG Inquiry, which intends this model for its own mandate to refer to "an ongoing process in which communities actively participate in a meaningful way," where Indigenous communities are sought "to have input into the design and implementation of a process throughout." Canada, The National Inquiry into Missing and Murdered Indigenous Women and Girls, *Interim Report*, 73.

304 Murdocca, *To Right Historical Wrongs*, 63.

305 Monture, "Confronting Power," 27.

306 Tuhiwai Smith, *Decolonizing Methodologies*, 153.

307 TRC, *Honouring the Truth, Summary*, 171.

308 Monture, "Confronting Power," 27.

309 NWAC, "What Their Stories Tell Us," 11.

310 Ibid., 12.

311 Hunter, "Violence that Indigenous Women Face," 34.

312 Monture, "Confronting Power," 26. Monture credits the work by the Task Force on Federally Sentenced Women [TFFSW] for modelling an example of how research into social problems can centrally position colonialism; see 28. See also TFFSW, "Creating Choices."

313 See Williams, "Intersectionality Analysis," 79.

314 Ibid., 94.

315 Ibid.

316 Maurutto and Hannah-Moffat, "Assembling Risk," 438. Maurutto and Hannah-Moffat write that risk assessment based on standardized, ostensibly objective criteria, "actuarial risk," "has taken on a hegemonic dominance that supercedes other models of governance, such as welfare and disciplinary forms of regulation."

317 Williams, "Intersectionality Analysis," 80, 92.

318 In the sentencing process, public safety is always germane to the determination of the sanction, and is an inherent concern in the sentencing principle that offenders must be separated from society where necessary; see Code, s. 718(c). In the federal prison domain, public safety is an express consideration within penitentiary placement decisions; see Corrections and Conditional Release Act, s. 28(a)(i).

319 For the provision of the Criminal Code of Canada dealing with pre-sentence reports, see Code, s. 721.

320 Balfour, "Do Law Reforms Matter?" 96.

321 For the Policy Bulletins and scoring tables (called the Custody Rating Scale) used by the Correctional Service of Canada to establish where to place each prisoner (in terms of the security level attached to the institution itself) and the level of security each prisoner should be assigned within that institution (minimum, medium, or maximum, involving escalating degrees of isolation and punitiveness), see Commissioner of the Correctional Service of Canada, "Security Classification." For a critical analysis of the increased penal dependence on and fidelity to risk assessments, see, e.g., Maurutto and Hannah-Moffat, "Assembling Risk." For a study of how the standardization of risk assessments obscures gender difference and may be problematic for women prisoners, see Hannah-Moffat, "Gendering Risk." For a thoughtful argument that the correctional process of assessing risk becomes gendered because women prisoners present different life histories and experience imprisonment differently from men, see Hannah-Moffat, "Moral Agent."

322 For an example of factors considered by provincial correctional authorities to inform security classification, see Alberta correctional legislation that empowers the director of a given prison in that province to establish various

classification processes for prisoners at that institution (Corrections Act, s. 11), and the associated regulations requiring certain baseline considerations for classification and assessment processes (Correctional Institution Regulation, s. 9).

323 Monture-Angus, "Women and Risk," 26.

324 Ibid., 27.

325 Ibid.

326 Williams, "Intersectionality Analysis," 92.

327 Ibid.

328 Ibid., 92–93.

329 Ibid., 94.

330 Ibid., 95.

331 Ibid. See also Williams, "Punishing Women," 285.

332 Comack, "New Possibilities," 165.

333 TFFSW, "Creating Choices."

334 Dell, Fillmore, and Kilty, "Looking Back 10 Years," 296.

335 Balfour, "Falling Between the Cracks," 102.

336 TRC, *Honouring the Truth, Summary*, 207.

CHAPTER 2: SENTENCING TRAUMA: *GLADUE* AND THE CONTINUUM, JUDICIAL NAVIGATIONS

1 House of Commons, *Subcommittee on Solicitation Laws,* 31.

2 Ibid., 32.

3 Ibid., 31.

4 *R. v. Masakayash*, para. 24.

5 *R. v. McNabb*, para. 56.

6 Ibid., para. 59.

7 *R. v. Firth*, para. 15.

8 Ibid., para. 12.

9 *R. v. First Charger*, para. 26.

10 *R. v. Chartier*, para. 1.

11 Ibid., para. 63.

12 Ibid., para. 64.

13 *R. v. Morgan*, para. 34.

14 Ibid., para. 61.

15 *R. v. McKenzie-Sinclair*, para. 27.

16 *R. v. RK*, para. 87.

17 There is no information about that child's death, other than the comment it happened "tragically." Ibid., para. 87.

18   Ibid., para. 86.

19   Ibid., para. 123.

20   Ibid., para. 124.

21   Ibid., para. 86.

22   Ibid. para. 124.

23   DeHart, "Pathways to Prison," 1375.

24   Brave Heart, "The Historical Trauma," 7.

25   *R. v. Lilley*, para. 3.

26   *R. v. Batisse*, para. 25.

27   *R. v. Chouinard*, para. 11.

28   Ibid., paras. 11 and 22.

29   Ibid., para. 22.

30   *R. v. Pépabano*, para. 20.

31   *R. v. George*, para. 2.

32   Ibid., para. 10.

33   Ibid., para. 2.

34   Ibid., para. 3.

35   Ibid., para. 5.

36   Ibid., para. 6.

37   Ibid.

38   Ibid., para. 7.

39   Ibid., para. 8.

40   Ibid., para. 10.

41   *R. v. Shenfield*, para. 5.

42   Ibid., para. 6.

43   Ibid., para. 2.

44   Ibid.

45   Ibid.

46   Ibid., para. 23.

47   Ibid., para. 6.

48   *R. v. Woods*, para. 5.

49   Ibid., para. 7.

50   Ibid., para. 11.

51   Ibid., para. 13.

52   Ibid., para. 13.

53   See ibid, paras. 13–14, 16.

54   Ibid., para. 16.

55 Ibid., para. 44.

56 Ibid.

57 Ibid., para. 49.

58 *R. v. Ipeelee*, para. 59.

59 *R. v. Woods*, para. 49.

60 Ibid.

61 *R. v. Ipeelee*, para. 84.

62 *R. v. Woods*, para. 49.

63 *R. v. Dennill*, para. 8.

64 Ibid., para. 33.

65 Ibid., para. 10.

66 Ibid., para. 10.

67 Ibid.

68 Ibid.

69 Ibid., para. 9.

70 Ibid., para. 11.

71 Ibid., para. 10.

72 Ibid., para. 34; emphasis added.

73 Ibid., para. 9.

74 Ibid., para. 34.

75 Ibid.

76 Ibid.

77 Ibid., para. 10.

78 Ibid., para. 11.

79 Ibid., para. 34.

80 *R. v. Chouinard*, para. 5.

81 Ibid., para. 7.

82 Ibid.

83 Ibid., para. 8.

84 Ibid., para. 22. It should be noted that in 1997 Justice Ratushny released a report reviewing the convictions of various women convicted of homicide resulting in the death of abusive partners, with a view to assessing the issue of self-defence. For a discussion of this report, see Canadian Association of Elizabeth Fry Societies [CAEFS], "Justice for Battered Women."

85 *R. v. Chouinard*, para. 15.

86 Ibid., para. 22.

87 Ibid.

88 Ibid.

89 Ibid., para. 19.

90 As I address in the Introduction, I do not distinguish the pathways perspective from the victimization-criminalization continuum, given my expansive interpretation of "victimization."

91 Brown, "Gender, Ethnicity," 143.

92 *R. v. Chouinard*, para. 18.

93 Ibid., para. 19.

94 *Daniels v. Canada*.

95 *R. v. Kahypeasewat*, para. 3.

96 Ibid., para. 2.

97 Ibid., para. 3.

98 Ibid., para. 4.

99 Ibid., para. 27.

100 Ibid., para. 3.

101 Ibid., para. 5.

102 Ibid., para. 12.

103 Ibid., para. 3.

104 Ibid., para. 6.

105 Ibid., para. 3.

106 Ibid., para. 8.

107 Ibid., para. 17.

108 Ibid.

109 Ibid., para. 27.

110 Ibid.

111 Ibid.

112 Ibid.

113 Ibid.

114 Ibid.

115 Ibid.

116 Pollock and Davis, "Continuing Myth," 17.

117 *R. v. Kahypeasewat*, para. 72.

118 Ibid.

119 Ibid.

120 Ibid.

121 Ibid., para. 27.

122 Ibid., para. 59.

123 Ibid., para. 72; emphasis added.

124 Ibid., para. 84.

125 Ibid., para. 61.

126 Tuhiwai Smith, *Decolonizing Methodologies,* 146.

127 Ibid., para. 72.

128 Koons-Witt, "Effect of Gender," 304.

129 CAEFS and NWAC, "Women and the Canadian Legal System," 386–87.

130 Sheehy, *Defending Battered Women,* 192–98.

131 Sheehy, "Defending Battered Women on Trial."

132 Public Inquiry into the Administration of Justice and Aboriginal People, *Report,* Volume I, Chapter 13.

133 Murdocca, *To Right Historical Wrongs,* 110.

134 CAEFS and NWAC, "Women and the Canadian Legal System," 386–87.

135 Ibid.

136 *R. v. Kahypeasewat,* para. 72.

137 CAEFS and NWAC, "Women and the Canadian Legal System," 386–87.

138 *R. v. Machiskinic; R. v. Waskewitch; R. v. Jack, Joyce Smith, and Nenette Smith; R. v. Michelle (R. v. AEM); R. v. Whitford,* 2008; *R. v. Hanley;* and *R. v. Masakayash.*

139 *R. v. Hanley,* para. 2.

140 *R. v. Masakayash,* para. 2.

141 *R. v. Martin, Evans & Laviolette,* para. 6.

142 Ibid., para. 3.

143 *R. v. Simms,* para. 3.

144 Ibid.

145 Ibid., para. 2.

146 Ibid., para. 3.

147 Ibid., para. 3.

148 Razack, "Gendered Racial Violence," 155.

149 Razack, *Looking White People,* 69.

150 *R. v. Simms,* para. 7.

151 Ibid., para. 7.

152 Public Inquiry into the Administration of Justice and Aboriginal People, *Report,* Volume I, Chapter 13.

153 *R. v. Elliott,* para. 9.

154 Ibid., para. 34.

155 *R. v. McClements,* para. 14.

156 *R. v. Bouchard,* para. 4.

157 Ibid., para. 7.

158 Ibid., para. 20.

159 *R. v. McNabb*, para. 58.

160 *R. v. Arcand*, 2014, para. 11.

161 *R. v. Johnson*, 2013, para. 40.

162 *R. v. Bourke*, para. 3

163 *R. v. Hansen*, para. 38.

164 *R. v. Good*, 2010, para. 22.

165 *R. v. Tippeneskum*, para. 6.

166 Ibid., para. 19.

167 Ibid.

168 *R. v. Gregoire*, para. 38.

169 *R. v. Pawis*, para. 86.

170 Ibid., para. 87.

171 *R. v. Good*, 2010. Good appealed her sentence "on the basis that the sentencing judge failed to consider her Aboriginal status pursuant to s. 718.2(e)," and that "the sentence was excessive and unfit because the judge overemphasized deterrence and denunciation to the exclusion of the objectives of rehabilitation and restorative justice," seeking the substitution of a provincial term of imprisonment (*R. v. Good*, 2012, para. 1). Her appeal was dismissed. The Yukon Court of Appeal held "the sentencing judge made no error in principle, and that the sentence imposed was fit" (*R. v. Good*, 2012, para. 47).

172 *R. v. Good*, 2010, para. 21.

173 Ibid., para. 22.

174 Ibid., para. 10.

175 Ibid., para. 34.

176 Ibid., para. 23.

177 Ibid., para. 34.

178 Ibid., para. 16.

179 Ibid., para. 34.

180 Ibid., para. 16.

181 Ibid., para. 20.

182 Ibid.

183 Ibid., para. 22.

184 DeHart, "Pathways to Prison," 1375.

185 Ibid., 1378.

186 *R. v. Good,* 2010, para. 26.

187 Ibid.

188 Ibid.

189 Ibid., para. 28.

NOTES TO PAGES 116-120

190 *R. v. Ipeelee*, para. 84.

191 Ibid., para. 87.

192 Ibid., para. 60.

193 *R. v. Redhead*, para. 9.

194 *R. v. Tippeneskum*, para. 8.

195 Ibid., para. 5.

196 Rutherford, "Attawapiskat Declares State of Emergency."

197 *R. v. Tippeneskum*, para. 6.

198 Ibid.

199 Ibid.

200 Ibid., para. 7.

201 Ibid., para. 19.

202 Ibid., para. 6.

203 Ibid., para. 19.

204 Ibid.

205 Ibid., para. 8.

206 Ibid.

207 Ibid., para. 20.

208 Justice DiGiuseppe cites Tippeneskum's domestic relationship with the complainant as an aggravating factor, in keeping with s. 718.2(a)(ii) of the Criminal Code. However, I would distinguish this case on its facts from those in the Introduction, wherein I registered my discomfort about uncritical application and weighting of s. 718.2(a)(ii) instead of more contextualized reasoning and balancing (in cases involving the violence of Indigenous women against intimate partners after histories of themselves being subjected to abuse in relationships). I would argue that this case speaks directly to the violation of trust issue that seems to animate s. 718.2(a)(ii); as Justice DiGiuseppe notes, Tippeneskum "repeatedly deceived" her partner "over a lengthy period of time" (*R. v. Tippeneskum*, para. 21) by failing to inform him about her HIV positive status.

209 *R. v. Tippeneskum*, para. 18.

210 *R. v. Gregoire*, para. 35.

211 Ibid., para. 7.

212 Ibid., para. 34.

213 Ibid.

214 Ibid., para. 38.

215 Ibid.

216 Ibid.

217 Ibid., para. 54.

218 Ibid., para. 50.

219 Ibid.

220 Ibid., para. 51.

221 Ibid.

222 *R. v. Pawis*, para. 2.

223 Ibid., para. 21.

224 Ibid., para. 1.

225 Ibid., para. 36.

226 Ibid., para. 42.

227 Ibid., para. 45.

228 Ibid., para. 53.

229 Ibid.

230 Ibid., para. 52.

231 Ibid., para. 86.

232 Ibid., para. 87.

233 Ibid., para. 102.

234 Ibid., para. 103.

235 Ibid., para. 104.

236 Ibid., para. 98.

237 Code, s. 718.2(a)(ii.1).

238 Ibid., s. 718.2(a)(iii).

239 *R. v. Pawis*, para. 98.

240 Ibid., para. 99.

241 Ibid., para. 100.

242 Justice Reinhardt lists other mitigating factors: "her attempt to have the child removed from her care, her immediate confession, her guilty plea, her stringent reporting conditions, the lack of alcohol or intoxicants as a precipitating factor, her receptivity to counselling and remedial programs offered by the aboriginal community in Toronto." Ibid., para. 107.

243 Ibid., para. 101.

244 Ibid.

245 Ibid., para. 106.

246 *R. v. Killiktee*, 2011.

247 *R. v. Littlecrow*, para. 20.

248 *R. v. Toews*, para. 11.

249 Ibid., para. 49.

250 Ibid., para. 63.

251 Ibid., para. 27.

252 *R. v. Dennis*, para. 57.

253 Ibid., para. 61.

254 *R. v. Serré*, para. 17.

255 Ibid., para. 63.

256 Ibid., para. 15.

257 Ibid., para. 56.

258 *R. v. Ross*, para. 17.

259 Ibid.

260 *R. v. Hansen*, para. 38.

261 See *R. v. Ipeelee,* paras 80–83.

262 Scott, "Reforming Saskatchewan's Biased Sentencing," 12.

263 *R. v. McCook*, para. 162.

264 Ibid., para. 163.

265 Scott, "Reforming Saskatchewan's Biased Sentencing," 20.

266 *R. v. Ipeelee*, para. 83.

267 Ibid.

268 *R. v. Johnson*, 2011.

269 Quigley, "Gladue Reports," 2.

270 Code, s. 721.

271 Holloway, "Gladue Reports," 2.

272 Ibid., 3.

273 Ralston and Goodwin, "*R v Drysdale,*" 116.

274 Holloway, "Gladue Reports," 2.

275 Quigley, "Gladue Reports," 3.

276 Hannah-Moffat and Maurutto, "Re-contextualizing Pre-sentence Reports," 266.

277 Ibid., 275.

278 Milward and Parkes, "Colonialism, Systemic Discrimination," 127.

279 Ralston and Goodwin, "*R v Drysdale,*" 116.

280 Milward and Parkes, "Colonialism, Systemic Discrimination," 124.

281 Office of the Correctional Investigator [OCI], *Annual Report, 2015–2016*, 45.

282 Milward and Parkes, "Colonialism, Systemic Discrimination," 126.

283 Ibid., 126.

284 Ibid., 125.

285 Ibid., 126.

286 Scott, "Reforming Saskatchewan's Biased Sentencing," 22.

287 Holloway, "Gladue Reports," 5.

288 Ibid., 4.

289 Ralston and Goodwin, "*R v Drysdale*," 116.

290 Quigley, "Gladue Reports," 6.

291 Scott, "Reforming Saskatchewan's Biased Sentencing," 22.

292 Quigley, "Gladue Reports," 7.

293 Ibid., 9.

294 Holloway, "Gladue Reports," 4.

295 Milward and Parkes, "Reforming Saskatchewan's Biased Sentencing," 121.

296 Holloway, "Gladue Reports," 7. For this template, see Legal Services Society of BC, *Gladue Submission Guide*.

297 *R. v. Peters*, para. 12.

298 Ibid.

299 *R. v. Ipeelee*, para. 62.

300 *R. v. Gladue*, para. 83; emphasis added.

301 *R. v. Ipeelee*, para. 60.

302 *R. v. Samson*, 2014, para. 67.

303 Ibid., para. 69.

304 *R. v. Dickson*, para. 7.

305 *R. v. Kanayok*, para. 15.

306 *R. v. Link*, para. 43.

307 *R. v. Smith*, 2012, para. 1.

308 Ibid., para. 18.

309 Ibid.

310 *R. v. Smith*, 2013 BCCA 173, para. 16.

311 *R. v. Serré*, para. 55.

312 Ibid., para. 57.

313 *R. v. First Charger*, para. 1.

314 Ibid., paras. 30–31.

315 *R. v. Gladue*, para. 84.

316 See ibid., para. 83; and *R. v. Ipeelee*, para. 60.

317 *R. v. Gladue*, para. 83.

318 *R. v. Ipeelee*, para. 60.

319 *R. v. Masakayash*, para. 9.

320 Ibid., para. 21.

321 Ibid., para. 8.

322 Ibid., para. 9.

323 *R. v. CT*, para. 15.

324 Ibid., para. 20.

325 *R. v. H*, para. 13.

326 *R. v. Hanley*, para. 10.

327 Ibid., para. 17.

328 Ralston and Goodwin, "*R v Drysdale*," 116.

329 *R. v. MAB*, para. 10.

330 Ibid.

331 Ibid., para. 8.

332 Ibid., para. 9.

333 Ibid., para. 14.

334 *R. v. McCook*, para. 58.

335 Ibid., para. 59.

336 Ibid., para. 52.

337 Ibid., para. 76.

338 Ibid., para. 77.

339 Ibid., para. 78.

340 See *R. v. Mattson*, para. 50; and *R. v. Napesis*, paras. 8–9, cited in *R. v. McCook*, paras. 72–73.

341 *R. v. Knockwood*, para. 8.

342 Ibid.

343 Ibid., para. 14.

344 Ibid.

345 Ibid., para. 72.

346 Ibid., para. 71.

347 Ibid., para. 72.

348 Ibid., para. 73.

349 *R. v. Toews*, para. 24.

350 *R. v. Florence,* 2013, para. 73.

351 Ibid., para. 50.

352 Ibid., para. 78.

353 *R. v. Florence*, 2015.

354 *R. v. Florence,* 2013, para. 75.

355 Ibid.

356 *R. v. Gladue*, para. 84.

357 *R. v. Whitford*, para. 10.

358 Ibid., para. 21.

359 Ibid., para. 10.

360 Ibid., para. 13.

361 Ibid., para. 21.

362 Ibid.

363 Ibid.

364 Ibid.

365 Ibid.

366 Ibid., para. 19.

367 Ibid., para. 18.

368 Ibid., para. 30.

369 Ibid., para. 33.

370 Ibid., para. 34.

371 Ibid., para. 21.

372 DeHart, "Pathways to Prison," 1378.

373 *R. v. Whitford*, para. 34.

374 Ibid., para. 33.

375 Ibid., para. 16.

376 See ibid., paras. 35–38.

377 Ibid., para. 40.

378 *R. v. Gladue*, para. 33.

379 *R. v. Ipeelee*, para. 72.

380 *R. v. Whitford*, para. 37.

381 Ibid., para. 40.

382 Ibid., para. 20.

383 Ibid., para. 40.

384 *R. v. Killiktee*, para. 2.

385 Ibid., para. 21.

386 Ibid., para. 5.

387 Ibid., para. 6.

388 Ibid., para. 7.

389 Ibid., paras. 10–11.

390 Ibid., para. 12.

391 Ibid., para. 13.

392 Ibid., para. 16.

393 Ibid., para. 17.

394 Ibid., para. 18.

395 Ibid., para. 26.

396 Ibid., para. 20.

397 Ibid., para. 24.

398 Ibid., para. 49.

399 Ibid., para. 42.

400 Ibid., para. 58.

401 Ibid., para. 66.

402 Killiktee subsequently appealed her sentence on the grounds that the judge failed to "give meaningful effect" to her Indigenous "status," although her appeal was dismissed, given Justice Ratushny's "great sensitivity" to *Gladue* principles and the determination that "public safety was paramount" (*R. v. Killiktee*, 2013, paras. 1, 3).

403 *R. v. Niganobe*, para. 64.

404 Ibid., para. 33.

405 Ibid., para. 34.

406 Ibid., para. 38.

407 Ibid., para. 46.

408 Ibid., para. 47.

409 Ibid.

410 Ibid., para. 74.

411 Ibid.; emphasis added.

412 *R. v. Ipeelee*, para. 73.

413 *R. v. Niganobe*, para. 74.

414 Ibid., para. 82.

415 Ibid., para. 83.

416 *R. v. Johnson*, 2011.

417 Ibid., para. 11.

418 Ibid.

419 Ibid., para. 10.

420 Ibid., para. 14. From the context of this statement, I infer Judge Cozens intended to say that in some instances the link is "more" rather than "less" tenuous.

421 Ibid., para. 16.

422 Ibid., para. 37.

423 *R. v. Jankovic*, para. 4.

424 Ibid., para. 8.

425 Ibid.

426 Ibid.

427 Paradies, "Beyond Black and White," 357.

428 Ibid.

429 Ibid.

430 Ibid., 361.

431 *R. v. Jankovic*, para. 8.

432 Ibid.; emphasis added.

433 Ibid., para. 10.

434 Brown, "Gender, Ethnicity," 152.

435 *R. v. Gladue*, para. 82.

436 *R. v. Jankovic*, para. 8.

437 Ibid.

438 Ibid.

439 *R. v. Bluebell*, para. 14.

440 Ibid., para. 15.

441 Ibid., para. 5.

442 Ibid., paras. 6–7.

443 Ibid., para. 14.

444 *R. v. Gladue*, para. 66.

445 *R. v. Bluebell*, para. 14.

446 *R. v. Ipeelee*, para. 66.

447 *R. v. Bluebell*, para. 22.

448 Ibid., para. 16.

449 *R. v. Ipeelee*, para. 84.

450 *R. v. Bluebell*, para. 15.

451 Ibid.

452 Ibid., para. 19.

453 See *R. v. Ipeelee*, paras. 81–83.

454 Ibid., para. 82.

455 *R. v. Collins*, para. 16.

456 Ibid., para. 17.

457 Ibid., para. 18.

458 Ibid., para. 22.

459 Ibid., para. 45.

460 Ibid., para. 48.

461 Ibid., para. 50.

462 Ibid., para. 23.

463 Williams, "Punishing Women," 280.

464 *R. v. Ipeelee*, paras. 81–83.

465 Ibid., para. 84.

466 *R. v. Collins*, para. 50.

467 Ibid., para. 62.

468 Ibid., para. 52.

469 *R. v. Ipeelee*, para. 83; emphasis added.

470 *R. v. Stevens*, para. 13.

471 Balfour, "Do Law Reforms Matter?" 98.

472 *R. v. Shore*, para. 3.

473 Ibid.

474 Ibid., para. 8.

475 Ibid., para. 10.

476 Ibid., para. 13.

477 Ibid., para. 24.

478 Ibid.

479 *R. v. Ipeelee*, paras. 81–83.

480 *R. v. Shore*, para. 24.

481 Ibid., para. 24.

482 Ibid., para. 40.

483 Ibid., para. 27.

484 Ibid., para. 29.

485 Ibid., para. 62.

486 Graydon, "Habilitation," 128.

487 See, e.g., *R. v. Shore*, para. 28.

488 Ibid., para. 27.

489 Ibid., para. 28.

490 Ibid.

491 Ibid., para. 29.

492 This case is unusual within the cases I selected for review, because it deals with the sentencing of an Indigenous woman who was already serving a life sentence when she committed the institutional offences that are the subject of this decision. Although a community sentence would not be possible in this context, the offences for which she pleaded guilty (extortion, assault causing bodily harm, and possession of a weapon) would have made this a more appropriate case for my study had these offences been committed on the outside. For this reason (alongside my general reasoning for including and not differentiating cases producing both provincial and federal sentences, as I explained in the Introduction), I have included this case. For reference, Justice Williams ordered a total sentence of thirty months' imprisonment for these offences (thirty months' imprisonment for extortion; twenty-four months for assault causing bodily harm; and eighteen months for weapon possession, all concurrent).

493 *R. v. SLN*, para. 33.

494 *R. v. Audy*, para. 1.

495 Ibid., para. 4.

496 Ibid.

497 Ibid.

498 Ibid., paras. 1, 5, and 8.

499 Ibid., para. 11.

500 Ibid., para. 15.

501 Ibid., para. 14.

502 Ibid., para. 12; emphasis added.

503 Ibid., para. 4.

504 Ibid., para. 13.

505 Ibid., para. 4.

506 Hannah-Moffat and Maurutto, "Re-contextualizing Pre-sentence Reports," 264.

507 Ibid., 275.

508 *R. v. Ussak*, para. 7.

509 Ibid., para. 40.

510 Ibid., para. 41.

511 Ibid., para. 11.

512 Ibid., para. 44.

513 Ibid., para. 24.

514 Ibid., para. 26.

515 Ibid., para. 36.

516 Ibid., para. 42.

517 Ibid., para. 70.

518 Code, s. 718.2(a)(ii).

519 *R. v. Ussak*, para. 71.

520 Ibid., para. 71. See also *R. v. Foy*, para. 77.

521 *R. v. Ussak*, para. 76.

522 Ibid., para. 65; emphasis added.

523 *R. v. Hansen*, para. 4.

524 Ibid., para. 45; emphasis added.

525 Ibid., para. 46.

526 *R. v. Rodrigue*, para. 14.

527 Ibid., para. 78.

528 *R. v. Elliott*, para. 27.

529 *R. v. Spence*, para. 35.

530 *R. v. Serré*, para. 63.

531 Ibid., para. 56.

532 *R. v. Littlecrow*, para. 20.

533 *R. v. Chamakese*, para. 8.

534 *R. v. Ussak*, para. 65.

535 *R. v. Florence*, 2013, para. 32.

536 *R. v. Ross*, para. 12.

537 Welsh and Ogloff, "Progressive Reforms," 495.

538 *R. v. Evaloardjuk*, para. 27.

539 *R. v. Elias*, 2009.

540 Ibid., para. 25.

541 *R. v. McClements*, para. 12.

542 Ibid., para. 34.

543 *R. v. Bourke*, para. 8.

544 Ibid., para. 10.

545 Ibid., para. 8.

546 *R. v. Keeping*, para. 36.

547 Ibid., para. 1.

548 Ibid., para. 4.

549 Ibid., para. 36.

550 *R. v. George*, para. 10.

551 *R. v. SMC*, para. 24.

552 *R. v. Gladue*, para. 33.

553 *R. v. Ipeelee*, para. 84.

554 Ibid., para. 87. See also para. 86.

555 *R. v. McIntyre*, para. 65.

556 *R. v. ET*, para. 23.

557 *R. v. Ipeelee*, para. 87; emphasis added.

558 *R. v. ET*, para. 7.

559 Ibid., para. 25.

560 Ibid., para. 26.

561 Ibid., para. 27.

562 *R. v. Gladue*, para. 79.

563 *R. v. Ipeelee*, para. 84.

564 *R. v. Sack*, para. 1.

565 Ibid., para. 8.

566 Ibid., para. 9.

567 *R. v. Peters*, para. 21.

568 *R. v. Saskatchewan*, para. 5.

569 Ibid., para. 15.

570 *R. v. MAB*, para. 19.

571 *R. v. Dennill*, para. 28; emphasis added.

CHAPTER 3: INCARCERATION WOUNDS: JUDICIAL DISCOURSES ABOUT HEALING

1 *R. v. Ipeelee*, para. 95.

2 Sapers, "A Preventable Death," para. 5.

3 Ibid., para. 28.

4 Ibid., para. 17.

5 Ibid., para. 3.

6 Ibid., paras. 17–18.

7 Ibid., para. 19.

8 Ibid., para. 24.

9 Ibid., paras. 70–73.

10 Jackson and Stewart, "A Flawed Compass," 185.

11 Sapers, "A Preventable Death," para. 5.

12 Ontario, Office of the Chief Coroner for Ontario, *Inquest Touching the Death*.

13 United Nations Office on Drugs and Crime, *Handbook on Prisoners*, 13.

14 Ibid.

15 Canadian Association of Elizabeth Fry Societies [CAEFS], *Submission . . . for the Special Report*, 19.

16 *R. v. McKenzie-Sinclair*, para. 30.

17 *R. v. Char*, 2007 CarswellBC, hereinafter *Char*.

18 *R. v. Pechawis*, para. 48.

19 Ibid., para. 5.

20 Ibid.

21 Ibid., para. 7.

22 Tyagi, "Victimization, Adversity," 134.

23 *R. v. Pechawis*, para. 48.

24 Ibid., para. 8.

25 Ibid., para. 41.

26 Roach, "Changing Punishment," 254.

27 *R. v. Fineday*, para. 8.

28 Ibid., para. 39.

29 Ibid., para. 40.

30 Ibid., para. 62.

31 Ibid., para. 42.

32 *R. v. Pawis*, para. 58.

33 Ibid.

34   Ibid., para. 94.

35   Ibid., para. 114.

36   *R. v. Woods*, para. 10.

37   Ibid., para. 45.

38   Ibid., para. 49.

39   Ibid.

40   Roberts and Gabor, "Living in the Shadow," 104.

41   *R. v. Woods*, para. 48.

42   *R. v. Tippeneskum*, para. 25.

43   Ibid., para. 15.

44   Ibid., para. 25.

45   *R. v. Kennedy*, para. 83.

46   Ibid., para. 90.

47   Ibid.

48   *R. v. Chartier*, para. 60.

49   Ibid., para. 63.

50   Ibid.

51   Ibid., para. 64.

52   Ibid., para. 76.

53   Ibid.

54   Ibid.

55   *R. v. LML*, para. 13.

56   Ibid., para. 35.

57   Linklater, *Decolonizing Trauma Work*, 101.

58   Turnbull and Hannah-Moffat, "Under these Conditions," 536.

59   CAEFS and NWAC, "Women and the Canadian Legal System," 97.

60   Pollack, "Taming the Shrew," 73.

61   *R. v. Nayneecassum*, para. 9.

62   Ibid., para. 10.

63   Ibid., para. 11.

64   Ibid., para. 19.

65   *R. v. Schinkel*, 2014, para. 5.

66   *R. v. Schinkel*, 2015, para. 29.

67   Ibid., para. 7.

68   Ibid., para. 8.

69   Ibid., para. 9; emphasis added.

70   Dej, "What Once Was Sick," 152.

71   *R. v. M(CA)*, para. 92.

72   Rumgay, "Scripts for Safer Survival," 411.

73   *R. v. Kendi*, para. 6.

74   *R. v. Kendi*, para. 9.

75   Ibid., para. 12.

76   Ibid., para. 44.

77   Ibid., para. 13.

78   Ibid., para. 10.

79   Ibid., para. 45.

80   Ibid., para. 51.

81   Ibid., para. 11.

82   Ibid., para. 13.

83   Ibid., para. 48.

84   Ibid., paras. 10, 12.

85   Ibid., para. 12.

86   Ibid.

87   Ibid., para. 13.

88   Ibid., para. 49.

89   Ibid., para. 6.

90   Ibid.

91   Ibid., para. 51.

92   Juristat, Johnson, *Outcomes of Probation,* 9.

93   *R. v. Char*, para. 10.

94   Ibid., para. 28.

95   *R. v. Char*, 2007 BCCA, para. 3.

96   *R. v. Char*, para. 32.

97   *R. v. Char*, 2007 BCCA, para. 3.

98   *R. v. Char*, para. 33.

99   Ibid., para. 35.

100 *R. v. Char*, 2007 BCCA, para. 4.

101 See, e.g., Renée Acoby's story in Fraser, "Life on the Instalment Plan." Kim Pate, the then executive director of CAEFS, explains that part of Acoby's institutional offences was driven by her anger at the Correctional Service of Canada for removing her daughter from her care. Pate comments broadly that "many women in prison, when they have that kind of devastation, will implode, start self-injuring, get depressed," and "some have suicided." But instead of self-destructing, Pate explains that Acoby "acts," she externalizes her rage, which often led to institutional charges (see p. 3). Kathleen J. Ferraro and Angela M. Moe find in their research that women's relationship with their children is often instrumental in their recovery from substance abuse, given the despair that accompanies the loss of those relationships. See Ferraro and Moe, "Mothering, Crime, and Incarceration," 28.

102 *R. v. Char*, para. 36.

103 Ibid.; emphasis added.

104 Ibid., para. 35.

105 Ibid., para. 36.

106 Ibid., para. 41.

107 Ibid.

108 Ibid.

109 Bouchard, "Mental Health," S44.

110 *R. v. Char*, para. 46.

111 *R. v. Char*, 2007 BCCA, para. 5.

112 *R. v. Char*, para. 46.

113 *R. v. Char*, para. 43; emphasis added.

114 Ibid., paras. 39–40.

115 Ibid., para. 41.

116 Ibid., para. 34.

117 *R. v. Char*, 2007 BCCA, 16.

118 Ibid.

119 Ibid., para. 10.

120 *R. v. Char*, para. 2.

121 Pollack, "'You Can't Have It Both Ways,'" 117.

122 Sapers, "Mental Health Challenges."

123 Ibid.

124 OCI, *Annual Report, 2016–2017,* 49.

125 Pollack, "'You Can't Have It Both Ways,'" 118.

126 *R. v. Diamond*, para. 8.

127 Ibid., para. 21.

128 Ibid., para. 14.

129 Ibid., para. 19.

130 Ibid., para. 17.

131 Ibid., para. 16.

132 Ibid.

133 Ibid., para. 11.

134 Ibid.

135 Ibid., para. 25.

136 Ibid., para. 28.

137 Ibid., para. 18.

138 Ibid.

139 CAEFS and NWAC, "Women and the Canadian Legal System," 97.

140 *R. v. Diamond*, para. 40.

141 *R. v. Woods*, para. 14.

142 *R. v. Diamond*, para. 25.

143 Welsh and Ogloff, "Progressive Reforms," 510.

144 Canada, Department of Justice, *What We Heard*, 16.

145 *R. v. Char*, para. 47.

146 *R. v. Diamond*, para. 25.

147 Hannah-Moffat and Maurutto, "Re-contextualizing Pre-sentence Reports," 264.

148 *R. v. Peeteetuce*, para. 34.

149 Ibid., para. 48.

150 Ibid.

151 Ibid.

152 *R. v. Killiktee*, 2011, para. 62.

153 Ibid., para. 66.

154 Ibid., para. 62.

155 Ibid.

156 Ibid., para. 66.

157 Shecapio had been drinking heavily for several days. She invited the deceased, a friend from the Native Friendship Centre of Montreal, to continue drinking with her at a neighbour's apartment. They left together after the deceased had an argument with the neighbour. In Shecapio's apartment, she and the deceased discussed her "medieval type dagger," which Shecapio later used to stab him once near the heart "after the beginning of another quarrel" (*R. v. Shecapio*, paras. 3–4). They had gone for a walk, and she had brought the dagger "concealed" (para. 4). After denying responsibility, Shecapio eventually told the police that she stabbed the deceased, "adding that she acted at his request because the victim was tired of his life and because he wanted her too much to love him" (para. 6).

158 *R. v. Shecapio*, para. 28.

159 Ibid., para. 10.

160 Ibid., para. 13.

161 Ibid., para. 14.

162 Ibid., para. 22.

163 Ibid., para. 23.

164 *R. v. Waskewitch*, para. 7.

165 Glass et al., "Non-Fatal Strangulation," 335.

166 *R. v. Waskewitch*, para. 14.

167 Ibid., para. 16.

168 Ibid., para. 36. For Elizabeth Sheehy's related work, see Sheehy, "Defending Battered Women on Trial": see also Sheehy, *Defending Battered Women*. For a feminist perspective on the context of violence against women, including Indigenous women, see, e.g., Sheehy, "Misogyny Is Deadly."

169 *R. v. Waskewitch*, para. 39.

170 Ibid., para. 25.

171 Ibid., para. 41.

172 Ibid., para. 44.

173 Ibid.

174 Ibid., para. 48.

175 Ibid.

176 Ibid., para. 42.

177 Ibid., para. 45.

178 Ibid., para. 43.

179 Bernier, "Breaking Down the Walls," 13.

180 *R. v. Waskewitch*, para. 49.

181 Ibid., para. 50.

182 Ibid., para. 25.

183 Hannah-Moffat and Maurutto, "Re-contextualizing Pre-sentence Reports," 274.

184 Ibid., 272.

185 Ibid., 274–75.

186 Ibid., 272.

187 Ibid., 273.

188 Ibid., 272.

189 Pate, Lecture on Mental Health.

190 *R. v. Rodrigue*, para. 38.

191 Ibid., para. 39.

192 *R. v. Waskewitch*, para. 50.

193 Ibid., para. 44.

194 Ibid., para. 46.

195 Regarding such judicial recommendations for other jurisdictions, the Correctional Investigator reports that "almost 1 in 4 women are from a province or territory that does not have a regional facility or healing lodge; 66% of those women are Aboriginal." Office of the Correctional Investigator [OCI], *Annual Report, 2014–2015*, 50.

196 Welsh and Ogloff, "Progressive Reforms," 510.

197 *R. v. Sinclair*, para. 1.

198 Ibid., para. 70.

199 Ibid., para. 17.

200 Ibid., para. 56; emphasis added.

201 Hannah-Moffat, "Moral Agent," 74; emphasis in the original.

202 United Nations Office on Drugs and Crime, *Handbook on Women and Imprisonment*, 4.

203 *R. v. Sinclair*, para. 64; emphasis in the original.

204 Comack, *Women in Trouble*, 136; emphasis in the original.

205 *R. v. Sinclair*, para. 70.

206 Ibid., para. 56.

207 Ibid., para. 70.

208 Ibid., para. 71.

209 *R. v. Pelletier*, 2011.

210 *R. v. Pelletier*, 2011, para. 25.

211 Ibid., para. 169.

212 Ibid., para. 36.

213 Ibid., para. 114.

214 Ibid., para. 115.

215 Ibid., para. 186.

216 Ibid.

217 Ibid., para. 211.

218 Ibid., para. 194.

219 Ibid., para. 103.

220 Ibid., para. 124.

221 Ibid., para. 125.

222 *R. v. Pelletier*, 2013, para. 8.

223 Ibid.

224 *R. v. Redhead*, para. 9.

225 Ibid.

226 Ibid., para. 24.

227 Ibid., para. 15.

228 Ibid., para. 16.

229 Ibid.

230 Hannah-Moffat, "Moral Agent," 80.

231 Shaw, Corrections Branch, Ministry of the Solicitor General, *Federal Female Offender*, 81.

232 Ibid., 83.

233 Ibid., 81; emphasis added.

234 Hannah-Moffat, "Moral Agent," 80.

235 *R. v. Gladue*, para. 68.

236 Monture-Angus, "Aboriginal Women and Correctional Practice," 52.

237 See the Task Force on Federally Sentenced Women [TFFSW], "Creating Choices."

238 Monture-Angus, "Aboriginal Women and Correctional Practice," 53.

239 Comack, "The Prisoning of Women," 121.

240 Shaw, "Women, Violence and Disorder," 61.

241 Ibid., 68.

242 *R. v. Redhead*, para. 24.

243 Ibid., para. 25.

244 *R. v. Chouinard*, para. 22.

245 Ibid.

246 Ibid., para. 25.

247 Ibid.

248 Ibid., para. 27.

249 Ibid., para. 22.

250 *R. v. Link*, para. 88.

251 *R. v. McCook*, para. 175.

252 *R. v. Redies*, para. 1.

253 Ibid.

254 Ibid., para. 13.

255 Ibid.

256 Ibid., para. 17.

257 Ibid.

258 Ibid.

259 See, e.g., *R. v. Proulx*, paras. 32–33.

260 *R. v. Redies*, para. 17.

261 Ibid., para. 22.

262 *R. v. Arcand*, 2014, para. 36.

263 *R. v. MAB*, para. 22.

264 Ibid.

265 Ibid.

266 *R. v. Link*, para. 141.

267 Ibid.

268 Ibid., para. 142.

269 *R. v. Smith*, 2012, para. 45.

270 Ibid.

271 *R. v. Smith*, 2013, para. 64.

272 Ibid., para. 1.

273 *R. v. Petawabano*, para. 43.

274 Ibid., para. 34.

275 *R. v. Brertton*, para. 25.

276 *R. v. McClements*, para. 24.

277 Ibid., para. 28.

278 Ibid., para. 43.

279 Ibid., para. 27.

280 Hartnagel, "The Rhetoric of Youth Justice," 369–70.

281 *R. v. Smith*, 2004.

282 Ibid., para. 1.

283 Ibid., para. 15.

284 Ibid., para. 17.

285 Ibid., para. 16.

286 Ibid., para. 18.

287 Ibid., para. 15.

288 Ibid., para. 18.

289 Ibid., para. 14.

290 Ibid., para. 25.

291 Ibid.

292 *R. v. Gladue*, para. 82.

293 *R. v. Ipeelee*, para. 85.

294 *R. v. Smith*, 2004, para. 23.

295 Ibid., para. 20.

296 Ibid., para. 24.

297 Ibid., para. 26.

298 Ibid., para. 27.

299 Ibid., para. 28.

300 Ibid., para. 29.

301 Ibid., para. 19.

302 Ibid., para. 21.

303 Ibid., para. 26.

304 Ibid., para. 25.

305 Ibid., para. 11.

306 Ibid., para. 25; emphasis in original.

307 Ibid., para. 12.

308 Ibid., para. 13.

309 Ibid., para. 21.

310 Ibid., para. 27.

311 Ibid.

312 Ibid., para. 12.

313 Ibid., para. 27.

314 *R. v. Aisaican*, para. 62.

315 *R. v. Isaac*, para. XIII.

316 Ibid., para. III.

317 Ibid., para. IV.

318 Ibid., para. XV.

319 Ibid., para. XVII.

320 *R. v. CGO*, para. 61.

321 The sentencing judge at the Provincial Court of British Columbia is Judge Marion Buller Bennett, and the judge authoring the written reasons for the British Columbia Court of Appeal is Justice Elizabeth A. Bennett. Hereafter, where I refer to "Judge Bennett," I am referring to the sentencing judge.

322 *R. v. CGO*, para. 38.

323 Ibid., para. 42.

324 Ibid., para. 4.

325 Ibid., para. 23.

326 Ibid., para. 56.

327 Ibid., para. 62.

328 Ibid., para. 65.

329 Ibid., para. 69.

330 Ibid., para. 74.

331 Ibid., para. 75.

332 Ibid., para. 56.

333 Ibid., para. 66.

334 Andersen, "Governing Aboriginal Justice," 309.

335 McFatter, "Sentencing Strategies," 1490.

336 *R. v. CGO*, para. 62.

337 *R. v. Pawis*, para. 106.

338 *R. v. Knockwood*, para. 36.

339 *R. v. Toews*, para. 19.

340 *R. v. Aisaican*, para. 33.

341 Ibid., para. 37.

342 *R. v. Ussak*, para. 52.

343 Ibid., para. 77.

344 *R. v. RCL*, para. 98.

345 Ibid., para. 99.

346 Ibid., para. 100.

347 Ibid.

348 *R. v. Gambler*, para. 22.

349 Ibid.

350 Ibid., para. 23.

351 Ibid., para. 17.

352 *R. v. Johnson*, 2013, para. 40; emphasis added.

353 Ibid., para. 23; emphasis added.

354 Sugar and Fox, "Nistum Peyako Séht'wawin Iskwewak," 476.

355 Ibid., 475.

356 *R. v. Johnson*, 2013, para. 39.

357 Ibid., para. 63.

358 Ibid.

359 Ibid., para. 31.

360 Ibid.

361 Ibid., para. 68; emphasis added.

362 *R. v. Papin*, para. 207.

363 Ibid., para. 187.

364 Ibid., para. 16.

365 Ibid., para. 51.

366 Ibid., para. 206.

367 Ibid., para. 16.

368 Comack, *Women in Trouble,* 153.

369 *R. v. Papin*, para. 165.

370 Ibid., para. 170.

371 Ibid., para. 136.

372 Ibid., para. 131.

373 Ibid., para. 44.

374 Ibid., para. 295.

375 Ibid., para. 287.

376 Ibid.

377 Ibid., para. 294.

378 United Nations Committee on the Elimination of Discrimination against Women, *Report*, 57.

379 *R. v. RCL*, para. 91.

380 Cull, "Aboriginal Mothering," 153.

381 Ibid., 144.

382 *R. v. RCL*, para. 98.

383 Ibid., para. 77.

384 Canada, The National Inquiry into Missing and Murdered Indigenous Women and Girls, *Interim Report*, 20; emphasis added.

385 Eljdupovic, Mitchell, Curtis, Jaremko Bromwich, Granger-Brown, Arseneau, and Fry, "Incarcerating Aboriginal Mothers," 46.

386 *R. v. McDonald*, para. 37.

387 *R. v. CT*, para. 3.

388 Public Inquiry into the Administration of Justice and Aboriginal People, *Report*, Volume I, Chapter 13.

389 *R. v. George*, para. 5.

390 *R. v. Killiktee*, para. 21.

391 *R. v. LML*, para. 8.

392 Ibid., para. 10.

393 *R. v. Johnson*, 2011, para. 16.

394 *R. v. Masakayash*, para. 24.

395 Ibid.

396 *R. v. Spencer*, para. 23.

397 Ibid., para. 33.

398 *R. v. Pijogge*, para. 8; see also para. 11.

399 Ibid., para. 30.

400 Ibid., para. 33.

401 Ibid., para. 49.

402 Ibid., para. 45.

403 Ibid., para. 50.
404 Ibid., para. 8.
405 Ibid., para. 22.
406 *R. v. Schinkel*, 2014, para. 10.
407 Ibid., para. 21.
408 Ibid., para. 22.
409 Ibid., para. 26.
410 *R. v. Schinkel*, 2015, para. 31.
411 *R. v. Key*, para. 13.
412 Ibid.
413 Ibid., para. 17.
414 Ibid., para. 19.
415 *R. v. Tizya*, para. 12.
416 *R. v. Firth*, para. 12.
417 *R. v. Elliott*, para. 40; emphasis added.
418 Ibid., para. 44.
419 Ibid.
420 *R. v. TAP*, 2013, para. 5.
421 Ibid., para. 16.
422 Ibid., para. 41.
423 Ibid., para. 71.
424 Ibid.
425 Ibid., para. 72.
426 Ibid., para. 74.
427 Ibid.
428 Ibid.
429 Ibid., para. 76.
430 Ibid., para. 77.
431 *R. v. TAP*, 2014.
432 *R. v. Hill*, para. 17.
433 Ibid., para. 30.
434 Ibid., para. 35.
435 Ibid., para. 40.
436 Ibid., para. 46.
437 Ibid., para. 42.
438 Ibid., para. 63.
439 *R. v. Sowden*, para. 54.
440 Ibid., para. 16.
441 Ibid., para. 43.
442 *R. v. Spence*, para. 44.

443   Ibid.

444   Ibid., para. 18.

445   Ibid., para. 21.

446   Ibid., para. 30.

447   Ibid., para. 48.

448   *R. v. Hansen*, para. 21; see also para. 36.

449   Ibid., para. 21.

450   Ibid., para. 12.

451   Ibid., para. 19.

452   Ibid., para. 49.

453   *R. v. Arcand*, 2014, para. 36.

454   Ibid., para. 32.

455   *R. v. Samson*, 2014, para. 70.

456   *R. v. Samson*, 2015, para. 33.

457   *R. v. Pham*, para. 11. Cited in ibid.

458   Davis, *Abolition Democracy,* 72.

459   Ibid., 73.

460   *R. v. Elliott*, para. 43.

461   *R. v. Link*, para. 132.

462   Ibid., para. 142.

463   *R. v. McClements*, para. 23.

464   Ibid., para. 41.

465   *R. v. Isaac,* para. XVII.

466   *R. v. Elias*, 2001, para. 101.

467   *R. v. Elliott*, para. 46.

468   *R. v. Proulx*, para. 54.

469   Code, s. 718.2(a)(vi).

470   *R. v. Sowden*, para. 41.

471   *R. v. Bouchard*, para. 13.

472   Ibid., para. 13.

473   Ibid.

474   Ibid.

475   *R. v. Bourke*, para. 11.

476   Ibid., para.12.

477   *R. v. Hill*, para. 63.

478   *R. v. LML*, para. 51.

479   *R. v. McClements*, para. 53.

480   Juristat, Johnson, *Outcomes of Probation,* 9.

481   *R. v. Proulx*, para. 39.

482   Roach, "Changing Punishment," 266.

483 *R. v. Elias*, 2009, para. 35.

484 *R. v. Isaac,* para. XX.

485 Bayes, "Harper's Crime Laws," 23.

486 Juristat, Johnson, *Outcomes of Probation,* 1, 8.

487 Turnbull and Hannah-Moffat, "Under these Conditions," 532.

488 Roach, "Changing Punishment," 266.

489 *R. v. Bourke*, para. 5.

490 *R. v. Abraham*, para. 25.

491 *R. v. Coombs*, para. 8.

492 *R. v. Merkuratsuk*, para. 28.

493 Ibid., para. 30.

494 *R. v. Link*, para. 125.

495 *R. v. Kanayok*, para. 19.

496 Ibid.

497 *R. v. McClements*, para. 43.

498 *R. v. Simms*, para. 55.

499 *R. v. Omeasoo*, para. 1.

500 Ibid., para. 8.

501 Ibid., para. 33.

502 Ibid., para. 37.

503 Ibid., para. 44.

504 Ibid., para. 31.

505 Ibid., para. 32.

506 Ibid.

507 *R. v. Firth*, para. 9.

508 Ibid., para. 11.

509 Milward and Parkes, "Colonialism, Systemic Discrimination," 139.

510 Juristat, Johnson, *Returning to Correctional Services,* 11.

511 Ibid.

512 Ibid., 12.

513 Ibid.

514 Ibid.

515 Ibid., 13.

516 Juristat, Brennan and Matarazzo, *Re-contact with the Saskatchewan Justice System.*

517 Reneé Gobeil and Meredith Robeson Barrett explain that "as women represent a small proportion of incarcerated offenders, they tend to receive less research attention relative to male offenders. This general trend applies to recidivism research as well. Indeed, several investigators have reported mainly aggregated recidivism rates (i.e., across genders) and have presented gender-specific data only in small, relatively superficial sections or in appendices." Gobeil and Robeson Barrett, "Research Report," 1.

518 Juristat, Johnson, *Returning to Correctional Services,* 8.

519 Ibid., 1.

520 Statistics Canada, *Women in Canada,* 36.

521 Gobeil and Robeson Barrett, "Research Report," 11.

522 OCI, *Annual Report, 2015–2016,* 43.

523 Ibid., 6–7.

524 Ibid., 11.

525 Ibid.

526 Ibid.

527 Ibid.

528 Aboriginal Corrections Policy Unit, Wesley, *Marginalized,* 20–21.

529 Shantz, Kilty, and Frigon, "Echoes of Imprisonment," 97.

530 Pollack, "'You Can't Have It Both Ways,'" 121.

531 Kilty, "Under the Barred Umbrella," 176. See also Bouchard, "Mental Health," S41.

532 See, e.g., Kilty, "'Under the Barred Umbrella,'"172. See also interview of Kim Pate by Hana Gartner (Gartner, "Interview: Kim Pate").

533 Haag, "Ethical Dilemmas," 96.

534 *R. v. Carter,* 2014, para. 19.

535 Ibid., para. 18.

536 Commission of Inquiry into Certain Events, Arbour, *Report,* 212.

537 Ibid.

538 Sugar and Fox, "Nistum Peyako Séht'wawin Iskwewak," 475.

539 Wesley, "Marginalized Report," 41.

540 Ibid., 18.

541 Sugar and Fox, "Nistum Peyako Séht'wawin Iskwewak," 477.

542 Peternelj-Taylor, "Conceptualizing Nursing Research," 350.

543 Statistics Canada, Canadian Centre for Justice Statistics, Gannon et al., *Criminal Justice Indicators: 2005,* 33.

544 Bernier, "Breaking Down the Walls."

545 BC Corrections, "Reducing Reoffending."

546 BC Corrections, "Reducing Reoffending: Cognitive Behavioural Programs."

547 Norwich et al., "Women Behind Bars."

548 Ibid.

549 Ibid.

550 Player, "Reduction of Women's Imprisonment," 428.

551 Sugar and Fox, "Nistum Peyako Séht'wawin Iskwewak," 476.

552 *R. v. Chamakese,* 2014 SKQB 44, para. 15.

553 *R. v. Toews,* para. 74.

554 Ibid., para. 26.

555 Ibid., para. 28.

556 Ibid., para. 75; emphasis added.

557 *R. v. Firth*, para. 16.

558 Ibid., para. 14.

559 Ibid., para. 13; emphasis added.

560 Ibid., para. 14; emphasis added.

561 *R. v. Good*, 2010, para. 17.

562 Ibid., para. 23.

563 Ibid., para. 34.

564 Ibid., para. 38.

565 Ibid.

566 Ibid., para. 39.

567 Ibid., para. 40.

568 *R. v. Pelletier*, 2011.

569 *R. v. Smith*, 2004.

570 *R. v. Connors*, para. 25.

571 *R. v. Abraham*, para. 32.

572 Ibid.

573 Ibid.

574 *R. v. Woods*, para. 47.

575 Ibid., para. 14.

576 Ibid, para. 15.

577 Ibid., para. 16. It does seem that Woods was highly motivated, as, after her release on an undertaking, she re-established positive relationships with family members and distanced herself from people mired in substance abuse and criminality (para. 15).

578 Ibid., para. 50.

579 The Truth in Sentencing Act, which entered into force on 22 February 2010, stipulates that judges can credit remand time only at a ratio of one to one, except where "the circumstances justify it," permitting credit for one and one-half days for each day spent in remand. See Canada, Bill C-25.

580 In April 2014, the SCC found in a judgment by Justice Andromache Karakatsanis that Parliament placed a cap of 1.5 to 1 on enhanced credit for pre-sentence custody, but did not limit or make exceptional the circumstances that could justify such credit (formerly, however, it was normal practice for judges to reduce the total sentence by a ratio of two to one for custody in remand). *R. v. Summers*, paras. 5, 7, and 57.

581 Milward and Parkes, "Colonialism, Systemic Discrimination," 138.

582 Eliason, Taylor, and Williams, "Physical Health of Women," 183.

583 Dirks, "Sexual Revictimization," 106.

584 Pollack, "'Taming the Shrew,'" 76. For a further reflection on how the pathologization of self-harming behaviour is often met with increased punitive measures such as institutional charges, see Kilty, "'Under the Barred Umbrella.'"

585 Pollack, "'Taming the Shrew,'" 76.

586 See, e.g., Sapers, "A Preventable Death," paras. 16–39.

587 Zaitzow, "Pastel Fascism," 40.

588 Shantz, Kilty, and Frigon, "Echoes of Imprisonment," 87.

589 Ibid., 97–98.

590 Jackson, *Justice Behind the Walls*, 18.

CONCLUSION: REFRACTED THROUGH INSTITUTIONAL LENSES

1   Ottawa, House of Commons, *Subcommittee on Solicitation Laws*, 31.

2   Ibid., 32.

3   Razack, *Looking White People*, 169.

4   *R. v. Stevens*, para. 14.

5   United Nations Committee on the Elimination of Discrimination against Women, *Report*, 42.

6   TRC, *Honouring the Truth, Summary*, 172.

7   Native Women's Association of Canada [NWAC], "Arrest the Legacy," 2 (in Insert 1).

8   Public Inquiry into the Administration of Justice and Aboriginal People, *Report*, Volume I, Chapter 13.

9   Ibid.

10 Hannah-Moffat, "Gendering Risk," 247.

11 Pollack, "'You Can't Have It Both Ways,'" 161.

12 Findlay, "Trouble in the Big House."

13 *R. v. Diamond*, 2006, para. 25.

14 *R. v. Whitford*, 2008, para. 28.

15 Ibid., para. 41.

16 The Office of the Correctional Investigator reports, "From research and experience, we know that when correctional programs are properly targeted and sequenced, well-implemented and delivered to meet earliest parole eligibility dates they can reduce recidivism, save money in the long run and enhance public safety." Office of the Correctional Investigator [OCI], *Annual Report, 2010–2011*, 43.

17 OCI, *Annual Report, 2009–2010*, 43.

18 Ibid., 44.

19 OCI, *Annual Report, 2014–2015*, 40.

20 OCI, *Annual Report, 2015–2016*, 45.

21 *R. v. Elias*, 2001, para. 105.

22 *R. v. Gladue*, para. 65.

23 Ibid.

24 *R. v. Ipeelee*, para. 61.

25 Ibid., para. 69.
26 Ibid.
27 Ibid., para. 61; emphasis added.
28 Juristat, Brzozowski, Taylor-Butts, and Johnson, *Victimization and Offending*, 15.
29 *R. v. Gladue*, para. 37.
30 *R. v. Ipeelee*, para. 74.
31 See also Shaw, "Women, Violence and Disorder," 68.
32 Hannah-Moffat, "Feminine Fortresses," 161n14.
33 *R. v. Hill*, para. 41.
34 Ibid., para. 48.
35 Ibid., para. 17.
36 *R. v. Sowden*, para. 21.
37 Ibid., para. 22.
38 *R. v. Ipeelee*, para. 67.
39 *R. v. Char*, para. 34.
40 Parkes et al., *Gladue Handbook*, 13–14.
41 Legal Services Society of BC, *Gladue Submission Guide*.
42 *R. v. Ipeelee*, para. 62.
43 *R. v. Dickson*, para. 7.
44 Canada, Department of Justice, *What We Heard*, 11.
45 Ibid., 15.
46 Bill S-251, An Act to amend the Criminal Code (independence of the judiciary) and to make related amendments.
47 *R. v. Ipeelee*, para. 63.
48 Ibid.
49 Scott, "Reforming Saskatchewan's Biased Sentencing," 10.
50 Public Inquiry into the Administration of Justice and Aboriginal People, *Report*, Chapter 10, "Alternatives to Incarceration."
51 Ibid.
52 Ibid.
53 *R. v. Ipeelee*, para. 66.
54 Ibid.
55 Public Inquiry into the Administration of Justice and Aboriginal People, *Report*, Volume I, Chapter 10.
56 Ibid., para. 68.
57 Ibid.
58 Ibid.
59 United Nations Committee on the Elimination of Discrimination against Women, *Report*, 51.
60 Ibid., 49.

61 *R. v. George*, para. 14, quoting *R. v. Vermette*, para. 39.

62 Balfour, "Do Law Reforms Matter?" 91.

63 Murdocca, *To Right Historical Wrongs*, 65.

64 Cited in Derrida, "Force De Loi," 1015.

65 Razack, *Looking White People*, 19.

66 *R. v. Sack*, para. 5; emphasis added.

67 Ibid.

68 *R. v. Hansen*, para. 55.

69 Ibid., para. 55.

70 Ibid., para. 56.

71 Murdocca, *To Right Historical Wrongs*, 92.

72 *R. v. Peters*, para. 20.

73 *R. v. Connors*, paras 16–24.

74 Ibid., para. 23.

75 *R. v. George*, para. 9.

76 In the following judgments, judges specifically comment that CSOs are no longer available due to amendments to the conditional sentencing regime: *R. v. Stimson*, paras. 13–14; *R. v. Connors*, para. 18; *R. v. Redies*, para. 12; *R. v. Audy*, paras 1, 5; *R. v. Arcand*, 2014, paras. 13, 15; *R. v. MAB*, para. 5; *R. v. SMC*, para. 3; *R. v. H*, para. 7; *R. v. Hansen*, para. 42; *R. v. Littlecrow*, para. 20; *R. v. Sandy*, para. 17; and *R. v. Ussak*, para. 59. Conditional sentences remain available in the following decisions because the various offence dates preceded amendments to the conditional sentencing regime, but the judges all comment that CSOs would otherwise no longer be possible: *R. v. Chartier*, para. 73; *R. v. Flett*, 2012, para. 28; and *R. v. McDonald*, para. 29. In another case, a judicial finding of fact is determinative on the issue of whether a CSO remains available given amendments: in *R. v. Link*, para. 121, contrary to the Crown position, the judge determines that a conditional sentence is still available despite the 2007 amendments because the judge finds the offence in issue is not a serious personal injury offence.

77 *R. v. Audy*, paras. 5–8.

78 *R. v. Smith*, 2012, para. 28.

79 Ibid., para. 29.

80 Ibid., para. 30.

81 *R. v. Smith*, 2013, BCCA 173, para. 57.

82 Ibid., para. 71.

83 *R. v. Smith*, 2012, para. 46.

84 *R. v. Simms*, para. 13.

85 *R. v. MAB*, para. 5.

86 Ibid., para. 6.

87 *R. v. Arcand*, 2014, para. 23.

88 Ibid., para. 23.

89   *R. v. RNS*, para. 21, cited in part in *R. v. Pijogge*, para. 36.

90   *R. v. SCM,* and *R. v. First Charger*.

91   Truth and Reconciliation Commission of Canada [TRC], *Honouring the Truth, Summary,* 174 and 324.

92   Balfour, "Do Law Reforms Matter?" 97.

93   Ibid.

94   Canada, Bill C-9, 1640.

95   Ibid.

96   Inquiry into the Administration of Justice and Aboriginal People, *Report,* Volume I, Chapter 13.

97   Monture-Angus, "The Lived Experience," 44.

98   Ibid., 45.

99   Parkes and Pate, "Time for Accountability," 258.

100 *R. v. M(CA)*, para. 81.

101 Sheehy, "Advancing Social Inclusion," 77.

102 Davis, *Are Prisons Obsolete?* 107.

103 *R. v. Elias*, 2001, para. 101.

104 Murdocca, *To Right Historical Wrongs*, 109.

105 Balfour, "Do Law Reforms Matter?" 93.

106 Ibid., 94.

107 CAEFS and NWAC, "Women and the Canadian Legal System," 97.

108 United Nations Committee on the Elimination of Discrimination against Women, *Report,* 41.

109 Ibid., 45.

110 Canada, The National Inquiry into Missing and Murdered Indigenous Women and Girls, *Interim Report,* 55.

111 "More Prisons to Be Expanded," CBC (10 January 2011). See also "Tories Announce $155.5M Prison Expansion," CBC (6 October 2010).

112 Bayes, "Harper's Crime Laws," 23.

113 The Task Force on Federally Sentenced Women [TFFSW], "Creating Choices," 28.

114 Carlen, *Sledgehammer,* 153; emphasis in original.

115 Balfour, "Do Law Reforms Matter?" 93.

116 *R. v. Peters*, para. 10.

117 Pollack, "'You Can't Have It Both Ways,'" 118.

118 Shantz, Kilty, and Frigon, "Echoes of Imprisonment," 101.

119 *R. v. Aisaican*, para. 9.

120 Dirks, "Sexual Revictimization," 111.

121 Pate, "Advocacy, Activism," 82.

BIBLIOGRAPHY

Primary Sources

BILLS, LEGISLATION, AND RELATED PROCEEDINGS

Canada. Bill C-9. An Act to amend the Criminal Code (conditional sentence of imprisonment). 1st Sess, 39th Parl, 2007 (Royal Assent on 31 May 2007). http://www.parl.gc.ca/LegisInfo/BillDetails.aspx?Language=E&Mode=1&billId=2172003.

———. Bill C-9. An Act to amend the Criminal Code (conditional sentence of imprisonment). 1st Sess, 39th Parl, 2007. http://www.parl.gc.ca/HousePublications/Publication.aspx?Language=E&Mode=1&DocI d=3294571.

———. Bill C-25. An Act to amend the Criminal Code (limiting credit for time spent in pre-sentencing custody), (The Truth in Sentencing Act). 2nd Sess, 40th Parl, 2009. http://www.parl.gc.ca/HousePublications/Publication.aspx?Language=E&Mode=1&DocI d=4172410&File=24#1.

———. Bill C-75, An Act to amend the Criminal Code, the Youth Criminal Justice Act and other Acts and to make consequential amendments to other Acts, 1st Sess, 42nd Parl, 2018. https://www.parl.ca/LegisInfo/BillDetails.aspx?Language=E&billId=9745407.

———. Bill C-32. An Act to Enact the Canadian Victims Bill of Rights and to amend certain Acts (Victims Bill of Rights Act), 2nd Sess, 41st Parl, 2015. https://www.parl.ca/LegisInfo/BillDetails.aspx?Language=E&billId=6503398.

———. Bill C-10. An Act to enact the Justice for Victims of Terrorism Act and to amend the State Immunity Act, the Criminal Code, the Controlled Drugs and Substances Act, the Corrections and Conditional Release Act, the Youth Criminal Justice Act, the Immigration and Refugee Protection Act and other Acts (Safe Streets and Communities Act). 1st Sess, 41st Parl, 2012. http://www.parl.gc.ca/HousePublications/Publication.aspx?Language=E&Mode=1&DocI d=5465759&File=62#11.

———. Bill C-10. An Act to enact the Justice for Victims of Terrorism Act and to amend the State Immunity Act, the Criminal Code, the Controlled Drugs and Substances Act, the Corrections and Conditional Release Act, the Youth Criminal Justice Act, the Immigration and Refugee Protection Act and other Acts (Safe Streets and Communities Act). 1st Sess, 41st Parl, 2012 (Royal Assent on 13 March 2012). http://www.parl.gc.ca/LegisInfo/BillDetails.aspx?Language=E&Mode=1&billId=512082 9&View=6.

———. Bill S-251. An Act to amend the Criminal Code (independence of the judiciary) and to make related amendments. 1st Sess, 42nd Parl, 2018. https://www.parl.ca/LegisInfo/BillDetails.aspx?Language=E&billId=9903593.

———. Bill S-3. An Act to amend the Indian Act in response to the Superior Court of Quebec decision in Descheneaux c. Canada (Procureur général), 1st Sess, 42nd Parl, 2017. https://www.parl.ca/LegisInfo/BillDetails.aspx?Language=E&billId=8532485.

Commissioner of the Correctional Service of Canada. "Security Classification and Penitentiary Placement: Commissioner's Directive 705-7 (2014-11-24). http://www.csc-scc.gc.ca/acts-and-regulations/705-7-cd-eng.shtml.

Controlled Drugs and Substances Act, SC 1996, c 19.

Correctional Institution Regulation, Alta Reg 205/2001.

Corrections Act, RSA 2000, c C-29.

Corrections and Conditional Release Act, SC 1992, c 20.

Criminal Code, RSC, 1985, c C-46.

Indian Act, RSC 1985, c I-5.

Ottawa. House of Commons. *Subcommittee on Solicitation Laws of the Standing Committee on Justice, Human Rights, Public Safety and Emergency Preparedness*, 38th Parl. 1st sess., No. 19 (31 March 2005). http://www.parl.gc.ca/HousePublications/Publication.aspx?DocId=1723237&Language=E&Mode=1&Parl=38&Ses=1#Int-1193178.

Parliament of Canada. Law and Government Division. *Legislative Summary:* Bill C-9: An Act to amend the Criminal Code (conditional sentence of imprisonment) by R MacKay (12 May 2006; revised 27 September 2007). https://lop.parl.ca/About/Parliament/LegislativeSummaries/bills_ls.asp?Language=E&ls= C9&Parl=39&Ses=1&source=library_prb.

CASES

Daniels v. Canada (Indian Affairs and Northern Development), 2016 SCC 12.

Descheneaux c Canada (Procureur Général), 2015 QCCS 3555.

First Nations Child and Family Caring Society of Canada et al. v. Attorney General of Canada (for the Minister of Indian and Northern Affairs Canada), 2016 CHRT 2.

R. v. Abraham, 2012 MBPC 77.

R. v. Aisaican, 2015 SKPC 11.

R. v. Allan, 2008 CanLII 35699 (ON SC).

R. v. Andrews, 2012 BCPC 486.

R. v. AQ, 2015 SKPC 51.

R. v. Arcand, 2010 ABCA 363.

R. v. Arcand, 2014 SKPC 12.

R. v. Armstrong, 2006 ABPC 5.

R. v. Asp (R. v. CMA), 2005 YKSC 58.

R. v. Audy, 2010 MBPC 55.

R. v. Batisse, 2008 CarswellOnt 8590 (Ont Sup Ct Jus) (WLeC).

R. v. Beaulieu, Beaulieu, Chief Zebrasky, 2007 MBPC 9.

R. v. Berner, 2010 BCPC 305.

R. v. Bird, 2008 ABQB 327.

R. v. Bisson, Kohl, and Hill, 2004 CanLII 12844 (ON SC).

R. v. Bittern, 2014 MBPC 51.

R. v. BKW, 2008 BCPC 418.

R. v. Bluebell, 2011 SKQB 203.

R. v. Borecky, 2012 BCSC 1338.

R. v. Bouchard, 2012 ONCJ 425.

R. v. Bourke, 2013 NWTTC 7.

R. v. Braun, 2006 BCPC 590.

R. v. Brertton, 2013 BCSC 1029.

R. v. Brooks, 2008 NSPC 58.

R. v. Burke, 2004 BCSC 1130.

R. v. Camara, 2012 ONCJ 232.

R. v. Capistrano, 2001 MBQB 60.

R. v. Carter, 2014 SKPC 150.

R. v. Carter, 2015 CarswellOnt 15573 (Ont Ct Jus) (WLeC).

R. v. CGO, 2011 BCPC 145.

R. v. Chamakese, 2014 SKQB 44.

R. v. Char, 2007 BCCA 346.

R. v. Char, 2007 CarswellBC 1489 (BC PC) (WLeC).

R. v. Charles, 2013 SKQB 139.

R. v. Chartier, 2015 MBPC 50.

R. v. Chouinard, 2005 CarswellOnt 10610 (Ont Sup Ct Jus) (WLeC).

R. v. Cleary, 2002 NWTSC 30.

R. v. Collins, 2009 CarswellOnt 9678 (Ont Sup Ct Jus) (WLeC).

R. v. Connors, 2010 NSPC 63.

R. v. Coombs, 2004 ABQB 621.

R. v. CT, 2014 BCPC 42.

R. v. Curran, 2001 ABPC 34.

R. v. Daybutch, 2015 ONCJ 302.

R. v. Daybutch, 2016 ONCJ 595.

R. v. Dennill, 2010 NWTSC 98.

R. v. Dennis, 2014 BCSC 692.

R. v. DEW, 2003 BCPC 488.

R. v. Diamond, 2006 QCCQ 2252.

R. v. Dick, 2002 BCPC 650.

R. v. Dickson, 2013 YKTC 27.

R. v. Dillon, 2004 NWTSC 39.

R. v. Elias, 2001 YKTC 501.

R. v. Elias, 2009 YKTC 59.

R. v. Elliott, 2013 BCPC 270.

R. v. ET, 2012 SKQB 169.

R. v. Evaloardjuk, 1999 CanLII 1156 (NU CJ).

R. v. Fineday, 2007 SKPC 2.

R. v. First Charger, 2013 ABPC 193.

R. v. Firth, 2012 YKTC 116.

R. v. Fisher, 2004 CanLII 10497 (ON SC).

R. v. Flett, 2012 MBQB 279.

R. v. Flett, 2013 MBQB 124.

R. v. Florence, 2013 BCSC 194.

R. v. Florence, 2015 BCCA 414.

R. v. Fox, 2015 ABPC 64.

R. v. Foy, 2002 CarswellOnt 6124 (Ont Sup Ct Jus) (WLeC).

R. v. Galloway, 2004 SKQB 130.

R. v. Gambler, 2012 SKPC 60.

R. v. George, 2012 ONCJ 756.

R. v. Gilpin, 2002 BCSC 1876.

R. v. Gladue, [1999] 1 SCR 688.

R. v. Good, 2010 YKTC 96.

R. v. Good, 2012 YKCA 2.

R. v. Gregoire, 2009 NLTD 21.

R. v. Guimond, 2010 MBPC 33.

R. v. H, 2014 BCSC 600.

R. v. Hachey and Selena Wiley, 2008 NBQB 52.

R. v. Hanley, 2014 BCSC 1373.

R. v. Hansen, 2014 BCSC 625.

R. v. Happyjack, 2006 QCCQ 8276.

R. v. Harry, 2013 MBQB 237.

R. v. Heavenfire, 2006 ABPC 228.

R. v. Hill, 2011 CarswellOnt 15782, 2011 ONCJ 859.

R. v. Icebound, 2006 QCCQ 2281.

R. v. Ipeelee, 2012 SCC 13.

R. v. Isaac, 2009 SKPC 111.

R. v. Jack, 2001 YKSC 55.

R. v. Jack, Joyce Smith, and Nenette Smith, 2008 BCPC 332.

R. v. Jankovic, 2004 ABPC 162.

R. v. John, 2004 SKCA 13.

R. v. Johnson, 2011 YKTC 11.

R. v. Johnson, 2013 YKSC 126.

R. v. Kahypeasewat (R. v. VK), 2006 SKPC 79.

R. v. Kanayok, 2014 NWTSC 75.

R. v. Keeping, 2012 CanLII 17398 (NL SCTD), 2012 CarswellNfld 130.

R. v. Kendi, 2010 NWTTC 8.

R. v. Kennedy, 2012 MBPC 60.

R. v. Key, 2014 SKPC 122.

R. v. Killiktee, 2011 ONSC 5910.

R. v. Killiktee, 2013 ONCA 332.

R. v. Knockwood, 2012 ONSC 2238.

R. v. Laliberte, 2000 SKCA 27.

R. v. Lilley, 2004 YKTC 38.

R. v. Link, 2012 MBPC 25.

R. v. Littlecrow, 2011 SKQB 393.

R. v. LLC, 2012 ABPC 103.

R. v. LML, 2012 ABPC 84.

R. v. MAB, 2014 ABPC 293.

R. v. Machiskinic, 2004 SKQB 358.

R. v. Martin, Evans & Laviolette, 2004 NWTSC 15.

R. v. Masakayash, 2015 ONCJ 655.

R. v. Mattson, 2014 ABCA 178.

R. v. M(CA), [1996] 1 SCR 500.

R. v. Quilt, 2014 BCSC 1060.

R. v. RCL, 2012 BCPC 53.

R. v. Redhead, 2009 MBQB 314.

R. v. Redies, 2009 YKTC 85.

R. v. RK, 2001 CanLII 26261 (MB PC).

R. v. Rodgers, 2012 SKQB 80.

R. v. Rodrigue, 2015 YKTC 5.

R. v. Ross, 2015 SKQB 150.

R. v. RNS, [2000] 1 SCR 149, 2000 SCC 7.

R. v. Sack, 2014 NSPC 107.

R. v. Saganash, 2006 QCCQ 2282.

R. v. Samson, 2014 YKTC 33.

R. v. Samson, 2015 YKCA 7.

R. v. Sandy, 2013 BCSC 2388.

R. v. Sans, 2004 NBQB 386.

R. v. Saskatchewan, 2015 ABPC 252.

R. v. Sayers and Elanik, 2003 NWTSC 69.

R. v. Schinkel, 2014 YKTC 42.

R. v. Schinkel, 2015 YKCA 2.

R. v. SCM, 2008 ABPC 214.

R. v. Serré, 2013 ONSC 1732.

R. v. Shecapio, 2006 QCCQ 13164.

R. v. Shenfield, 2008 ABPC 47.

R. v. Shoenthal, 2006 SKQB 177.

R. v. Shore, 2002 SKPC 42.

R. v. S(IMD), 2000 YTSC 19.

R. v. Simms, 2013 YKTC 60.

R. v. Sinclair, 2014 MBPC 13.

R. v. SLN, 2010 BCSC 405.

R. v. Small Eyes and Hunt, 2008 ABPC 300.

R. v. SMC, 2014 BCPC 144.

R. v. Smith, 2004 YKTC 14.

R. v. Smith, 2012 BCPC 440.

R. v. Smith, 2013 BCCA 173.

R. v. Smith, 2013 BCCA 192.

R. v. Sowden, 2013 CarswellOnt 18652; 2013 ONCJ 746.

R. v. Spence, 2014 SKQB 171.

R. v. Spencer, 2013 SKQB 183.

R. v. Stevens, 2009 NSPC 46.

R. v. Stimson, 2010 CarswellAlta 2644 (ABPC) (WLeC).

R. v. Stonechild, 2009 SKPC 122.

R. v. Summers, 2014 SCC 26.

R. v. Swan, 2004 CanLII 29564 (MB PC).

R. v. TAP, 2013 ONSC 797.

R. v. TAP, 2014 ONCA 141.

R. v. Tapaquon, 2009 SKQB 142.

R. v. Tippeneskum, 2011 ONCJ 219.

R. v. Tizya, 2013 YKTC 104.

R. v. Toews, 2013 BCSC 2474.

R. v. Travers, 2001 CanLII 17782 (MB PC).

R. v. Ussak, 2013 NUCJ 9.

R. v. Vermette, 2001 MBCA.

R. v. Waskewitch (R. v. DLW), 2007 SKPC 151.

R. v. Wells, [2000] 1 SCR 207.

R. v. Whitford, 2005 BCSC 1110.

R. v. Whitford, 2008 BCSC 1378.

R. v. Woods (R. v. CIW), 2007 SKPC 54.

GOVERNMENTAL AND NON-GOVERNMENTAL REPORTS

Aboriginal Corrections Policy Unit. Public Safety Canada. *Marginalized: The Aboriginal Women's Experience in Federal Corrections,* by M. Wesley. Ottawa: Public Safety Canada, 2012. https://www.publicsafety.gc.ca/cnt/rsrcs/pblctns/mrgnlzd/mrgnlzd-eng.pdf.

The Aboriginal Healing Foundation. *Reclaiming Connections: Understanding Residential School Trauma Among Aboriginal People: A Resource Manual.* Ottawa: Aboriginal Healing Foundation, 2005. http://www.ahf.ca/downloads/healing-trauma-web-eng.pdf.

Blackstock, Cindy, et al. *Keeping the Promise: The Convention on the Rights of the Child and the Lived Experiences of First Nations Children and Youth.* Ottawa: First Nations Child and Family Caring Society of Canada, 2004.

Canada. Department of Justice. *What We Heard: Transforming Canada's Criminal Justice System: A Report on Provincial and Territorial Stakeholder Consultations: Criminal Justice System Review.* Ottawa: Minister of Justice and Attorney General of Canada, 2018. http://www.justice.gc.ca/eng/rp-pr/other-autre/tcjs-tsjp/WWH_EN.pdf.

————. The National Inquiry into Missing and Murdered Indigenous Women and Girls. *Interim Report: Our Women and Girls Are Sacred.* Ottawa: National Inquiry into Missing and Murdered Indigenous Women and Girls, 2017. http://www.mmiwg-ffada.ca/wp-content/uploads/2018/04/ni-mmiwg-interim-report-en.pdf.

————. Office of the Correctional Investigator [OCI]. *Annual Report of the Office of the Correctional Investigator 2009–2010.* Ottawa: The Correctional Investigator Canada, 2010. http://www.oci-bec.gc.ca/cnt/rpt/pdf/annrpt/annrpt20092010-eng.pdf.

————. Office of the Correctional Investigator [OCI]. *Annual Report of the Office of the Correctional Investigator 2010–2011.* Ottawa: The Correctional Investigator Canada, 2011. http://www.oci-bec.gc.ca/cnt/rpt/pdf/annrpt/annrpt20102011-eng.pdf.

————. Office of the Correctional Investigator [OCI]. *Annual Report of the Office of the Correctional Investigator 2013–2014.* Ottawa: The Correctional Investigator Canada, 2014. http://www.oci-bec.gc.ca/cnt/rpt/pdf/annrpt/annrpt20132014-eng.pdf.

————. Office of the Correctional Investigator [OCI]. *Annual Report of the Office of the Correctional Investigator 2014–2015.* Ottawa: The Correctional Investigator Canada, 2015. http://www.oci-bec.gc.ca/cnt/rpt/pdf/annrpt/annrpt20142015-eng.pdf.

————. Office of the Correctional Investigator [OCI]. *Annual Report of the Office of the Correctional Investigator 2015–2016.* Ottawa: The Correctional Investigator Canada, 2016. http://www.oci-bec.gc.ca/cnt/rpt/pdf/annrpt/annrpt20152016-eng.pdf.

————. Office of the Correctional Investigator [OCI]. *Annual Report of the Office of the Correctional Investigator 2016–2017.* Ottawa: The Correctional Investigator Canada, 2017. http://www.oci-bec.gc.ca/cnt/rpt/pdf/annrpt/annrpt20162017-eng.pdf.

————. Royal Canadian Mounted Police [RCMP]. *Missing and Murdered Aboriginal Women: A National Operational Overview.* Ottawa: Her Majesty the Queen in Right of Canada, RCMP, 2014.

————. Royal Canadian Mounted Police [RCMP]. *Missing and Murdered Aboriginal Women: 2015 Update to the National Operational Overview.* Ottawa: Her Majesty the Queen in Right of Canada, RCMP, 2015.

————. Royal Commission on Aboriginal Peoples [RCAP]. *Bridging the Cultural Divide: A Report on Aboriginal People and Criminal Justice in Canada.* Ottawa: Canada Communication Group Publishing, 1996.

————. Royal Commission on Aboriginal Peoples [RCAP]. *Report of the Royal Commission on Aboriginal Peoples.* Volume I: *Looking Forward, Looking Back.* Ottawa: Royal Commission on Aboriginal Peoples, 1996. http://www.collectionscanada.gc.ca/webarchives/20071115053257/www.ainc-inac.gc.ca/ch/rcap/sg/sgmm_e.html.

————. Special Committee on Violence Against Indigenous Women. *Invisible Women: A Call to Action: A Report on Missing and Murdered Indigenous Women in Canada.* (41st Parl, 2nd Sess, Chair: Stella Ambler). Ottawa: House of Commons, 2014. http://publications.gc.ca/collections/collection_2014/parl/xc2-411/XC2-411-2-1-1-eng.pdf.

————. Truth and Reconciliation Commission of Canada [TRC]. *Honouring the Truth, Reconciling for the Future: Summary of the Final Report of the Truth and Reconciliation Commission of Canada.* Winnipeg: Truth and Reconciliation Commission of Canada, 2015. http://www.trc.ca/websites/trcinstitution/File/2015/Findings/Exec_Summary_2015_05_31_web_o.pdf.

Canadian Association of Elizabeth Fry Societies [CAEFS]. *Submission of the Canadian Association of Elizabeth Fry Societies to the Canadian Human Rights Commission for the Special Report on the Discrimination on the Basis of Sex, Race and Disability Faced by Federally Sentenced Women.* Ottawa: CAEFS, 2003. http://www.caefs.ca/wp-content/uploads/2013/04/CAEFS-Submission-to-the-Canadian-Human-Rights-Commission-for-the-Special-Report-on-the-Discrimination-on-the-Basis-of-Sex-Race-and-Disability-Faced-by-Federally-Sentenced-Women.pdf.

————. *CAEFS' Oral Submission to the Canadian Human Rights Commission 2003 [Part 1].* http://www.caefs.ca/resources/issues-and-position-papers/human-rights/submissions-to-chrc/., and https://www.youtube.com/watch?v=LY-M8GBBXMw&feature=youtu.be.

Canadian Bar Association. National Criminal Justice Section. "Bill C-9—*Criminal Code* Amendments (Conditional Sentence of Imprisonment)." September 2006. https://www.cba.org/CMSPages/GetFile.aspx?guid=cbb3dcc4-fd9d-4368-9463- 0f660e9eaafc.

Commission of Inquiry into Certain Events at the Prison for Women in Kingston. *Report of the Commission of Inquiry into Certain Events at the Prison for Women in Kingston.* Commissioner: Arbour J. Ottawa: Public Works and Government Services Canada, 1996. http://www.justicebehindthewalls.net/resources/arbour_report/arbour_rpt.htm.

Corrections Branch. Ministry of the Solicitor General. *The Federal Female Offender: Report on a Preliminary Study.* Prepared by Margaret Shaw. Ottawa: Solicitor General Canada, 1991.

Dell, Colleen Anne, and Roger Boe. "Research Reports: An Examination of Aboriginal and Caucasian Women Offender Risk and Needs Factors." December 2000. http://www.csc-scc.gc.ca/research/092/r94_e.pdf.

Gobeil, Renée, and Meredith Robeson Barrett. "Research Report: Rates of Recidivism for Women.Offenders." September 2007. http://www.csc-scc.gc.ca/research/r192-eng.shtml.

Holloway, Rod. "Gladue Reports and the Legal Services Society: How to Get a Gladue Report." (2016). Copy on file with author.

Jackson, Michael, and Graham Stewart. "A Flawed Compass: A Human Rights
    Analysis of the Roadmap to Strengthening Public Safety." September 2009.
    http://www.justicebehindthewalls.net/news.asp?nid=78.

Legal Services Society of BC. *Gladue Submission Guide*. Prepared by Judy Clarke,
    Jennifer Hepburn, and Carol Herter. September 2017. https://www.lss.bc.ca/
    resources/pdfs/pubs/Gladue-Submission-Guide-eng.pdf.

Native Women's Association of Canada [NWAC]. "Arrest the Legacy: From
    Residential Schools to Prisons." 2012. http://www.nwac.ca/gendering-
    reconciliation.

———. "Culturally Relevant Gender Based Models of Reconciliation." March
    2010. https://nwac.ca/wp-content/uploads/2015/05/2010-NWAC-
    Culturally-Relevant-Gender-Based-Models-of-Reconciliation.pdf.

———. "What Their Stories Tell Us: Research Findings from the Sisters in Spirit
    Initiative." 2010. https://nwac.ca/wp-content/uploads/2015/07/2010-
    What-Their-Stories-Tell-Us-Research-Findings-SIS-Initiative.pdf.

Ontario. Office of the Chief Coroner for Ontario. *Inquest Touching the
    Death of Ashley Smith: Jury Verdict and Recommendations*. Coroner: Dr
    John Carlisle. Ontario: Queen's Printer for Ontario, 2013. http://www.
    caefs.ca/wp-content/uploads/2014/01/A.S.-Inquest-Jury-Verdict-and-
    Recommendations1.pdf.

Parkes, Debra, et al. *Gladue Handbook: A Resource for Justice System Participants
    in Manitoba*. September 2012. https://law.robsonhall.com/wp-content/
    uploads/2015/10/Gladue_Handbook_2012_Final-1.pdf.

Provincial Association of Transitional Houses and Services of Saskatchewan
    [PATHS]. *Restorative Justice: Is it Justice for Battered Women?: A Report
    on the Proceedings of a Forum to Explore Restorative Justice Issues Related to
    Violence Against Women*. Saskatoon: PATHS, 2000. http://pathssk.org/wp-
    content/uploads/2011/04/PATHS-Report-Restorative-Justice-Is-It-Justice-
    for-Battered-Women.pdf.

Public Inquiry into the Administration of Justice and Aboriginal People. *Report
    of the Aboriginal Justice Inquiry of Manitoba*. Commissioners: Justices Alvin
    C. Hamilton and C. Murray Sinclair. Winnipeg: Aboriginal Justice Inquiry,
    1991. http://www.ajic.mb.ca/volume.html.

Representative for Children and Youth for BC [RCYBC]. "Delegated Aboriginal
    Agencies: How Resourcing Affects Service Delivery." Prepared by Bernard
    Richard. Victoria: Office of the Representative for Children and Youth,
    2017. http://www.rcybc.ca/sites/default/files/documents/pdf/reports_
    publications/rcy-daa-2017.pdf.

Sapers, Howard. (Correctional Investigator of Canada) "A Preventable Death."
    20 June 2008. http://www.oci-bec.gc.ca/cnt/rpt/pdf/oth-aut/oth-
    aut20080620-eng.pdf.

Task Force on Federally Sentenced Women. "Creating Choices: The Report of the Task Force on Federally Sentenced Women." Correctional Service of Canada, April 1990. http://www.csc-scc.gc.ca/women/toce-eng.shtml.

United Nations Committee on the Elimination of Discrimination against Women. *Report of the Inquiry Concerning Canada of the Committee on the Elimination of Discrimination against Women under Article 8 of the Optional Protocol to the Convention on the Elimination of All Forms of Discrimination against Women.* New York: United Nations, 2015. https://digitallibrary.un.org/record/836103/files/CEDAW_C_OP.8_CAN_1-EN.pdf.

United Nations Office on Drugs and Crime [UNODC]. *Handbook on Prisoners with Special Needs.* Criminal Justice Handbook Series. Prepared by Tomris Atabay. New York: United Nations, 2009. https://www.unodc.org/pdf/criminal_justice/Handbook_on_Prisoners_with_Special_Nee ds.pdf.

———. *Handbook on Women and Imprisonment. Second Edition, with Reference to the United Nations Rules for the Treatment of Women Prisoners and Non-custodial Measures for Women Offenders (The Bangkok Rules).* Criminal Justice Handbook Series. Prepared by Tomris Atabay. New York: United Nations, 2014. https://www.unodc.org/documents/justice-and-prison-reform/women_and_imprisonment_-_2nd_edition.pdf.

OTHER GOVERNMENT SOURCES: STATISTICS

Canada Statistics Canada. *Adult Correctional Services in Canada 2008/2009.* Prepared by Donna Calverley. Fall 2010. http://www.statcan.gc.ca/pub/85-002- x/2010003/article/11353-eng.htm#a7.

———. Statistics Canada. *Adult Correctional Statistics in Canada, 2015/2016.* Prepared by by J. Reitano. Ottawa: Minister of Industry, 2017. http://www.statcan.gc.ca/pub/85-002-x/2017001/article/14700-eng.pdf.

———. Statistics Canada. *Criminal Victimization in Canada, 2014.* Prepared by by S. Perreault. Ottawa: Minister of Industry, 2015. http://www.statcan.gc.ca/pub/85-002-x/2015001/article/14241-eng.pdf.

———. Statistics Canada. *Criminal Victimization in the Territories.* Prepared by S. Perreault and T. Hotton Mahony. 26 January 2012. http://www.statcan.gc.ca/pub/85-002-x/2012001/article/11614-eng.pdf.

———. Statistics Canada. *The Incarceration of Aboriginal People in Adult Correctional Services.* Prepared by by S. Perreault. Ottawa: Minister of Industry, 2009. http://www.statcan.gc.ca/pub/85-002-x/2009003/article/10903-eng.pdf.

———. Statistics Canada. *Outcomes of Probation and Conditional Sentence Supervision: An Analysis of Newfoundland and Labrador, Nova Scotia, New Brunswick, Saskatchewan and Alberta, 2003/2004 to 2004/2005.* Prepared by S. Johnson. Ottawa: Minister of Industry, 2006. http://www.statcan.gc.ca/pub/85-002-x/85-002-x2006007-eng.pdf.

———. Statistics Canada. *Re-contact with the Saskatchewan Justice System.* Prepared by A. Brennan and A. Matarazzo. http://www.statcan.gc.ca/pub/85-002-x/2016001/article/14633-eng.htm.

———. Statistics Canada. *Returning to Correctional Services after Release: A Profile of Aboriginal and Non-Aboriginal Adults Involved in Saskatchewan Corrections from 1999/00 to 2003/04.* Prepared by S. Johnson. Ottawa: Minister of Industry, 2005. http://www.statcan.gc.ca/pub/85-002-x/85-002-x2005002-eng.pdf.

———. Statistics Canada. *Victimization and Offending Among the Aboriginal Population in Canada.* Prepared by J.-A. Brzozowski, A. Taylor-Butts, and S. Johnson. Ottawa: Minister of Industry, 2006. http://www.statcan.gc.ca/pub/85-002-x/85-002-x2006003-eng.pdf.

———. Statistics Canada. *Victimization of Aboriginal People in Canada, 2014.* Prepared by J. Boyce. Ottawa: Minister of Industry, 2016. http://www.statcan.gc.ca/pub/85-002-x/2016001/article/14631-eng.pdf.

———. Statistics Canada. *Violent Victimization of Aboriginal Women in the Canadian Provinces, 2009.* Prepared by S. Brennan. Ottawa: Minister of Industry, 2011. http://www.statcan.gc.ca/pub/85-002-x/2011001/article/11439-eng.pdf.

Statistics Canada. *Aboriginal Peoples in Canada: Key Results from the 2016 Census. The Daily,* 25 October 2017. http://www.statcan.gc.ca/daily-quotidien/171025/dq171025a-eng.pdf.

———. *Aboriginal Statistics at a Glance,* 2nd ed. Ottawa: Minister of Industry, 2015. http://www.statcan.gc.ca/pub/89-645-x/89-645- x2015001-eng.pdf.

———. Centre for Justice Statistics. *Adult Correctional Statistics in Canada, 2010/2011.* Prepared by M. Dauvergne. Ottawa: Minister of Industry, 2012. http://www.statcan.gc.ca/pub/85-002-x/2012001/article/11715-eng.pdf.

———. Canadian Centre for Justice Statistics. *Criminal Justice Indicators: 2005.* Ottawa: Minister of Industry, 2005. http://www.statcan.gc.ca/pub/85-227-x/85-227-x2002000-eng.pdf.

———. *Women in Canada: A Gender-based Statistical Report: First Nations, Métis, and Inuit Women.* Prepared by P. Arriagada. Ottawa: Minister of Industry, 2016. http://www.statcan.gc.ca/pub/89-503-x/2015001/article/14313-eng.pdf.

———. Canadian Centre for Justice Statistics. *Victimization and Offending in Canada's Territories.* Prepared by S. de Léséleuc and J.-A. Brzozowski. Ottawa: Minister of Industry, 2006. http://www.statcan.gc.ca/pub/85f0033m/85f0033m2006011-eng.pdf.

———. *Women in Canada: A Gender-Based Statistical Report: Women and the Criminal Justice System.* Prepared by T. Hotton Mahony. Ottawa: Minister of Industry, 2011. http://www.statcan.gc.ca/pub/89-503-x/2010001/article/11416-eng.pdf.

———. *Women in Canada. A Gender-based Statistical Report: Women and the Criminal Justice System.* 7th ed. Prepared by T. Hotton Mahony, J. Jacob, and H. Hobson. Ottawa: Minister of Industry, 2017. http://www.statcan.gc.ca/pub/89- 503-x/2015001/article/14785-eng.pdf.

Secondary Sources

Adjin-Tettey, Elizabeth. "Sentencing Aboriginal Offenders: Balancing Offenders' Needs, the Interests of Victims and Society, and the Decolonization of Aboriginal Peoples." *Canadian Journal of Women and the Law* 19, no. 1 (2007): 179–216.

Alexander, Michelle. *The New Jim Crow: Mass Incarceration in the Age of Colorblindness,* Rev. ed. New York: The New Press, 2012.

Andersen, Chris. "Governing Aboriginal Justice in Canada: Constructing Responsible Individuals and Communities through 'Tradition.'" *Crime, Law and Social Change* 31 (1999): 303–26.

Balfour, Gillian. "Do Law Reforms Matter? Exploring the Victimization-Criminalization Continuum in the Sentencing of Aboriginal Women in Canada." *International Review of Victimology* 19, no. 1 (2012): 85–102.

———. "Falling Between the Cracks of Retributive and Restorative Justice: The Victimization and Punishment of Aboriginal Women." *Feminist Criminology* 3, no. 2 (2008): 101–20.

———. "Re-Imagining a Feminist Criminology." *Canadian Journal of Criminology and Criminal Justice* 48, no. 5 (2006): 735–52.

Bayes, Shawn. "Harper's Crime Laws." *Canadian Dimension* 41, no. 2 (March 2007): 22–24.

BC Corrections. "Reducing Reoffending." http://www2.gov.bc.ca/gov/content/justice/criminal-justice/corrections/reducing-reoffending.

———. "Reducing Reoffending: Cognitive Behavioural Programs." http://www2.gov.bc.ca/gov/content/justice/criminal-justice/corrections/reducing-reoffending/cognitive-behavioural.

Belknap, Joanne. "'Offending Women': A Double Entendre." *The Journal of Criminal Law and Criminology* 100, no. 3 (2010): 1061–97.

Bernier, Jennifer. "Breaking Down the Walls: Building a Case for Community-Based Alternatives to Incarceration that Better Meet the Needs of Criminalized Women." *Network Magazine* 13, no. 1 (Fall/Winter 2010–11). http://www.cwhn.ca/en/node/42825.

Blaze Baum, Kathryn, and Tavia Grant. "Missing and Murdered Indigenous Women Toll 'Way Bigger' than 1,200: Minister." *Globe and Mail,* 15 February 2016. http://www.theglobeandmail.com/news/politics/toll-of-missing-and-murdered- indigenous-women-way-bigger-than-1200-minister/article28761649/.

Botsford Fraser, Marian. "Life on the Instalment Plan: Is Canada's Penal System for Women Making or Breaking Renee Acoby?" *Walrus,* March 2010. http://thewalrus.ca/life-on-the-instalment-plan/.

Bouchard, Françoise. "Mental Health (A Health Care Needs Assessment of Federal Inmates in Canada)." *Canadian Journal of Public Health* 95, Suppl. 1 (2004): S1-S63.

Bracken, Denis C., Lawrence Deane, and Larry Morrissette. "Desistance and Social Marginalization: The Case of Canadian Aboriginal Offenders." *Theoretical Criminology* 13, no. 1 (2009): 61–78.

Brave Heart, Maria Yellow Horse. "The Historical Trauma Response Among Natives and Its Relationship with Substance Abuse: A Lakota Illustration." *Journal of Psychoactive Drugs* 35, no. 1 (2003): 7–13.

Brave Heart, Maria Yellow Horse, and Lemyra M. DeBruyn. "The American Indian Holocaust: Healing Historical Unresolved Grief." *American Indian and Alaska Native Mental Health Research* 8, no. 2 (1998): 60–82.

Britton, Dana M. "Feminism in Criminology: Engendering the Outlaw." *Annals of the American Academy of Political and Social Sciences* 571 (2000): 57–76.

Brown, Marilyn. "Gender, Ethnicity, and Offending over the Life Course: Women's Pathways to Prison in the Aloha State." *Critical Criminology* 14, no. 2 (2006): 137–58.

Brownridge, Douglas A. "Understanding the Elevated Risk of Partner Violence against Aboriginal Women: A Comparison of Two Nationally Representative Surveys of Canada." *Journal of Family Violence* 23, no. 5 (2008): 353–67.

Burgess-Proctor, Amanda. "Intersections of Race, Class, Gender, and Crime: Future Directions for Feminist Criminology." *Feminist Criminology* 1, no. 1 (2006): 27–47.

Cameron, Angela. "Stopping the Violence: Canadian Feminist Debates on Restorative Justice and Intimate Violence." *Theoretical Criminology* 10, no. 1 (2006): 49–67.

Campbell, Allison. "Federally Sentenced Women and Security Classification." July 2006. http://citeseerx.ist.psu.edu/viewdoc/download?doi=10.1.1.541.4676&rep=rep1&type=pdf.

Campbell, Larry, Neil Boyd, and Lori Culbert. *A Thousand Dreams: Vancouver's Downtown Eastside and the Fight for its Future.* Vancouver: Greystone Books, 2009.

Canadian Association of Elizabeth Fry Societies [CAEFS] and Native Women's Association of Canada [NWAC]. "Women and the Canadian Legal System: Examining Situations of Hyper-Responsibility." In *First Voices: An Aboriginal Women's Reader*, edited by Patricia A. Monture and Patricia D. McGuire, 382–99. Toronto: Inanna, 2009.

———. "Women and the Canadian Legal System: Examining Situations of Hyper-Responsibility: Discussion Paper by the Canadian Association of

Elizabeth Fry Societies (CAEFS) and the Native Women's Association of Canada (NWAC)." *Canadian Woman Studies* 26, nos. 3, 4 (Winter/Spring 2008): 94–104.

Canadian Association of Elizabeth Fry Societies [CAEFS]. "Justice for Battered Women— Denied, Delayed . . . Diminished: Jails Are Not the Shelters Battered Women Need." http://www.caefs.ca/wp-content/uploads/2013/04/Justice-for-Battered-Women.pdf.

Carlen, Pat. *Sledgehammer: Women's Imprisonment at the Millennium.* London: Macmillan Press Ltd., 1998.

CBC. "8th Fire: Indigenous in the City." CBC *Doc Zone, 8th Fire.* http://www.cbc.ca/8thfire/2011/11/indigenious-in-the-city.html.

Chan, Wendy, and Dorothy Chunn. *Racialization, Crime, and Criminal Justice in Canada.* Toronto: University of Toronto Press, 2014.

Chesney-Lind, Meda. "Patriarchy, Crime, and Justice: Feminist Criminology in an Era of Backlash." *Feminist Criminology* 1, no. 1 (2006): 6–26.

Chewter, Cynthia. "Book Review of *In Conflict with the Law: Women and the Canadian Justice System.*" *Canadian Woman Studies* 19, nos. 1, 2 (Spring/Summer 1999): 215–16.

Chrisjohn, Roland, Sherri Young, and Michael Maraun. *The Circle Game: Shadows and Substance in the Indian Residential School Experience in Canada.* Syilx Territory on the Penticton Indian Reserve, BC: Theytus Books, 2006.

Comack, Elizabeth. "Introduction." In *Criminalizing Women: Gender and (In) Justice in Neo-Liberal Times,* edited by Gillian Balfour and Elizabeth Comack, 58–78. Winnipeg: Fernwood Publishing, 2006.

———. "The Prisoning of Women: Meeting Women's Needs." In *An Ideal Prison? Critical Essays on Women's Imprisonment in Canada,* edited by Kelly Hannah-Moffat and Margaret Shaw, 117–127. Halifax: Fernwood Publishing, 2000.

———. "New Possibilities for a Feminism 'in' Criminology? From Dualism to Diversity." *Canadian Journal of Criminology* 41, no. 2 (1999): 161–71.

———. *Women in Trouble: Connecting Women's Law Violations to Their Histories of Abuse.* Halifax: Fernwood Publishing, 1996.

Conaghan, Joanne. "Intersectionality and the Feminist Project in Law." In *Intersectionality and Beyond: Law, Power and the Politics of Location,* edited by Emily Grabham et al., 21–48. New York: Routledge-Cavendish, 2009.

Constable, Marianne. "The Silence of the Law: Justice in Cover's 'Field of Pain and Death.'" In *Law, Violence, and the Possibility of Justice,* edited by Austin Sarat, 85–100. Princeton: Princeton University Press, 2001.

Cover, Robert. "Violence and the Word." *Yale Law Journal* 95, no. 8 (1986): 1601–29.

Crenshaw, Kimberlé. "A Tale of Two Movements: Intersectionality, Gender, and the Prison Industrial Complex." Lecture delivered at the UCSB

Multicultural Centre Theatre, 18 May 2006., Regents of the University of California. http://www.youtube.com/watch?v=d1v9E83yTNA.

Cull, Randi. "Aboriginal Mothering Under the State's Gaze." In *"Until Our Hearts Are On The Ground": Aboriginal Mothering, Oppression, Resistance and Rebirth*, edited by D. Memee Lavell-Harvard and Jeannette Corbiere Lavell, 141–56. Toronto: Demeter Press, 2006.

Cunliffe, Emma, and Angela Cameron. "Writing the Circle: Judicially Convened Sentencing Circles and the Textual Organization of Criminal Justice." *Canadian Journal of Women and the Law* 19, no. 1 (2007): 1–36.

Darnell, Regna. "Nomadic Legacies and Contemporary Decision-Making Strategies between Reserve and City." In *Aboriginal Peoples in Canadian Cities: Transformations and Continuities*, edited by Heather A. Howard and Craig Proulx, 39–51. Waterloo: Wilfrid Laurier University Press, 2011.

Davis, Angela. *Abolition Democracy: Beyond Empire, Prisons, and Torture: Interviews with Angela Y. Davis.* Toronto: Seven Stories Press, 2005.

———. *Are Prisons Obsolete?* New York: Seven Stories Press, 2003.

DeHart, Dana D. "Pathways to Prison: Impact of Victimization in the Lives of Incarcerated Women." *Violence Against Women* 14, no. 12 (2008): 1362–81.

Dej, Erin. "What Once Was Sick Is Now Bad: The Shift from Victim to Deviant Identity for Those Diagnosed with Fetal Alcohol Spectrum Disorder." *Canadian Journal of Sociology* 36, no. 2 (2011): 137–60.

Dell, Colleen Anne, Catherine J. Fillmore, and Jennifer M. Kilty. "Looking Back 10 Years after the Arbour Inquiry: Ideology, Policy, Practice, and the Federal Female Prisoner." *The Prison Journal* 89, no. 3 (2009): 286–308.

Denham, Aaron R. "Rethinking Historical Trauma: Narratives of Resilience." *Transcultural Psychiatry* 45, no. 3 (2008): 391–414.

Derrick, Justice Anne S. "Address." Remarks for her swearing-in ceremony, delivered at the Nova Scotia Court of Appeal, Halifax, 15 September 2017. Unpublished.

Derrida, Jacques. "Force De Loi: Le Fondement Mystique De L'Autorité" [Force of Law: The Mystical Foundation of Authority]. Translated by Mary Quaintance. *Cardozo Law Review* 11, nos. 5/6 (1990): 920–1046.

Dirks, Danielle. "Sexual Revictimization and Retraumatization of Women in Prison." *Women's Studies Quarterly* 32, nos. 3/4 (2004): 102–15.

Donovan, Sadie. "Challenges to and Successes in Urban Aboriginal Education in Canada: A Case Study of Wiingashk Secondary School." In *Aboriginal Peoples in Canadian Cities: Transformations and Continuities*, edited by Heather A. Howard and Craig Proulx, 123–42. Waterloo: Wilfrid Laurier University Press, 2011.

Doob, Anthony N., and Cheryl Marie Webster. "Countering Punitiveness: Understanding Stability in Canada's Imprisonment Rate." *Law and Society Review* 40, no. 2 (2006): 325–67.

Duff, R. Antony, and David Garland. "Introduction: Thinking about Punishment." In *A Reader on Punishment*, edited by Antony Duff and David Garland, 1–43. Oxford: Oxford University Press, 1994.

Eliason, Michele J., Janette Y. Taylor, and Rachel Williams. "Physical Health of Women in Prison; Relationship to Oppression." *Journal of Correctional Health Care* 10, no. 2 (2004): 175–203.

Eljdupovic, Gordana, Terry Mitchell, Lori Curtis, Rebecca Jaremko Bromwich, Alison Granger-Brown, Courtney Arseneau, and Brooke Fry. "Incarcerating Aboriginal Mothers: A Cost Too Great." In *Incarcerated Mothers: Oppression and Resistance*, edited by Gordana Eljudupovic and Rebecca Jaremko Bromwich, 43–58. Bradford, ON: Demeter Press, 2013.

Faith, Karlene, and Anne Near, eds. *13 Women: Parables from Prison*. Vancouver: Douglas and McIntyre, 2006.

Faith, Karlene. *Unruly Women: The Politics of Confinement and Resistance*. Vancouver: Press Gang Publishers, 1993.

Ferraro, Kathleen J., and Angela M. Moe. "Mothering, Crime, and Incarceration." *Journal of Contemporary Ethnography* 32, no. 1 (2003): 9–40.

Findlay, Stephanie. "Trouble in the Big House: How Mandatory Minimum Sentencing Could Make It Worse for Women in Prison." *Maclean's*, 17 January 2011. http://www2.macleans.ca/2011/01/17/trouble-in-the-big-house/.

Flynn, Lindy-Lou. "Plains Indian Ways to Inter-tribal Cultural Healing in Vancouver." In *Aboriginal Peoples in Canadian Cities: Transformations and Continuities*, edited by Heather A. Howard and Craig Proulx, 227–44. Waterloo: Wilfrid Laurier University Press, 2011.

Galloway, Gloria. "Senate Backs Down from Standoff over Indian Act Amendment." *Globe and Mail*, 13 November 2017. https://www.theglobeandmail.com/news/politics/senate-backs-down-from-standoff-over-indian-act-amendment/article36901420/.

Glass, Nancy, et al. "Non-Fatal Strangulation Is an Important Risk Factor for Homicide of Women." *The Journal of Emergency Medicine* 35, no. 3 (2008): 329–35.

Golder, Ben, and Peter Fitzpatrick. *Foucault's Law*. New York: Routledge, 2009.

Gone, Joseph P. "Reconsidering American Indian Historical Trauma: Lessons from an Early Gros Ventre War Narrative." *Transcultural Psychiatry* 51, no. 3 (2014): 387–406.

Government of Canada. "Government of Canada Launches Inquiry into Missing and Murdered Indigenous Women and Girls." News release, 8 December 2015. https://www.canada.ca/en/indigenous-northern-affairs/news/2015/12/government-of-canada-launches-inquiry-into-missing-and-murdered-indigenous-women-and-girls.html.

Graydon, Charalee F. "Habilitation: Sentencing of Female Offenders." *Canadian Journal of Law and Jurisprudence* 5, no. 1 (1992): 121–41.

Green, Joyce. "Balancing Strategies: Aboriginal Women and Constitutional Rights in Canada." In *Making Space for Indigenous Feminism*, edited by Joyce Audry Green, 140–159. Black Point, NS: Fernwood Publishing, 2007.

———. "Taking Account of Aboriginal Feminism." In *Making Space for Indigenous Feminism*, edited by Joyce Audry Green, 20–32. Black Point, NS: Fernwood Publishing, 2007.

Haag, Andrew M. "Ethical Dilemmas Faced by Correctional Psychologists in Canada." *Criminal Justice and Behavior* 33, no. 1 (2006): 93–109.

Hannah-Moffat, Kelly. "Feminine Fortresses: Woman-Centered Prisons?" *The Prison Journal* 75, no. 2 (1995): 135–64.

———. "Gendering Risk at What Cost: Negotiations of Gender and Risk in Canadian Women's Prisons." *Feminism and Psychology* 14, no. 2 (2004): 243–49.

———. "Re-Forming the Prison—Rethinking our Ideals." In *An Ideal Prison? Critical Essays on Women's Imprisonment in Canada*, edited by Kelly Hannah-Moffat and Margaret Shaw, 30–40. Halifax: Fernwood Publishing, 2000.

———. "Moral Agent or Actuarial Subject: Risk and Canadian Women's Imprisonment." *Theoretical Criminology* 3, no. 1 (1999): 71–94.

Hannah-Moffat, Kelly, and Paula Maurutto. "Re-contextualizing Pre-sentence Reports: Risk and Race." *Punishment and Society* 12, no. 3 (2010): 262–86.

Hartnagel, Timothy F. "The Rhetoric of Youth Justice in Canada." *Criminal Justice: The International Journal of Policy and Practice* 4, no. 4 (2004): 355–74.

Howard, Heather A. "The Friendship Centre: Native People and the Organization of Community in Cities." In *Aboriginal Peoples in Canadian Cities: Transformations and Continuities*, edited by Heather A. Howard and Craig Proulx, 87–107. Waterloo: Wilfrid Laurier University Press, 2011.

Howard, Heather A., and Craig Proulx. "Transformations and Continuities: An Introduction." In *Aboriginal Peoples in Canadian Cities: Transformations and Continuities*, edited by Heather A. Howard and Craig Proulx, 1–21. Waterloo: Wilfrid Laurier University Press, 2011.

Howard, Heather A., and Craig Proulx., eds. *Aboriginal Peoples in Canadian Cities: Transformations and Continuities.* Waterloo: Wilfrid Laurier University Press, 2011.

Hunter, Anna. "The Violence that Indigenous Women Face." *Canadian Dimension* 39, no. 2 (March/April 2005): 34–35.

Ignass, Marianne. "'Why Is My People Sleeping?' First Nations Hip Hop between the Rez and the City." In *Aboriginal Peoples in Canadian Cities: Transformations and Continuities*, edited by Heather A. Howard and Craig Proulx, 203–26. Waterloo: Wilfrid Laurier University Press, 2011.

Jackson, Michael. *Justice Behind the Walls: Human Rights in Canadian Prisons.* Vancouver: Douglas and McIntyre, 2002.

Kilty, Jennifer M. "Under the Barred Umbrella: Is There Room for a Women-Centered Self- Injury Policy in Canadian Corrections?" *Criminology and Public Policy* 5, no. 1 (2006): 161–82.

Kirmayer, Laurence J., Gregory M. Brass, and Caroline L. Tait. "The Mental Health of Aboriginal Peoples: Transformations of Identity and Community." *The Canadian Journal of Psychiatry* 45, no. 7 (2000): 607–16.

Koons-Witt, Barbara A. "The Effect of Gender on the Decision to Incarcerate Before and After the Introduction of Sentencing Guidelines." *Criminology* 40, no. 2 (2002): 297–328.

Kuokkanen, Rauna. "Myths and Realities of Sami Women: A Post-Colonial Feminist Analysis for the Decolonization and Transformation of Sami Society." In *Making Space for Indigenous Feminism*, edited by Joyce Audry Green, 72–92. Black Point, NS: Fernwood Publishing, 2007.

LaRocque, Emma. "Métis and Feminist: Ethical Reflections on Feminism, Human Rights and Decolonization." In *Making Space for Indigenous Feminism*, edited by Joyce Audry Green, 53–71. Black Point, NS: Fernwood Publishing, 2007.

Linklater, Renée. *Decolonizing Trauma Work: Indigenous Stories and Strategies*. Halifax: Fernwood Publishing, 2014.

Macdonald, Nancy, and Meagan Campbell. "Lost and Broken." *Maclean's*, 13 September 2017. http://www.macleans.ca/lost-and-broken/.

Manson, Allan, et al. *Sentencing and Penal Policy in Canada: Cases, Materials, and Commentary*. 2nd ed. Toronto: Emond Montgomery Publications, 2008.

Marchetti, Elena. "The Deep Colonizing Practices of the Australian Royal Commission into Aboriginal Deaths in Custody." *Journal of Law and Society* 33, no. 3 (2006): 451–74.

———. "Intersectional Race and Gender Analyses: Why Legal Processes Just Don't Get It." *Social and Legal Studies* 17, no. 2 (2008): 155–74.

Martel, Joane, and Renée Brassard. "Painting the Prison 'Red': Constructing and Experiencing Aboriginal Identities in Prison." *British Journal of Social Work* 38, no. 2 (2008): 340–61.

Maurutto, Paula, and Kelly Hannah-Moffat. "Assembling Risk and the Restructuring of Penal Control." *British Journal of Criminology* 46 (2006): 438–54.

Maynard, Robyn. "Criminal (in)justice: State Violence and the Criminalization of Indigenous Women in Canada. An Interview with Gillian Balfour." *Briar Patch* 40, no. 2 (1 March 2011). http://briarpatchmagazine.com/articles/view/criminal-injustice.

McFatter, Robert M. "Sentencing Strategies and Justice: Effects of Punishment Philosophy on Sentencing Decisions." *Journal of Personality and Social Psychology* 36, no. 12 (1978): 1490–1500.

Milward, David, and Debra Parkes. "Colonialism, Systemic Discrimination, and the Crisis of Indigenous Over-Incarceration: Challenges of Reforming the Sentencing Process." In *Locating Law: Race, Class, Gender, Sexuality, Connections*, edited by Elizabeth Comack, 116–142. 3rd ed. Halifax: Fernwood Publishing, 2014.

Mirchandani, Kiran, and Wendy Chan. "From Race and Crime to Racialization and Criminalization." In *Crimes of Colour: Racialization and the Criminal Justice System in Canada*, edited by Wendy Chan and Kiran Mirchandani, 9–22. Toronto: Broadview Press, 2002.

Monture, Patricia A. "Confronting Power: Aboriginal Women and Justice Reform." *Canadian Woman Studies* 25, nos. 3, 4 (Summer 2006): 25–33.

Monture-Angus, Patricia. "The Lived Experience of Discrimination: Aboriginal Women Who Are Federally Sentenced." 2002. http://www.caefs.ca/ wp- content/uploads/2013/04/The-Lived-Experience-of-Discrimination-Aboriginal-Women-Who-are-Federally-Sentenced-The-Law-Duties-and-Rights.pdf.

———. "Aboriginal Women and Correctional Practice: Reflections on the Task Force on Federally Sentenced Women." In *An Ideal Prison? Critical Essays on Women's Imprisonment in Canada*, edited by Kelly Hannah-Moffat and Margaret Shaw, 52–60. Halifax: Fernwood Publishing, 2000.

———. "Women and Risk: Aboriginal Women, Colonialism, and Correctional Practice." *Canadian Woman Studies* 19, nos. 1, 2 (Spring/ Summer 1999): 24–29.

———. *Thunder in My Soul: A Mohawk Woman Speaks.* Halifax: Fernwood Publishing, 1995.

"More Prisons to be Expanded." CBC, 10 January 2011. http://www.cbc.ca/news/ politics/story/2011/01/10/tories-prison-infrastructure.html.

Muftic, Lisa R., Jeffrey A. Bouffard, and Leana Allen Bouffard. "An Exploratory Study of Women Arrested for Intimate Partner Violence: Violent Women or Violent Resistance?" *Journal of Interpersonal Violence* 22, no. 6 (2007): 753–74.

Murdocca, Carmela. *To Right Historical Wrongs: Race, Gender, and Sentencing in Canada.* Vancouver: University of British Columbia Press, 2013.

National Inquiry into Missing and Murdered Indigenous Women and Girls [MMIWG]. "Background." http://www.mmiwg-ffada.ca/en/about-us/background/.

Newhouse, David R. "Urban Life: Reflections of a Middle-Class Indian." In *Aboriginal Peoples in Canadian Cities: Transformations and Continuities*, edited by Heather A. Howard and Craig Proulx, 23–38. Waterloo: Wilfrid Laurier University Press, 2011.

Norwich, Marni. "Women Behind Bars." *The Straight,* 2 November 2006. http:// www.straight.com/article/women-behind-bars.

O'Neil, John. "Editorial: Aboriginal Health Governance." *Journal of Aboriginal Health* 1, no. 1 (2004): 4–5.

Paradies, Yin C. "Beyond Black and White: Essentialism, Hybridity and Indigeneity." *Journal of Sociology* 42, no. 4 (2006): 355–67.

Parkes, Debra, and Kim Pate. "Time for Accountability: Effective Oversight of Women's Prisons." *Canadian Journal of Criminology and Criminal Justice* 48, no. 2 (2006): 251–85.

Pate, Kim. "Interview: Kim Pate" by Hana Gartner. CBC's *The Fifth Estate*, 26 November 2010. http://www.cbc.ca/fifth/blog/interview-kim-pate.

———. "Advocacy, Activism and Social Change for Women in Prison." *Canadian Woman Studies* 25, nos. 3, 4 (Summer 2006): 81–84.

———. "Lecture on Mental Health and Sentencing." Lecture delivered to the Canadian Chapter of the International Association of Women Judges at the Judging Women: Aging, Mental Health and Culture conference held by the National Judicial Institute and the Faculty of Law, University of British Columbia at the Fairmont Pacific Rim Hotel, Vancouver, 11 May 2011.

Peternelj-Taylor, Cindy A. "Conceptualizing Nursing Research with Offenders: Another Look at Vulnerability." *International Journal of Law and Psychiatry* 28, no. 4 (2004): 348–59.

Player, Elaine. "The Reduction of Women's Imprisonment in England and Wales: Will the Reform of Short Prison Sentences Help?" *Punishment and Society* 7, no. 4 (2005): 419–39.

Poister Tusher, Chantal, and Sarah L. Cook. "Comparing Revictimization of Two Groups of Marginalized Women." *Journal of Interpersonal Violence* 25, no. 10 (2010): 1893–1911.

Pollack, Shoshana. "'You Can't Have It Both Ways': Punishment and Treatment of Imprisoned Women." *Journal of Progressive Human Services* 20, no. 2 (2009): 112–28.

———. "'I'm Just Not Good in Relationships': Victimization Discourses and the Gendered Regulation of Criminalized Women." *Feminist Criminology* 2, no. 2 (2007): 158–74.

———. "Taming the Shrew: Regulating Prisoners through Women-Centered Mental Health Programming." *Critical Criminology* 13, no. 1 (2005): 71–87.

Pollock, Joycelyn M., and Sareta M. Davis. "The Continuing Myth of the Violent Female Offender." *Criminal Justice Review* 30, no. 1 (2005): 5–29.

Poole, Nancy. "Integrating Trauma with Addiction Research and Treatment." In *Transforming Addiction: Gender, Trauma, Transdisciplinarity*, edited by Lorraine Greaves, Nancy Poole, and Ellexis Boyle, 36–49. New York: Routledge, 2015.

Presser, Lois. "The Narratives of Offenders." *Theoretical Criminology* 13, no. 2 (2009): 177–200.

Quigley, Tim. "Gladue Reports: Some Issues and Proposals." (2016). Unpublished, copy on file with author.

Raeder, Myrna S. "Domestic Violence in Federal Court: Abused Women as Victims, Survivors, and Offenders." *Federal Sentencing Reporter* 19, no. 2 (2006): 91–129.

Ralston, Benjamin, and Christine Goodwin. "*R v Drysdale*: A Gold Standard for the Implementation of *R v. Gladue.*" *Criminal Reports* 33, 7th (2017): 114–24.

Razack, Sherene H. "Gendered Racial Violence and Spacialized Justice: The Murder of Pamela George." In *Race, Space, and the Law: Unmapping a White Settler Society*, edited by Sherene H. Razack, 121–56. Toronto: Between the Lines, 2002.

———. *Looking White People in the Eye: Gender, Race, and Culture in Courtrooms and Classrooms.* Toronto: University of Toronto Press, 1998.

Roach, Kent. "Changing Punishment at the Turn of the Century: Restorative Justice on the Rise." *Canadian Journal of Criminology* 42, no. 3 (2000): 249–80.

Roberts, Julian V., and Thomas Gabor. "Living in the Shadow of Prison: Lessons from the Canadian Experience in Decarceration." *British Journal of Criminology* 44, no. 1 (2004): 92–112.

Ruby, Clayton C., Gerald J. Chan, and Nader R. Hasan. *Sentencing.* 8th ed. Markham: LexisNexis Canada, 2012.

Rumgay, Judith. "Scripts for Safer Survival: Pathways Out of Female Crime." *The Howard Journal of Criminal Justice* 43, no. 4 (2004): 405–19.

Rutherford, Kate. "Attawapiskat Declares State of Emergency over Spate of Suicide Attempts." CBC, 9 April 2016. http://www.cbc.ca/news/canada/sudbury/attawapiskat-suicide-first-nations-emergency-1.3528747.

Sapers, Howard. "Mental Health Challenges in Federal Corrections." Lecture delivered to the North Shore Schizophrenia Society at West Vancouver Memorial Library, 7 November 2011. https://www.youtube.com/watch?v=oBWmv07HRYU.

Scott, James T.D. "Reforming Saskatchewan's Biased Sentencing Regime." Updated version of paper delivered at Legal Aid Saskatchewan's Annual Conference, September 2014. Unpublished. Archived at http://www.spmlaw.ca/scdla/JimScott_sentencing_bias_2014.pdf.

Shantz, Laura, Jennifer M. Kilty, and Sylvie Frigon. "Echoes of Imprisonment: Women's Experiences of 'successful (Re)integration.'" *Canadian Journal of Law and Society* 24, no. 1 (2009): 85–106.

Shaw, Margaret. "Women, Violence and Disorder in Prisons." In *An Ideal Prison? Critical Essays on Women's Imprisonment in Canada*, edited by Kelly Hannah-Moffat and Margaret Shaw, 61–70. Halifax: Fernwood Publishing, 2000.

Sheehy, Elizabeth. *Defending Battered Women on Trial: Lessons from the Transcripts.* Vancouver: University of British Columbia Press, 2014.

———. "Defending Battered Women on Trial: 'Not a Battered Woman': Jamie Gladue." Lecture delivered at the Faculty of Law, University of British Columbia, Vancouver, 1 April 2011.

———. "Misogyny Is Deadly: Inequality Makes Women More Vulnerable to Being Killed." *Canadian Centre for Policy Alternatives Monitor* 17, no. 3 (2010): 18.

———. "Advancing Social Inclusion: The Implications for Criminal Law and Policy." *Canadian Journal of Criminology and Criminal Justice* 46, no. 1 (2004): 73–95.

Simon, Jonathan. "The Vicissitudes of Law's Violence." In *Law, Violence, and the Possibility of Justice,* edited by Austin Sarat, 17–48. Princeton: Princeton University Press, 2001.

Smith, Andrea. "Native American Feminism, Sovereignty and Social Change." In *Making Space for Indigenous Feminism,* edited by Joyce Audry Green, 93–107. Black Point, NS: Fernwood Publishing, 2007.

Smith, Andrea, and Luana Ross. "Introduction: Native Women and State Violence." *Social Justice* 31, no. 4 (2004): 1–7.

St. Denis, Verna. "Feminism Is for Everybody: Aboriginal Women, Feminism and Diversity." In *Making Space for Indigenous Feminism,* edited by Joyce Audry Green, 33–52. Black Point, NS: Fernwood Publishing, 2007.

Stastna, Kazi. "Shacks and Slop Pails: Infrastructure Crisis on Native Reserves." CBC, 26 November 2011. http://www.cbc.ca/news/canada/story/2011/11/24/f-first-nations-infrastructure.html.

Sugar, Fran, and Lana Fox. "Nistum Peyako Séht'wawin Iskwewak: Breaking Chains." *Canadian Journal of Women and the Law* 3, no. 2 (1989–90): 465–82.

Tasker, John Paul. "Confusion Reigns over Number of Missing, Murdered Indigenous Women." CBC, 16 February 2016. http://www.cbc.ca/news/politics/mmiw-4000-hajdu-1.3450237.

———. "Ottawa Announces $800M Settlement with Indigenous Survivors of Sixties Scoop." CBC, 5 October 2017. http://www.cbc.ca/news/politics/ottawa-settle-60s-scoop-survivors-1.4342462.

"Tories Announce $155.5M Prison Expansion." CBC, 6 October 2010. http://www.cbc.ca/news/politics/story/2010/10/06/toews-prison-construction.html.

Tuhiwai Smith, Linda. *Decolonizing Methodologies: Research and Indigenous Peoples.* London: Zed Books Ltd, 2008.

Turnbull, Sarah, and Kelly Hannah-Moffat. "Under These Conditions: Gender, Parole and the Governance of Reintegration." *British Journal of Criminology* 49, no. 4 (2009): 532–51.

Tyagi, Smita Vir. "Victimization, Adversity and Survival in the Lives of Women Offenders: Implications for Social Policy and Correctional Practice." *Canadian Woman Studies* 25, nos. 1, 2 (Winter 2006): 133–38.

Vowel, Chelsea. *Indigenous Writes: A Guide to First Nations, Métis, and Inuit Issues in Canada.* Winnipeg: HighWater Press, 2016.

Welsh, Andrew, and James R.P. Ogloff. "Progressive Reforms or Maintaining the Status Quo?: An Empirical Evaluation of the Judicial Consideration of Aboriginal Status in Sentencing Decisions." *Canadian Journal of Criminology and Criminal Justice* 50, no. 4 (2008): 491–517.

Williams, Toni. "Intersectionality Analysis in the Sentencing of Aboriginal Women in Canada: What Difference Does It Make?" In *Intersectionality and Beyond: Law, Power and the Politics of Location*, edited by Emily Grabham et al., 79–104. New York: Routledge-Cavendish, 2009.

———. "Punishing Women: The Promise and Perils of Contextualized Sentencing for Aboriginal Women in Canada." *Cleveland State Law Review* 55 (2007): 269–87.

Zaitzow, Barbara H. "Pastel Fascism: Reflections of Social Control Techniques Used with Women in Prison." *Women's Studies Quarterly* 32, nos. 3, 4 (2004): 33–48.

Zehr, Howard. *The Little Book of Restorative Justice.* Intercourse, PA: Good Books, 2002.

INDEX